World Religions

A Guide to the Essentials

Thomas A. Robinson & Hillary Rodigues

EDITORS

World Religions: A Guide to the Essentials, with CD-ROM
© 2006 by Hendrickson Publishers, Inc.
P. O. Box 3473
Peabody, Massachusetts 01961-3473

ISBN 978-1-56563-317-9

Printed in the United States of America

Second Printing – December 2006

Library of Congress Cataloging-in-Publication Data

World religions : a guide to the essentials / Tom Robinson . . . [et al.].
    p. cm.
  Includes index.
  ISBN 1-56563-317-2 (alk. paper)
  1. Religions–Textbooks. I. Robinson, Thomas A. (Thomas Arthur), 1951-
  BL80.3.W645 2006
  200–dc22
                                        2005031515

This book is dedicated to the Religious Studies students
at the University of Lethbridge

Table of Contents

About the Authors

This project was conceived some years ago by professors Tom Robinson and Hillary Rodrigues of the Department of Religious Studies at the University of Lethbridge, Lethbridge, Alberta, Canada. As the project neared completion, the Department hired two new faculty members, James Linville and John Harding, who contributed to the project. The final product is a joint effort by all members of the Department.

TOM ROBINSON has a PhD in Judaism and Christianity in the Greco-Roman Era from McMaster University, and teaches courses in the history of Christianity and in koine Greek. He has contributed the Introduction and the chapters on Judaism, Christianity, Islam, Sikhism, and Other Religions. He has also developed the accompanying software, with the assistance of the other contributors to the project.

HILLARY RODRIGUES has a PhD in Hinduism from McMaster University, and teaches courses in various Eastern Religions and in aspects of Asian philosophy and literature. He has contributed the chapters on Hinduism, Buddhism, Jainism, and Chinese Religions.

JAMES LINVILLE has a PhD in Hebrew and Old Testament from the University of Edinburgh, and teaches courses in Hebrew Bible literature, mythology, and Judaism. He has contributed the chapter on Ancient Religions.

JOHN HARDING has a PhD in Japanese Religion from the University of Pennsylvania, and teaches Buddhism and East Asian Religions with an emphasis on modern Japanese religions and the cross-cultural exchange between Asia and the West. He has contributed the chapter on Japanese Religions.

CHAPTER ONE   Introduction

WHAT IS RELIGION?

Religion is a characteristic of the human species, stretching from antiquity to the present, from simple societies to the most complex, from the unlearned to the educated, from the weak to the powerful, from the young to the old, from the peripheral to the centers of powers. Yet religion is notoriously difficult to define. Some scholars would argue that no definition can be adequate, since religion as expressed throughout the world and throughout human history is simply too diverse and complex to be neatly captured in a short definition that identifies a common condition. Indeed, most of the common assumptions about religion fail when we try to apply them to all traditions we normally think of as religious.

Surely gods must be present in religion, one might think. No, for some religions deny either the existence of gods or their relevance. Surely an afterlife must be important in religion. No, for some religions either deny an afterlife or do not divide present and future existence in this way. Perhaps a moral code of some kind captures a common element in religion. No, for in some societies, morality is primarily dealt with by philosophers rather than priests, by the academy rather than the temple; among some peoples, codes of behavior provide social order and create stable societies without appeal to religious motives or motifs. Perhaps the common feature among religions is some sense of the "Other"—an awareness of a dimension beyond the visible and the ordinary. But that definition, even if true, is too vague, open-ended, and without sufficient content to provide substance to our definition of religion.

Another problem makes it difficult to find a precise definition of religion: it is sometimes not possible to distinguish neatly the religious dimension from the non-religious. For example, many political ideologies have offered a comprehensive vision of the world and demanded sweeping commitment of their members, differing little from the sense and scope of religious claims. Or consider the world of sports. Normally it provides small adventures of escape into the realm of play and relative meaninglessness; sometimes, however, it becomes warped into a comprehensive world of conviction and commitment by which an individual's life is inspired and value and meaning determined, and where good and evil battle on the playing field for the souls of fans.

The difficulty in finding a fully adequate definition of religion should not lead us to the conclusion that the concept of religion is without substance. There is enough commonality among things that are not easily grouped under any other category to suggest that some broad phenomenon lies behind them. Further, such matters cross diverse cultures and span vast periods, giving us a sense that at some level religion is a profound part of the human experience.

RELIGION AND RELIGIONS

So difficult is it to specify the defining features of religion that often the study of religion focuses on individual religious traditions themselves, treating each religious tradition as a separate study. It is not religion, *per se,* that is studied, but a variety of religions, each a subject in its own right. That is largely our approach in this book.

We examine each major religion individually, as a self-contained system. We observe the complex and sometime quite distinctive features that have come together to create each religion. We recognize and attempt to understand the world of coherence and meaning that each religion has created for its adherents. In some ways, then, we are examining religion more in the concrete than in the abstract. Our hope is that by taking this approach, the answer to the more difficult question "What is *religion?*" will become clearer, as we observe *religions* in their sometimes varied and sometimes strikingly similar expressions.

There are, of course, other ways to introduce the subject of religion. Rather than looking at each religion as a unique entity, as we have done in this text, we could have examined the *phenomenon* of religion, looking for those common elements that make religions religious–the religious essence of things. An equally worthwhile approach would have been to introduce religion by looking at the various ways religion is studied across a number of disciplines. These matters are taken up briefly in this introductory chapter, providing a glimpse into the essence of religion and the nature of the academic discipline of Religious Studies. After that, we turn to the main core of our text–separate chapters for each major religious tradition.

WHAT IS A "WORLD" RELIGION?

The list of religions that one studies in introductory courses on world religions varies widely on the periphery but is undisputed at the core. Four religions account for the overwhelming majority of religious adherents–some 70% of the world's population, or 85% of the religious population. These are Hinduism and Buddhism (Eastern Religions) and Christianity and Islam (Western Religions). About 15% of the world's population is classed as non-religious, leaving 15% that belong to other religions. Of these smaller religions, Judaism, Jainism, and Sikhism are usually treated in introductory texts, along with Taoism, Confucianism, and Shinto, whose adherents can be less precisely calculated.

> **WORLD RELIGIONS**
> *Coined in 1800s, the term World Religions included only Buddhism, Christianity, and Islam. Later it was expanded to include Hinduism, Confucianism, Taoism, Judaism, and Shinto. The term is much more flexibly used today.*

> **WESTERN RELIGIONS**
> **Western Religions:** Those religions that have roots in the religious perspective of the Hebrew Bible (Old Testament). The primary western religions are Judaism, Christianity, and Islam.
> **Judaism:** Based on the religion of the ancient Hebrews; largely reflecting major reforms after the destruction of first Jewish temple in the 500s B.C.E. and other reforms after the destruction of the second temple in 70 C.E. (rabbinic Judaism).
> **Christianity:** A reform movement growing out of Judaism in the first century C.E.; became the religion of the Roman Empire in 300s; from 1500s, expanded globally.
> **Islam:** A reform movement in the Arabian Peninsula in the 600s C.E.; within a hundred years, dominant power from Spain and the North African coast to the Indian Ocean; suffered as western Europe expanded from the 1500s.

It should be noted that it is extremely difficult to get an accurate count of religious adherents. The figures usually do not discriminate between those who regularly attend religious events and closely observe religious practices and those who do not–between the *devotee* of a religion and the *resident* of a country in which that religion is dominant. Further, the figures appear to be counting different things in different traditions (e.g., residents in the Christian count but devotees in the Shinto count).

Comparative counts of adherents, then, are highly problematic, though the figures we have used here are the ones most often offered in reference works. More discriminating, problem-free criteria need to be developed if we are to make more accurate statements about the size of religious traditions.

Other matters need to be noted in calculating the number of adherents. Many of the larger religions have sub-groups that have many more members than some religions that are counted as distinctive world religions in their own right. Judaism, for example, is smaller than a great number of the distinctive traditions within Christianity.

Further, some religions that are counted as world religions are largely confined to a particular people or location (e.g., Hinduism, Sikhism, Judaism, and Shinto). This is changing, however, as patterns of population shift in an increasing mobile modern world, marked by considerable emigration of people from their traditional homelands. Even so, only the three great "missionary" religions (Buddhism, Christianity, and Islam) have a substantial worldwide reach across peoples, cultures, and places.

WHY STUDY RELIGIOUS TRADITIONS?

Religion is so much a part of the experience of being human that few areas of human activity and reflection are without some religious influence or association.

Personal and Group Identity

The majority of people define who they are and what they value, partly at least, on a framework of religion. Efforts to understand humans and their behavior will be incomplete unless we recognize the religious component, which is often at the center of an individual's or a society's reflection and which is rarely so peripheral that it can be simply dismissed as inconsequential. In some cases, religion is so closely intertwined with the larger culture that the line between the two is blurred, as in the case of Sikhism and Shinto, and for periods of its history, of Judaism.

Religion and the Global Neighborhood

In a time not so long ago, neighbors were those who shared assumptions and goals. Backgrounds were similar; moral sensibilities were largely the same. Neighbors met not only over their backyard fences but also in the same social and religious establishments. This is no longer true. Movements of people often have made neighborhoods more diverse than uniform, reflecting the varied nature of the global village. New neighbors bring with them their cultures and religious sensibilities. To understand neighbors in the modern neighborhood, some sense of how they think and what they value is essential.

The frequency, speed, and ease of travel also have helped to bring diverse perspectives together. Travelers to foreign lands usually will acquaint themselves with a map so that unfamiliar geography becomes familiar. They often will refer to a phrasebook so that they can communicate somewhat in the local language. They routinely will consult a guidebook to become familiar with the local culture and points of interest. For most cultures, religion will be a prominent part of a tourist's experience of a foreign country. Religious sites likely will make up a large part of the tourist's must-see places. Cultural taboos and behaviors, by which a culture is most commonly recognized, often are rooted in religious sensibilities. We would rarely venture into a foreign country without a map of the road system and the streets. If we visit a foreign country without learning something of the religious dimensions of its people, we will be traveling without an adequate mental map of the people we encounter.

Political Tensions

Journalists and their news networks often focus on conflicts. Frequently we first hear of a country because some conflict has broken out there.

EASTERN RELIGIONS

Eastern Religions: Imprecise division; generally religions of Asia, though Islam is usually treated as western.

Hinduism: A generic term for an array of religions native to India that recognizes the Vedas; largely restricted to India and its emigrant communities.

Buddhism: A rejection of Vedic religion, developed by the Buddha in 500s B.C.E. in northeast India; expanded eastward, becoming the dominant religion of southeast Asia; based on the "Four Noble Truths" and the "Eightfold Path."

Jainism: Founded in 500s B.C.E. by Mahavira in eastern India; rejected Vedas; emphasized asceticism to free soul of karmic matter; confined to India.

Confucianism: Founded in 500s B.C.E. by Confucius; emphasized social order and responsibility and reverence of family; largely restricted to East Asia.

Daoism: Shadowy beginnings (ca. 500s B.C.E.?); associated with Laozi; teaches about the path (tao), consisting of maintaining a harmony of opposite forces and the natural order; largely restricted to China and Chinese communities.

Shinto: The indigenous traditions of Japan, distinguished particularly from foreign implants such as Buddhism; emphasizes ancestors and the kami, mysterious divine powers that inspire awe.

Sikhism: Hindu reform movement, with elements of Islam, begun by Nanak in 1500s C.E.; primary text is Adi Granth; largely confined to the Punjab area of northwest India and emigrant communities.

Sometimes a religious element plays a role in the conflict, either as a primary identifying mark for the different sides of the dispute or as the direct cause that sparked the conflict. Even when religion plays a more peripheral role, it often serves as a convenient loyalty around which a group may be rallied. Efforts to understand societies and their relations with other peoples usually will require some knowledge of the religious dynamics of the situation.

METHODOLOGIES IN THE STUDY OF RELIGION

No one methodology dominates the field of Religious Studies. Scholars in the discipline use a variety of methodologies, generally borrowed from other disciplines, though sometimes adjusted to the particular needs of the student of religion.

Although Religious Studies as a discipline uses a number of methodologies, each Religious Studies scholar generally can be identified by a dominant methodology. For example, Religious Studies scholars can be anthropologists, historians, sociologists, theologians, philosophers, psychologists, archaeologists, linguists, or members of a number of other professional disciplines. Sometimes, departments of Anthropology, Sociology, History, or Philosophy, for example, will have a specialist in Religion, although just as often such scholars are housed in departments of Religious Studies.

Part of the reason for the considerable scope of approaches in Religious Studies is that religion, as a dominant human experience, influences human behavior and environment at a variety of levels. Below, we discuss briefly the major approaches in Religious Studies, in no particular order of importance. Even within these approaches, methodologies can differ widely.

Anthropology of Religion

Certain subjects once dominated the anthropological study of religion. The experience of "primitive" or tribal cultures, often untouched by previous contact with the "outside" world, was idealized as offering the oldest—and purest—forms of religion. Also of interest was *folk religion*, a term that identifies the religious sensibilities of the common people, often mixed with the ideas of the larger institutionalized religions but beyond the control or approval of the religious specialists of these traditions. Certain themes dominated early anthropological investigation: rituals, shamanism, altered states, magic, and kinship. Today the themes remain but the subjects have changed. More mainstream religious traditions (or elements within them) are being studied. The familiar and the home environment is as likely a context for the anthropological researcher as the foreign and the far. Moreover the "great" traditions (major world religions, such as those studied in this book) now compete for scholarly attention with the "little" traditions, which previously had been the subjects of choice.

Sociology of Religion

People live in societies. Since religion is one of the primary defining human experiences, we can expect religion to have some clear social dimension. Sociologists of religion study how religion shapes societal conditions and, conversely, how societal factors shape religion. They attempt to understand religious groups as social phenomena and to understand the religious dynamic within the larger society. Sociologists debate among themselves whether the deepest and most accurate insights into the societal dimension of religion are gained by quantitative approaches (large-scale uniform statistical surveys of adherents) or qualitative approaches (closer observation and individualized discussion with a few of the adherents).

History

Cultures rise and fall; nations conquer and collapse. Within this ebb and flow of life, religion exists in a variety of conditions. Sometimes religion simply

GENERAL TERMINOLOGY

Ablution: A ceremonial washing of the body or of objects

Agnostic: (lit., "not" + "knower"). In common usage, synonym for skeptic

Allegorical: A method of interpretation that finds hidden or coded meaning in texts

Amulet: An object believed to possess special protective powers, often carried on a person

Ancestor Worship: Religious actions that are concerned with the spirits of dead relatives

Animism: Belief that spirits inhabit inanimate objects and natural phenomena

Anthropomorphic: A representation of gods with human form or characteristics

Apocalyptic: Matters related to the cataclysmic end of the world and final judgment

Apologist: A defender or advocate for a particular viewpoint

Apostasy: The rejection of the faith that one once held

Ascetic: One who rejects ordinary social life for exceptional religious discipline, which often involves poverty, celibacy, and seclusion

Atheist: A non-theist; one who believes that gods and the spiritual world do not exist

Blasphemy: Contemptuous or irreverent act or word concerning a deity or something sacred

Canon: The sacred and authoritative scriptures (writings) of a religious group

Celibacy: A rejection of the sexual aspects of life in the interests of focused religious devotion

Dualism: Belief in two primary and competing cosmic powers of good and evil

dies with its culture; sometimes religion sparks a transformation and en-livens a once-dying culture into a renewed dynamic force; sometimes re-ligion carries vital elements from a collapsing society into a new society. Historians of religion attempt to understand the development and trans-formation of religion as part of the historical process and to understand how religion shapes and is shaped by other forces within the historical process.

Philosophy of Religion

Religions make truth claims, from statements about the existence of God, the moral order of the cosmos, the nature of evil, immortality and the afterlife to the very nature of truth and knowledge (sometimes ex-pressed in terms of reason and revelation). Philosophers of religion exam-ine the rational basis of religious truth claims, often focusing on the nature of religious language.

Theological Approaches

Universities and colleges are not the only places where religion is studied. A vigorous study of religion existed *within* religious traditions themselves long before academics attempted to understand religion as *outsiders* to the traditions. In this *theological* or *confessional* study of religion, there is often a clear search for the answer to the question of human sig-nificance and meaning, and a conviction that the religious tradition under study offers clarity and comfort about these matters. There may, however, be disputes within the tradition as to what the right answers are.

THE "INSIDER'S" OR "OUTSIDER'S" VIEW

The discipline of Religious Studies attempts to understand the reli-gious dimension of human experience. Religious Studies scholars have debated how this is best done, generally recognizing but debating the sig-nificance of the difference between the view of an insider and that of an outsider, between the view of a participant and that of an observer, be-tween the subjective perspective and the objective. Although Religious Studies scholars have been unable to come to a consensus as to the most appropriate approach, they generally recognize the need to examine each tradition on its own merits, as a system that provides a world of coherence and meaning for its adherents. This means that generally Religious Studies professors will not advocate one religious tradition over another, even if they have religious commitments themselves, nor will the assumptions of any one tradition be permitted to lay the ground rules for the discussion or have priority.

Approaching the study of religion from the assumptions of one particular religion is called the confessional perspective. The main concern that arises for Religious Studies scholars is how one's understanding of one's own religion and the religions of others is affected by using confessional compared to non-confessional assumptions. Working from the assumptions of any one tradition would seem to create an uneven playing field for the other religious traditions.

Some other disciplines have similar problems. For example, in a Political Science class on Marxism, students may have political affiliations quite opposed to Marxism, yet there is a reasonable expectation that this will not prevent them from understanding Marxism and treating it with fairness and balance. The same is a reasonable expectation for a Religious Studies class. This does not mean there cannot be rigorous debate about religious issues and claims. It does mean that the assumptions of any one tradition will not have pride of place, as is the case in confessional approaches.

TOLERANCE AND RELIGIOUS COMPETITION

Religions are always confessional to some extent: they offer a vision of the world that makes sense and offers coherence, based on a set of often explicitly declared assumptions. Their

---

GENERAL TERMINOLOGY
(continued)

Eschatology: (lit., "study of last things"). A term for concepts related to the end of the world and the human order

Exorcism: A ritual to drive out evil forces (demons) from places or people

Henotheism: Worship of one god but does not deny the *existence* of other gods

Heresy: The counter to orthodoxy; beliefs or practices that are rejected as destructive to the essence of a religious tradition. A negative label imposed by the majority tradition

Iconoclast: Someone opposed to the use of religious images

Martyr: One who dies, usually voluntarily, for a cause

Monasticism: The practice of asceticism and poverty in order to devote life to constant religious service; often communal

Monotheism: Belief in one divine being or god

Mysticism: A quest for deeper religious truth, bringing about a sense of union with the divine

Myth: Stories reflecting the great deeds of the gods, which function as foundational stories for religious traditions

Orthodoxy: (lit., "correct belief"). The counter to heresy; the essential beliefs and practices by which a religious community defines itself; the determination of essential beliefs and practices generally made by the majority tradition

Pagan: A pejorative term, once commonly used by western religions for adherents of polytheistic religions

adherents find a compelling, comprehensive meaning to life and the world about them by that set of assumptions. It is natural that adherents use these assumptions to evaluate the larger world about them. This means that rarely will religions seem to take a "neutral" position, as Religious Studies scholars often strive to do. Sometimes the dialogue between religions has been sharp, and history offers a long list of conflicts in which religion has played a prominent role.

Many individuals, both inside and outside religious traditions, have tried to encourage greater tolerance and dialogue between religious communities. In this context, attempts by any religion to advance their religion at the expense of other religions are often viewed as offensive.

It is unlikely, however, that religious competition will disappear. Much of the course of history has been influenced by the growth of one religion at the expense of another. Some religious traditions have a clear missionary thrust at their core. Indeed, over seventy percent of those who belong to a religious tradition are adherents of religions that have grown at the expense of other religions. That process can hardly be reversed, and a good case can be made that the process should not be halted. Suppose we were to freeze the state of religion as it is today, with each religion content with its present membership. We would not necessarily have created a better, richer, or more authentic religious environment. We would simply have frozen, in a most arbitrary way, a historical process.

Religion, as part of human experience, is a dynamic force. Just as empires and societies rise and fall, expand and shrink, so religious traditions undergo change in the ebb and flow of life. They debate within themselves and with each other. They offer worlds of coherence and meaning that are fresh options for some and failed options for others. That is likely to continue.

THE IDEAL AND THE REAL

There is a tendency in brief summaries of a religious tradition to present the religion in terms of the ideal it expresses. But religions, as lived, at best approximate any such ideal. We might compare it to the difference between a play as written and a play as performed. Both have value; both are "the play." Equally so, a religion is both what is preached and what is practiced, both what is prescribed and what is performed. The academic study of a religious tradition, then, should not focus exclusively on the elite literary record (the prescribed and the preached) or search for the period that supposedly expresses most authentically the essence of that religion. The whole history of a religion constitutes that religion, from its past to its present, and to whatever it may become in the future. All the adherents of a religion constitute the religious community, from the priestly elite, to the contented devotee, to the protestor on the periphery.

Religions are not static, frozen in a moment of purity and perfection. Religions both change with the times and force the times to change, being renewed and renewing. Rarely are all individuals within a religion content with every aspect of their tradition. Some see particular elements as stale or distorted, in need of reform. Such challenge and critique are as much part of the dynamism of a religion as the carefully guarded orthodoxy of a content majority.

ASPECTS OF AUTHORITY

For most traditions, religious authority tends to rest in an ancient text and a contemporary priesthood. The text often is considered to be the very voice of God or an expression of the will of God. It is treated as truth of a high order, and its insights are considered to provide a reliable guide to the large questions of life.

The text is usually preserved and interpreted by a body of priests, or clergy, who form the religious hierarchy. Such individuals are selected to act as the religious representatives of the society. These individuals are considered to be the religious experts, trained and authorized to handle certain aspects of the religious apparatus of the tradition. There is often

GENERAL TERMINOLOGY
(continued)
Pantheism: View that the universe as a whole is God or is part of God
Pantheon: Full assembly of gods and goddesses in a religion
Pilgrimage: Journey to a sacred place, done as a religious act
Polytheism: Belief in a divine world of many gods and spiritual forces
Prayer Beads: (sometimes also called rosary in Christianity). String of beads or knots that aids an individual in performing a cycle of prayers
Priest: A religious official; a range of offices may be found in evolved priesthoods
Profane: The counter to sacred; the everyday; the ordinary; more negatively: to violate the sacred state of things
Proselyte: A convert from another religion
Purity: A state in which a person or object will not cause the sacred domain to be polluted
Reincarnation: Rebirth of the person (or soul) into one or more successive lives; largely an eastern concept
Revelation: Knowledge gained by God disclosing truth to humans, often through a text or inspired speech
Rites of Passage: Rituals that mark a change in status of a person within a community, e.g., birth, puberty, marriage, death
Sacred: The counter to profane; the quality of things (places, objects, times, events, etc.) associated with the domain of the gods
Sacrilege: Any intentional violation of a sacred object

a sense of a danger inherent in religious rituals and objects, which may produce harm if handled by a person who is not formally empowered to act in the religious sphere. Empowered, or ordained, individuals often are called priests, though many traditions have dozens of religious functionaries with distinctive titles, ranks, and specific duties. Members of the religious hierarchy are likely to be primarily concerned with the preservation and performance of the tradition's current practices and beliefs.

But religious practice and belief are sometimes challenged. Challenge may be led by individuals who have no recognized status as clergy or by clergy who act beyond the boundaries assigned to them by their religious commission. Such persons often claim to speak a message directly from God; usually the message is characterized by a call for reform. This reform may have the character of innovation; just as often, though, it calls for restoration of the religion to the principles of a perceived ancient golden age.

Some smaller societies have what anthropologists term shamans. These are largely independent religious operators. They exhibit an unusual sense of the world of the invisible, and they are felt by others to have power within the world of the gods. Those who have anxieties arising from either spiritual or physical needs often seek out such individuals to act as intermediaries with the gods.

SACRED SPACE AND SACRED TIME

Religious traditions call attention to the religious aspects of life by creating domains of sacred space and time, which interrupt or regulate the flow of everyday life. Various methods are used to create these sacred dimensions.

Sacred space is created by assigning a particular quality of holiness or religious significance to a location. Temples and churches are prominent examples of created sacred space, though rivers, groves, mountains and stones can be endued with a sacred aura and thus provide sacred space. In some cases, entire cities or countries are considered sacred.

Sacred time often follows an annual calendar, with specific days observed as holy by generation after generation. Sometimes one day of the week is given special status, as with the Jewish Sabbath or the Christian Sunday. Often sacred time is clearly demarcated by performances that create boundaries for sacred time, such as an opening prayer or a closing benediction that frequently marks a Christian assembly, for example.

In whatever way sacred space and time is created by a tradition, it is expected that adherents will conduct themselves in appropriate ways when they approach the sacred. Attention to such matters does not merely serve to remind adherents of the religious dimensions of life; most traditions consider that sacred space and sacred time in some way secure and sanitize the broader reaches of space and time, guaranteeing humans a more beneficial engagement with the world around them.

RITUAL BEHAVIOR

Humans communicate by language. That is obvious to everyone. What we tend at times to overlook is that language, broadly defined, consists of far more than words. We are familiar enough with facial expressions and body gestures as perfectly clear means of communication. Some areas of human behavior are particularly rich in such gestures of meaning. Consider the world of sports, for example. The officials specify the boundaries of the game and the status of the players. In baseball, the game does not start until the umpire calls "Play ball!" Time is altered from the point of that call. Pitches now become "balls" or "strikes," not mere throws of a ball. Players are either "safe" or "out." Marked as they are by a specific pattern, purpose and place, such ritualized actions create and control a complete and structured world of meaning.

Religion, like many other aspects of human interaction, frequently uses a varied world of rituals and symbols, by which it creates and controls dimensions of space and time distinct from of the world of the ordinary. Making the sign of the cross in Christian traditions is in many ways little different from a military salute. The ceremony for the ordaining of a monk or priest is little different from a convocation for conferring a university degree or the ceremony at which a monarch confers a knighthood. Life is filled with such ritualized actions.

Rituals have certain distinguishing features. As actions that are intended to communicate, they must be patterned and repeatable; otherwise such actions would be nothing more than random movements. As a

---

GENERAL TERMINOLOGY (continued)

Saint: One who has displayed a heightened degree of devotion or religious accomplishment

Sanctuary: Sacred space, such as a temple or a church

Scripture: The sacred writings of a religion, usually having primary authoritative status

Shaman: A religious healer and wonderworker who often appears to be possessed by divine spirits and who is perceived to have power within the realm of the invisible

Taboo: A prohibition of a behavior or a restriction on the use of a particular object

Theodicy: An effort to explain the presence of evil in a world created by a god who is good

form of language, the meaning of ritual generally must be learned, just as the meaning of words must be learned. The meaning of a ritual is generally not self evident in much the same way that the meaning of a given combination of letters is not evident until meaning is assigned to it, making it into what is commonly called a word. Further, as language, ritual is given its meaning within a particular context. Simply because a particular combination of letters such as "c-a-t" may be assigned the meaning "feline" in one language, there is no reason to expect that the very same combination of letters in another language will mean the same thing in the second language. (Indeed, even within the same language the same combination of letters may have another seemingly unrelated meaning in another context.) In the same way, one must be aware that the meaning of a ritual is assigned by the group using it; it has no universal meaning. For example, religious traditions often feature some kind of washing. One cannot assume that the meaning of a washing in one tradition (Christian baptism, for example) is the same as the meaning of a ritual washing in another religion—or, indeed, even within sub-groups of the same religion.

Finally, ritual often is used at major points of transition in the life of a religious adherent. Initiation and ordination rituals, for example, alter the status of the adherent both in the eyes of the one undergoing the ritual and the eyes of the entire community where the ritual has meaning. Consider marriage ceremonies, whether secular or religious: these show a similar sense of a change in status of the participants, both in their eyes and in the eyes of the wider community.

Rituals, then, are powerful tools by which a society sets boundaries, confers status, and marks changes in some state of affairs. Rituals are particularly useful for religion, as it often plays with the world of the unseen, and carves out domains of space and time for that world out of the world of the ordinary.

ETHICS & MORAL SYSTEMS

Religion has played a prominent role in the regulation of human behavior. Almost every religious tradition discriminates between acceptable and unacceptable conduct, sometimes capturing the essentials of conduct in a short, easily remembered list, such as the Ten Commandments.

Regulated conduct generally includes aspects of moral and of ritual behavior, though different traditions may emphasize one more than the other. Primary moral principles are often shared widely among religions, with clear prohibitions against such actions as lying, stealing, and killing. Often sexual propriety is addressed. Sometime, a range of taboos concerning consumption of certain foods and levels of social contact are specified.

Frequently religious traditions will associate rewards and punishment with good and bad conduct, though the connection is more ambiguous in some traditions than in others. Belief in an afterlife or in reincarnation often is featured in the broad discussion of behavior and its consequences. Also related to this discussion are questions of human nature and the human dilemma, and the character of good and evil.

TECHNICAL TERMINOLOGY AND JARGON

We have attempted to keep this text as jargon-free as possible. All academic disciplines struggle to maintain the right balance in the use of technical terminology, or what might be called the jargon of the discipline. Sometimes common English words can communicate as clearly as the jargon of the discipline. Too much jargon reshapes normal dialogue into coded and peculiar language that only the initiated can understand. Such jargon is bad jargon.

> **DATING SCHEMES**
> **A.D.** (from Latin phrase *anno Domini*, meaning "in the year of our Lord"). This dating scheme was developed in the 500s C.E. It dates all events from the birth of Jesus, and is paired with the abbreviation B.C. Since it has a Christian coloring, most Religious Studies scholars use the more neutral abbreviation C.E. (*see below*) in its place.
> **A.H.** (abbreviation for "after *Hijra*" or "in the year of the *Hijra*" [Latin: *anno hegirae*]). This is used in the Muslim calendar, which dates all events from the year of Muhammad's flight (*hijra*) from Mecca to Medina.
> **B.C.** (abbreviation of the phrase "before Christ"). Paired with A.D. First used in the 1600s C.E. It is used to count dates in years prior to the birth of Jesus. Since it has a Christian coloring, most Religious Studies scholars use the more neutral abbreviation B.C.E. in its place (see below).
> **B.C.E.** (abbreviation of the phrase "before the Common Era"). Used in place of the conventional B.C. Paired with C.E. (*see below*).
> **C.E.** (abbreviation of the phrase "Common Era"). Used in place of A.D., an abbreviation that has Christian confessional coloring. Paired with B.C.E. Some speak of the B.C.E. and C.E. abbreviations as "before the Christian Era" and "Christian Era," without the confessional element.

On the other hand, technical terms often capture in one word a complex concept that might otherwise be expressed only by a long paragraph—or an even longer discourse. Obviously, such terms are useful shortcuts in communication.

Even the best terminology does not carry a fixed meaning for all users at all times. The student must always be aware of the context in which documents are written and statements made. Even people within a religion may use the same term in quite different ways. When the same term is used by different religions, one must be especially careful to con-sider the term's context.

In keeping with our interests to produce a text that is as jargon-free as possible, we have opted to use simple spelling of foreign words. That means restricting the spelling to the twenty-six letters of the English al-phabet, unlike many books that attempt to reproduce foreign sounds or letters by using non-alphabetical symbols such as the apostrophe or single quote mark as letters. It is doubtful that such "letters" assist the be-ginning reader. For those who are interested, we have provided an appen-dix of alternative spellings and pronunciations for many foreign terms.

DATING SCHEMES

In a guest editorial in *CIVILIZATION: The Magazine of the Library of Congress* (June/July 1999), Kofi A. Annan, the Secretary-General of the United Nations, spoke of writing on the eve of the third millennium. He commented on his use of the term "third millennium":

> You might say that the millennium is simply a date in the calendar of one civilization. Many other calendars are used in different parts of the world. And yet the Christian calendar no longer belongs exclusively to Chris-tians. People of all faiths have taken to using it simply as a matter of conve-nience. There is so much interaction between people of different faiths and cultures—different civilizations, if you like—that some shared way of reckoning time is a necessity. And so the Christian Era has become the Common Era.

It is increasingly the case that publications in Religious Studies use the abbreviations B.C.E. (before the Common Era) and C.E. (Common Era) in place of the traditional abbreviations B.C. (before Christ) and A.D. (*anno Domini*, Latin for "in the year of our Lord"). The new abbreviations first ap-peared in the late 1800s, and were adopted widely by Jewish scholars and more gradually in the wider culture. Such abbreviations avoid the clearly Christian confessional terms such as "Christ" and "Lord" used in the traditional dating scheme with reference to Jesus and his birth.

The contention that the new abbreviations identify a "common era" is, however, a bit of an academic fiction, since the dates are still set in terms of the assumed year of the birth of Jesus. Some scholars use the new abbreviations, but speak of B.C.E. as "before the Christian Era" and C.E. as "Christian Era," recognizing that the dates mark no significant start-ing point for any tradition but the Christian.

A FINAL WORD

In an introductory textbook to ten major religious traditions, it is not possible to give more than a general or broad view of each religion. Thus the description of the beliefs and practices of a particular religion in such a text as ours is likely to apply more fully to the majority tradition or to the tradition considered to be the most original or orthodox. Each major religion is likely to have several subgroups, and these are often further subdivided. Some religions have hundreds—even thousands—of separate groups, each of which understands itself as distinct from all the other groups of that religion.

Many factors account for the differences between groups within the same religious tradition. These can range from cultural and linguistic to structural and theological. The consequences of the differences extend from the insignificant to the serious. Some subgroups see themselves as the only true form of their religion—all other subgroups are heretical or tainted in some way. Others see their subgroup as one of a multitude of valid forms of their religion, with their particular form appropriate for the particular social or cultural context. The fine nuances of belief and practice of the smaller subgroups generally are the subject of study in more senior courses in a university.

Our aim in this text is to present a clear and condensed portrait—the essentials—of the major religious traditions and to give a sense of the importance and scope of religion in the human experience. Ten chapters deal with specific religious traditions. Each chapter is roughly divided into three equal parts: History, Beliefs, and Practices. Boxes on the right side of right-facing pages provide short summaries of the major features of each religion; these are designed as quick study aids and a fast entry into the world of religious traditions.

CHAPTER TWO

Ancient Religions

THE LEGACY OF ANCIENT RELIGIONS

All religions have histories. They change and develop over time. They both borrow from and exert influence upon the religions around them. At times the shifts in a people's religious beliefs and practices can be dramatic; at other times, religious worldviews adapt to changing cultural and intellectual environments through more gradual evolutions of thought. No religion appears on the scene without a history. In this chapter, we examine the ancient worldviews that influenced many current world religions. We will concentrate on the influences on the Western traditions, but many of the ideas we will encounter are far more widespread.

Eastern religions generally are not hesitant to recognize their links to more ancient religious aspirations, and this continuity can be readily traced by scholars. For example, modern Hinduism, Buddhism, and Jainism have their roots deep in ancient India—a legacy that none of these religions seeks to disown, even though it is obvious the traditions have changed over the millennia. The religions of China and Japan likewise draw on ancient visions of the world from their own locales. Western religions (Judaism, Christianity, and Islam), however, tend to disassociate themselves from the ancient religions that preceded them. They see themselves as unique revelations from God, breaking in upon and radically replacing (or sometimes reforming or fulfilling) more "primitive" or less sophisticated kinds of religion that had been dominant in the area. A casual observer might agree that there does seem to be considerable discontinuity between these religions and the religions they replaced. The ancient religions had many gods; the western religions but one. In Athens, the city that still bears the name of the goddess Athena, most people are now Greek Orthodox Christians, who are hardly likely to think of the goddess as actually existing. Vatican City in Rome is now the seat of power of Catholic Christianity, no longer part of a sprawling metropolis with a semi-divine emperor and in whose coliseum Christians were brutally murdered for sport. The Pyramids, the great structures intended to grant immortality to the pharaohs, now share Egypt with a predominantly Muslim population that would be outraged to discover anyone praying to the ancient gods.

Yet, even in the West the past lives on. The ancient Persian (Iranian) religion of Zoroastrianism was the religion of mighty emperors who once held sway over the whole Middle East, from the borders of Greece into Egypt. It is still practiced some 2,500 years later, although its adherents now number in the thousands, not millions. Modern Judaism has roots that go back well over two thousand years. Yet, scholars see it arising from the slow development of monotheism from an earlier polytheistic Israelite society, not the instantaneous introduction of a fundamentally new "ethical monotheism" onto the scene when the early Israelite ancestors began to form the nation of Israel. This is one of very many areas in which religious claims about the past (here Judaism and Christianity) are challenged by modern, critical scholarship. Christianity and Islam have their own connections with the ancient Near East, both through the religion of ancient Judaism and through other associations such as their sacred writings. Further, in spite of their sense of discontinuity with the past, all the western religions reflect some of the mentality common in ancient religions of the Mediterranean and Mesopotamian regions in which they developed.

Both areas developed impressive civilizations early, particularly in Egypt along the fertile Nile River and in the equally fertile area along the Tigris and the Euphrates, the two great rivers of Mesopotamia (literally the "Land Between the Rivers"), present-day Iraq and Syria. There the great religions of Sumer, Assyria, and Babylonia developed. And one must not forget the renowned pantheon of the Greek and Roman Olympian gods, and the high cultural achievements associated with these peoples. Although western traditions have consciously and clearly broken from the worldview of these ancient civilizations, elements of ancient religious reflection linger on in our modern faiths. This chapter will explore some of the general features of ancient religion to identify continuities and discontinuities with the prominent religions of the modern world.

RELIGION OF THE POOR AND RELIGION OF THE POWERFUL

The ancient world had many cultures and many religions. There was also diversity within regions. Although we speak of, for instance, "Mesopotamian Religion," we should really be saying "Mesopotamian Religions," for they were many. We have at best a one-sided picture of any religion from these areas. For one thing, little data has survived the ravages of time, and what has survived is often not easy to interpret. For another, in the ancient world, very few people could read or write, so the religious sensibilities of most people, particularly the poor and illiterate, are almost entirely beyond recovery now. The myths, incantations and hymns that survive do so only because of that wonderful technology called writing, and writing has largely been the tool of the rich and the leisured. We simply do not know the stories, legends, songs and traditional teachings of the non-literate common citizens of these lands— the ninety percent or more of the population of the ancient world. Something of their religion can be pieced together from other artifacts that have survived, but the oral traditions that expressed their sense of the world and what those artifacts really meant to them are in large part lost forever. It is, therefore, the religions of the powerful elite of city-states and empires that are best attested, not the beliefs of the subsistence farmers barely scratching out a living from their backbreaking work.

MAJOR ANCIENT NEAR-EASTERN CIVILIZATIONS

Sumerian: (3500-2000 B.C.E.). The oldest Mesopotamian civilization. Its many city-states were the first to develop cuneiform writing.

Assyrian: (2300s-612 B.C.E.). Assyria had a long history but is most famous for being Israel's arch-enemies during its latter period. Many of its cities, including Nimrud and Nineveh, have provided rich finds in artifacts and texts, some of which are prophetic oracles.

Babylonian: (1900s-500s B.C.E.). Many phases of dominance and weakness. Hammurabi's (1728-1686 B.C.E.) law-code is a milestone of the powerful Old Babylonian civilization, while Nebuchadnezzar of the brief Neo-Babylonian period conquered Jerusalem in 587 B.C.E., a significant event in Israelite history.

Persian: (550-331 B.C.E.). Incorporating the Medes into its structure, Persia defeated Babylonia and became a vast empire from India to Greece. Its westward expansion was halted by the Greeks at the Battle of Marathon.

Classical Greece: (400s-338 B.C.E.). Various confederations of city-states in Greece and the Aegean. Its mythology, art, architecture, philosophy, and science shaped much of the thinking in the western world.

Hellenistic: (333-30 B.C.E.). The empire of Alexander the Great, which spread Greek culture throughout the eastern Mediterranean and the Middle East.

Roman: The last great Mediterranean empire. Christianized by the 300s C.E., the western empire fell in the 400s and the eastern (Byzantine) in the 1400s.

We can assume, however, some overlap of the rural and the urban, of the elite and the people they governed. The extent of the overlap and the unique perspectives of the non-literate are largely indeterminable. Both would be concerned with similar ideas: prosperity, health, and security for one's family and community. Yet, since religion tends to adapt to its environment, we would expect some differences in answers to these questions, and indeed even different sets of questions in some areas. The limited world of the low-level agriculturalists, who would rarely travel far from their fields, shaped a religion that concentrated on the factors that made for a meaningful, good life on those small parcels of land and tiny villages. There seems to have been a strong connection with nature: rituals had to be performed to make sure the crops grew and to guarantee that the deities and spirits of the ancestors looked after the worshipper's own community and region.

The connection between nature and human society, of course, is represented in the religion of the powerful, but in a rather different form. The city-state, kingdom, or empire had more on its mind than the well-being of villages and crops, although these remained vitally important. There was the need for the gods' help in maintaining political control over larger territories and even contested lands. Armies were needed and taxes were raised to pay for them. There was the need for the organization of masses of labor for irrigation and city building, manufacturing, and crafts. Scribes were needed to keep records and files, and so forth. All of these spheres of life required specialists. Therefore, the religions of the most powerful were somewhat removed from the actual tasks of working the fields and performing the basic labor upon which society depended.

All of these factors made their mark on the religions. The urban centers could afford, indeed, required specialization in religious duties: priests and other temple functionaries, such as various diviners and prophets who would speak in the name of the deities, accountants (temples could also function as banks and tax collecting agencies), scribes and so forth. The religion had to legitimize a complex political structure, and to express the hopes, fears, and ambitions (sometimes *ruthless* ambitions) of powerful elites. This was usually done by presenting the king as the representative of the deity on earth. Myths and rituals helped the king establish his power as the legitimate ruler and his relationship with the gods. Such mythology could have a great impact on the economy of a country. For example, the giant pyramids placed a tremendous burden on Egypt's financial and material resources and labor which otherwise could have been employed toward other tasks.

INCLUSIVE AND EXCLUSIVE

Western people tend to think of religions as exclusive: that is, a person belongs to only one religion at a time. Indeed, the Jewish and Christian Bibles and the Islamic Quran teach against mixing the "true" religion with beliefs and practices from foreign faiths. This exclusivity is a prominent concern in monotheistic religions, and it reaches back into the early period of our western religions. But that was not the dominant view in the ancient religious world of polytheism, which naturally reflected an inclusive attitude, providing due reverence to all the gods and receiving from them benefits in the domains they controlled.

In the ancient world there were often a number of different religious centers in one kingdom, each with its own unique rituals, mythology, and patron deity. Each could expect some support from the local rulers, and each would in turn lend their support to the leadership. In Egypt, for example, priests in different centers offered different views of creation that attributed creative acts to the deities worshipped at their particular shrine. At Heliopolis in northern Egypt, creation was related to the sun god appearing on a mound that arose in the midst of a watery chaos called Nun. The sun created two other gods, associated with the air and water, and these two gave birth to two more, the earth (Geb) and the sky (Nut) who, in turn, engendered four more deities, including Isis and Osiris. These nine deities could still, however, be considered aspects of a single divine

MAJOR ANCIENT NEAR EASTERN TEXTS

Baal Cycle: Important Canaanite myths tell of Baal's quest for a suitable palace and his battles with Yamm (Sea) and Mot (Death).

Book of the Dead: Written on tomb walls and on papyrus, this text provides spells for the deceased to use to survive the tests and judgments of the dead. Praises to the gods are also included.

Enuma Elish: Often referred to as the Babylonian creation story, it tells the tale of Marduk, who becomes the chief god after killing Tiamat. Her body was used to create heaven and earth.

Epic of Gilgamesh: Often referred to as the Babylonian flood story, it recounts the mythical adventures of a Mesopotamian king and his friend Enkidu. One of the stories recounts a great flood. It is one of the oldest recorded stories on earth, known as early as the third millennium B.C.E.

Hammurabi's Code: From the eighteenth century B.C.E., one of the earliest known legal codes. The laws deal with various property and commercial regulations, violence, marriage, and social order. Codes like this are often seen as providing models for the biblical collections of Israelite laws.

The *Iliad* and the *Odyssey*: Greek epics traditionally ascribed to the poet Homer (700s B.C.E.), telling tales of the battle at Troy (of Trojan horse fame) and the travels of one of the heroes returning from the war. Deities play major roles.

Rosetta Stone: A multi-lingual stone inscription from the 100s B.C.E., discovered in 1799. It was the key to deciphering Egyptian hieroglyphic writing system.

power, which was explicitly located in the power of the king. On the other hand, the Memphis theology distinguished itself from nearby Heliopolis in that the god Ptah, holding within himself eight other deities, created the world through his speech. At Thebes, in central Egypt, creation was spoken of as having four aspects, each represented by a pair of deities. A mound emerged within the unformed chaos. The sun god Amun emerged from an egg. So, too, in Mesopotamia; rival mythologies and temples could co-exist. At times there may have been animosity and tensions between them, but for the most part each was taken as revealing some measure of sacred truth that should not be ignored.

We often do not know how much elite or imperial concerns dictated religion to the masses. At times, a new political power would let the common-folk carry on as they had done previously, so long as the people did not resist the new elite or openly defy the religious claims made by it. Anyone associated with the power-structure itself, however, could be expected to adopt the general ideology of the rulers. On rare occasion, there were even attempts to force a religious exclusivity on people. The Egyptian Pharaoh Akhenaten rejected the existing belief in the sun as one of the major deities in favor of a radical monotheism. For him, the sun god, Aten, was the only god. His attempt to suppress all other forms of worship, however, failed. After his death, the old priesthoods reasserted themselves, and they did their best to wipe the memory of the "heretic king" from history. Another famous case is celebrated to this day. In the last few centuries B.C.E., many Jews were frustrated at the encroachment of Hellenistic (Greek-influenced) culture and religion upon their communities. When Hellenism was forced on Judah and Jerusalem, considerable resistance arose, and war erupted in 167 B.C.E. when the Hellenistic king desecrated the Jewish temple in Jerusalem by sacrificing pigs on the altar. The Jewish zealots, led by Judas Macabbeus, finally recaptured and rededicated the temple in late 164 B.C.E. The rededication is celebrated every year at the Jewish festival of Hanukkah. For the Jewish rebels, exclusivity of worship was something for which they were willing to die in order to preserve against a rival exclusivist position.

Despite all of this, it must be remembered that religious differences could often exist without open hostility, and given changing political and cultural circumstances, various new forms of religion could emerge. Only rarely did this result in a fundamentally new religion: often traditions would evolve and myths would be rewritten to express the new relationships between the gods worshipped by different groups of people or in different locales.

THE GODS

As noted already, Middle Eastern *polytheism* (literally, "many gods") gave way to *monotheism* (i.e., "one god"), although the actual history of this change is very uncertain, and one must be careful not to oversimplify the situation. There are other kinds of theology, which, in some ways, fall between polytheism and strict monotheism. Indeed, many ancient people may be best described as *henotheists*, that is, believers in one god as primary in their lives or their region, although the existence of other deities as being worthy of worship by other people or in other regions is accepted without any difficulty. More strictly, *monolatry* refers to the acceptance that only one god is worthy of worship, while all other deities are somehow inferior, and this may actually be the best term to describe ancient Israelite religion. All of these forms, and many kinds of belief in between, existed at various times in the ancient Near East, although for most of its history, a strict monotheism or monolatry were relatively rare.

Even though the modern western religions declare themselves to be monotheistic, one cannot take *monotheism* at face value as a permanent fixture of these traditions from their beginnings. The ancient Hebrews (Jews) once believed in various gods, and some parts of the Jewish Bible seem concerned to link a few of these names together, to affirm that YHWH (often translated as "The Lord") is one and the same as Elohim ("God"). The Hebrew Bible also repeatedly and explicitly accuses the ancient Hebrews of "prostituting" themselves by worshipping other gods. Modern

---

MESOPOTAMIAN DEITIES

Hundreds of Mesopotamia deities and non-human powers are known. Many prominent Babylonian deities can be correlated with Sumerian ones. The latter names are in parentheses.

Assur: Patron deity of the city of Assur and of the Assyrian civilization which identified his consort as Ishtar. Worship of Assur was closely related to Assyrian royal ideology.

Ea (Enki): Master of the primeval watery abyss, Ea, like many other deities, is assocated with fertility.

Enlil (Ellil): A powerful god and father of many of the gods, he guards the sacred "Tablet of Destiny," which records the fate of everything.

Ishtar (Inanna): Goddess of fertility and war. Identified as the planet Venus. Myths tell of her descending to the underworld and of her lover Dumuzi or Tammuz who must spend six months of the year in the realm of the dead.

Marduk: The god of the city of Babylon became the chief god after fighting and slaying Tiamat.

Shamash (Utu): Although the sun-deity was not as central a figure in Mesopotamia as in Egypt, Shamash was widely worshipped. Later Assyrian kings consulted him through diviners for advice on political and military affairs.

Tiamat: A goddess who tried to destoy the other gods but was herself destroyed by Marduk. Her body was cut into two pieces, which were used to create heaven and earth. Her tears created the Tigris and Euphrates Rivers.

Zoroastrians would be insulted if they were considered anything other than monotheists but the ancient Persian religion has a strong *dualist* idea of opposite cosmic principles or spirits of good and evil. Judaism, Christianity, and Islam all accept a multitude of angels. Christianity and Islam also have long-held dualist beliefs between the righteous God and his cosmic enemy Satan, or Iblis. These beliefs grew out of an ancient Jewish concept of God's battle with rebel angels. What is more, Christians describe their single god as "Father, Son, and Holy Spirit"—the Trinity. The three persons of the trinity are one, and Christians find no trouble in describing themselves as monotheists. For the Muslims, however, the idea of the trinity has the ring of polytheism to it, and they criticize Christianity for not adequately maintaining the oneness of God.

The greatest example of blurring the distinction between monotheism and polytheism comes from Hinduism. For most Hindus, there are very many gods—so many that some writers speak of millions of them. Yet, there is also a sense in Hinduism that a number of these are only different aspects of one of the great deities who has some dealing with other of the great gods and goddesses. The chief gods, then, each take up particular aspects of reality, and worshippers may belong to a sect devoted to one god or another. For some, the greatest god is Vishnu, for others it is Shiva, and still others, the great goddess Devi, who goes by many different names. In this sense Hinduism can be henotheistic or even monolatrous. On an even more philosophical level, these great deities are often described as only aspects of a single deity regardless of what name a worshipper may use. In this sense, Hinduism can be, at least for some practitioners, monotheistic. The ancient Indian sages went yet further, articulating a mystical philosophy in which no gods really exist as outside of the universe. For them, all is god (*pantheism*). It should be clear, then, that the categories used to classify religions should not be employed in a heavy-handed way. One has to be careful to make sure the categories fit the evidence, instead of forcing the evidence to fit the categories, which is often the easier task and usually the most simplistic and inadequate.

MYTHOLOGY

One of the most fascinating, if not frustrating, topics in ancient religions is mythology. Often ancient texts are badly damaged and written in languages that are difficult to decipher. Many times what is published in modern books of mythologies are best-guesses at translation, or are modern retellings with only a superficial connection with the originals. Another problem is that the ancient storytellers did not leave us essays explaining what their myths meant. Sometimes they wrote instructions on how and when to recite the text in the course of a ritual, but it is a tough job sorting through the layers of symbolism without a clear guide from the ancients explaining the world behind the symbols. And this raises the most difficult issue of all: what is *mythology* anyway?

Mythology is notoriously hard to define: there are always stories which seem to deserve the title *myth* but do not fit into one's technical description. In non-academic contexts myth often means a lie, a falsehood, or a fairy story. But scholars of religion use the word in an entirely different way. For academics, there is an unclear line between "legends," "folk-stories," and "myths." To call a religious story a myth is not to dismiss it or to imply that it is not worthy of belief. Indeed, to call such a story a myth is to acknowledge that a community does, or did, *accept it as true* in a most profound sense. Myths capture, in symbolic ways, a people's sense of the way the world really is. In this sense, even biblical stories of the flood or the creation of the world can rightly be called myth, without implying anything other than people down through the ages have believed those stories to carry vitally important religious truths.

A number of theories have been advanced to explain what myths are or what they do. All of the theories at least explain *some* myths, but never all of them. Some scholars have proposed that myths are all related to the working of nature—a kind of primitive science. Often the earth is represented by a goddess, such as Ishtar in Babylon. Yet some myths seem to have no immediate connection to nature. They seem more

EGYPTIAN DEITIES

Egyptians had over fifty deities. Most were native. Only a few of the primary gods are listed here.

Amun: An early primeval deity, worshipped as a creator and sustainer of the universe, typically shown with a tall feathered crown.

Aten: Akhenaten of the New Kingdom established a monotheism dedicated to the sun disk, Aten, which had only recently been deified.

Atum: Another primeval creator deity who became associated with the sun and was represented in human form.

Hathor: A universal mother goddess also associated with death. Often portrayed as a woman with horns or as a cow, she is associated with sun iconography.

Horus: Son of Osiris and Isis. The sky god, who avenged his father's death. Closely associated with royalty and depicted in hawk form.

Isis: The divine mother and queen of heaven. Wife and sister of Osiris, who gathered her slain and dismembered husband Osiris.

Osiris: Husband and brother of Isis. He was killed by his brother Seth. He became lord of the underworld and judge of the dead.

Re: The sun deity had many names and forms. Re was the most important and was considered a creator and sustainer. He was often merged with other deities, such as Re-Atum. Re was depicted in human form.

Seth: God of storms and violence. He murdered his brother Osiris.

concerned with deeper issues of human values and meaning of life. Other myths appear to be "charters" for social customs or institutions: that is, they provide a rationale for the existence of specific kinds of ritual actions, forms of social structure and the like. Other scholars note that myths seem to be closely linked to rituals. The great scholar of the History of Religions, Mircea Eliade, argued that by enacting a myth in a ritual, the individual or community believes it can access the creative divine powers the myth describes. He called this process of returning to the sacred time the "myth of the eternal return." Eliade's theory can explain many features of myth and ritual, but not all. Myths of cultural heroes are frequent exceptions. Other theories, psychological in focus, such as those of Joseph Campbell and Carl Jung, hold that myths are metaphorical projections of universal concepts that govern the human unconscious. However insightful at some level, such theories ignore the vast cultural and historical differences in human experience.

None of these theories, in any of their many variants, can really explain the whole range of mythology. Rather than start with a firm theory, then, it is better to use the most appropriate elements of the various theories that have been offered, and to interpret the stories from a number of perspectives. No one theory seems to hold the key to the rich world of myth.

Just as there is a range of theories attempting to make sense of the world of myth, the myths themselves range widely across subject and theme. We have seen a number of Egyptian creation accounts, in which the pharaoh and the gods were closely linked. The life and death of the king and the rise of his successor was seen to parallel a myth of a god whose death could bring new life. Osiris was murdered by Seth, his body cut up into pieces and scattered on the earth. His widow, Isis, gathers up the pieces and with the help of magical incantations, brings him back to life long enough for the pair to have a child, Horus. Thus, upon death, the Pharaoh would be associated with Osiris, and his successor became the embodiment of Horus. In this way, the death of a king became a reason to affirm stability and not chaos: the transition is only the playing out of a primordial truth. One can see many possible explanations: it explains the continuation of divine presence in the monarchy, it validates the new pharaoh, it links the fate of the royal line to the natural cycles of the earth. The myth engages meaning on many levels.

THE WORLD

In many ancient religious systems, the world is viewed as having been created by one god or group of gods, but it is ruled by others. A number of myths tell how creation was initiated by a single deity, or the merger of two deities, who in turn produce other gods through a variety of means. In other instances, however, gods fight inter-generational wars, which result in a much younger deity winning the right to rule as monarch over the other gods. The royal god then completes the creation of the natural world, including humanity. This pattern is known from Greece to Mesopotamia and beyond. For example, the Babylonian myth *Enuma Elish* is a creation story telling how Marduk won control of the primordial heavens and the "tablet of fate" after a terrible battle with the goddess Tiamat. Her body was cut up to create the heavens and the earth. Her demon champion, Qingu, was slain, and his blood used to create humanity. In the ritual performed during the New Year festival, the king would be enthroned as Marduk's fitting representative on earth, after having been slapped and humiliated by the officiating priests. His reaction to this part of the ritual would be an omen for how the upcoming year was to turn out. Despite this, the ritual was all about the king's power. His governors would have to ritually submit, in emulation of the gods' symbolic acceptance of Marduk's sovereignty.

Other creation myths speak of creation as organic, that is, creation is spontaneous and the creator paradoxically appears as a part of what is being created. In these myths, some kind of chaotic matter pre-exists (often represented as water), which separates to reveal physical matter and a group of deities who set in motion a series of creative acts.

THE GRECO-ROMAN PANTHEON

The twelve Olympian gods formed a family of deities, who ruled following their conquest of older gods called the Titans. Sometimes deities were added, sometimes dropped, and Hades, god of the underworld, was often excluded. The Roman name for a Greek deity is in brackets.

Zeus [Jupiter]: The chief god, who overthrew his father, Cronos. He ruled the sky. His symbol was the thunderbolt. With his brothers Poseidon and Hades, the three gods divided the rule of the universe (heavens, sea, and underworld).

Poseidon [Neptune]: Brother of Zeus and Hades, he was the second-most powerful god and ruler of the sea. His symbol was the trident.

Hades [Pluto]: Brother of Zeus and Poseidon. He was god of the underworld and king of the dead.

Hera [Juno]: Wife of Zeus and mother of some of his children. Most of the gods and goddesses in the Olympian family were children of Zeus from illicit affairs, which provoked the jealousy of Hera.

Other Olympian Deities:
Aphrodite [Venus]
Apollo [Apollo]
Ares [Mars]
Artemis [Diana]
Athena [Minerva]
Hermes [Mercury]
Hestia [Vesta]
Hephaestus [Vulcan]

Sometimes included:
Demeter [Ceres]
Dionysus [Bacchus]

The concept of "creation from nothing," in which the creator god is perfectly timeless and fully separated from the created world (that is, he is transcendent), is very familiar to adherents to Judaism, Christianity, and Islam. It is, however, not shared by many ancient religions and is probably quite a late development in the history of religions. Hinduism and Chinese religions, for example, still embrace variations of the organic mythology of creation.

Often mythology attempts to explain the workings of the universe. Gods associated with vegetation, weather, technology, and even death act in dramas expressing the often enigmatic nature of life. Frequently a powerful deity is temporarily defeated by gods representing chaos or death, only to recover his strength and his throne in the end. Such were the most important myths of Ugarit, a city on the northern shore of Syria, which was abandoned around 1200 B.C.E. The storm god Baal sought a palace from the father god, El, but before taking his place as the heavenly king he had to face the wrath of Mot (death) and Yam (the sea). Several centuries later, Baal would be viewed as the arch-rival of the ancient Israelite god. Much of the Jewish Bible (Christian Old Testament) warns the Israelites not to worship him.

Although there are many variations on the theme, the world was widely conceived of as having three basic layers. The natural world was on the middle one, surrounded by an ocean or river. The heavens were above (sometimes multi-layered) and an underworld beneath where the dead lingered in a shadowy half-existence—if they had any existence at all.

All three levels of reality were interrelated and interconnected. Pits and caves might lead to the underworld, and sacred mountains could find their tops in the heavens. The ancient world knew of many such mountains: Olympus in Greece, Zaphon in northern Syria, Zion in Jerusalem. The Pyramids and Mesopotamian Ziggurat temples were figures of sacred mountains, reaching into the realm of the heavens. Temples were other places where the various levels of the universe could meet. Priests could enter the throne room of the gods by entering the most sacred recesses of the temple.

THE HUMAN CONDITION

As opinions differ on the nature of the gods in world religions, so too do opinions vary on humanity and the meaning of human life. In some ancient Babylonian mythology, humans were intended to be the servants of the gods, primarily by bringing sacrifices to feed them. This has sometimes rather unfairly been called a pessimistic view of the human condition and purpose, particularly when compared to the ancient Israelite account in the book of Genesis, in which God creates humanity "in his own image." In that story, humanity's ties with the divine are not through the blood of a demon, as in some ancient accounts, but through being the ultimate creation of a deity who somehow makes humans a picture of himself. Humanity's first job is to tend the Garden of Eden, a paradise. Even in this supposedly positive story, though, humans soon sin, and they are expelled from the garden. Now humans must work, not to feed the gods as in the *Enuma Elish*, but to feed themselves. And the work will be hard.

In other stories from Babylonian mythology, we see many points in common as well as some shocking differences with the Biblical stories. One of the most intriguing books from the ancient world, the *Epic of Gilgamesh*, includes an episode closely resembling the biblical story of the great flood and Noah's ark. Both books talk of divine outrage at humanity, the instructions to one man to build a boat to save his family from a flood, the sending of birds from the vessel to test if any dry land had reappeared, and the offering of sacrifices afterwards. Yet, the books differ greatly. Gilgamesh's version has the gods upset at the noise and commotion humanity creates. In the Bible, God is angry at human sin and wants to save the family of the one righteous person who is left. The biblical myth occurs in the context of the greater story of how the

CANAANITE DEITIES

The best known Canaanite city was Ugarit on the Mediterranean coast in Northern Syria. It was destroyed in the late thirteenth century B.C.E., but the so-called "Canaanite" culture was widespread throughout the eastern border of the Mediterranean Sea for many centuries afterward. Its language was close to Hebrew, and its literature has many affinities with the Hebrew Bible. Even so, the Israelite god has its own affinities with both El and Baal.

Asherah: A form of the Mesopotamian goddess Isthar (Ashtarte), she is associated with the morning star. Well-known from biblical tradition, some ancient inscriptions combine worship of Yahweh with the goddess or with some ritual item called an *asherah*.

Anath: A major goddess, associated with sexuality and violence. She is an ally of Baal in a number of important myths. Her mourning for Baal after he was swallowed by Mot is a significant theme.

Baal: The most important deity is associated with storms, rain, and fertility. Myths tell of his adventures in obtaining a temple and combating Yamm (Sea) and Mot (Death). In the Bible, Baal is the Israelite deity's chief rival.

El: The elderly, wise father of the gods, he is less active in mythological dramas than Baal and Anath. He holds authority over the other members of the pantheon. In Hebrew, the word *el* can be both a proper name for a deity, and a common noun indicating "god."

Kothar: Craftsman for the other deities with associations with the underworld.

initial created world changed into its present state, with different peoples scattered here and there and human life limited to a relatively short span of years, and God willing to go to great lengths not only to punish the wicked, but to preserve the righteous and the pious. Gilgamesh's flood is told in retrospect, as an explanation why the hero will never attain immortality: it was granted only to the flood's survivor, Utnapishtim, as a once-only boon. Gilgamesh is doomed to die.

DIVINE KINGSHIP

In many instances, an individual could stand out from the rest of humanity and enjoy a special relationship to the gods. Usually this individual was the king, who was held to be the gods' representative on earth, and sometimes even as a divine being in his own right. As the only individual with such links to the divine, society depended on the king to render in his ritual acts and person appropriate service to the gods to ensure the stability and renewal of human society and nature. The figure of the divine king is, not surprisingly, a common fixture in the urban societies in the ancient world. The flip side of this special relationship is that organized religion became an instrument of the state.

Although it is difficult for the modern mind to imagine such identification of the ruler as one of the gods or as having a divine nature, one need not look far to find vestiges of that ancient worldview in modern society. Consider the status of the Emperor in Japan. Until the middle of the twentieth century, he was revered as divine by his subjects; indeed, not until the peace treaty imposed on Japan to end World War II did the Emperor renounce his divine status. The emperors of China were expected to perform vital rituals to ensure the security and prosperity of the kingdom and the world. These rituals were performed in China up to the overthrow of the imperial system in the early twentieth century. Traces of divine kingship are found in the status conferred on the Queen of England at her coronation. She was not crowned by the British Parliament, but by the Archbishop of Canterbury. Of course, in practical terms, her right to rule is granted by the British people, who have not sought to remove her. The royal ideology, however, says her right to rule comes from God, and it is she, and not the archbishop, who is the head of the Church of England (Anglican Church).

In times of threat, even elected national leaders of secular states sometimes sound more like religious leaders than politicians. What they often imply in speeches is that one should remain faithful to the *national* cause because it is a *religious* duty: the country's cause is just in the eyes of God. Many modern religious leaders attribute perceived national decline to failing religious adherence. In the western world, this is often the legacy of early Jewish thought as preserved in the Bible, but the ancient Israelites were not the only people to make the connection between ethics and religious observation, on the one hand, and social, political, and economic fortunes on the other. In these areas, then, the modern world remains very much like the ancient one.

IMMORTALITY

An integral feature of Christianity, Islam, and Judaism is a belief in an afterlife in which the pious and righteous believers will enjoy a paradise in the presence of God while a bitter fate awaits disbelievers and wicked people. Each of the three monotheistic faiths has its own variation on this theme (in Judaism it is far less pronounced than in the others). These are, of course, ancient beliefs, and they can be found in ancient Egyptian thought, for example. Yet, they are only part of a larger complex of thought about the nature of life and death.

There were other conceptions of what happens after one dies. In many cases, dead ancestors could linger on as spirits or ghosts and influence the affairs of the living (not always to their benefit). Offerings would be made to provide food and other goods to the spirits in order to win their favor. When such offerings or the memory of the deceased ended, so too did their shadowy existence. Great heroes or kings might be eventually regarded as gods, but most people were convinced they

PRIMORDIAL AND HEROIC CHARACTERS

Adam: In the Genesis tradition, the first human. He lived with his wife Eve in the Garden of Eden, the primordial paradise, until expelled for disobedience, popularly portrayed as "eating the forbidden apple."

Adapa: A great Mesopotamian sage before the flood. Brought culture to humanity. He provided food for the gods, but incurred some disfavor after breaking the wing of the divine South Wind in a storm.

Aqhat and **Danel:** Heroes of two different Ugaritic (Canaanite) legends. (Danel's story is named after his ill-fated son Aqhat.) Both stories involve the loss of one's children and of offending the deities.

Atrahasis, Utnapishtim, Ziusudra: Heroes of Mesopotamian legends and myths of a great flood. The hero is instructed to save himself, his family and the animals by building a great boat.

Etana: The king of Kish who ascended on an eagle to Ishtar to request a son. Fearing for his life, he returned to earth, later succeeding in his hopes for fatherhood.

Gilgamesh: A king who became the hero of the legendary *Epic of Gilgamesh*. He is viewed as partly divine and had initially been a poor ruler. He reformed, and his story recounts a series of adventures as he tries and fails to win immortality.

Noah: In the Genesis tradition, the man who built an ark to save humans and animals from a great flood.

themselves would go to the underworld upon death. In some conceptions, the deceased faced a trial or judgment before being admitted to the afterlife. Egyptian coffins and tombs were often decorated with texts containing magical spells to help the deceased through the dangerous journey to the great beyond. In Greco-Roman thought, the worthy could find a paradise in the Elysian Fields, although, unlike later Christian and Islamic thought, this was still in the underworld and not in a heaven imagined in the sky.

As noted already, the *Epic of Gilgamesh* deals with the impossibility of eternal life. Many ancient myths tell of journeys to the underworld to try to win back the life of a loved one, and Gilgamesh goes in search of his friend Enkidu. These journeys are not typically successful: at best, the underworld requires compensation in the form of a replacement or gives up her dead on a temporary basis. In some cases, this temporary respite is linked to symbolism of seasonal cycles of vegetation.

Some ancient philosophers wondered about the meaning of life and death. To them, human efforts in this world seemed to have no effect on one's ultimate fate. Even in the Jewish Bible there is sometimes a sense that in death, both the righteous and wicked can expect the same treatment:

> But all this I laid to heart, examining it all, how the righteous and the wise and their deeds are in the hand of God; whether it is love or hate man does not know. Everything before them is vanity, since one fate comes to all, to the righteous and the wicked, to the good and the evil, to the clean and the unclean, to him who sacrifices and him who does not sacrifice. As is the good man, so is the sinner; and he who swears is as he who shuns an oath (Ecclesiastes 9:1-2, New Revised Standard Version).

Beliefs in a judgment and an afterlife did grow in some cultures. Such beliefs became well developed in Persian Zoroastrianism and in Judaism of the second temple period (ca. 500 B.C.E.-70 C.E.) and from there into Christianity and Islam. In the Judaism of the last few centuries B.C.E., belief in the judgment of the soul developed into a more pronounced dualist worldview. All of creation was locked in a struggle between God and rebel angels. Numerous expressions of such beliefs were recorded and they typically predicted how God would ultimately be victorious. This often required the destruction of the entire earth and the virtual creation of a new paradise reserved for God's pious followers. All others will face destruction outright or eternal torment in Hell.

It is these apocalyptic views that influenced early Christians, and they believed that Jesus rose from the dead in a victory that all believers could share in: the body would die, but at the end of the age the body would be raised and the believer would live forever with God. The belief in bodily resurrection also persists in traditional Judaism, even if apocalyptic thought, for the most part, waned as the common era progressed. Islam, likewise, has its own vision of an apocalyptic future and of the resurrection of the dead. An undercurrent of thought in more mystical sectors of western religion, however, accepts reincarnation. That is, the soul of the individual can be born into a succession of physical bodies. Belief in reincarnation is very typical of Indian religions such as Hinduism, Buddhism, and Jainism. It is plausible that, at least to some extent, Eastern religious thought may have influenced Mesopotamian and Mediterranean belief. Yet, it would be going too far to say that all Western notions of reincarnation are the result of such importation of exclusively Indian conceptions.

RITUAL INTERACTION WITH NATURE AND WITH THE DIVINE

The world for the ancients was typically an interconnected organic whole. The heavens were intimately linked to the earth, and humanity had to stay in balance with both. Myth and ritual expressed this relationship and these desires. The myths were often violent, representative of the apparent arbitrariness of life and great forces of nature that seemed beyond human control. Often rituals were performed to reawaken the creative energy of the original event, in which the cosmic enemy was defeated, chaos structured or restructured, and order and life brought to the world.

As noted above, in the ancient world the fate of the universe was often seen as dependent on the king's performance of certain rituals. Just

TERMINOLOGY

Cuneiform: (lit., "wedge shape"). The oldest written script, invented by the Sumerians about 3000 B.C.E. Wedge-shaped characters are mainly found on clay cylinders and tablets in various cultures of Mesopotamia.

Hieroglyphics: (lit., "sacred picture"). The script of ancient Egypt. The discovery in 1799 of a multilanguage inscription (the Rosetta Stone) allowed scholars to decipher the language.

Ostraca: A fragment of a clay pot on which material has been written. The scrap paper of the ancient world.

Papyrus: Paper on which many ancient documents were written. The dryness of the Egyptian desert preserved thousands of papyri fragments of ancient documents, in various languages.

Stele: An upright stone slab, on which inscriptions are carved. Something like an ancient billboard, often with official pronouncements.

Tel: (lit., "hill" or "mound"). A technical term in archaeology for a mound formed by a settlement lived in and rebuilt over time that leaves a hill reflecting various strata of settlement.

Ziggurat: The typical temple architecture in Mesopotamia, shaped as a stepped tower and seen as linking heaven and earth.

as the heavens could not function without the deities, so nature could not function without the king and the royal institutions of priests, scribes, and so forth properly performing their duties for the gods and goddesses. This intricate linking of human royalty and heavenly control over nature seems almost a universal feature of pre-modern urban religion.

The endless cycles of nature, the unknowable powers behind it, and the uncertainties and ambiguities of human life were mysteries to the ancients, yet they perceived some kind of harmony as the ideal. Ritual often tried to influence these powers by replicating something of the cycles of life and death, and to show the divine powers that humanity is aware that it is not by their own power that they live. To this end, the gods were offered countless sacrifices and offerings. Sacrifices could consist of different things: crops or wine were often used, as well as incense or even gifts of gold or silver. In many cases, however, the gods demanded blood sacrifices. Animals were ritually slaughtered and at least part of the animal was burned on altars. Often, some of the meat went to the priests, and some could even be distributed back to the people. The Christian New Testament, for example, advises Christians to avoid eating meat that had been sacrificed to "idols": the standard biblical way of describing sacrifices to non-Christian deities. Sacrifices can be offered to glorify a deity, to win the favor of a deity, to mark important dates, or to pay for the sin of a person or the whole nation.

Countless books have been written trying to explain the cultural and psychological origins of sacrifice, and there is probably no end in sight to this significant part of religious studies. From a modern standpoint, most troubling is the fact that occasionally cultures would require a human sacrifice. Most famous of all are the religions of ancient Mexico and central and South America, in which thousands of people, often prisoners of war, but sometimes members of the society itself, were sacrificed to ensure the prosperity of the culture. In many cases this seems to have been a response to terrible stresses: the less gruesome system of animal offerings no longer seemed to earn the people reliable weather and harvests, so more drastic measures were called for. The ancient Near East was also the location for at least some human sacrifice, although there were probably more accusations than there was practice of it. Such charges were a good way of demonizing one's enemy.

Sacrifices and ritual killing have marked the religious routine of many cultures. Such ideas run deep in many mythologies. Often the universe comes into being through the death of a primordial being, where sometimes the world is created from the carcass of a slain god, who sometimes is portrayed in the form of a person. The ancient Norse (Vikings) spoke of Odin creating the world from the body of the giant Ymir. The *Enuma Elish* says Tiamat's corpse was split to make heaven and earth. Ancient Hindu texts told of the self-sacrifice of the primordial person, Purusha. Most probably, animal sacrifice stems from the awareness that life and death are inextricably linked: human sacrifice is an extreme form of this awareness. In some religions, there are conscious attempts to denounce human sacrifice, or to symbolize it in other, less costly ways. Some Hindu texts rewrite myths in a way that seeks to establish animal replacements for an apparent requirement for human sacrifice. Still later texts express how one may even use plants as a replacement for animals in sacrifice. One thing can symbolize another, even in sacrifices. Indeed, the Passover sacrifice of ancient Judaism is no longer practiced, but it is symbolized by a placing a shank-bone on a plate at the *seder* meal.

Many contemporary religions continue to offer animal sacrifice. Some forms of Hinduism specify sacrifices, for example, and the Samaritans in northern Israel still celebrate their Passover with the traditional sacrifice of a lamb. In North and Central America, the religions derived from the African practices of those caught up in the slave trade sometimes make such offerings. During the great pilgrimage to Mecca, Muslims sacrifice a sheep or other animal on the Festival of Sacrifice (Id al-Adha) to symbolize the patriarch Abraham's willingness to sacrifice his son at the insistence of God. In Islam human sacrifice is abhorrent, as it is in Judaism and Christianity: God stopped Abraham from carrying out this order at the last moment, giving him a sheep to sacrifice instead. While the Islamic festival offends the sensibilities of many Westerners for religious or animal-rights reasons, the meat itself is put to good use. Traditionally, part of it is retained for the family of the sacrificer, while the remainder is offered to neighbors and the poor. Therefore, it also expresses Islamic concern for the plight of the hard-pressed.

In ancient Judaism, many sacrifices were offered for the remission of sins. Such is not done anymore since the temple, which had become the only authorized place for sacrifice in Judaism, is no longer standing. Yet, many Jewish festivals still symbolize the rituals in which such offerings were made: most importantly, Yom Kippur, the Day of Atonement. Early Rabbinic writings, made in the aftermath of the fall of the temple in 70 C.E., seek to find replacements for the sacrifices in an increased accent on prayer and acts of mercy and kindness. In Christianity, sacrifice is not acceptable, although Christian theology often speaks of Christ as the "lamb of God," whose death was the one acceptable sacrifice for the remission of the believer's sins. The ritual of the Eucharist is a symbol of Christ's sacrifice, established according to the New Testament by Christ himself on the evening before his death. In Catholic theology, the wine and bread is believed to become the actual blood and body of Christ. While Western Religions have long since abandoned blood sacrifice as a means of "feeding" a god, the old ideas of the atoning value of sacrifice and the willingness to offer up to God what is most precious continues.

MAGIC / ASTROLOGY

Because of the perceived interconnection between the realm of the deities, of nature, and of human society, ancient people began trying to understand how it all worked as a unity. Beliefs arose that by studying certain natural phenomena, or patterns that resulted from seemingly random actions, one could learn the secrets of the universe. Ancient religions from China through the Middle East and into Europe embraced many different kinds of divination and astrology. In many cases, political decisions depended on the patterns of stars, phases of the moon, patterns of cracks in heated bones, or even the pattern of markings on the internal organs of sacrificed animals. Illnesses and misfortune could be ascribed to demons and evil magicians. Gods or the spirits of the dead would be invoked to help one attain one's desires or to protect one from malicious magic. Sometimes, the gods would speak to prophets who would deliver advice, warnings, or threats to a king. These often reflected the king's concerns over security and power.

It is too easy to dismiss this kind of religiosity in the modern world as silly or superstitious. But what is often denigrated as superstition is actually a misunderstanding about another person's religion. Behind magic and astrology is a worldview that the universe is interconnected and at least partially knowable and predictable, if only to those willing to become initiated into the mysteries. And more than echoes of this ancient worldview remain with us. New concerns about the environment and the global community have led many people to try to reclaim some of the ancient conceptions about a fully integrated universe. Concerns of this nature explain, in part, the appeal of Buddhism and Hinduism to many in the technologically advanced but depersonalized Western world. The so-called neo-pagan and Wiccan movements are based on ritual activities meant to connect the practitioner with the earth (often imagined as "Goddess" or "Gaia"). These rituals include magical acts meant to bring harmony and balance into the life of the practitioner. Alongside this, astrology and other forms of divination are gaining a new audience.

The similarity between these new religions and the ancient faiths they claim they are recovering can easily be overestimated, but the underlying perception about the world is, to a large extent, comparable. The ancient world was full of beliefs about astrology and divination. The modern Zodiac was developed from earlier Mesopotamian models. The *Enuma Elish* discusses the establishment of these arts through creating an ordered universe and Marduk securing for himself the "Tablet of Destiny." Witchcraft and magical protection from witches were certainly a part of the religious landscape across the ancient world. Texts have been discovered offering incantations to remedy many kinds of illness, toothaches, and even hangovers. It is uncertain how many modern, new age witches actually believe their spells can have a material effect on the world, but the basic premise of an integrated universe and the power of symbols to influence one's interaction with it connects them with a long history of human religious practice. Religions throughout time have been marked by the fear of so-called "occult" practices as a kind of inversion of "true" religion. The Jewish and Christian Bibles take a sharp stance against any practice of magic. Many Christians to this day believe that the realm of the magical and demonic are substantial, though deformed, aspects of reality. Magic for them is very real: it is a tool of the devil. Exorcisms, the removal of evil spirits dwelling in people, are, for many, no Hollywood fantasy.

THE ROAD AHEAD

Books could be written on the persistence of ancient ideas in modern religions, and here we have but a sampling of some of the main ideas. The field is likely only to grow: answers are sometimes harder to come by than new questions. Yet, when you read the other chapters in this book, try to think of how stories are used to express beliefs about the world, and humanity's place in it. Consider how similar themes pop up in different contexts with radically different meanings. All of the difficult questions we face in our lives were the very kinds of issues the ancients were confronted with too. Trying to understand the cultural and historical reasons why people have produced so many different religious responses to these issues is part of what makes Religious Studies so fascinating.

Western Religions

HISTORY

Judaism & Ancient Hebrew/Israelite Religion

Scholars of the Jewish religion frequently draw a distinction between Judaism on the one hand and the religion of the ancient Hebrews or Israelites on the other. The distinctive terms remind us that Judaism is a particular interpretation and development of the traditions of the ancient Israelites. For our purposes in this book, however, that kind of distinction need not be made. When we speak of Judaism, we include in it the full spectrum of a religious tradition reaching back to the ancient Hebrews and forward to present-day Judaism.

A Word About Sources

The Hebrew Bible (what Christians call the "Old Testament") is the oldest literature of the Jewish people. Among others things, it provides a sketch of the Jewish people from their beginnings down to efforts to restore their homeland and religion after their devastating defeat by the Babylonian Empire in the 500s B.C.E. That story covers nearly two millennia, from about 2000 B.C.E. to near the turn of the eras.

A problem arises in that, although the stories of the Hebrew Bible span this considerable period, the composition of these stories in a final form more or less familiar to us today probably did not occur until the last few hundred years or so of that period (500 B.C.E.–100 C.E.). About two hundred years ago, scholars became concerned about this gap between the time of the composition of the stories and the time of the events the stories purport to record. The worth of these stories in reconstructing the history of ancient Israel was hotly debated, and the debate continues. Some argue for a reasonable accuracy of the stories; others treat the stories as idealized constructs reflecting the interests of the scribal community responsible for the final compilation of these stories. The most widely recognized view that rose out of these debates is called the "Documentary Hypothesis." It identifies the main sources behind the Torah (the first part of the Jewish Bible) by the letters J (Yahwist, from the German Jahweh), E (Elohist), D (Deuteronomist), and P (Priestly writer), each reflecting different dates, environments, and perspectives in which the biblical traditions took their shape.

No hypothesis has gained universal acceptance, and the scholarly debate is sometimes quite heated. In the treatment that follows, the storyline of the Bible is recounted, with occasional reference to major scholarly controversies.

The Patriarchs

The earliest traditions of the Hebrews are recounted in family stories called the Patriarchal Narratives. Much of Genesis, the first document in the Bible, consists of stories about these patriarchs, or founding fathers, of the Hebrews: Abraham, his son Isaac, his grandson Jacob (also called Israel), and Jacob's twelve sons, who came to constitute the heads of the "Twelve Tribes of Israel." A favorite son, Joseph, gets special attention, with stories featuring him making up almost half of the Patriarchal Narratives.

These stories are set in the nomadic world of the Middle East in the earlier half of the second millennium B.C.E., and in Egypt. The date of the earliest telling of these narratives is debated. The date of their incorporation in the written biblical narrative is more certain—sometime in the 500s and 400s B.C.E. These stories provide a portrait of Israel as a divinely instituted tribal confederation, and it is with that confederation (or nation) that Jewish identity has been defined throughout its history. Scholars debate to what degree such stories are to be considered historical, legendary, or an invented history, shaped by the agenda and interests of the post-exilic Jewish community whose literary efforts produced the Hebrew Bible.

Moses, the Law-Giver

Although Abraham is presented as the father of the Hebrews, it is Moses, the national liberator, religious reformer, and law-giver, who is credited with providing the most substantial elements of Hebrew religion.

Moses' story begins when the Hebrews were at a low point in their history, whether that "history" is legendary or not. They were slaves in Egypt and their very existence as a people threatened, as their newborn boys were killed by government decree. According to the story in Exodus (the second document in the Bible), Moses was rescued from this fate by the daughter of the Pharaoh, ruler of Egypt, and raised as a member of the royal house in Egypt. But unable or unwilling to forget his Hebrew heritage, Moses rose against the Egyptians and led the Hebrews through the Red (or Reed) Sea to freedom. According to the biblical tradition, this escape, called the Exodus, ended more than 400 years of residence in Egypt. The Exodus is one of the highlights of the Jewish calendar, and is celebrated in the Passover (Pesach) festival. Its theme of liberation has stimulated the imagination of Jews through long periods of oppression, exile, and wandering.

The story continues with the formation of the freed Hebrews into a religious nation, under solemn oath to obey Yahweh, their newly revealed God, and to follow Torah, Yahweh's newly revealed law. This law, expressed in condensed form, is popularly known as the Ten Commandments or Decalogue (lit., "ten words").

"Conquest" and the Judges

TEXTS OF TORAH (LAW)

(in order of composition)

Torah: The first five books of the Hebrew Bible, the primary source for Torah. Also called Pentateuch.

Tanak (Tanakh): An acronym for the three parts of the Hebrew Bible: Torah [Law] + Neviim [Prophets] + Ketuvim [Writings]. Commonly called the Hebrew Bible or simply the Bible (= Christian "Old Testament").

Mishnah: (lit., "repetition"). The primary collection of oral Torah, complementing the written Torah of the Tanak. Compiled around 200 C.E. from older traditions.

Talmud: (lit., "study"). The Mishnah combined with commentary (called the *gemara*) comprises the Talmud. Two versions were compiled: one in Palestine, called the Jerusalem Talmud (300s C.E.); the other (more influential) in Babylon (400s C.E.). Medieval commentaries are incorporated into present texts of the Talmud. Those by Rashi (1040-1105) and Maimonides (1135-1204) are particularly influential.

Responsa: Collections of written replies from rabbis to questions about the Torah, after the completion of the Talmud. There are over 1,000 volumes of responsa.

Shulchan Aruch: (lit., "The Prepared Table"). Originally a Sephardic work from the 1500s, it was annotated in the same century with Ashkenazi alternative practices. It is the most used guidebook for Torah observance among observant Jews.

According to the biblical account, Moses died before a permanent home for the new nation had been established, but the idea of a nation in a covenant relationship with Yahweh continued to inspire the Hebrews, as they came into possession of the land of Canaan (Palestine), or what came to be called the Promised Land. Scholars debate whether the Hebrew presence in Canaan represents a conquest from the outside, a lower class social revolution from the inside, or a less dramatic evolutionary population shift from urban centers to more nomadic and rural lifestyles, due perhaps to economic or environmental pressures.

Whatever the case, the biblical account indicates that initially the Hebrews experimented with various forms of tribal alliances and leadership under charismatic military heroes, in a period referred to as the time of the judges. As time passed, the tribes recognized the usefulness of a union under one leader, and they established a monarchy.

The First Temple Period (900s-500s B.C.E.)

It is with the monarchy that we move into a more documented period of history for the Hebrews, although even here there is scarce mention of the Hebrews outside of their own writings. Most of the literature from this time is now lost, but portions of that literature are thought to be preserved in the later theologically motivated, sweeping national histories (the biblical books of Kings and Chronicles), completed after the monarchy had collapsed in the 500s. It is not possible to determine to what degree these writers reshaped the earlier materials to their agenda. One should remember that histories are interpretations of the past; the histories of ancient Israel are interpretations of the Israelite past, viewed from a perspective of national crises, collapse, and exile in the 500s and 400s B.C.E.

According to the biblical story, the early monarchy struggled to unite and control the groups in the tribal alliance. Success was brief, lasting roughly one century (900s B.C.E.), under the reigns of Saul, David, and Solomon. After that, the discontent and isolation of the northern tribes from the centralized palace power in the south fueled a civil war that split the Hebrews into northern and southern rival monarchies. Many scholars think that the biblical story has reversed the roles of the north and the south: it was the north that developed first and dominated. The biblical account does recognize that the north, called Israel, was the stronger and larger, but it emphasizes the religious unfaithfulness and political instability of the north, which was ruled by several short-lived dynasties. Indeed, the history of the monarchy in the north was largely the story of the rise and reign of a strongman, followed by a brief and incompetent reign of a weak son, which ended in a palace coup. The northern kingdom came to an end in 722 B.C.E., when the Assyrians marched through the region, lying waste to land and people. In the southern territory, called Judah, the monarchy had greater prestige, largely because of its connection to the great king David and to the temple. David's dynasty survived until the defeat of Judah by the Babylonians in 586 B.C.E. Both Assyrian and Babylonian accounts speak of these collapses. To this day many Jews anticipate the reestablishment of the dynasty of David, and Christians, an offshoot of Judaism, still speak of their leader, Jesus, as the son, or descendant, of David.

The Exile (500s B.C.E.)

The loss of independence and the exile of Judah's elite to Babylon constituted one of the most severe crises in the history of the Hebrews. The tribes of the north had been absorbed so completely into the land of their exile that they disappeared from history, other than as the legendary "Ten Lost Tribes." This was not to be the fate of Judah, although the loss of homeland, the collapse of the Davidic monarchy, and the destruction of the Temple had made that prospect likely. Fortunately, the exile was short-lived: the Babylonians fell quickly to the Persians, who favored resettlement of displaced captives. Further, a religious revival took place among the Jews in exile, prompted by prophets and a renewed interest in Torah. An interest in collecting, editing, and composing Hebrew literature marked this period, producing what would come to be known, with further additions, as the Hebrew Bible. This body of rich and varied literature stands as the most significant accomplishment of the Jewish people, and

LEADERS (BIBLICAL)
Abraham: The father of the Hebrews, who with his son Isaac, his grandson Jacob (also called Israel), and Jacob's twelve sons are counted as the Patriarchs.
Moses: Law-giver who presented the Torah and covenant to Israel and founded the nation.
David: (900s B.C.E.). The idealized king, whose dynasty is featured as one of the key elements in the restoration of Israel.

LEADERS (MEDIEVAL)
Maimonides: (1138-1204). A Spanish Jewish philosopher and commentator on the Talmud, he formulated thirteen principles of Judaism.
Rashi: (1040-1105). French rabbinic commentator on the Bible and the Talmud.

LEADERS (MODERN)
Moses Mendelssohn: (1729-1786). German philosopher; leader of the Jewish Enlightenment.
Abraham Geiger: (1810-1874). German rabbi; founder of the Reform movement.
Samson R. Hirsch: (1808-1888). German rabbi; leader of the neo-Orthodox movement, which challenged Reform innovations.
Zacharias Frankel: (1801-1875). German rabbi; founder of the positivist-historical school, which influenced Conservative Judaism in North America.
Theodor Herzl: (1860-1904). Austrian journalist; founder of World Zionist Organization; sought to create a Jewish state.
Mordecai Kaplan: (1881-1983). American rabbi and founder of Reconstructionist Judaism.

it still influences contemporary thinking on powerful religious themes such as monotheism, ethics, and social justice.

Babylonia became fertile ground for Jewish speculation. Even after Persia conquered Babylonia and permitted Jews to return to Palestine, many Jews remained in Babylonia, where a rich Jewish culture was developing. Indeed, Jewish scholars in Babylon were to become leading contributors to developments within Judaism for about 1,500 years.

It is thought that during this time Judaism added a number of beliefs popular in Zoroastrianism, the religion of the Persians. Concepts of angels, Satan, the resurrection of the dead, and final judgment all are prominent in Persian religion and become prominent in Judaism only after contact with the Persians.

The Second Temple Period (late 500s B.C.E.–70 C.E.)

Those Jews who returned to Palestine from Babylonian exile faced a number of crises. The capital city, Jerusalem, had been destroyed and the temple lay in ruins. New families of influence had arisen, and Jews who had escaped deportation had intermarried with peoples of questionable parentage. The returning exiles took kindly to none of this, and, in their rebuilding of the city and the society, they instituted a policy of exclusion and defined borders of purity more rigorously. This created tension with the population already in the area, whose rights and status became more and more restricted. The Samaritans, whom we meet later as a distinctive society, grew out of this alienation.

Little is known about the returnees and their new society. We know they completed the rebuilding of the temple in the late 500s B.C.E. or shortly thereafter (thus the period that followed is often referred to as Second Temple Judaism). They instituted a rigorous application of Torah under Ezra and developed a more uncompromising monotheism. These were significant religious accomplishments. But politically the new society was of no account, their territory having been reduced to little more than a twenty-five mile square around Jerusalem.

Although the promise of a homeland and nation is a prominent feature of the covenant that Yahweh made with Israel, many of the exiled Jews chose to remain in Babylonia, the only land that they knew.

The Persian Empire, under whom the Jews were permitted to return to Palestine, was conquered by Alexander the Great and his Macedonian/Greek Empire. Many of the Jewish elite became attracted to aspects of Hellenism, the Greek culture that followed in the wake of Alexander's conquests. The attraction was sometimes so overpowering that it threatened the distinctive identity of Jews. For example, even something as important to Jewish identity as circumcision was disregarded by some Jews. After almost two centuries of Greek influence, a Hellenistic king attempted to outlaw Judaism. This move backfired, sparking the successful Maccabean Revolt (167–164 B.C.E.). Jews gained their independence for the first time in 400 years.

But many Jews found Jewish rule hardly more pleasing than foreign rule, for the Maccabees came to control the high-priesthood and throne, neither of which they were qualified to hold according to the prescription of the Jewish scriptures. This situation led to the formation of a number of groups with varying agenda. Sadducees, the elite who controlled the temple and much of the commerce, supported the status quo. Pharisees focused on Torah, providing at times a religious critique of the elite; their political involvement and influence varied as situations changed. The Essenes offered a more sweeping critique of both temple and palace, apparently removing themselves to the banks of the Dead Sea in protest. After the Romans conquered Palestine in the first century B.C.E., further groups formed, the Christian movement being one, and the militant Zealots being another. During this period of political struggles and disappointments, many of the new groups in Judaism developed an apocalyptic mentality: despair with the present conditions; anticipation of the intervention of God to establish his own rule (the "kingdom of God"); and the punishment of evildoers and the reward of the pious at the final Great Judgment.

This apocalyptic mentality energized opposition to Rome, and in 66 C.E., Jews attacked Roman troops in Palestine and massacred their

ANCIENT GROUPS

The following groups (except for the Samaritans) arose in the Maccabean period. Most were wiped out by the Jewish revolts against Rome in the first and second centuries C.E.

Maccabees: The nickname of the Hasmoneans, a priestly family who led the revolt against the Seleucid Greeks, and liberated Palestine for a few decades before the Roman conquest of the East.
Essenes: Often identified with an apocalyptic sect, discontent with life under the Maccabees, who formed an isolated ascetic, scribal, and priestly community near the Dead Sea at Qumran. The Dead Sea Scrolls were part of their library.
Pharisees: A non-priestly group, whose concern about religious purity and the study of Torah and oral traditions gave them popular influence in the society. Their traditions influence rabbinic Judaism.
Sadducees: The religious elite, controlling the Jerusalem temple and its economy. They rejected the oral Torah and some of the newer ideas in Judaism.
Samaritans: A group in central Palestine, with obscure Jewish ancestry. They used the Pentateuch and expected a prophet-like messianic figure.
Zealots: A collection of diverse discontents and apocalyptic militants, who led the revolt against Rome.

non-Jewish neighbors in many towns. The Romans and non-Jews retaliated in kind. In 70 C.E., Jerusalem was captured and razed, the temple destroyed, and countless thousands of Jews killed or sold into slavery. Thus ended the second temple period, and some two thousand years later, Jews still conduct their religion without a temple, although that institution had long been a cornerstone of Jewish piety.

Rabbinic Judaism

The impact of the failure of the Jewish Revolt was profound. Many groups on the Jewish political and religious map simply disappeared. Revolutionaries were exterminated. The governing elite lost the temple, council, and influence. Apocalyptic dreams became nightmares when God did not ride to the rescue. What had been a multi-textured society became much more uniform, under the direction of a group of expert teachers of the Jewish Torah. These teachers, called rabbis, were most closely connected to a pre-revolt group, the Pharisees. The tradition developed by these teachers is called Rabbinic Judaism.

Three features mark the perspective of the rabbis. One: the fate of Jews and the Jewish nation is tied directly to obeying the precepts of Torah. Two: Torah is to be guarded by building a "fence" about it, consisting of detailed supplementary laws. Three: Torah consists of both written Torah (the Bible) and oral Torah (traditions passed on orally by the sages). Both, according to the rabbis, originated with Moses.

Slightly over a hundred years after the destruction of the temple, much of the oral Torah was collected and organized into a written work, called the Mishnah. This large work, divided into six sections, covered a range of topics discussed by the rabbis, from the temple, sacrifice, Sabbath, festivals, civil and criminal matters, to agriculture and women's issues (marriage, divorce, etc.).

The Mishnah itself became the subject of further discussion, and a body of commentary (*gemara*) grew up around the discussion of the Mishnah. This commentary came to be included in the manuscripts of the Mishnah, creating a composite and much larger collection called the Talmud. Two Talmuds were published, one in Palestine and the other in Babylonia. The Babylonian version, completed by 500 C.E., became the more influential.

The Talmud itself then became the chief text for study, surrounded by additional discussion in the form of great medieval commentaries. Such discussions were incorporated into manuscripts of the Talmud. This has made each page of the Talmud look somewhat like a patchwork, with the text of the Mishnah and the *gemara* at the center, and the various commentaries on the Mishnah in blocks around it.

For about 1,700 years, up to the time of the Enlightenment, Judaism was dominated by the Rabbinic perspective, and even today large numbers of Jews follow the detailed specifications of rabbinic legislation.

Changes and Challenges to Rabbinic Judaism

Although Rabbinic Judaism held sway until the modern age, it was not without its challenges. A group of Jews called the Karaites (lit., "readers") were formed in Babylonia in the early 700s, just after the area came under Muslim rule. The Karaites rejected the authority of the rabbis and disregarded oral Torah, emphasizing instead the authority of the Pentateuch. Their influence, which was considerable, declined in the 1100s as Jews in Spain revitalized the rabbinic traditions in various philosophical and practical directions, although Karaites remain a presence to this day.

> **MEDIEVAL GROUPS**
>
> **Karaite:** A group of Babylonian Jews in the 700s, who rejected the authority of the Talmud and the Rabbinic tradition. They emphasized a more literal approach to Hebrew scripture.
>
> **Kabbalist:** A general term for a Jewish mystic, who sought the hidden meaning behind the external realities and the coded meaning of texts. Kabbalism did much to revitalize Judaism from the 1200s, at a time when European expulsion of Jews was beginning.
>
> **Ashkenazi:** Jews of German background, including most east European Jews. Yiddish was their language, and Christianity the dominant culture under which they took their shape.
>
> **Sephardic:** Jews largely of Spanish background, who migrated to the Ottoman Empire, Italy, and the Netherlands, when they were deported from Spain. Ladino was their language, and Islam the dominant culture under which they took their shape.

Kabbalism began in the 1100s, developing from older mystical roots in Judaism. While it required strict adherence to the Talmud, it explored dimensions of mysticism and sought the hidden or coded meaning in texts far beyond the usual speculations of the rabbis. Although Kabbalism revitalized Judaism during the centuries of European persecution and expulsion of Jews that followed, the esoteric and secret teachings often brought it under suspicion from Talmudic authorities.

Messianic movements had been characteristic of Judaism through much of its history, but developments in Kabbalistic thought in the 1500s stirred messianic interests into a frenzy. The most influential was the Sabbataian movement of the 1600s. Jewish populations throughout Europe and the Ottoman Empire were swept along by a pitch of messianic expectation and excitement sparked by the preaching of Shabbetai Tzevi. The movement lost much–but not all–of its influence when the leader, under pressure, converted to Islam.

Messiahs and mystics have the potential to challenge the authority of the rabbi. So does the miracle-worker. The rabbinic movement faced such a challenge from a simple laborer, who came to be known as Ba'al Shem Tov (lit., "Master of the Good Name"). Displaying charismatic and miraculous powers, he preached that God cherished the pious simplicity of the common Jew over mastery of the Talmudic legislation, which had become an impossible attainment for the average Jew. This eighteenth-century movement, called the Hasidism (lit., "pious"), created powerful expressions of enthusiasm, prayer, dance, and heartfelt worship of God in the humble, ordinary activities of life. Although initially seen as a threat to rabbinic Judaism, the movement soon became its strongest supporter, reacting to the radical reforms of some Jews during the 1800s as a result of the Enlightenment. Indeed, the Hasidic movement now is considered ultra-orthodox—the strongest adherent to rabbinic Judaism. Numerous Hasidic groups still exist, usually centered around a holy man (tsaddiq), whose position is hereditary.

European Expulsions

Jews lived a precarious existence in lands where they took up residence. Since Jews were not assimilated but maintained their identity as a distinctive people—by choice and by force—they were readily viewed as foreign and their practices scorned as alien and even subversive. Further, in Christian nations, Jews were often branded as "Christ-killers" for, according to traditions in the Christian Gospels, Jews were involved in the plot to execute Jesus. This made Jews easy scapegoats when the local economic or political situation became unstable, for whatever reason. In 1290, Jews were expelled from England. Over the next 300 years, Jews who would not convert to Christianity were expelled from most European lands. In Spain, where the largest community of European Jews resided, deportation came in 1492—a date easy to remember, for Columbus was setting sail at the same time as Spanish harbors were crowded with fleeing Jews. Ironically, Columbus was to discover a "new world," which in time would become the home for the largest Jewish community in the world.

Even Jews who had converted often did not escape. Many of the converts continued to practice Judaism secretly, and all were suspected of doing that. In Spain, for example, Jewish (and Muslim) Conversos (converts to Christianity) often were tagged with the disparaging label Marranos (lit., "pigs"), and many suffered under the Spanish Inquisition.

Many of the Jews who were expelled from Spain (Sepharadic Jews) found homes in the Ottoman Empire, North Africa, Italy, and the Netherlands. Many of the Jews expelled from elsewhere in Europe (Ashkenazic Jews) found residence in Poland and, when Poland was divided, in areas of recent Russian conquest. In the late 1800s, however, Russian Jews faced massacres, pogroms, and deportations. The mood of this period is captured in the musical *The Fiddler on the Roof.* The inspiration of the Zionist movement owed much to the plight of these Jews.

The various persecutions of Jews in Europe led to considerable immigration to North America. Presently, roughly one-half of the world's Jews live in North America, about one-quarter in Israel, and one-quarter remain in Europe (which had held the main concentration of Jews until the genocide of the Holocaust in the mid-1900s).

Ashkenazim and Sephardim

Two main traditions developed in rabbinic Judaism. The primary difference relates to the lands in which they took their shape. The Ashkenazim trace much of their cultural influences to Germany and eastern European lands, where Christianity was dominant; Yiddish is their distinctive language. The Sephardim trace their influences to Spain, and later to North Africa and lands of the Ottoman Empire, where Islam was dominant, and to Italy and the Netherlands. Ladino is their language.

On most matters, there are slight differences in the details of the laws and vocabulary between the two groups of Jews. At one time these differences considerably strained relations between the

MODERN GROUPS

Hasidic: A mystical movement founded by Baal Shem Tov (1700-1760) in Poland. Particularly important to eastern European Jews. It emphasized devotion and joy of the common Jew over the learning of the rabbis as a means of harmony with God.

Reform: Founded in 1800s; emphasizes an ethical monotheism rather than ritual, law, and messianic expectations. Such change allowed Jews to identify more easily with western enlightenment society. They view Judaism as always needing a reforming spirit in order to be authentic.

Conservative or **Positive-Historical:** Founded in 1800s as reaction to Reform Judaism's radical discarding of tradition; stands mid-way between the Reformed and Orthodox. Judaism is to be reformed, but not on rationalist principles. Historical scholarship is the tool used to determine the non-binding elements in Judaism practice.

Orthodox: Also called "neo-orthodox"; maintains traditional practices and beliefs, making it the most loyal group to rabbinic Judaism. Judaism is eternal and divinely given, thus not subject to change.

Reconstructionist: Founded on the principle of Judaism as an evolving religious culture, subject to change. Views Judaism as a human construct, as Reform Judaism does.

Zionist: Founded by Theodor Herzl. Primarily a secular movement, whose goal was to establish a Jewish homeland.

two communities. But today the orthodox of both groups refer to the same reference work on Torah, called the *Shulchan Aruch* ("The Prepared Table"). This was originally a Sephardic work from the 1500s, which attempted to provide a practical guidebook for Torah observance. It was annotated in the same century with Ashkenazi alternative practices, and thus made to serve both communities.

The Ashkenazim, centered in Europe, were most affected by the Enlightenment, and the Jewish groups growing out of that, such as Reform, Conservative, Reconstructionist, and neo-Orthodox, are part of the Ashkenazi tradition.

The Enlightenment (Haskalah)

As a result of the Enlightenment, European and American Jews were forced to rethink their religious and cultural world. Previously, the options for Jews were limited. They had been excluded from most cultural, professional, and educational institutions, unless they became converts to Christianity.

A new range of possibilities for Jews in modern western society opened as a result of the changes in the political and intellectual landscape of Europe. The American and French Revolutions proclaimed a spirit of brotherhood and equality, and Napoleon's armies liberated Jews from ghettos throughout Europe, reversing policies of discrimination. In this "emancipation," Jews could become lawyers and teachers; they could vote and sit in the national parliaments; they could attend the universities. (The rise of national states after the defeat of Napoleon, however, sometimes revived anti-Jewish sentiments.)

Jews were expected, in return for "emancipation," to identify more closely with the national society and the national interest. Citizenship and its promises came, therefore, at a cost to traditional Jewish religious and cultural interests. Jews reacted in various ways to this new tolerance, as they attempted to appropriate their religious heritage in the context of the modern world. Many rejected much of their Jewish tradition; these groups were usually based in urban areas. Other groups in urban areas, as well as Jews from villages and rural areas more generally, maintained a more vigorous loyalty to ancient beliefs and practices.

Zionism, the Holocaust (Shoah), and the Modern State of Israel

Not all modern Jewish movements are religious. In the last years of the 1800s, reestablishing the nation of Israel became a priority among secular Jews of diverse orientations. It was this driving force, called Zionism, more than the aspirations of religious Jews, that pushed the issue of a homeland for the Jews onto the world stage. These Jews recognized that in many areas of the world, the position of Jews continued to be precarious, and even in lands in which Jews were emancipated, an ugly anti-Semitism often lay close to the surface. The only real security was in an independent Jewish homeland.

Zionism's perception of a latent anti-Semitism in European society was confirmed in the most horrific way when Nazi Germany declared a "Final Solution" to the "Jewish Question." The Holocaust death camps became the final home for some six million Jews (one-third of Jews worldwide), and a new word, *genocide*, was coined to describe the policy to eliminate all individuals in an ethnic group. Under such dark conditions, even those Jews who had dismissed the effort to establish a Jewish homeland as outdated became sympathetic supporters of the cause, although they themselves often lived comfortably in their own lands and had no desire themselves to take up residence in a Jewish state. Fifty years after the founding of the Zionist movement, the modern state of Israel was established, in 1948.

But there were disappointments. Traditionally, Jews had believed that the rebuilding of Israel would be associated with the coming of the Messiah. Yet it had been secular socialists who dominated the Zionist movement, and it was the socialist kibbutz, or collective, that became the distinctive pattern of settlement

FESTIVALS

Rosh Hashanah: (lit., "beginning of the year"). Jewish New Year, in September or October. Begins a 10-day solemn period of repentance and self-examination, which ends on Yom Kippur.

Yom Kippur: (lit., "Day of Atonement"). The holiest day of the Jewish calendar, marked by fasting, prayer, and repentance.

Sukkot: "Tabernacles" or "Booths." A seven-day harvest festival, linked to the wandering of the Hebrew exiles in the desert after their escape from Egypt.

Pesach: (lit., "to pass over"). Commonly known as Passover. Celebrates the escape of the ancient Hebrews from Egyptian slavery (Exodus). A special meal (the *seder*) with various foods, including unleavened bread (*matzah*), is the highlight.

Hanukkah: "Dedication." Celebrates the victory of the Maccabees over Syrian Greek overlords, who had outlawed Judaism. The name makes reference to the light from a miraculous eight-day burning of holy oil. A special eight-branch candlestick is used.

Purim: "Lots." Recalls the Queen Esther story in which Persian Jews were saved when the drawing of lots exposed a plot to kill them. Costumes and boisterous plays are featured.

Shavuot: "Weeks." Commonly known as Pentecost (lit., "fifty"), celebrated fifty days after Passover. Commemorates the giving of Torah.

Sabbath: Seventh day of the week, designated for rest and pious reflection. Connected to both the creation of the world and the giving of Torah.

in the new state. The secular character of the new Jewish state and its leaders fell far short of what many pious Jews had anticipated.

From the perspective of all Jews, whether religious or not, there is a disappointment that the new homeland was unwelcomed by its neighbors. The displacement of Palestinians as a result of the creation of a new Jewish state and the Palestinians' own quest for a homeland pose considerable hurdles in the politics of the region to this day.

BELIEFS

God

"Hear, O Israel, the Lord our God is one." These are the opening words of the most common prayer in Judaism, called the *Shema*. Jews, therefore, are constantly reminded of the uniqueness of God. There is one God; there is no other. God (the creator) stands as distinct from everything else (the creation). That is the fundamental boundary, separating the vast expanse of being into two profoundly distinct realities. The same idea, in seed form, is expressed in the first of the Ten Commandments: "You shall have no other gods." This monotheistic perspective distinguished Judaism from the various polytheistic religions of the ancient Near East, and it has become an equally important belief of Christianity and Islam, the two world religions that borrowed extensively from Judaism.

Monotheism seems to have been a gradual development in the religion of the Hebrews. Initially, the Hebrews were forbidden from worshipping other gods, which did not mean that they denied the existence of other gods. Later, some of the Hebrew prophets declared outright that no other gods existed. They contrasted their living god who created all things with the gods of wood and stone, which were human-made (or "made with hands," as they said). Jews were often quite mocking of pagan gods, who, they said, had eyes but could not see and ears but could not hear.

So fundamental was the monotheistic perspective for Jews that they sought and often received special exemptions from the civil authorities in the lands of the Diaspora. For example, under the Roman Empire Jews were not required to offer sacrifices to Rome and the Caesar or to local gods.

Jews speak of the "Thirteen Attributes" of God, or the Thirteen Attributes of Mercy. The list comes from a passage in Exodus (34:6–7), in which the mercy, loving-kindness, and forgiveness of God are emphasized. Although that does not provide a full portrait of God in Jewish reflection, it is important to understand that this emphasis on the mercy of God is fundamental to Judaism. Sometimes that aspect of Jewish belief is overlooked, particularly since Christianity has come almost to monopolize the theme of the mercy of God as the mark of its distinctive identity, at least in popular thinking.

The more mystical and speculative forms of Judaism sometimes have pressed the monotheistic boundaries. Gnosticism, which held a sharp dualism between the spiritual and the physical worlds, had a Jewish coloring, and perhaps a Jewish origin. Gnostics posited a long chain of emanations between God and the physical world, as did Kabbalism. In Kabbalism, ten beings, called *sefirot* (lit., "numbers"), separate the unlimited and unknown God (*Ein Sof*) from the created world.

The Human Condition

All three western religions posit a Golden Age (Garden of Eden or Paradise) at the beginning of human existence, based on the story of creation of Adam and Eve, which is found in the first few pages of the Hebrew Bible. All three also have some sense of a loss of Paradise and an exile from Eden. A widely accepted doctrine in Christianity emphasizes the grave consequence of the sin of the primal parents—a moral deformity (original sin) in all of human posterity. Islam tends to emphasize the opposite pole: humans are ignorant of what they should do; they are not inherently sinful. Judaism generally takes a middle position, recognizing the importance of the influence of both good and evil inclinations in the human struggle.

OFFICES

Cantor: (lit., "singer"). Leader of music and prayer in synagogue services. The duties vary from congregation to congregation. The office was established in the Middle Ages, when more complex music became the fashion.

Exilarch: Political head of the Jewish community in Babylonia until the thirteenth century, when the Muslim empire there fell.

Gaon: (lit., "eminence"). Originally used as a title of respect for the head of Babylonian academies for Torah study. Now widely used for a rabbi expert in Torah.

High Priest: An office during the temple period. The chief priest was to be a descendent of Aaron, the first high priest.

Mohel: A person trained in the procedure of circumcision.

Levite: An assistant to the priest, with various temple duties. After the destruction of the temple, they lost a role in Judaism, although their identity as Levites has been maintained.

Priest: A descendent of Aaron. A few roles continue, although the temple has not existed for 2,000 years.

Prophet: The Israelites had both official and unofficial prophets, who supported or challenged temple and palace. One section of the Hebrew Bible incorporates the messages of some of these prophets.

Rabbi: A teacher of Torah, and spiritual advisor and leader in the synagogue. Primary Jewish leader after the destruction of the temple.

Whatever the exact nature of the human condition, the strained relationship between God and his human creation was not quickly healed. In fact, according to the primeval history presented in the first part of Genesis (the first document in the Hebrew Bible), things went from bad to worse, forcing God at one point to destroy everything that he had made. One individual, Noah, found favor with God, however. By means of an ark (boat), Noah, his family, and pairs of animals were saved from the Great Flood, and the world was able to renew itself. But the lesson was not long remembered, and humans challenged God again, attempting to reach into God's domain by constructing a massive tower on the plains of Babel. God responded, dividing and confusing the human effort by splitting human speech into a babble of multiple, mutually incomprehensible languages.

Salvation and the Covenant

The bleakness of the primeval story is countered, however, by God's continued effort to reestablish a relationship with humans. Finally, after relationships with a few noble individuals, such as Enoch and Noah, God took special interest in Abraham, who was to become the father of the Hebrew people. The relationship was formalized by a covenant and marked by the rite of circumcision. This covenant was later renewed with Abraham's descendants under the leadership of Moses at Mount Sinai.

When God reaffirmed his covenant with the Hebrew nation under Moses, a law code (the Ten Commandments or Decalogue) was provided, and God's unique name, Yahweh, was revealed. The law code, or Torah, showed the double-sided nature of the relationship between Yahweh and the Hebrews. Yahweh would provide the Hebrews with land and security; the Hebrews would worship only Yahweh, and they would keep his commandments. The covenant, thus, had a conditional aspect.

The conditional nature of the covenant became a theme of religious reformers, who connected the fate of the nation with faithful observance of Torah. The prophets often predicted future disaster or explained present crises by pointing to violations of Torah by those who were bound by a covenant oath to obey Torah. Over the centuries, such explanations usually offered a satisfactory account of the circumstances of the nation or the individual, but sometimes the connection between the behavior of the people and their fate strained the faith of even the most pious. The Holocaust, in which many observant Jews were exterminated, forced some Jews to rethink the nature of Judaism and the covenant.

The Chosen People

The story of God's choice of Abraham and his descendents has shaped Jewish self-identity profoundly. Jews are the "chosen people." But the claim by Jews to be God's chosen people sometimes has offended the peoples among whom they lived. Both the Hebrew prophets and the rabbis have speculated on the reason for God's choice of the Hebrews, as well as the consequences of that choice. Generally Jews see their election by God as laying a special responsibility on Jews to the nations about them—they are God's witness in the world. One rabbinic explanation of the special status of the Jews states that God offered the Torah to numerous groups before offering it to the Jews. All the other groups declined the offer. Jews are almost chosen by default.

In the emancipation of Jews during the Enlightenment, the idea that God would have a special people (particularism) was at odds with the spirit of universalism of the age. Many Jews sought their identity as citizens of the countries in which they resided rather than in a distinctive status as God's chosen people.

In many ways, monotheism itself has implicit universalist claims. If there is but one god, that god must be the god of everyone, and everyone must be, in some way, the people of that god.

Revelation

SITES

Temple: The first, called Solomon's temple, was destroyed by the Babylonians in 586 B.C.E.; the second temple was destroyed by the Romans in 70 C.E.

Synagogue: A community center in which numerous activities take place, the most important of which is the weekly Sabbath services. Reform Jews call their synagogues "temples," implying that synagogues serve fully the religious needs of the Jews.

Zion: The hill on which the temple was situated. Considered the center of the cosmos, God's holy hill. Muslim Dome of the Rock stands there now.

Mount Sinai: The mountain in the Sinai Desert where, according to tradition, Moses received the Ten Commandments and Yahweh made a covenant with the Israelites.

Diaspora: (lit., "dispersion"). A term used for the areas outside of Israel in which Jews resided. Until modern times, this often meant a resident-alien status.

Israel: Land and independence were especially cherished by people whose beginnings were that of nomadic strangers. Jews called Israel the "Promised Land." In 1948, Israel became an independent Jewish nation, for the first time in almost 2,000 years.

Western Wall (Wailing Wall): The western wall of the Second Temple complex. With the temple destroyed, Jews throughout the centuries came to this location to pray for the restoration of Israel.

For most of the history of Judaism, a central belief was that God revealed his purpose by spoken or written word in unusual encounters with selected individuals. Moses encountered God and returned to the people with written commandments; the prophets were commissioned by God to announce "a word of the Lord" to the people. This understanding of God's chief mechanism of communication with the people has elevated the word (or *scripture*, the written word) to primary authority.

Except for Reform Jews, Jews agree in principle with the concept of revelation. Dispute arises over which of the various documents have authoritative status, with Orthodox Jews arguing for the whole corpus of the Bible and the Talmud, and other groups either dismissing parts of this wide collection or qualifying the application of particular parts. Such disputes have had a long history in Judaism. The first-century Sadducees, for example, appear to have granted revelatory status only to the Pentateuch, as did the Samaritans, and the Karaites.

Reform Jews do not appeal to the revelatory character of religious texts. As the primary appropriators of the assumptions of the Enlightenment, religious texts have their power and their truthfulness in so far as they mesh with reason and reflect universal principles.

Torah

Torah is generally taken to mean *law*, but it also has a sense of *instruction*. The term can be applied narrowly to the Pentateuch, to the whole Bible, or to the full Talmudic legislation.

The Ten Commandments represent a brief summary of Torah. But the Hebrew Bible contains many more commandments—Jews identify 613 specific commands and prohibitions in the Hebrew Bible. These are expanded on in the Mishnah and the Talmud, producing much larger volumes of Torah.

Jews distinguish material in their literature that is legally binding from what is merely explanatory, such as stories, parables, prayers, etc. If the material has the character of law, it is called *halakah*; otherwise, it is called *aggadah*. *Halakah* is largely contained in the Mishnah and Talmud; *aggadah* is found scattered throughout the Mishnah and Talmud, and in a wide variety of other Jewish literature, such as the Midrash.

God's Dwelling Place

Much of Jewish religious life had been focused around the Temple, built on one of the hills in Jerusalem. It was there that God met the people. It was there that powerful religious apparatus and relics could be found, such as the Ark of the Covenant—Hollywoodized in the movie *Raiders of the Lost Ark*.

But the Hebrews rarely had stable government; usually they were surrounded by much more powerful neighbors. The temple suffered the fate of the people, being destroyed by the Babylonians in the sixth century B.C.E., rebuilt, then destroyed again, this time by the Romans in the first century C.E. For two thousand years, Judaism has functioned without its primary religious facility, the only place where valid sacrifice could be made. This was clearly a significant loss. Jews have made the ruins of the Western Wall of the platform on which the temple stood—a site near the holiest place in their temple—into a sacred place, gathering there to pray, in particular for the restoration of Israel.

Two changes in perspective made it possible for Judaism to survive the profound loss of their temple. For one thing, from early on some prophets had challenged what they saw as defiled temple practices, and they called at times for a less cult-centered worship. For another, after the Roman destruction of the temple, the rabbis argued that, in the absence of the temple, prayer had replaced sacrifice as the means by which humans maintained contact with God. The synagogue, which had existed even before the destruction of the Temple, became the place of religious and social assembly.

Yet Jews were always aware of their great loss, and much of Jewish prayer and liturgy expresses the desire for a rebuilding of Jerusalem and the Temple. Not all Jews are comfortable with such ideas of restoration. Reform Jews call their synagogues "temples," an explicit rejection of the belief that the Temple must be restored for Judaism to be able to perform its religion adequately and fully.

DIVINE NAMES

As monotheists, the Jews did not have a pantheon of gods; however, various names were used for their god. In particular, Jews sought ways to avoid pronouncing the name YHWH, using various circumlocutions.

YHWH: The Tetragrammaton. Often seen with the vowels (Yahweh). It is the personal name of the Hebrew god, which was revealed to Moses. The word "Jehovah" is an artificial Christian construct based on these consonants, with "J" used instead of "Y" (under German influence). The omission of the vowels is intended to protect against pronouncing the name of God. Often the English word "God" is written without a vowel ("G-d").

Adonai: Hebrew, meaning "Lord." This word is often pronounced wherever the letters YHWH occur in the Bible.

Elohim: A generic name for god in Semitic languages. Often used for God in the Hebrew scriptures, and its abbreviated form "El" was often used in compounds (e.g., El-Shaddai—"God Almighty").

Ein Sof: ("the Unlimited"). The name given to the unknowable and limitedless God of kabbalistic speculation.

Ha-Shem: (lit., "the Name"). Another common circumlocution for the name of God.

Diaspora

For most of Jewish history, the majority of Jews have lived away from their homeland of Palestine, in what is termed the Diaspora (dispersion). After the destruction of the Second Temple in 70 C.E., only a handful of Jews remained in Palestine.

Some lived in the Diaspora by choice as they sought better economic opportunities. Often, however, Jews found themselves in the Diaspora as a result of war, transported there as slaves. They frequently lived a precarious existence as strangers and aliens. Sometimes hostility to the Jewish presence was so great that Jewish communities suffered near extinction, as in the mid 1900s when the Nazis adopted a plan to exterminate the Jews. On the other hand, in some periods Diaspora Jews experienced a brilliant cultural flowering, as occurred in Babylonia, where they developed into a leading center of Jewish renewal that was to shape much of Judaism for over 1,500 years, and in Spain under Muslim rule, where medieval Judaism was renewed.

The fortunes of the Jews changed in 1948, when the modern state of Israel was established. Although the "Law of Return," enacted in 1950, gives to any Jewish person the right to immigrate to Israel, about 75% of Jews still live in the Diaspora. Most are likely to continue to live outside of Israel, for generally Diaspora Jews are now fully absorbed as citizens in the various countries in which they have taken up residence.

Eschatology: Reflection on the End of the World

Generally speaking, western religions have a linear view of history; eastern religions have a cyclical view. The difference is that western religions see the historical process moving on to a final conclusion, at which point a new and permanent order will be established. Eastern religions tend to see human history as merely a segment of a process of decline and renewal of the cosmos that has no beginning and no imminent end.

Since Persian times, Jews have reflected on the matter of the afterlife. The belief in the resurrection of the dead and a final judgment became prominent features in Jewish thinking, although a wide range of speculation about these matters has been accommodated within Judaism. Usually two ideas are central in traditional Jewish thinking. One: there is a "World to Come," a messianic age, something of a restored "Garden of Eden," into which the righteous will enter. Two: a brief period of punishment, lasting no more than twelve months, will occur prior to this; few, except for the exceptionally righteous, will escape this punishment entirely. But beyond that, opinions vary considerably.

Whatever the specific details, the resurrection of the dead has been one of the central beliefs of Judaism. Jews were often mocked for this belief during the Greco-Roman times, but in the Christian and Muslim worlds that replaced the Roman Empire, the idea was not considered strange, for both Christianity and Islam had made belief in the resurrection of the dead central to their own religious systems too. In the medieval period, when the Jewish scholar Maimonides outlined the "Thirteen Principles" of Judaism, the resurrection of the dead is featured in the thirteenth principle, and the eleventh and twelfth principle imply such a resurrection. Indeed, Jews are reminded daily of the resurrection of the dead, each time they repeat the Amidah prayer.

As with many Jewish beliefs, a considerable difference of opinion separates Reform from the Orthodox, as a result of innovations since the Enlightenment. The idea of the physical resurrection of the dead is rejected by the Reform, and they modify the liturgical prayers to reflect this.

RITES/RITUALS

Circumcision (Bris): As a sign of the covenant, Jewish baby boys have the foreskin of the penis removed in a ceremony when they are eight days old. They are named at this time too. Male converts are also required to undergo this procedure. A *mohel* performs the surgery.

Bar Mitzvah: (lit., "son of the commandment"). The ceremony that declares a Jewish boy of age thirteen to be a full member of the community. The event is celebrated in the synagogue, with the boy reading from the Torah.

Bat Mitzvah: (lit., "daughter of the commandment"). A ceremony for girls, on parallel with the Bar Mitzvah ceremony, found in all forms of Judaism except the Orthodox.

Sitting Shivah: A seven-day period of mourning after the death of a close relative. The family restricts its activities and friends visit. Mourners sit on low stools or on the floor.

The Passover Seder: A highly ritualized meal, in which Jews recall the Exodus of the Hebrews from Egyptian slavery. Specific foods are used to illustrate aspects of the story.

Messiah

The concept of the Messiah is connected in Judaism to the restoration of Israel. After the exile, Jews began to anticipate the day in which Jerusalem would be restored and the people of Israel gathered back to their land. By the Roman period, Jews were beginning to think in terms of an agent from God (called the "Messiah" or "anointed one") who would appear to accomplish this mission, although the precise details varied.

A number of messianic claimants arose throughout the centuries. The most famous are Jesus, whom Jews consider a messianic pretender, and Shabbetai Tzevi, a rabbi who stirred messianic expectations widely, but then shattered them by converting to Islam after he was arrested in 1666 in Constantinople, where he had tried to claim his kingdom.

The idea is still prominent in Orthodox Judaism, where the arrival of the Messiah is connected with the resurrection of the dead and the gathering of Jews to Israel. References to Elijah speak of the same hope, for Elijah is understood to be the forerunner of the Messiah. The chair of Elijah is a fixture of the circumcision ceremony and Elijah is anticipated as a guest at each Passover *seder*. Jewish prayers reflect this hope too.

Purity

In the rabbinic tradition, purity and pollution became crucial considerations. Thousands of minute specifications developed to separate the clean from the unclean, to prevent the clean from becoming polluted by the unclean, and to reestablish a condition of cleanness for whatever had become defiled. Rabbinic legislation specifies degrees of uncleanness and defines the extent that particular levels of uncleanness can be transferred by second- and third-hand contact, and so forth. In some ways, ritual pollution as described by rabbinic tradition has the character of a contagious disease, which can be carried from one to another, and thus must be contained.

An understanding of clean and unclean conditions helps make sense of a multitude of regulations that specify permissible levels of physical and social contact in Judaism, particularly in regard to corpses and women during their menstrual period. Further, since ritual pollution can be transferred some distance from the actual point of first contact, one can appreciate the observant Jew's concern to minimize social contact with unobservant Jews and non-Jews, who may well compromise the status of purity sought by the observant Jew. One example will suffice to show the level of attention observant Jews will take to maintain ritual purity. They will dispose of fingernail clippings carefully, burning them or flushing them down the toilet, so that, as carriers of ritual pollution, the clippings will not render people unclean who might accidentally come into contact with them.

The diligent and detailed quest for purity appears to arise out of the rabbinic concern that, with the loss of temple, the laws of purity for priests needed now to be maintained by all of Israel.

A Fence about Torah

Rabbinic Judaism's concern for ritual purity and strict obedience to the commandments led rabbis to build what they called "a fence about Torah." In practice, this has meant providing a considerably more detailed exposition of Jewish law than is found in the biblical text, which oftentimes offers a general command or prohibition, but leaves the specifics to be worked out.

For example, one of the Ten Commandments specifies that the Sabbath Day is to be kept holy, and work should not be done on that day. That kind of statement does not provide clear comment on what, precisely, is *work*. In the Mishnah, that matter is taken up with vigor. One tractate focuses solely on the issue of the Sabbath, listing what kinds of activity are considered work (thirty-nine general actions are mentioned), and then it goes into detail on a number of matters of a more specific nature. These are further illuminated in the *gemara* (commentary on the Mishnah, which, with the Mishnah, constitutes the Talmud), and the rabbis provide further illumination in the form of Responsa (answers to questions about the Talmudic legislation). For example, the Mishnah specifies that one cannot light a fire on the Sabbath; in the modern world, this has generally been understood by Orthodox Judaism to prohibit one from turning on an electric light on the Sabbath. Many observant Jews will turn on lights prior to the beginning of the Sabbath and leave them burning throughout the Sabbath, or they will use a light switch timer, which they set prior to the onset of the Sabbath.

THE TEN COMMANDMENTS
(1) I am the LORD your God, who brought you out of the land of Egypt, the house of bondage:
(2) You shall have no other gods beside Me. You shall not make for yourself a sculptured image, or any likeness of what is in the heavens above, or on the earth below, or in the waters under the earth. You shall not bow down to them or serve them. . . .
(3) You shall not swear falsely by the name of the LORD your God; for the LORD will not clear one who swears falsely by His name.
(4) Remember the sabbath day and keep it holy. Six days you shall labor and do all your work. But the seventh day is a sabbath to the LORD your God; you shall not do any work—you, your son or your daughter, your male or female slave, your livestock, or the alien resident in your towns. For in six days the LORD made heaven and earth, the sea, and all that is in them, but rested the seventh day; therefore the LORD blessed the sabbath day and consecrated it.
(5) Honor your father and your mother, that you may long endure on the land which the LORD your God is giving you.
(6) You shall not murder.
(7) You shall not commit adultery.
(8) You shall not steal.
(9) You shall not bear false witness against your neighbor.
(10) You shall not covet your neighbor's house: You shall not covet your neighbor's wife, or his male or female slave, or his ox or his ass, or anything that is your neighbor's.
Exodus 20:2-14 (*Tanakh: The Holy Scriptures*, © Jewish Publication Society, 1985)

The simple Sabbath legislation of the Bible offers no clarity on these matters. A fence to protect that Sabbath legislation is built by these wide-ranging regulations.

PRACTICES

Torah Obligations: Men and Women

The full responsibility of Torah traditionally had been considered the obligation of adult males (defined as males thirteen years of age or older). That is why in Orthodox congregations the coming of age is celebrated formally only for boys, in a Bar Mitzvah or "Son of the Commandment" event. It is also why only male members can be counted to determine quorum (minyan) for religious events. It is also why orthodox Jewish women do not generally attend Sabbath synagogues services, and why they are separated from men when they do attend synagogue functions.

Modern forms of Judaism have frequently challenged such exclusion of women. Some groups have created a Bat Mitzvah ("Daughter of the Commandment") service, to celebrate the adulthood of a Jewish girl. In some groups, women sit with men in the synagogue and women can become rabbis.

The Calendar

The Jewish calendar takes the creation of the world as its starting point. This date is calculated from various genealogical lists in the Bible, and corresponds to the year 3760 B.C.E. of the Christian calendar. Twelve lunar months of thirty days make up each year, with the addition of an extra month seven times in every nineteen-year cycle. To calculate the current date on the Jewish calendar, simply add 3,760 to the Christian (western) calendar date. If the date is after the Jewish New Year (in September or October), add an extra year.

Annual Celebrations

Jews celebrate a range of events in the annual cycle, all of which recall some circumstance in the history of the Hebrew people. The oldest festivals focus on a short period from the escape of the Hebrews from Egyptian slavery through their wanderings in the Sinai Desert before coming into the Promised Land (Palestine). The dates for these festivals mesh nicely with the harvest cycle in Palestine, suggesting that the Hebrews appropriated indigenous agricultural feasts, and modified the content with stories from their pre-history.

Rosh Hashanah. The New Year, Rosh Hashanah ("Beginning of the Year"), is the first day of a ten-day period of solemn reflection, self-examination, and repentance. The first and last day (Yom Kippur) of this period are considered the "high holy days" of the religious year. Rosh Hashanah is celebrated in September or October. Tradition has it that God created humans on Rosh Hashanah and annually reviews each individual's performance on that day. To reflect God's forgiveness, Jews customarily wear white. In some ways, Rosh Hashanah provides Jews with a clean slate to begin the new year. Jews often try to pay off debts and make amends before this day, and on this day they often go to a lake or river and symbolically throw away their sins. The blowing of the *shofar* (ram's horn) is a highlight of the synagogue service on this day.

Yom Kippur. The tenth day after Rosh Hashanah marks the high point of the solemn period of repentance. The day is called Yom Kippur (Day of Atonement). It serves as a focal point for communal confession of sins before God and for individual forgiveness of others. In the Bible, a goat (the scapegoat) was selected to carry the sins of Israel away into the wilderness on this day. At the end of the synagogue service on Yom Kippur, Jews greet each other with the call "Next year in Jerusalem!"–a reminder of restoration for Israel and the coming of the messiah.

CREED

Jews have no formal creed, although some Jewish scholars have drawn up lists of primary articles of faith. A popular list is Maimonides' "Thirteen Principles," from the 1200s. The most popular form is the hymn Yigdal (lit., "May He be magnified"), found in Jewish prayer books.

Thirteen Principles:

(1) God exists.

(2) There is only one god; there is no other.

(3) God does not have physical form, nor is he subject to physical needs.

(4) God is eternal–the first and the last.

(5) Prayer is to be directed to God alone. No other is worthy of such acts.

(6) God communicates with humans through prophets.

(7) Moses is the primary prophet.

(8) The Torah was given by God to Moses.

(9) There will be no other Torah.

(10) God observes all deeds and thoughts of humans.

(11) God rewards those who keep his commandments and punishes those who violate his commandments.

(12) The Messiah will come. One is to wait daily, no matter how long until Messiah comes.

(13) The dead will be resurrected, when God pleases.

In addition to these high holy days, three primary ancient festivals, often called pilgrim festivals, are celebrated by Jews, as well as some minor ones from antiquity and some quite new. The three pilgrim feasts are closely tied to the harvest cycle, and were positioned to allow Jews to make a pilgrimage to Jerusalem to celebrate the feasts there. While the temple was standing, Jews from distant places in the Diaspora often would make a pilgrimage to Jerusalem. This meant that Jerusalem was frequently crowded with excited pilgrims. Indeed, it was at one of these pilgrim festivals (Passover) that Jesus was crucified in Jerusalem and at another (Pentecost) that the early Christian movement, an offshoot of Judaism, started.

Sukkot. Five days after Yom Kippur, Jews celebrate Sukkot (lit., "Tabernacles" or "Booths"). The feast was associated with the end of the harvest cycle and is sometimes known as the "Feast of Ingathering" or "Feast of the Harvest." The harvest aspect is somewhat overshadowed by an event in Hebrew history that came to be celebrated at this time. According to biblical tradition, after escaping from Egypt the Hebrews wandered in the desert for forty years before entering the Promised Land. To identify with the impermanent condition of their ancestors, Jewish families construct a temporary shelter outdoors, in which they either reside for the seven-day festival, or in which they take their meals.

Pesach (Passover). Passover is the second of the three pilgrim festivals. It is often called the "Feast of Unleavened Bread," for the feast commemorates the Exodus, the rushed escape of the Hebrews from Egyptian slavery, when they hastily baked bread for the journey, not having time to add yeast or allow the dough to rise. While the temple was standing, this feast featured the sacrifice of a paschal lamb for each family, recalling the escape of the Hebrew first-born sons from the Angel of Death in the final plague on Egypt. For Jews, the Exodus marks their beginnings as a free people.

The Passover is celebrated by several special actions. Of first importance is the thorough cleaning of the home of all yeast and foods in which yeast is found. In place of normal bread, unleavened *matzah* bread is eaten. There is then the preparation of the Passover meal (*seder*). Strict Jews will have a complete set of Passover dishes and tableware that are used only on this occasion, being securely boxed away until the next Passover. Some Jews have a separate set of trays for their dishwasher and fridge to hold the Passover dishes. The Passover meal itself is rich with symbolism. It follows a set order of readings from the *Passover Haggada*, and of eating and drinking, all recalling the escape of Jews from Egypt. The door of the house is opened in the middle of the meal, in anticipation of the arrival of Elijah, the forerunner of the messiah.

Elements of the biblical Exodus story of escape from slavery to freedom have been appropriated by even non-Jewish groups, particularly in the spirituals of American slave music and by liberation theology of Christian revolutionary movements in Latin America.

Shavuot. Seven weeks (fifty days) after Passover is the third pilgrim feast, called Pentecost (Greek for "fifty") or Shavuot (weeks). Thus it sometimes is referred to as the "Feast of Weeks." The feast celebrates the giving of Torah, which according to tradition occurred fifty days after the Exodus. The feast is sometimes called "First fruits," an early harvest feast. This reflects the agricultural roots common to most of the older Jewish feasts.

Several other celebrations or commemorations mark the Jewish calendar. A few of the more important or better-known ones are discussed below. Some are ancient; others are from the twentieth century.

Hanukkah. This feast is also called "Dedication" or the "Feast of Lights." It occurs shortly before the Christian celebration of Christmas, and has sometimes taken on some of the non-religious features of the Christmas festivities, such as gift-giving. But the holiday is really not parallel at its core. The holiday celebrates the rededication of the temple after the Greek Seleucid king prohibited the practice of Judaism and polluted the temple by sacrificing pigs there (160s B.C.E.). The Maccabean Revolt won freedom for the Jews, but when they prepared the temple for Jewish use again, they found only one day's supply of sacred oil for the candlestick (*menorah*), one of the key articles of temple. According to the story, this oil miraculously lasted for eight days, until a new supply could be made. The eight Hanukkah candles, lit by Jewish families

SYMBOLS

Star of David: (more correctly: *Magen* ["shield"] of David). The most common symbol of modern Judaism, featured on the flag of Israel. Gained popularity as a symbol for Judaism after Zionism adopted it in 1897.

Menorah: A seven-branched candlestick, found in the temple; represents the seven days of creation. It has been the most recognizable symbol of Judaism from ancient times. A special eight-branched *menorah* is used for Hanukkah.

Tetragrammaton / Tetragram: (lit., "four letters"). The four consonants in the Hebrew word "Yahweh," the personal name of the Jewish God.

Yarmulke / Kippah: A skull cap worn by Jewish men. Orthodox Jews cover their heads in all public places; Conservative Jews (and some Reform) when at prayer.

Kosher: Many symbols indicate *kosher* foods, depending on which of various Jewish agencies supervised the procedure.

Tallit: Prayer shawl, with four corners and fringes on each corner. A smaller one is worn by Orthodox Jews, somewhat as an undershirt.

Tefillin/Phylactery: Small leather boxes containing portions of the Torah, bound to the forehead and right arm during prayer.

Mezuzah: (lit., "doorpost"). Portions of Torah in a small container attached to the doorposts of a Jewish home.

around the same time as Christians are hanging out Christmas lights, bring joy to the darkness of winter.

Purim. Another feast of similar antiquity is Purim (Lots). It is based on the story of Esther, the Jewish wife of the king of Persia, who saved the Jews from a plot to exterminate them. The feast is a time of rowdy merriment: eating special desserts, dressing in costumes and acting out the story of the villain Haman and the good Queen Esther, and consuming lots of wine—all part of the festivities.

Newer Annual Celebrations. Two special days have been established in the mid-1900s. One, Yom Ha-shoah was established as a day of remembrance of the victims and the heroes of the Holocaust (Shoah) by the Israeli Parliament in 1951. Since no particular date stood out as the most critical date of the Holocaust, a date within the Warsaw Ghetto uprising was selected. This falls a week after Passover, in the Spring. A week later is the state of Israel's Independence Day.

Shabbat (Sabbath). All the days of celebration and commemoration described above are annual events. The celebration for which Jews have been most recognized and distinguished from their neighbors is the weekly Sabbath. Two explanations for this observance are offered: (1) God's rest on the seventh day of creation, and (2) the giving of Torah. Work is forbidden on the Sabbath, and rabbinic legislation goes to great length to specify what that encompasses. Orthodox Jews will not cook, turn on lights, drive vehicles, and the list goes on, with every imaginable activity and situation addressed. Reform Jews initially replaced the Sabbath (Saturday) with Sunday for their religious meetings, although even Reform synagogues now generally meet on the Sabbath.

Rites of Passage

Judaism celebrates four primary rites of passage: birth, adulthood, marriage, and death. All emphasize religious themes, and it is the religious aspects of these rites that we emphasize here.

Circumcision. The ceremony of circumcision (*bris* or *brit*) celebrates the birth of each male child. It takes place on the eighth day after birth, and in addition to the procedure of circumcision, the child is named, usually after a relative. In some ways, circumcision celebrates less the birth of the child than the admission of that child into the membership of a religious people. Circumcision is the sign of the covenant between God and Abraham, and as a descendant of Abraham, the child enters into the covenant community by the same sign as all male members in the past have entered. The rite is probably the oldest Hebrew ritual that survives today.

A *mohel*, a Jew trained and ordained to do the procedure, performs the circumcision, acting in the place of the father, who traditionally had the obligation to circumcise his sons. The child is seated briefly on a chair designated as the "chair of Elijah," which reflects messianic expectations.

In the 1800s, Reform Jews rejected circumcision, some calling it a "bloody, barbaric" act. Today, Reform Judaism encourages circumcision, but does not require it, as do Conservative and Orthodox Judaism.

Since the 1970s, birth celebrations for girls, frequently called "Joy of the Daughter" or something similar, have become popular in some groups.

Bar Mitzvah. The next rite takes place when the boy reaches puberty (considered age thirteen). The transition of a boy to manhood is celebrated in the Bar Mitzvah ceremony. As with the birth ceremony, the religious aspect is emphasized. Indeed, the term "Bar Mitzvah" means "son of the commandment," again recalling the covenant by which Jewish identity is prescribed. It is at this point that the full injunctions of Torah become binding on the boy. The Bar Mitzvah event features the young candidate being "called up" to read from the Bible, usually a Torah passage, in the synagogue service following his birthday. Often a grand party is part of the celebrations afterwards.

A parallel event for girls (the Bat Mitzvah) has become popular in all but the Orthodox traditions. The first such celebration was provided by the founder of Reconstructionist Judaism for

PRAYER
The Eighteen Benedictions (Blessings): also called Amidah (lit., "standing"), Tephillah (lit., "prayer"), or Shemoneh Esrei (lit., "eighteen"). The principal prayer in the Jewish liturgy, going back 2000 years, made up of nineteen blessings, the twelfth having been added to the original eighteen sometime in the early period. The following is a brief summary of the main features of the blessings and petitions.
1. God's greatness as God of the fathers/patriarchs
2. God's power in a variety of situations
3. God's holinesss
4. God's gift of knowledge
5. God's gift of repentance
6. God's gift of pardon and forgiveness from sin
7. God's redemption of Israel from its struggles
8. God's healing of the sick
9. God's blessings of the various produce of the ground
10. God's gathering of the dispersed of Israel
11. God's restoration of righteousness and justice
12. God's punishment of the wicked and heretics
13. God's reward of the pious
14. God's rebuilding of the city of Jerusalem
15. God's restoration of the royal house of David
16. God's acceptance and response to prayers
17. God's restoration of worship at the Temple in Jerusalem
18. Extensive thanks and blessings to God
19. God's peace on Israel.

his daughter in 1922. The celebration for boys is at least as old as the 1500s C.E., though the concept is older.

Marriage. Unlike some religions that idealize celibacy and asceticism, Judaism encourages marriage and family life. While much in the Jewish marriage ceremony has some parallels with non-Jewish rites of marriage (rings, wedding document or vows, toasts), an unusual action interrupts the joyous occasion. The groom crushes a glass under his foot, reminding Jews, in their moment of great joy, of the shadow of sorrow that befell all Jews when the Temple in Jerusalem was destroyed.

Although marriage is honored, should a marriage break down, divorce is permitted and remarriage encouraged. Monogamy has been the law for Ashkenazi Jews since the 900s. For Sepharadic Jews, whose influences reflect a Muslim context, polygamy was permitted until the 1950s.

A major problem confronting Jews in the modern world is mixed marriage, which often has resulted in the Jewish partner leaving Judaism. Further, the majority of children of such marriages do not identify with Judaism. A further problem of mixed marriage is the problem it creates for identifying a member of the Jewish community. Traditionally, Jewish identity has been matrilineal, but Reformed Jews have argued for either matrilineal or patrilineal descent.

Death. Death is handled with a degree of simplicity and haste. Generally, burial is done on the day of the death. The coffin is simple; the burial shroud is the same for rich and poor. Mourning is regulated, and the first week the family sits *shiva*, where they remain at home and are visited by friends. The end of formal mourning takes place in a ceremony one year after the death. Cremation is not permitted, and some Jews in the Diaspora have themselves buried in Israel. There is a belief that the resurrection of the dead at the end of the age will occur in Israel, and those buried elsewhere will need to journey through underworld caverns to reach Israel, from which they then will participate in the resurrection.

Religious Officials

As long as the Temple existed, most formal religious offices were connected to that institution. A high-priest stood at the head, and that office was largely hereditary, although on occasion political intrigue installed other claimants. At times a dispute might arise over which family of the high-priest lineage (from Moses's brother Aaron) had valid rights to that office. The community that wrote the Dead Sea Scrolls seems to have distanced themselves from the temple in Jerusalem for some such reason.

A body of priests (*cohen*) served on a part-time basis in the temple, often with rotating obligations. Even two thousand years after the destruction of the temple and the loss of most of the priestly functions, some limited role for the priest has continued. Priests have the first right to be called up to read the Torah passage in a Jewish service, and priests still serve in a rite related to the status for a first-born child. The surname Cohen identifies a member of a Jewish priestly family, as do names such as Kaplan, Katz, and Kohn, among others.

Levites assisted priests in the temple. Today, they are the second to be called up to read the Torah, in the absence of a *cohen*. Jewish surnames such as Levi, Levy, Levine, Levitt, and Segal, among others, usually identify a Levite.

> **TERMINOLOGY**
> **Matrilineal:** In Judaism, only those born to a Jewish mother were considered Jewish by birth.
> **Parve (pareve):** (lit., "neutral"). This word, or an abbreviation "P" appears on *kosher* labeling for products that may be eaten either with meat or dairy dishes.
> **Yeshiva:** (lit., "sitting"). The academy for study of the Torah leading to ordination as a rabbi.
> **Yiddish:** The term is an English form of the German word *jüdisch* ("Jewish"). Yiddish is a dialect of German spoken by Ashkenazi Jews. Most of the vocabulary is German; the script uses the Hebrew alphabet.

Along with priestly offices, ancient Israel had a king. Whereas the temple lasted for about a thousand years, the monarchy lasted only half that long. But the idea of a restored dynasty or House of David (the ideal Jewish king) has sparked the imagination and expectation of Jews through the ages, especially in its messianic images.

Another group, the prophets, seem to have been attached to the temple and court, although details of their role are vague. More clear and influential in the history of Judaism is the role of those who, often without office, spoke as prophets—special mouthpieces of God. Often their messages were counter-cultural, blasting temple and palace and predicting doom on the nation. Those who recognized the voice of God in the declarations of these prophets sometimes formed communities of support, to preserve and transmit these messages. A large part of the Hebrew Bible consists of writings from such communities.

After the destruction of the temple by the Romans in 70 C.E., the teacher (rabbi) gradually became the prominent authority in Judaism. Although the precise lineage of the rabbis is unclear, Judaism had developed a scribal community quite early, which produced an influential body of literature. Such scribal skills appeared among the rabbis, who produced an immense body of commentary on the Torah. Today, the rabbi is most importantly a teacher and an expert in the Torah. Although the rabbi's role may expand to include other religious duties similar to those generally performed by priests or clergy in other religions, many such duties are not done, or need not be done, by the rabbi in Judaism. The rite of initiation (circumcision), for example, is handled by a specialist trained in the procedure. The marriage ceremony can be conducted by anyone, provided a quorum (*minyan*) is present, although for legal reasons, a licensed rabbi usually performs the ceremony, making the marriage valid both religiously and civilly. Priests still perform a few rites, although their primary functions had revolved around the temple, which has not existed for 2000 years. It is common practice, however, to have a rabbi present at these various events, since, as an expert in the law, the rabbi can assure that the rites are done according to the specifications of Torah.

The position of cantor (lit., "singer"), a leader in synagogue prayer and music, developed sometime in the medieval period. The cantor often serves as a teacher of Hebrew too. The duties can vary widely from congregation to congregation.

Jewish circumcision traditionally has been performed by a *mohel*, a Jew trained and ordained for the procedure. In non-Orthodox branches of Judaism, a woman may be so trained. She is called a *mohelet*.

Dietary Laws (Kashrut)

Judaism has developed an extensive range of dietary taboos, beyond what one finds in any other major religion. The prohibition against pork is but one of many restrictions on meat; that taboo happens to be so well known only because pork is a common meat among most societies, and Jews' refusal to eat pork thus stands out. Pork falls under a general prohibition against meat of animals that either do not have a split hoof or do not chew their cud. As well, Jewish law prohibits the eating of birds of prey or of seafood that does not have both scales and fins. Observant Jews also have rules concerning wines and the specific foods to be used at the Passover *seder*.

The restriction on meat is extended further. The meat of acceptable animals is considered *kosher* ("clean") only if the animal has been killed, cleaned, and cooked according to specific rules. That being the case, animals killed in hunting fail to meet the conditions of *kosher* slaughtering and thus are unacceptable, as is meat from all but *kosher*-certified meat packers.

Two main concerns control the slaughter, preparation, and consumption of *kosher* meat. Both concerns are based on a broad reading of legislation in the Bible. One commandment forbids the consumption of blood, thus a particular method of slaughter that drains most of the blood is specified; further the meat is salted and washed to draw out any remaining blood. The second commandment relevant here is that meat and milk dishes cannot be prepared together, or, according to developed Jewish legislation, even consumed together. Observant Jews will have two sets of dishes and cookery, one for meat dishes and one for milk or dairy. Such Jews will even observe a specific length of time between the consumption of meat and milk dishes (three to six hours), and between the consumption of milk and meat dishes, they will at least rinse their mouth and some will wait an hour, depending on local custom.

Jews keep various degrees of *kosher*. The Orthodox are *kosher* at home and in public; other Jews often maintain certain aspects of *kosher*, but not the full range. Reform Jews had rejected the idea of *kosher* altogether, but more recently some have returned to a measure of *kosher* observance.

In North America in particular, thousands of packaged food products bear a *kosher* certification symbol, from one of dozens of certifying agencies. The certification started in the 1920s to assist Jewish families who wished to keep *kosher* in an increasingly diverse ethnic environment. In order to distinguish dairy products where there could be confusion, the letter D (dairy) is sometimes used; products that may be consumed with either dairy or meat dishes are either unmarked or marked by the word *parve* or *pareve* (neutral).

Distinctive Dress

The stereotype of Jewish dress portrayed in movies and the press frequently features black hats (brimmed or fur) and dark clothing; untrimmed beards; long curled hair (forelocks) in place of sideburns. These are features only of a small segment of Orthodox Jews, the Hasidic. The clothing style is largely reflective of customs in Poland and other places where the Hasidic tradition developed in the 1700s. The beard and curls stem from a particular rabbinic interpretation of passages in the Hebrew Bible. Even in these matters, Hasidic customs vary. For the most part, however, Jews are indistinguishable from non-Jews in terms of dress; both groups buy clothes from the same designers and are swayed by the same fashions.

There are, however, a few items of attire that Jews wear primarily in liturgical contexts. While the temple existed, the most distinctive dress was that which separated the priest and temple staff from the people, although even while the temple was standing, certain articles of religious dress began to be worn by some Jews who were not temple functionaries.

After the destruction of the temple, some of these items became standard for all Jews in liturgical situations, and for some Jews even outside the liturgical context. The following are fairly standard.

Prayer Shawl (Tallit). There are two forms. One is a shawl worn over the head in prayer. The other, worn by Orthodox Jewish men, is a smaller version, and is worn much like an undershirt. Both articles have four corners, with a fringe on each corner.

Phylactery (Tefillin). Small leather boxes containing passages from the Torah are bound to the forehead and right arm of the Orthodox Jew in prayer. They are generally worn only during the morning prayers.

Yarmulke (Kippah). A round skullcap is worn at prayer by most Jews. The Orthodox Jews wear a yarmulke at all times. The origin of the custom is uncertain. In some areas, such head coverings were not required even as late as the 1100s.

Modern Jewish Divisions

As a result of the Enlightenment and emancipation from European ghettos, Jews developed various ways to relate to and participate in the larger world. Many scholars divide modern Judaism into four distinct groups: Reform, Conservative, Orthodox, and Reconstructionist. Some caution must be used with such simplification.

Such categorization works best in describing the situation in the United States. Further, in the latter half of the twentieth-century, particularly because of the Holocaust, some groups that had discarded many elements of Jewish tradition are returning to more traditional practices, thus reducing some of the earlier sharp differences that had been used to distinguish the groups. In 1999, for example, Reform Judaism encouraged its members to consider keeping Sabbath and *kosher* regulations, which it had rejected outright a hundred years earlier. One can trace this return to more traditional practices in Reform Judaism by comparing important declarations made over the last century or so: the Pittsburg Platform (1885), the Columbus Platform (1937), and the Centenary Perspective adopted at San Francisco (1976). There are, as well, Jews who do not belong to any of these four groups; they see their Judaism in purely ethnic and secular terms. Secular Jews account for about 30% of Jews. The four positions discussed below are all religious. Conservative is the largest at 30%; Reform stands at 25%; Orthodox at 14%; and Reconstructionist at 1%.

Reform Judaism. This branch of Judaism is called Liberal Judaism in Great Britain. It encompasses the more radical religious responses to the Enlightenment. It tends to highlight the universal and ethical aspects of

Judaism and its monotheism and to discard ritual aspects, which had sharply distinguished Jews from the national cultures in which they lived. A similar liberalizing trend was at work in many Protestant traditions in Europe, particularly in Germany, when Reform Judaism first established itself, and Reform Judaism came to share many of these features. Reform Jews changed the Sabbath services to Sundays, replaced the Hebrew biblical text with vernacular translations, disregarded *kosher* laws, discarded distinctive dress, no longer performed circumcision, and substituted the longing for a restored temple and homeland with full citizenship in the countries in which they resided. The general sense was that Judaism was a system in evolution, and needed constantly to be reformed to be effective and relevant.

But there was some danger in this approach. How much of Jewish tradition could be lost without the death of Judaism itself? How close to Christianity could Judaism come without destroying a place for itself? Indeed, many Jews found that they could be comfortable in the Protestant liberalism of the day, and simply left Judaism completely, becoming Christian converts. The seventeenth-century philosopher Moses Mendelssohn, whose ideas helped spark the Reform Movement, illustrates the danger. Mendelssohn was a practicing Jew; his son became a convert to Christianity; his grandson, the renowned composer Felix Mendelssohn, featured the anti-Jewish Christian hero, St. Paul, in his first oratorio, and married the daughter of a Protestant minister.

Conservative. Many within Judaism sought a more secure way to appropriate the wider culture without risking the identity of Jews or Judaism. In Germany, the perspective was called positive-historical; in its later North American form, it is called Conservative Judaism. Rather than rejecting outright ritual and tradition as alien or unnecessary to the essence of religion, Zacharias Frankel (1801-1875), the father of the conservative movement, insisted on a critical examination of the traditions of Judaism with a view to determining what was part of the core and what was merely the cultural husk in which the regulation was first expressed. Thus Conservative Jews retain traditional elements (e.g., Sabbath, *kosher*), but the form of these could vary from past practice. This balancing between preservation and modification of tradition makes Conservative Judaism quite diverse, ranging from fairly observant to minimally so.

Orthodox. Although the roots of Reform and Conservative Judaism lie in Europe, these movements have had their greatest success in North America. European Jews tended to maintain the traditional practices and beliefs of Judaism, and the term "Orthodox" came to be applied to them to distinguish them from Reform Judaism. A "neo-orthodox" movement

permitted elements from the wider culture, while at the same time retaining all elements of the tradition. Orthodox Jews represent only about
14% of the Jewish population today, though prior to the Holocaust, in
which many Orthodox Jews perished, they were the dominant force.
Their relatively small size is disproportionate to their influence: in Israel,
they wield considerable political power, and some of the ritual practices
that they most faithfully maintained are being adopted again by less
orthodox Jewish traditions.

Reconstructionist. Reconstructionist Judaism is usually given a place
in discussions of groups within Judaism, for its ideas have influenced
American Judaism widely, although numerically it is insignificant. Ideas
of a "chosen" people, of revelation, and of a personal messiah were rejected. It sees Judaism as an evolutionary culture, a product of human
reflection, and subject to change in the context of a democratic community. Religion is but one part of the Jewish complex.

CONCLUSION

The oldest of the surviving "western" religions is now the smallest,
although its unintended offspring, Christianity and Islam, make up over
half of the world's population. Judaism has learned to live in the lands of
these offspring, sometimes sharing fully in their cultural successes; sometimes expelled, excluded, or limited to a restricted range of interchange.

Not only has Judaism had profound influence on religious thinking
generally because of its novel ideas and emphases, it has itself been subject to the religious influences of the wider religious world in which it
found itself frequently scattered. Much of the diversity in Judaism today
reflects the struggle to come to terms with the larger world, while retaining what gives Judaism its distinctive identity. Among Jews, the elements
of that essential Jewish identity have been hotly debated since the Enlightenment, although the experience of the Holocaust has, in some ways,
reemphasized some of the traditional elements of Judaism.

CHAPTER FOUR   Christianity

HISTORY

The Christian Claim

The term "Christianity" is coined from a title that Christians applied to their leader, Jesus, from the early days of their movement. They claimed that Jesus was the ultimate link to God, being God's Christ or Messiah (lit., "anointed one" from Greek and Hebrew respectively). In the language of the day, that meant that Jesus was God's commissioned agent, who by word and action proclaimed God's will and accomplished God's purposes. So closely allied was Jesus with the purposes of God, according to Christian perception, that he came to be routinely described as God's son.

The Jewish Context

According to early Christian writings, Jesus was born in Bethlehem, a town in southern Palestine near Jerusalem, and he grew up in Nazareth, about sixty-five miles to the north, in an area of Palestine called Galilee. Both were small towns.

Jews traced their ancestry back over more than a thousand years to Palestine. Their holy city, Jerusalem, was there. Their temple was there, bustling with pilgrims from all areas of the Mediterranean and Mesopotamia. Memorials of the renowned King David and his dynasty were there. At the time of the birth of Jesus, however, much of Jewish glory lay idealized in the distant past. The Davidic dynasty had collapsed six hundred years before, humbled by the mighty Babylonian Empire. For most of Jewish history, the Jewish territory was little more than a twenty-five-mile square around Jerusalem, the capital. In the century before Jesus' birth, Jewish fortunes briefly improved under the Maccabees, a family of priests and warriors who gained Jewish independence, and expanded Jewish territory into the north, where stories of Jesus have their setting. Most Jews lived elsewhere, however, in what was called the Diaspora, where they had migrated during the half-millennium before. All Jews, however, whether living in Palestine or the Diaspora, revered Jerusalem as home to God's people, God's king (when he should appear), and God's temple. Pious Jews made long pilgrimages to Jerusalem and its temple, as Jesus himself did, according to stories in early Christian accounts.

The Roman Context

The success of the Maccabean independence movement had encouraged expectations of a restored Jewish nation comparable to the idealized kingdom of David from the distant past. Hopes for such glorious restoration were crushed, however, when Rome, the new power on the Mediterranean scene, marched through the area, conquering Palestine in 63 B.C.E. Aspirations of Jewish independence that survived were forced underground as Rome clamped down on any hint of rebellion. The Roman presence and the Roman response to revolution could not have escaped Jesus' attention, nor could the restorationist ideas in popular Jewish thought.

Different attitudes developed in Palestine to the Roman presence, from the accommodating to the defiant. Apocalyptic literature, which spoke of the end of the present order and of a cosmic restoration in the coming reign of God, fueled much of the speculation of this period.

A number of charismatic men raised bands of revolutionaries against Roman rule. Each met a similar fate, as the Roman army, at the height of its power, held the territories it had recently conquered in close check. The most celebrated revolt, commonly called "the Jewish War," lasted from 66 to 73 C.E. It resulted in the destruction of Jerusalem and the temple, and the horrific slaughter and enslavement of tens of thousands of Jews.

It was in such a charged political climate that Jesus lived, and that earliest Christianity was established.

Jesus

The birth of Jesus, which marks the beginning of the Christian story, is one of the best-known dates in history. The Christian calendar (which has near universal use in the international community because of global western influence) treats the birth of Jesus as the critical moment of history. All that occurred before Jesus' birth is assigned to a "past" and labelled B.C. (before Christ)—an abbreviation not used until the 1600s. All that comes "after" is counted in years from Jesus' birth and is labeled A.D. (Latin: *anno Domini*, meaning "in the year of our Lord"). The calendar reflecting this division of history is attributed to a monk named Denis (Greek: Dionysius) the Little, who lived five hundred years after the birth of Jesus. Due to errors in his information, he started the dating about half a decade too late; this explains the seemingly odd date of Jesus' birth in 6 B.C.

The pivotal point of history that the birth of Jesus marks in the Christian calendar stands in sharp contrast to Jesus' obscure and humble beginnings. The early Christians themselves, when they told the story of Jesus, admitted their founder's humble birth in a barn and his ethnic identity as a Jew (a minority often on the margin of social status and power in the Roman Empire). Even the Christian story of the wise men (*magi*) coming from the east bearing gifts for Jesus, the new-born "king," highlighted the irony of the less-than-princely status of Jesus, who lived in a world that, according to early Christian writers, largely failed to recognize him.

The earliest Christian writings report almost nothing of Jesus' childhood or his adult life until he began his career as a religious teacher and

MAJOR TEXTS

Bible: Two collections in one: the Hebrew Bible of the Jews (which Christians call the "Old Testament") and new Christian writings (which they call the "New Testament"). [See sidebar "CANON"]

Church History: (early 300s). The work of Eusebius, bishop of Caesarea. Written as the Roman Empire shifted towards Christianity, it outlines the history of Christianity in its first 300 years. Eusebius quoted his sources extensively, and as a result we have substantial passages from many early Christian authors whose works are otherwise lost.

The City of God: (early 400s). Written by Bishop Augustine, as the Roman Empire was beginning to fall to the barbarian tribes. It outlines a view of church and state.

Summa Theologica: (1200s). The massive work of Thomas Aquinas, and a high point in medieval scholarship. It has shaped much of Catholic thinking to the present.

The Ninety-Five Theses: (1517). Short debating points by Luther primarily regarding abuses in the indulgence system. It sparked the Protestant Reformation.

The Institutes of the Christian Religion: (1500s, in various versions). A work of John Calvin, which provides the basis for the development of much of Protestant theological reflection.

reformer. Two gospels, Matthew and Luke, however, do provide a birth narrative, from which the various details of the popular Christmas story come: Mary and Joseph, shepherds, a chorus of angels, *magi*, a trip to Bethlehem. These gospels also include some less well known events. Luke, for example, adds a story about Jesus' exceptional understanding of religion by the age of twelve, when he engaged in discussions with leading teachers of the day. In the second century, many more stories about Jesus were composed, often filling in the gaps of Jesus' youth with tales of the miraculous and bizarre. These are called "Infancy Gospels," part of a collection of Christian writings largely from the second and third centuries known as the "New Testament Apocrypha."

But the heart of the story as told by the earliest writers focuses simply on Jesus and his religious career, when he was about thirty years old. Some ninety stories about Jesus make up the first-century evidence, and these are almost entirely restricted to four documents called "Gospels" (Matthew, Mark, Luke, and John). The stories provide a portrait of Jesus as a religious reformer who had a sense of a special relationship with God and a special role in God's plan. Numerous stories report healings and exorcisms, and a few report what are called "nature miracles," involving some dramatic suspension of natural law (e.g., turning water into wine; walking on water).

Besides the colorful narratives, much of the material about Jesus purports to recount his teaching. Some 1,500 sayings are attributed to Jesus in the early Christian writings. A central theme is the coming of the kingdom of God, which sometimes has an apocalyptic, end-of-the-world tone to it, often challenging notions of who will benefit from God's reign. According to Jesus, God's reign brings hope to those who are excluded by traditional religious boundaries; prostitutes and the hated tax collectors are invited into the circle of Jesus' friends. Early Christian writings report that such actions by Jesus caused scandal among circles of pious Jews. Such scandal was intensified by Jesus' controversial treatment of food laws (*kosher*) and Sabbath legislation. How could one who showed carelessness about God's laws (Torah) claim to speak for God?

Events turned ugly, and during a Passover, one of the great annual pilgrim feasts of the Jews, Jesus was arrested in Jerusalem, tried, convicted, and executed. Whatever the Jewish involvement in the death of Jesus, the earliest Christian writings reflect the Christian suspicion that Jews were behind the plot. This led Christians in later centuries to charge Jews with deicide (the killing of God), and often to treat Jews as "Christ-killers" and agents of the devil.

The Early Church

Jesus was executed–a fate common enough for those who were perceived to threaten the stability of the volatile Palestinian area. With their leader dead, rebel groups usually disbanded and their leader's name quickly was forgotten except as a byword. But the Jesus movement did not disband, though there are some clues in the early stories that it almost did. Curiously, it reappeared, with its members boldly declaring that God had raised Jesus from death and had appointed him as cosmic judge and savior. Jesus was, they said, the Messiah (or the Christ), a word that identified, for them, the agent of God in the dramatic new reign of God. They pointed to the Jewish scriptures, particularly to the section called the Prophets, where scores of passages, they claimed, spoke of Jesus as the Messiah. The first converts were Jews who believed that message.

One of the new converts, Paul, who had been at first a persecutor of Christians, became a leader of a group within the Christian movement that argued for unrestricted acceptance of Gentiles (non-Jews) as full members. Gone was the earlier expectation that Gentile converts to Christianity would follow a Jewish lifestyle, particularly difficult because of its food and Sabbath laws and the requirement of circumcision. This new stance led to a rapid distancing of Christianity from Judaism, so that by the end of the first century, non-Jews probably constituted the majority of members in the Christian movement.

That is not to say that Christianity lost its Jewish roots. Quite the contrary.

CANON: VERSIONS AND SECTIONS

Bible: (lit., "books"). Main term for Christian canon, consisting of the Old Testament (the Jewish Bible) and the New Testament.

New Testament: Collection of early Christian writings of various kinds, consisting of four gospels, thirteen letters attributed to Paul, and a few other documents, largely written in the last fifty years of the first century.

Gospels: (late 60s-90s C.E.). The first four books of the New Testament (Matthew, Mark, Luke, and John), mainly consisting of stories and sayings of Jesus. The first three are called *synoptic*, because of similar structure and content.

Septuagint (LXX): (100s B.C.E.). Greek translation of the Hebrew Bible, used by Greek-speaking Jews. This was the first Bible of early Christians.

Vulgate: Jerome's Latin translation of the Bible (in the 400s). This became the Bible of the western church until the Protestant Reformation of the 1500s, when it was challenged by vernacular translations.

Apocrypha: (lit., "hidden"). Books in the Vulgate but not in the present Jewish canon. Some are accepted by Catholics and Orthodox; Protestantism rejects them all.

Authorized Version: (1611). More popularly known as the King James Version (KJV). A translation of the Bible into English at the high point in English literature (Elizabethan/Shakespearian times). Used widely in the English world until newer translations began to replace it in the twentieth century.

Christianity retained so much of its Jewish heritage that the Greco-Roman society initially seem to have treated the Christian movement as a sect of Judaism. Both Jews and Christians were monotheists; both used the same religious texts, the Hebrew Bible (which Christians came to call the Old Testament); both used the same religious vocabulary; both followed similar ethical practices, which often set them apart from their Gentile neighbors.

As Christianity became more demarcated from Judaism, rumors circulated about the new movement—even charges of sexual immorality and cannibalism. Christians also were accused of being atheists, largely because they lacked most of the apparatus of ancient religion: sacrifices, temples, images, and a proper priesthood. Christianity refuted such charges, mainly through the literary activities of a group of second-century Christian intellectuals called the Apologists.

During the third century, the church experienced considerable growth, so much so that the imperial government on occasion organized empire-wide attacks on the Christian churches, leading to hundreds, and perhaps thousands, of martyrs. Although there had always been sporadic persecutions, these more intense attacks helped to create a company of martyrs or saints in sufficient numbers to provide an impressive contingent of heroes for the developing Christian calendar. The date of the death of a martyr was celebrated as their "birth date" into paradise. Any physical remains of these martyrs or objects associated with them became cherished relics and the graves of martyrs became holy space, in contrast to the defilement that generally had been associated with death and cemeteries by pagans and Jews.

Christianity as the State Religion

At the height of the most intense persecution, Christians experienced the most dramatic reversal of fortune. A new Roman emperor, Constantine, declared religious toleration and began a successful campaign of promoting the Christian church. So successful was this new alliance that by the end of the 300s, Christianity had become the state religion, and classical paganism had largely admitted defeat.

Most, but not all, saw the alliance between church and state as a good thing. Pagans, of course, did not, nor did Jews. Some evidence suggests that paganism lived on at various levels: among some of the elite, in rural communities, and often just beneath the surface of Christian believers. Whatever the merits of these observations about continuing pagan attachments, the reality is that belief in Jesus as the key to social and spiritual wellbeing became the dominant conviction of the vast majority in the Roman Empire. Elements of older beliefs that survived in Christian thinking had largely a secondary, though not necessarily meaningless, character.

Some Christians, however, became alarmed at the church/state alliance under Constantine, as crowds of former pagans, untutored in Christian belief or behavior, flocked into the church. Some joined the monastic movement, which provided an environment where one could live devotedly to God, undisturbed by the new secular influences on the church that seem to be inescapable in the new relationship with the state.

Christianity, as the state church, also encountered difficulties with dissenting Christian groups, whose views often were suppressed, as uniformity as well as unity became prized goals of the imperial church. The suppression of these groups, whose divergence often had a regional coloring, fostered political as well as religious resentment, sometimes resulting in the rise of national movements and churches opposed to the imperial church.

East and West

Christianity enjoyed its initial success primarily in the eastern areas of the Roman Empire. The eastern Mediterranean was predominantly Greek-speaking, having been under Greek influence from at least the time of Alexander the Great in the 300s B.C.E. The earliest Christian literature was written almost exclusively in Greek, though gradually Latin

MAJOR LEADERS

Jesus: Born in Palestine about 6 B.C.E. The records about him (mainly the Christian Gospels) indicate a brief career as a religious reformer, healer, and exorcist. Executed around 30 C.E.

Paul: (10?-64 C.E.). Originally an opponent of the new Christian movement, he became a leading member and an advocate for allowing non-Jews to join. Many of his letters are preserved in the New Testament.

Constantine: (ca. 272-337). Called the first Christian emperor, he proclaimed religious toleration [313] and promoted the church with resources of the state.

Augustine: (354-430). The leading theologian, writer, and bishop of the 400s, his views have shaped much of Christianity to the present in both the Catholic and Protestant traditions. He emphasized predestination and original sin.

Gregory the Great: (540-604). Pope from 590 to 604. He is associated with major innovations in the liturgy of the church (Gregorian Chants). He defended the primacy of the bishopric of Rome.

Thomas Aquinas: (1225-1274). The leading scholar of Scholasticism, he did much to synthesize the developing beliefs of the western (Roman Catholic) church.

Martin Luther: (1483-1546). A controversial German monk who opposed the secular tendencies of the Renaissance popes and their money-raising schemes. These concerns helped to spark the "Protestant" Reformation, the major schism in the western (Roman Catholic) church.

took hold in the Christian assemblies of the west, and regional languages sometimes generated a body of expressive Christian literature. The linguistic difference between the Greek church in the east and the Latin church in the west led to differences in liturgy, theological vocabulary, and theological interests and speculation. Other differences, such as the treatment of religious images, sometimes brought tensions to a boiling point between the Eastern and Western churches.

The East and West also faced different problems. The East (Byzantine Rite or the Orthodox Church) had been christianized for a longer time, and serious theological differences had developed there, in particular regarding the nature of the Trinity and the specific nature of the divinity of Jesus. The Byzantine church dismissed these variations as heresy, suppressing groups such as the Nestorians and Monophysites, whose views often became associated with regional interests (Syrian and Egyptian, in particular). When Islam conquered these areas in the 600s and 700s C.E., oppressed Christian groups there often welcomed the Muslims as liberators. The West (Latin or Roman Rite or "Catholic" Christianity), on the other hand, faced either unchristianized peoples or, in some cases, Christians of Arian belief, the only major "deviant" theological perspective with which both the West and East had to deal. Arianism proposed a lower status for the Son of God or the Logos (a term Christians had borrowed from Greek philosophy) than what came to be the official position of the imperial church. After the fourth century, Arians were found mainly among the Germanic "barbarian" tribes, and these were either converted to Roman orthodoxy or defeated by the Franks, the one Germanic tribe that had converted directly from paganism to Catholic Christianity.

As the western empire collapsed in the 400s, the Byzantine Empire in the east underwent renewal, particularly under Justinian in the 500s. The East was able to briefly free some of the western territory that had fallen to the barbarians. But the Eastern Emperor and Western Pope sometimes clashed over Byzantine policy and influence in the West. When Islamic conquests in the 600s weakened the Byzantine Empire, even the limited help the Pope might expect from the East was uncertain. The Pope finally turned to the Franks, a barbarian tribe that had settled in Gaul (France). Even though the Byzantine Empire suffered considerable setbacks, its capital, Constantinople, remained a brilliant center of culture and theological speculation.

For many centuries, in spite of occasional strain, the Eastern and Western churches considered themselves to be in union with the other, and saw themselves together making up the full body of the Christian church. They were able to maintain that sense of unity by the adoption of a common creed and participation in ecumenical councils. But growing differences in religious emphases and slight differences in practice, coupled with conflicting political ambitions and personal conflicts, fractured the communities, resulting in a formal schism in 1054 C.E. The Crusades further strained the relationship, when western crusading armies plundered Constantinople in the 1200s. The city was able to regain some strength, resisting the encircling Turkish (Muslim) armies until 1453. By this time, the Russian Church, centered in Moscow, had become the primary representative and defender of Eastern Christianity.

Western Medieval Christianity

Medieval is the Latin form of the word middle, and historians frequently speak of a Medieval period or the Middle Ages, when speaking of European history. The period roughly runs from 500-1500, covering the years between the ancient world and the modern world.

The first half of the medieval period was marked by significant losses. About a century after Christianity became the main religion of the Roman Empire, the Mediterranean world suffered various political setbacks and upheavals, lasting for over a half millennium. In the 400s, barbarian invasions from the north brought an end to the Roman Empire in the west (476 C.E.). In the 600s and 700s, the new Muslim Empire conquered much of the Byzantine Empire, including all of the land bordering the south and east coasts of the Mediterranean Sea, all of Spain, and most of the Mediterranean islands. In the 800s

SACRED OFFICES

The early church developed over two dozen offices in its first four centuries.

Apostle: The earliest leaders of the Christian church, apostles were sometimes identified with the twelve disciples of Jesus. The office died out after the first generation, and the new office of bishop took its place in the second century.

Bishop: (lit., "overseer"; Greek: *episcopos*). In various areas of Christianity by the early second century, a person by the title bishop was the chief officer over the churches in a city. There was a sense that the bishop was linked to the apostles by an "apostolic succession."

Presbyter: (lit., "elder"). Directly beneath the bishop were the presbyters, who served the small multiple congregations that made up the corporate church of the city. They later are known as priests.

Deacon: (lit., "servant"). The last of the ordained clergy, their tasks were more administrative while the tasks of priests were more religious and liturgical. Deacons served the bishops directly. In many areas, their number was restricted to seven.

Pope: (Greek *Pappas*, "father"). A term that came to be used in the Western Church exclusively for the Bishop of Rome from the eleventh century. It is a common term for priest in the Eastern Church.

Patriarch: The head of national Eastern Orthodox churches. The title has been used since the sixth century.

and 900s, invasions came from the far north, as the Norse (Normans or Vikings) plundered much of Europe and the Mediterranean, and then settled there.

This long 500-year period had been referred to as the Dark Ages. The term is rarely used now, for it obscured the positive side of life during these times. In particular, a significant period of cultural flowering is associated with Charlemagne (Charles the Great) and his Carolingian Age (800s), as the center of the western world shifted from the Mediterranean to northern and western Europe. The Carolingian empire later came to be known as the Holy Roman Empire, and lasted in name, if sometimes in little else, for over a thousand years. Emperors and popes sometimes battled each other over the right to influence the church and control its appointments during this time.

The latter half of the medieval period reflected a growing confidence in Europe. New monastic orders ushered in a period of religious reform and renewal (900s-1200s). Innovative intellectual exploration and theological systemization marked a period called Scholasticism (1200s). New military muscle made the west again a power to be reckoned with, and the Crusades against the Muslims (1100s-1200s) demonstrated that renewed confidence. Daring voyages of discovery came at the end of the period, with unimaginable wealth to advance the political ambitions of European rulers and with vast multitudes of unchristianized peoples to spark the missionary zeal of the Church.

At the end of the Middle Ages, western Europe, though geographically a small part at a remote edge of the world, came soon to dominate the globe. Much of the world became westernized. And in a somewhat parallel and related advance, much of the world became Christianized, making Christianity today the largest religion in the world, at over thirty percent.

The Protestant Reformation

As western Europe was on the verge of becoming the leading world power and Christianity the major religious force, Christianity in Europe suffered a major rift. In the 1400s, the western church, under the leadership of the Bishop of Rome, had become major patrons of the Renaissance, a cultural movement inspired by the golden age of classical Greece and Rome. Huge building projects, such as St. Peter's Basilica, were part of a grand renewal of the city of Rome. In order to fund such projects, the church used various schemes, some of dubious merit. Many princes resented wealth from their regions flowing to Rome. This political concern became linked with criticisms by religious reformers, who questioned the church's wealth and focus. Such combined complaints frequently developed into a restriction on the authority of the Pope, with key decisions now made by a council, as was done in earlier periods of Christian history. This reform effort, the Conciliar Movement, was most effective in the early 1400s.

Some more radical reform efforts rejected the authority of both Pope and Council. In the 1500s, various groups, later called Protestants, broke from the authority of the Catholic Church, and established churches that recognized the authority of the Bible (scripture) alone. This new basis of authority was not without its own problems, as Protestants frequently found themselves split by disagreements over the correct meaning of some key passages from the Bible. The German monk Martin Luther, the "father" of the Reformation, opted for moderate reform, seeking to change a limited number of church practices. The movement shaped by his perspective came to be called Lutheran, and developed into state churches in much of Germany and Scandinavia. The reform in Switzerland was led by the Swiss priest Zwingli and later by the French theologian Calvin. They opted for more sweeping reform of belief, practice, and church structure. This movement, later called Reformed or Calvinist, established pockets of followers in numerous countries, and became the state church in various Swiss cantons, in the Netherlands, and in Scotland (where they were called Presbyterians). England experimented with a "middle way" after Henry VIII's political break from the Catholic Church. They tried to distance themselves from the

MAJOR DIVISIONS

Roman Catholic: ("catholic" = "universal"). Christians under the authority of the Bishop of Rome (pope), whose roots lie in the western Roman empire and whose primary language is Latin. Catholics represent over half of Christians.

Orthodox: ("orthodox" = "correct belief"). The counterpart to the Catholics. Their roots lie in the eastern Roman Empire (Byzantine). Their primary language was Greek, though soon autonomous national churches developed, featuring their national language. Its center had been Constantinople; after 1453, it shifted to Moscow and the Russian Orthodox Church.

Monophysite: (lit., "one" + "nature"). A largely Egyptian schism from the Byzantine church in the 400s, though it had adherents widely in the East. It argued that Christ had one nature (the divine); this left it open to the charge that Jesus was not really human, but only appeared to be.

Nestorian: A largely Syrian schism from the Byzantine church in the 400s. Its distinction between Jesus the man, born of Mary, and Christ the Son, left it opened to the charge that God did not really become human (the Orthodox view), but merely indwelt and inspired the human Jesus.

Protestant: A name applied generally to all non-Catholic western Christians, whose roots lie in the religious and political protests of the 1500s.

Uniate: Any Eastern rite church in communion with the Church of Rome.

extremes of both Catholicism and Protestantism. This tradition is called the Anglican. Reformed elements in England under the Puritans, and under similar groups elsewhere, pressed for more sweeping Protestant reforms. Most radical of the Protestant reformers were the Anabaptists ("re-baptizers"), initially a schism from the Swiss Reformed movement. They insisted that the only valid baptism was of adult candidates, because only adults could be accountable for their decision to join the church. These re-formers, therefore, rebaptized those who had been previously baptized as children. This action challenged state churches (whether Catholic or Prot-estant), which assumed that anyone born in the state would be a member of the state church. Anabaptists were generally pacifists, too, at a time when Catholic and Protestant states battled each other. Those unwilling to fight for the cause of faith and country fell under further suspicion. These Ana-baptist groups (Mennonite, Amish, and Hutterite) experienced persecu-tion by Catholics and Protestants alike, and they were forced to flee from country to country for safety.

The Reformation changed the map of Europe: northern Europe be-came largely Protestant; southern Europe remained dominantly Catholic, with borders marked loosely by the Rhine and Danube rivers. This bor-der also marked a linguistic divide, with Germanic languages to the north and Romance languages to the south, which loosely falls along the an-cient Roman and barbarian borders, established well before Christianity was a factor of any kind there.

Modern Christianity

The split between Catholics and Protestants and the further splits among the various Protestant groups contributed to a devastating Thirty Years War (1618-1648). The brutal consequence of religious and politi-cal hostilities forced some to question the focus that the church often seemed to place on divisive religious nuances. They proposed a less com-plex, more generic religion, which emphasized a remote creator deity and a world operating under natural law, a perspective called Deism. Mir-acle and divine intervention were largely dismissed. This new perspec-tive challenged basic Christian dogma of the divinity of Jesus. About the same time, science more and more offered an explanation of what had been identified as supernatural activity in the world, and often sharply challenged the biblical view of the world. In the 1800s, a movement called Biblical Criticism raised further questions about the miraculous elements in stories in the Bible and questioned the authorship of some of biblical documents. These new perspectives tended to weaken the authority of the Christian scriptures, and serious disagreements about these matters often divided Christian churches even further.

Reflecting another trend, various pietistic movements, such as the Methodists, arose in the 1700s, calling for deep changes to personal behavior as a result of often dramatic experiences of conversion. In the 1800s, particularly in North America, a number of restorationist movements arose, calling for a return to the supposed simplicity and purity of the age of the apostles. Some created utopian communities, such as the Shakers; others anticipated the imminent arrival of the "Second Coming" of Jesus, when God's kingdom would be established (Disciples of Christ, Mormons, Seventh-Day Adventists, Jehovah's Witnesses, and Pentecostals).

In the twentieth century, the struggle with the modern age has resulted in an informal and sometimes fuzzy division between "liberal" and "conservative" churches. To some degree, the differences have been reduced as a result of the impact of the Charismatic Movement (Pentecostalism) in mainstream churches in the last half of the twentieth century and by efforts of evangelicals to participate more fully in broad Christian movements from which they had been previously excluded or with which they had earlier refused to participate.

Globalization

Christianity in the modern period is marked by two features that were foreign to it throughout most of its history. One is the rise of more secular or rational

---

MAJOR PROTESTANT GROUPS

Lutheran: (1517). First group of the Protestant Reformation. Led by Martin Luther, it became the state church in most areas of northern and central Germany and in all of Scandinavia.

Reformed: (1521). Founded by Zwingli (Swiss) and later led by Calvin (French). Emphasized predestination and a presbyterian form of church governance. Became the state church in the Netherlands, Scotland, and in areas of Switzerland.

Anabaptist: (1525). Mennonites, Hutterites, and Amish. Also called the "Radical Reformation," because of their rejection of church/state ties, their pacifism, and their requirement of adult baptism.

Anglican: (1534). The Church of England, formed as a result of King Henry VIII's break from the authority of the pope. Anglicanism came to see itself as a "middle way" between Catholicism and Protestantism. Puritan influence in the 1600s gave it a more Protestant character.

Methodist: A movement emphasizing personal piety and social action; founded by an Anglican priest, John Wesley, and his brother Charles.

Baptist: A diverse Protestant group, started in England with Anabaptist and Puritan influences. Largest Protestant group in the United States. Emphasizes adult baptism rather than the more common practice of infant baptism.

Pentecostal: The most recent and largest Protestant group. It emphasizes baptism in the Holy Spirit (often with speaking in tongues) and the Second Coming of Jesus.

approaches to religion, brought on by the European Enlightenment of the 1700s. The other is the global character of the church and the diverse cultures of its members.

The rapid global expansion of Christianity stemmed from two key efforts: first came the Catholic missionary efforts on the heels of the European explorers and colonizers of the 1500s. This missionary effort affected the Americas and some of the colonial outposts in India and China. The second wave of missionary activity came in the 1800s and 1900s, with Protestants now involved and the base of missions much less restricted. Africa and Asia became dotted with Christian missions. At the end of the twentieth century, Europe represented only a small part of the worldwide Christian church, a significant change from the 1500s.

The fractured state of the western Christian church complicated its missionary efforts. Christian schism and competition in non-Christian lands often discredited the Christian cause, which led many churches to explore the possibility of cooperative, rather than competitive, missionary efforts. In time, this cooperation flowered into ecumenical movements promoting unification in the western church, the largest and most lasting being the World Council of Churches, founded in 1948.

BELIEFS

The Jewish Influence

The first Christians retained much of the religious world they had grown up with in Judaism. So sweeping was their incorporation of Judaism into Christianity that the first Christians were able to use the Jewish Bible (what Christians called "The Old Testament") as their only scripture for many decades, until some of the writings of Christian leaders began to be circulated and read. Even then, the Jewish Bible maintained its status among Christians, as it does to this day. Individuals from the Hebrew Bible color the Christian story: Adam and Eve, Abraham, Moses, David, Isaiah, and Daniel appear as frequently in Christian teaching as in Jewish. Christians, such as Marcion in the second century, who suggest discarding the Jewish Bible, generally have been treated as heretics.

As one would expect, Christian use of the Hebrew scriptures has a clear Christian slant. Given that Christians view Jesus as God's agent in human salvation selected before the world even existed, God's revelation to the Hebrews must have reflected that intention in some way. Christians look for the message about Christ in the Hebrew Bible by applying various interpretative techniques. From early on, Christians pointed out that the Hebrew prophets spoke of an age of restoration under God's agent (the Messiah or the Christ), and they identified passage after passage that, they contended, predicted Jesus' action or character as Messiah. They also used and developed the allegorical method, by which objects and events in the Hebrew Bible were seen to carry in seed or shadow form the reality that was fully expressed in Jesus.

Sometimes a Christian group will attempt to structure its behavior around a more literal reading of the Hebrew scriptures. Jewish food laws are sometimes followed and church meetings are held on Saturdays (the Jewish Sabbath) rather than on Sundays. Such groups have had little influence on the larger Christian community's more selective appropriation of Judaism.

The Jewish Torah

The earliest Christians were Jewish. Initially, it appears, all obeyed the Jewish Torah. The debate over the admission of Gentiles (non-Jews) into the Christian movement raised sharp questions about the purpose of Torah and the obligation of Christians to obey it. The strongest arguments against Torah observance came from Paul, a Jew who initially had persecuted the church and imprisoned its followers. After a dramatic experience, Paul converted to Christianity, and within a few years of the church's beginning had become a chief advocate against retaining Torah observance. Paul's argument ran something like this: if Jesus was in fact God's agent of salvation (as all Christians believed),

---

KEY FESTIVALS

(*following the calendar order*)

Epiphany: [January 6]. The date originally marked the birth of Jesus in the Eastern Church. When the Eastern Church adopted the western date of December 25, they kept January 6 for the celebration of Jesus' baptism. The West celebrates the visit of the magi on January 6.

Lent: In the West, a forty-day period of fasting or self-denial and penance, beginning on Ash Wednesday. In the East, the period is longer, resulting from how a forty-day fast period is calculated leading up to Easter. The East still has rigorous fasting rules, restricting food to one meal each day during this period.

Easter: The primary and oldest Christian festival, celebrating the death and resurrection of Jesus, held in the Spring. This was connected to the Jewish Passover. Many churches reserve baptism until Easter celebrations. Good Friday commemorates Jesus' death.

Pentecost: (lit., "fiftieth"). Also called Whitsunday. A Sunday celebration fifty days after Easter, commemorating the descent of the Holy Spirit on the disciples. It is understood as the start of the world mission of the church. Connected to Jewish Shavuot ("Feast of Weeks")."

Christmas: [December 25] (lit., "Christ's mass"). Celebration of the birth of Jesus. First celebrated ca. 336 under Constantine. The date was chosen to coincide with the birthday of the "unconquered sun."

then the Torah (the Jewish law) must have had shortcomings as a vehicle for salvation. If Torah was not adequate and Jesus was, then Jews had no greater advantage than non-Jews. And if Torah was not adequate for the salvation of Jews, why make it necessary for non-Jews, who had a fully adequate vehicle to salvation in Jesus?

Some Jewish Christians continued to observe Torah. In the second century, they were referred to as Ebionites. They became increasingly isolated as the church's membership became increasingly non-Jewish.

God

Christians and Jews declare that there is but one God. That perspective set both groups apart from the larger religious world of the ancient Mediterranean, which, while not teeming with divinities, had an extended family of gods (about two dozen) and a host of demigods in their rich mythology.

The Christian commitment to monotheism is reflected in how early Christians dealt with the world of paganism. They refused to worship the traditional gods, in spite of the threat of martyrdom. Christians could have escaped such a fate simply by offering a sacrifice to pagan gods, but they would not do so because they sensed that such action would be disloyal to Christ. Further, Christians borrowed heavily from Judaism for their attacks on pagan gods. Such arguments were rooted in a monotheistic consciousness, and would have made little sense outside of that perspective. To polytheists, such exclusivity in the worship of one god and the hostility and mockery directed at all other gods were offensive and dangerous attitudes, for each god deserved worship, at the appropriate times and places.

For Christians, their God was the same God as the Jewish God. He was creator and sustainer of the world, and he would hold the world accountable before him in a final judgment. Yet, this God, from both Jewish and Christian perspective, was a God of mercy and forgiveness. Some early Christians, however, saw considerable contrast between the God revealed by Jesus and the God of the Hebrew Bible. The Marcionites, mentioned earlier, rejected the Hebrew Bible and its vision of God.

The Trinity

Jews and Muslims have faulted Christian monotheism as not adequately monotheistic. The charge stems from how Christians have incorporated Jesus into their understanding of the divine.

Christians had to reconcile their monotheism with the high status that they ascribed to Jesus. For two centuries (200s and 300s), this debate held center-stage. A resolution was reached at the Council of Nicea (325) and, after various shifts in positions in the 300s, was finally and effectively confirmed at another council, at Constantinople in 381. That resolution and its creed (Nicene) have become the most familiar theological statement of Christians to this day, being repeated weekly in most Christian groups. This is called a trinitarian position, where the one God consists of the Father, the Son, and the Holy Spirit. Charges that this is a polytheist position have always been strenuously rejected by Christians.

Jesus

The Early Debates. The focus of much of early Christian theological debate, particularly in the east, focused on problems raised by the status of Jesus. The first question was how monotheism could be maintained with Jesus elevated to high status. The poles of the debates portrayed Jesus either as a man, inspired by God, or merely a mode or aspect of God, not a distinct being. These debates, largely in the third century, have been labeled, somewhat wrongly, as monarchianism—emphasizing the one ultimate ruler of the cosmos, perhaps against Gnostic speculations of two opposite primal forces. Most Christians argued for something somewhere in the middle, however, maintaining a distinction between the Father and

KEY RITUALS

The two rituals shared by most Christian groups are baptism and the Eucharist. The Roman Catholic tradition has seven sacraments, as well as a variety of rituals associated with special festivals.

Baptism: The rite of initiation in the Christian community. Practiced from the first century onwards, it underwent various transformations, which have resulted in diverse practices within Christianity. The main modern debates are over candidates and mode: whether it should be administered to children or restricted to adults, and whether it should be by pouring, sprinkling, or immersion. The ancient debate centered on whether the baptism of schismatics was valid.

Eucharist: This rite is known by a number of names (Communion, the Mass, the Last Supper, the Lord's Supper, the Table, the Breaking of Bread . . .). Based on the story of Jesus' "Last Supper" with his disciples on the night prior to his execution; bread and wine are used, referring to the flesh and blood of Jesus in his sacrificial death. Christians have debated whether the bread and wine are symbols or something more substantial.

The Seven Sacraments: The Council of Trent in the 1500s affirmed seven sacraments as essential to the Roman Catholic faith. They are: Baptism, Confirmation, Eucharist, Penance (sometimes called Reconciliation), Anointing of the Sick (sometimes called "Extreme Unction" or "Last Rites"), Holy Orders, and Matrimony.

the Son (Jesus), while maintaining that Jesus was fully God. They found the Greek concept of the Logos useful in describing the Son.

The rejection of monarchian positions then led to speculation regarding the nature of the Son (Logos). While agreeing that the Logos was more than human, a group called the Arians argued that the Logos was not eternal. But that seemed to suggest that the Logos was not fully God, for an essential characteristic in the Christian definition of God was that he was eternal. Against Arianism, the argument was made that the Logos was in every way the same as God: "co-eternal" or "eternally-begotten," as they put it. This position (called the Nicene) won the debate and became the definition of orthodoxy in the fourth century at the Council of Nicea (325 C.E.).

With the divine status of the Son entrenched in the creedal formulas, the nature of the incarnation (the Logos in human form) then required attention. The Nestorians emphasized the human side of the incarnation, condemning the popular piety that spoke of Mary as the "Mother of God." On the opposite side, the Monophysites argued that the incarnated Logos had only a divine nature. Both positions were rejected by the majority: the Nestorian position was judged as not adequately uniting the human and the divine aspects; the Monophysite position was rejected for not maintaining a sufficiently substantial human element in the incarnation. Orthodoxy (the majority position) expressed itself in the Chalcedon Definition of Faith (451 C.E.), which held that both human nature and divine nature were uniquely united in unmixed form in Christ—Christ was both fully human and fully divine. The alternative positions, however, gained some national support against the central authority of the Byzantine Empire and Church. To this day, the Monophysite position is the Christianity of the Syrian (or Jacobite) and Egyptian (Coptic) churches; the Nestorian position is maintained by smaller Christian communities in Iraq, Iran and Syria.

The Historical Jesus. The traditional view of Jesus as the Son of God, and thus divine, meant that the miracle stories associated with Jesus presented no problems for Christians. Indeed, in the expansion of the church, such stories usually were featured as compelling evidence of the truth of the Christian message. Under the influence of the Enlightenment, both the possibility of miracles and the divine nature of Jesus became sharp issues of contention within the Christian community. Such debates were furthered by a new approach to the biblical literature, which treated the texts as any other historical texts, subjecting them to such questions as date, sources, authorship, etc. No more were the biblical texts treated as unique sources of revelation: they were viewed as documents shaped by the assumptions of their ancient pre-scientific environments. Many theologians argued that the Bible needed to be demythologized if it was to speak to the modern post-Enlightenment age. This meant that Jesus had to be stripped of supernatural powers. Many portraits of Jesus since the 1800s emphasize a religious reformer of ethics rather than the divine cosmic savior of traditional Christian thinking.

The Cosmos

In a monotheistic universe, God must be the cause of all that exists, and all that exists must have its purpose with reference to God. Since Christians use the Hebrew Bible as the first part of their canon, they share an account of origins with Jews: the creation story, featuring Adam and Eve and the Garden of Eden. From this story, several of the primary assumptions of Christianity are shaped. The cosmos, as God's creation, is good. Humans, as God's paramount creation, bear the divine image. At least, that is the first page of the story.

> **KEY CREED**
> **The Apostles' Creed:**
>
> I believe in God,
> the Father almighty,
> creator of heaven and earth.
>
> I believe in Jesus Christ,
> God's only Son, our Lord,
> who was conceived
> by the Holy Spirit,
> born of the Virgin Mary,
> suffered under Pontius Pilate,
> was crucified,
> died,
> and was buried;
> he descended to the dead.
> On the third day he rose again;
> he ascended into heaven,
> he is seated at the right hand
> of the Father,
> and he will come to judge
> the living and the dead.
>
> I believe in the Holy Spirit,
> the holy catholic Church,
> the communion of saints,
> the forgiveness of sins,
> the resurrection of the body,
> and the life everlasting.
> Amen.

The Human Condition

The cosmos has suffered grave damage, however, according to the traditional Christian understanding, for humans have rebelled against God. Humans and the human home have been profoundly disabled as a result. What was once Paradise has become "Paradise Lost." Humans have been expelled from Eden; the Golden Age has ended. Humans have pursued their own desires rather than the will and pleasure of God. Death, rather than life, is to be their end.

The story of Adam and Eve eating the "forbidden fruit" captures that disobedience. The story is similar in tone to the Greek tale of Pandora's box, where the disobedience of one individual led to disaster for the whole race.

While Christians traditionally have maintained that Adam's sin, or "The Fall" as they call it, has had serious consequences for the human condition, they have disagreed regarding the extent to which humans have been impaired by sin. One view stresses that humans have a free will: in other words, humans are not so impaired that they cannot choose between good and evil. This makes humans more responsible for their actions and their destiny. The other view stresses the gravity of the human condition, denying any capacity in humans to choose the right path or any goodness that would merit salvation. This places the destiny of humans starkly in God's hands. Since none deserve favor, those who are selected have only God's mercy to thank. This theological position is called predestination. Augustine was the most forceful exponent of the latter view, and most of the early Protestant reformers made it central to their theology.

Salvation

According to both Jews and Christians, after the expulsion of Adam and Eve from the Garden of Eden, God maintained a relationship with humans through selected righteous individuals, such as Noah, Abraham, Moses, David, and others. Each had some message or function that aided in the communication between God and the human family.

According to Christians, such mediators or agents were minor players in the grand scheme, all being overshadowed by Jesus, God's own Son, who permanently healed the breach between God and humans. Christians generally understand the death of Jesus to be a crucial element in the resolution of the alienation of humans from God, and they celebrate the death and resurrection of Jesus annually in Good Friday and Easter Sunday ceremonies. This is the major theme of Christian art too.

Christians have held various views on the meaning of the death of Jesus, however. To some, Jesus' willingness to die primarily demonstrates the ultimate commitment to God, an example of obedience that is to mark the daily attitude of all believers. To others, the death is a quasi-legal event, by which the sins of humans are transferred to God's Son, who then stands in the place of humans under the just judgment of God. Jesus' death then delivers humans from the sentence of death, which God had decreed as the punishment for sin. Some medieval theologians argued that the death of Jesus was a ransom God paid to the devil for the release of human souls, and others debated whether the death of Jesus was the only solution possible for the human dilemma, or whether God could have used any mechanism he wished to cure the human condition.

But whatever the nuanced explanation of the death of Jesus, it is clear that Christians do not treat Jesus' death as some tragic martyrdom; it is central to the resolution of the human problem. Christians frequently capture that importance by speaking of Jesus as the "sacrifice," using a near-universal religious image that signifies the effort to settle any debt to God or to heal any alienation from God.

Religious Images

One of the most distinctive features that set Judaism apart from Greco-Roman religion ("paganism") was that Jews had no image of their God. Greco-Roman religion and culture teemed with religious images. Jews often mocked the inadequacy of pagan gods, who had ears but could not hear and eyes but could not see. Of course, pagans took quite a different view of their images.

Christians largely borrowed the polemic of Jews against the "idols" of the pagans. But when Christianity became the state religion and paganism ceased to be a threat, the use of religious images began to flourish within Christianity. Scenes from the Old and New Testament were featured, including images of Jesus. Although religious images were not universally accepted by Christians, the first serious conflict over images seems not to have arisen until after the establishment of Islam. Muhammad had destroyed the religious images in Mecca, and Islam developed a cautious approach to religious art. In the 700s and 800s, the Byzantine church, which saw many of its churches fall under Muslim rule and sensibilities,

SACRED PLACES

Bethlehem: A small town about five miles south of Jerusalem and the traditional birthplace of Jesus. An Old Testament prophecy states that a ruler of Israel would come from that town, and early Christian writers emphasized that link.

The Holy Land: All of Palestine, first described as the Holy Land by Christians (not by Jews). After Constantine's conquests, his mother Helena promoted pilgrimages to sites associated with Jesus and the apostles. Palestine still has thousands of Christian pilgrims each year, visiting the traditional tomb of Jesus and Calvary, the site of Jesus' execution.

Mount Athos: From 1927, a self-governing monastic territory on a 30x6 mile peninsula in northeastern Greece. For centuries it has been the traditional center of eastern monasticism. According to tradition, no female (human or animal) may enter the territory.

Vatican City: A city-state and smallest country in the world (about 110 acres); the residence of the Bishop of Rome and the headquarters of the Roman Catholic Church. It was formally established in 1929, after the Italian independence movement of the 1800s seized most of the papal lands from the church.

Hagia Sophia: Built by Emperor Constantine and rebuilt by Emperor Justinian, this church in Constantinople (Istanbul) was once the largest domed building in the world.

St. Peter's Basilica: Built during the Renaissance, this stands as the primary church of Christendom.

was split by the Iconoclastic ("Image-Breaker") Controversy. Both sides in the debate appealed to scripture and to past practice. The final resolution permitted religious images, though the Eastern Church restricted itself largely to icons—religious images of Jesus and the saints painted on flat surfaces. Three-dimensional art, such as statutes, became foreign to Eastern worship. The Western Church, where the debate was far less pressing, allowed the full range of religious art. In all cases, images could be venerated (honored), but they could not be worshipped.

From time to time, iconoclastic tendencies were sparked in the Western Church too. In the time of the Reformation, many Protestants destroyed religious art. Sometimes the only art that remained in Protestant-controlled churches was the stained glass window. So plain did many Protestant churches become that Reformed churches have sometimes been described as "four bare walls and a sermon."

Asceticism

Early Christianity generally approved of ascetic behavior. It did not require a rigorous asceticism for all of its members, however, and it attempted to prohibit or control extreme forms of asceticism among those who chose that path. The two clearest expressions of asceticism in Christianity are monasticism and celibacy, though other forms, such as fasting, demonstrate ascetic behavior as well.

Monasticism began in the mid-200s and received its first surge of growth in the period immediately after the conversion of Constantine in the 300s. Many felt that the moral standards of the church were weakened by the influx of converts jumping on the imperial bandwagon. Monasticism frequently reaped the benefits of this discontent, as individuals disengaged from the secular world in order to engage in religious contemplation unencumbered by the affairs of the world or tainted by the multitudes now in the church. Moreover, with the once hostile Empire now in league with Christianity, the Christian ideal of martyrdom was no longer a possibility. Extreme asceticism became as close a substitute for martyrdom as could be had in a Christian empire. Some early forms of monasticism reached levels of extreme asceticism (eating only grass, going naked, living for years on pillars). Such extremes prompted the creation of monastic rules, which were intended to eliminate bizarre behavior, prevent excessive competition in monastic communities, and bring monks under the discipline and authority of the church hierarchy. The Rule of Benedict (500s) became standard in the west, requiring vows of poverty, celibacy and obedience. The piety associated with such asceticism often provided monastics with popular authority, which allowed monasticism to become a powerful tool of reform in the church at various times. Monasticism also became a powerful tool in Christian missions.

Celibacy was another mark of Christian asceticism. Even as early as the first century, celibacy was praised; by the 1100s, it had become a requirement of all clergy in the Western Church. In the Eastern Church, it is an obligation only of higher clergy.

Protestantism generally has rejected both monasticism and celibacy as necessary or meaningful expressions of Christian devotion and dedication.

Church and State

For the first three centuries of Christianity, the state was largely either ambivalent to Christianity or actively hostile. Even under the latter circumstances, the Christian attitude to the state was not uniformly negative.

When Emperor Constantine converted to Christianity, the fortunes of the church were dramatically reversed. The state, once the fearsome enemy of the church, became its staunch protector and promoter. Christians generally saw the new relationship as positive, and often spoke glowingly of the bond. A few protests have been raised from time to time against the relationship, and it is possible to find some Christian groups even in the modern period speaking of the church/state link under Constantine as the "fall" of the church.

SYMBOLS

Cross: Various kinds of crosses have been used in Christian art, recalling the death of Jesus by crucifixion.

Chi-Rho: A monogram formed by two Greek capital letters "X" (*chi* [the "CH" sound] and "P" (*rho* [the "R" sound]) superimposed one on the other. The letters are the first two Greek letters in the Greek word for "Christ." This sign came to be associated with Constantine, the first Christian emperor, and with the imperial church.

IHS: An old abbreviation for the Greek transliteraton of the name Jesus, from the first three Greek capital letters (I-H-S) of that name. Some have attempted to find an abbreviation for three Latin words behind the letters: either a short form for "in this sign" or for "Jesus, Savior of Men."

IHC: Abbreviation for Jesus, consisting of the first three letters of the Latin name for Jesus.

INRI: Abbreviation of Latin words for "Jesus of Nazareth, King of the Jews," from the Latin inscription on the cross according to tradition.

Dove: The dove is used frequently to represent the Holy Spirit in Christian iconography.

Fish: An early symbol of Jesus, often associated with the Eucharist. The symbolism may have come about from the Greek word for fish, ΙΧΘΥΣ ("I-CH-TH-U-S"). This serves as an acrostic for "Jesus-Christ-God's-Son-Savior."

Lamb: Christians view the death of Jesus as a final sacrifice for sin.

The Good Shepherd: The (pre-Christian) image of a shepherd carrying a lamb is appropriated by Christians as a symbol of Jesus.

In the East, the church and state were firmly linked under the power and prestige of the emperor. In the west, the collapse of imperial authority in the 400s as the barbarians advanced over more and more of the Roman lands created a political vacuum of sorts. The pope, as Bishop of Rome and the only western Patriarch, took on, by necessity, some of the duties that had belonged to the imperial court. Moreover, an ambiguous and frequently strained relationship came to exist between the western church and the eastern emperors. The pope finally turned to one of the recently converted barbarian tribes, the Franks, for a political ally. In time, the church promoted the Franks to imperial dignity, crowning Charlemagne as the Roman Emperor in the west on Christmas Day, 800, some three centuries after the last western emperor had reigned.

Charlemagne's effort to revive the old Roman Empire in the west helped to produce a "Holy Roman Empire" in the centuries to follow, powerful enough to play a major role in the affairs of Europe and often of the Church. The emperors often saw themselves as guardians of the church against control by powerful Roman noble families. On occasion, emperors appointed members of their own staff as pope. The church, which was rescued on occasion by the emperor, sometimes found itself in need of being rescued from the emperor. Battles and debates between pope and emperor over conflicting spheres of authority marked medieval Christianity in a debate known as the Investiture Controversy. The resolution demarcated areas of authority more clearly, generally to the benefit of the papacy, and established a protocol for imperial and papal supervision of religion in the late 1000s and early 1100s.

The relationship between church and state usually led to a state church. That meant that only one church was allowed and dissenters lost civil rights. The main branches of the Protestant Reformation did little to alter this arrangement, though the more radical elements challenged the church-state connections, usually at their peril. The early settlement of North America was colored by such tensions. Puritans established their colonies so that they could worship as they saw fit; others established settlements in which not only they but any group could worship without fear of repression. Gradually, the voices of religious toleration gained a wider hearing. Today, religious dissenters generally operate in Christian countries with full civil rights.

Development and Purity

All religions struggle with the heritage of their past and the degree to which development must remain faithful to the ancient essence. Christianity has dealt with the matter in two main ways. One is to emphasize the continuity with the past through religious officials, by whom the primitive traditions are faithfully transmitted and in whom the power of the early authorities rest. By the end of the second century, Christians spoke of an "apostolic succession" that linked the church back to the apostolic tradition of the earliest period through the church's bishops. This emphasis allowed for controlled and gradual change, and it has been generally within that framework that Christianity has developed.

Sometimes all development is seen as suspect. Present practice is compared to the practice of the primitive period—a kind of Golden Age associated with the apostles. The goal of such comparison is to restore the church to the often idealized purity of the past. For example, monastic groups in the medieval period often criticized the wealth of the church and contrasted it with the poverty of Jesus and the apostles. Other groups, often utopian in perspective, have similarly appealed to "primitive" Christianity, and have assumed that the most primitive practice was "pure." In the 1800s and early 1900s in North America, numerous "restorationist" movements made that claim, from Mormons, Disciples of Christ, and Jehovah's Witnesses to Pentecostals. Often the growth of such movements has been remarkable. Pentecostalism, for example, hardly a hundred years old, is now the largest Protestant group in the world.

> **THE BEATITUDES**
>
> *Ethical teachings of Jesus*
>
> - Blessed are the poor in spirit, for theirs is the kingdom of heaven.
> - Blessed are those who mourn, for they will be comforted.
> - Blessed are the meek, for they will inherit the earth.
> - Blessed are those who hunger and thirst for righteousness, for they will be filled.
> - Blessed are the merciful, for they will receive mercy.
> - Blessed are the pure in heart, for they will see God.
> - Blessed are the peacemakers, for they will be called children of God.
> - Blessed are those who are persecuted for righteousness' sake, for theirs is the kingdom of heaven.
> - Blessed are you when people revile you and persecute you and utter all kinds of evil against you falsely on my account.
> - Rejoice and be glad, for your reward is great in heaven, for in the same way they persecuted the prophets who were before you. (Gospel of Matthew, Chapter 5, New Revised Standard Version)

Eschatology: Reflection on the End of the World

Christians have a linear view of history, as do the other western traditions. That means that Christians quite naturally bring a religious understanding to bear on the end (*eschaton*) of the historical process.

Details are suggestive rather than precise. Christian eschatological language speaks of a "new age," a "new heaven and earth," a "New Jerusalem," a "Thousand Years of Peace," "The Millennium"—concepts that imply a paradise regained or a Golden Age restored. Jesus, who came once to the world, will come again—in a "Second Coming"—and the forces of evil will be vanquished. The dead will be resurrected and all will face the Great Judgment. The righteous will inherit eternal life; the wicked will be punished.

Sometimes eschatological reflection has been intensified at particular moments of perceived crisis in Christian society. Certain that the cosmos is about to collapse, some have spoken of full-blown apocalyptic doom, predicting the exact date of the end of the world and identifying some contemporary figure as the wicked Antichrist, whose mark is the number 666, and who will terrorize the helpless world.

Various debates over eschatological details have colored Christian debate as early as the teaching of Jesus himself and the writings of Paul. Sometimes the debate has focused on whether eschatological language should be taken literally or figuratively. The victory of Christianity in the Roman world or the spread of Christianity in the modern world has been sometimes understood as the intent of the eschatological claims of Christianity. Post-enlightenment thought has caused many Christians to reject any literal eschatological vision; on the other hand, many of the modern restorationist movements within Christianity have made eschatology part of their distinctive theological perspective.

Revelation

God speaks. Humans hear. Western traditions generally have emphasized that religious knowledge of the most certain kind comes from God's deliberate action to communicate divine and eternal truth, whether through Moses on the mountaintop or Muhammad in a cave. Christians accepted the concept of that kind of revelation, but they located the revelation in Jesus and intensified the concept. Jesus was viewed from early on as not a transmitter of God's words, but as the "Word of God" himself, the Logos. Thus the incarnation—God becoming human—lies at the core of the Christian concept of revelation.

PRACTICES

Structures of Authority

Early Christians developed several mechanisms of authority. Such mechanisms did much to give Christianity a unity and uniformity that it might not otherwise have had. Four elements stand out, all of which have roots in the second century, if not earlier. These are: canon, creed, council, and clergy. All four, in various ways, have been used as tests for exposing heresy and schism.

Canon. At first, Christians used the Hebrew Bible in Greek translation (Septuagint) as their Bible. They developed special ways of treating it in order to make it speak meaningfully to their increasingly non-Jewish movement. The Hebrew prophets, with their critique of Hebrew religion and their anticipation of renewal, provided adequate voice for early Christian criticism of Judaism and the Christian proclamation of Jesus as God's agent. Soon, under Jewish and Greek influence, Christian theologians developed methods of allegorical interpretation, by which the whole of the Hebrew Bible might have application to specific interests in Christianity.

From early on, Christians produced literature of their own too. By the second century, Christians had begun to use some of this literature in liturgical settings, giving prominence to two special collec-

> **MAJOR PRAYERS**
>
> **The Lord's Prayer:** (also called the "Our Father" or the "Pater Noster").
> *Our Father who art in heaven,*
> *Hallowed be thy name.*
> *Thy kingdom come.*
> *Thy will be done,*
> *On earth as it is in heaven.*
> *Give us this day our daily bread;*
> *And forgive us our debts,*
> *As we also have forgiven our debtors;*
> *And lead us not into temptation,*
> *But deliver us from evil.* (Matthew 6:9-13; an alternative form of this prayer is found in Luke)
>
> **Hail Mary:** (sometimes called the "Angelical salutation" or the "Ave Maria," the latter from the first words of the prayer in Latin; it is a distinctly Roman Catholic prayer).
> *Hail Mary, full of grace,*
> *the Lord is with thee.*
> *Blessed art thou amongst women*
> *and blessed is the fruit*
> *of thy womb, Jesus.*
> *Holy Mary, Mother of God,*
> *pray for us sinners,*
> *now,*
> *and in the hour of our death.*
> *Amen.*

tions, the Gospel and the Apostle (the writings of Paul). Canonical lists were compiled of the documents that had status as authoritative texts, and the usual criterion was the apostolic authorship or commissioning of a document. By the end of the second century, canonical lists looked much like what constitutes the New Testament today; by the mid-fourth century, formal canonical lists defined exactly the content of the New Testament, which has remained unchanged to this day—shared by Western and Eastern Christians and by Catholics and Protestants.

The content of the Old Testament is another matter. As early as the second century, Jews and Christians debated over the content of the Hebrew Bible. Christians used the Septuagint, the popular Greek translation of the time. Jews produced new Greek translations. These were based on a smaller core of Hebrew texts. During the Protestant Reformation, Protestants opted for the smaller Jewish canon; Catholics retained the larger canon, which had been used by Christians since the first century. The texts in the Catholic collection that are not in the Protestant collection are called the Apocrypha or the Deuterocanonical writings. Eastern Christians use parts of the larger collection.

Creed. So important is *belief* in the Christian tradition that adherents to Christianity are often called simply *believers.* The first demarcation of Christians from Jews was expressed in terms of whether one believed that Jesus was the Christ. When Christians identify their religion as "The Faith," they are capturing that character of belief that is central to the definition of Christianity.

In Latin, the word for "I believe" is *credo.* From this word, we get the English word *creed.* The creed, a list of short statements of essential belief, is used by Christians as the touchstone of orthodoxy. As early as the first century, Christians were defining themselves in terms of what they believed; in the second century, they spoke of the Rule of Faith and developed creedal formulas; and in the early fourth century, at their first ecumenical (empire-wide) council, they established a creed that endures in the majority of Christian circles to the present.

Since creeds provide a summary of the essential beliefs of Christianity as defined by the majority, the creed was a convenient tool to test the adequacy of the beliefs of those in Christianity who were not part of the mainstream. Thus, there have always been Christian groups whose beliefs failed the test of the primary Christian creeds. These groups, however, represent a small minority. Most Christians, east or west, Catholic or Protestant, affirm the creeds approved by the early Christian councils.

Councils. The bishop was the leader of the Christian churches of a city. When matters affected Christianity more widely, bishops met in councils, or synods, to examine and resolve the problem. The sense was that the decision of the majority of bishops was to carry weight over the whole church, and frequently the councils of bishops were able to reach near consensus conclusions. Councils often issued *canons,* statements generally addressing some matter of practice. Such canons, or rules, became the law under which the church saw itself operating.

Councils could be limited to a small area, but frequently they were provincial, presided over by the bishop of the chief city of the province, who was called the metropolitan. After the conversion of Constantine and under his influence, empire-wide councils were held. These came to be known as "Ecumenical (universal) Councils."

Clergy. According to the earliest records of the church, Jesus had twelve disciples, who, sometimes along with others, are called apostles. But these offices were not continued beyond the first century, and scholars have debated why that was. We do know with certainty that by the early years of the second century, a three-part hierarchy of office was developing, and the structure was so successful that by the end of that century, it was largely universal. That structure had a bishop (lit., "overseer") at the head of the church in each city. Beneath him were presbyters (lit., "elders"), from which the word "priest" comes. The third order, called deacons (lit., "servants"), was generally viewed as inferior to the presbyters, but since they more directly served the various administrative needs of the bishop, a deacon sometimes was elected to succeed a bishop, a right the presbyters usually claimed.

> **TERMINOLOGY**
>
> **Autocephalous:** (lit., "self" + "head"). Refers to the structure of the Eastern Orthodox Churches, where each national church has its own head, without one overall authority, as is found in the Western Church in the Bishop of Rome (pope).
>
> **Eschatology:** Speculation about the end of the world or of humankind. In Christianity, often related to the "Second Coming" of Jesus and the "Final Judgment."
>
> **Incarnation:** (lit., "in flesh"). The belief that God took on real human characteristics in Jesus. The specifics of that event are debated by Christians.

Through most of Christian history, it has been the bishops who have governed and directed the church, and it is in the bishops that apostolic authority and succession is thought to lie.

Beneath these three offices, dozens of others developed, from readers and singers to widows, virgins, and deaconesses to gravediggers, doorkeepers (a little like modern-day bouncers), and offices related to monasteries. The church appears to have been fairly creative in shaping its structure, and attempts to find similar hierarchies in the ancient secular or religious world have failed, though an occasional parallel can be found.

The Roman Empire was divided into a number of provinces (the number fluctuated), and one city in each province was considered the chief city, or metropolis. In Christianity, the bishop in the chief city came to be called a metropolitan, and to him fell certain responsibilities over the bishops in his province. Provinces were grouped by the church into larger units, of which there came to be five in Christianity by the end of the fourth century (with chief cities Rome, Constantinople, Alexandria, Antioch, and, as a courtesy, Jerusalem). The bishop of the chief city in each quarter of the empire was called the Patriarch, a term still in use in eastern Christianity.

The most recognized official in the Christianity hierarchy is no doubt the pope. That title simply means "father," and it was not used exclusively for the Bishop of Rome until the eleventh century. As bishop of the chief city in the west and as the proclaimed successor of Peter, the pope gained considerable power. Given that Catholics constitute over one half of all Christians, those of non-Christian traditions frequently view the pope as the leader of Christianity, not just of western or Catholic Christianity. In the eastern churches, the term pope is widely used for all priests, just as the word father is used of priests in the west.

Church Hierarchal Structure

Episcopal. The dominant structure of hierarchy in Christian groups is *episcopal.* The word is a transliteration of the Greek *episcopos,* which means "overseer" or "superintendent." The English word bishop is used to identify someone holding the episcopal office. Bishops and councils of bishops are the primary authorities for determining belief and practice. The Eastern Church is episcopal; the Western Church is largely episcopal, though a debate over structure did develop within Protestantism. Lutherans (largely in Germany and Scandavania) and the Church of England (Anglican) retained the episcopal structure. In the United States within a decade of the American Revolution, the term Episcopal became the official name for the Church of England—a necessary change given the suspicions following the war. Most state churches are episcopal in structure.

Presbyterian. Reformed elements of the Reformation favored the presbyterian form of government. Under this system, the minister and the elders (Greek: *presbyteroi*) of the church form the local governing body. These individuals are elected by the members of the local assembly. Various bodies of representatives from these local presbyteries form larger provincial and national bodies. A fair amount of diversity exists in these structures, but the main emphasis remains: the membership elects their representatives, and these representatives provide the governance of the church. Most churches that are Presbyterian in structure are Calvinist in doctrine, following the fusion of these ideas by John Calvin in experiments in Geneva, where religion dominated the political structures.

Congregational. In congregational church government, each local church acts democratically and autonomously through its members. This presented a challenge to the central authority of state churches. In England, where congregationalism had wide expression, it was often associated with "Independents" and other "Non-Conformists," and its ministers and members frequently suffered repression.

Religious Buildings

Christians have no central building as a special abode of the divine presence. From their first days, they claimed that God did not dwell in temples made with hands (an attack on both Judaism and classical paganism). Where Christians gathered in groups of as few as two or three, there, they said, Jesus was present.

For the first two hundred years of their existence, Christians met for corporate religious activities in the homes of their members, and often a wealthy member appears to have served as patron of the group, providing ample room for religious meetings and general hospitality. By the mid-200s, Christians were renovating or constructing buildings solely for religious use. After the emperor converted to Christianity in the early 300s, much of the construction in cities and towns was religious, as the quickly growing Christian movement expressed the grandeur of their new status and attempted to accommodate the flood of new members.

Often these new churches had relics of martyred saints buried or housed on the site, bringing further dignity and a heightened sense of sacredness to the location. The church in which the bishop preached, called the cathedral, gained further status from the bishop's presence. The most famous cathedral is St. Peter's Basilica, in Rome, the residence of the pope, the Bishop of Rome. The head of the Church of England, called the Archbishop of Canterbury, sits in Canterbury Cathedral.

The churches built under Constantine adopted the familiar Roman style of public administration, the basilica. Christians made no use of the pagan religious architecture of the Greek columned temples. Other styles developed, from Romanesque to Gothic to Baroque. Sometimes a church will reflect a mixed style. Christian churches became the most distinctive feature, and often the only feature, in the skyline of medieval European cities.

The Religious Cycle

Early Christians developed a few rituals that helped define and empower their community. Frequently the chief Christian rituals are referred to as sacraments, sacred signs of inward grace. These rituals were viewed as the vehicles by which spiritual empowerment was provided to the individual. Three widely shared sacraments are Baptism, the Eucharist, and Ordination.

Baptism. Baptism, a ritual washing that is encountered in many religious traditions, marked the formal initiation of an individual into the Christian community. But, in that the rite was a one-time event, it became more highly charged than the typical ritual washing. Generally, young children are baptized in Christianity, though some Christian groups, such as the Anabaptists, have argued that only adults can make a conscious choice to join the church and thus only they should be baptized. Some differences exist, too, regarding the means of baptism: should it be by sprinkling or pouring, or full immersion.

Eucharist. Another early ritual was a weekly symbolic meal, called the Eucharist. A cup of wine and a loaf of bread were shared among the baptized. The language and the objects of the Eucharist remind partakers of the death of Jesus, the event upon which the community was founded and by which the individual member receives spiritual nourishment. In the Protestant Reformation of the 1500s, the nature of the Eucharist was hotly debated. Catholics maintained that the bread and wine of the Eucharist ceremony were transformed into the body and blood of Jesus; many Protestants saw the bread and wine as merely symbols of the body and blood of Jesus.

Ordination. A third early ritual, somewhat more obscure in its origins and less defined in its practice, was the "laying on of hands" or ordination to religious office (later called the sacrament of Holy Orders). By this ceremony, the candidate is transferred from the laity into the clergy and empowered to conduct the rites of the church. Early Christians tended not to use terminology of paganism for their religious officials, though under the influence of Jewish scriptures, priestly images can sometimes be found. Some Protestant traditions, emphasizing the "priesthood of all believers," do not consider clergy to be empowered more than the laity (non-clergy), since all are filled with the Holy Spirit. Even so, most Protestant churches have specialized and trained leadership, which is akin to ordained ministry.

As the Christian church developed, other practices became institutionalized and ritualized. In the 1200s, the heyday of theological refinement and systemization in Christian Europe, the present Catholic position on sacraments was formalized. Seven sacraments were recognized: baptism, Eucharist, holy orders, confirmation, penance, marriage, and last rites. Each provided divine empowerment at moments of crisis or at stages of transfer from one status to another. The terms have changed over the years, but the substance remains the same. Today, "last rites" is often referred to as the "anointing of the sick," and penance is called "reconciliation."

Protestantism tended toward a more simple ritualism, and generally only baptism and the Eucharist counted as sacraments there. But the treatment of marriage and ordination in many Protestant traditions strongly resemble sacraments, in practice if not in theory.

Annual Celebrations

Easter. The average person on the street, and many people in Christian churches, would probably identify Christmas as the primary Christian celebration. For most of Christian history and in most Christian traditions even today, however, Easter is the primary Christian celebration. It was the first annual celebration instituted by Christians, perhaps as early as the first century. Whereas Christmas celebrates Jesus' birth, Easter celebrates Jesus' death and resurrection, crucial events in the early Christian understanding of salvation.

Lent. Easter was the central part of a much longer period of Christian observance. By the fourth century, a forty-day period of fasting, called Lent (lit., "springtime"), preceded Easter, and the Easter cycle was not ended until the Feast of Pentecost fifty days after Easter. Traditions vary as to how the days are to be counted and what foods are permitted.

Christmas. The celebration of the birth of Jesus on December 25th appears first in the west in the 300s. It is thought to have been celebrated on that day to counter the popular festive celebrations of the birth of the Sun. By the middle of the 400s, most of the east had taken up the western date, although earlier the East had celebrated the birth of Jesus in the Feast of the Epiphany, on January 6. That feast, which had also celebrated the baptism of Jesus, came to be associated with the visit of the *magi* in the western nativity celebrations.

Many features in the modern celebration of Christmas in the English-speaking world reflect the influence of Charles Dickens' writings and German traditions popularized by the British monarchy in the 1800s. The Santa Claus tradition comes largely from the Dutch celebration of St. Nicholas, an early bishop and the patron saint of children.

Dietary Concerns

Early Christian tradition presents Jesus in conflict with Jewish dietary legislation, and Paul, who argued the case for admission of Gentiles into the church, largely rejected Jewish food laws. As more and more Gentiles joined the church, Jewish dietary concerns came to have even less hold on Christianity. Given these conditions at the beginning of the Christian movement, Christianity developed almost no food taboos.

Christians did, however, confront a problem with meat sold in the market places of Greco-Roman towns. Much of the meat would have come from animals sacrificed to pagan gods. Christians debated whether such meat was tainted and thus to be avoided. That problem died out as paganism ceased to be practiced in the Roman Empire, and Christiantiy came to center stage as the state religion.

Occasionally, small Christian sects have introduced food taboos into their movements, usually by attempting to follow Jewish food taboos prescribed in the Old Testament, but no Christian group has looked to the rabbinic legislation or observed strict *kosher* regulations. Some groups also have prohibited intoxicants, or coffee, tea, or tobacco. These taboos have had little impact on the dietary behaviors of the majority of Christians.

The only significant food taboo is one associated with the fast, when no food or limited food may be eaten. This is more a restriction on the time that food can be eaten, not with the kind of food that can be eaten. In the early period, Christians were encouraged to fast on Wednesdays and Fridays, a measure to distinguish Christians from Jews, who fasted on Mondays and Thursdays. The restriction may have been intended also to reduce social contact with Jews. As well, a Lenten season developed fairly early (300s). This period of introspection and repentance leading up to Easter has a number of food restrictions associated with it, varying from group to group as to what may be eaten, how the length of the fast is to be measured, and the number of meals that can be taken.

The best-known food taboo in Christianity is the prohibition against eating meat on Friday, the primary fast day in the Western Church. Fish was exempt under the category of meat, thus making fish a popular, and almost required, dish for Catholics on Friday. Vatican II, a reforming council in the 1960s, removed that taboo.

CONCLUSION

Christianity confronts two major challenges as it enters the twenty-first century. One problem concerns its fundamental definition; the other concerns its relationship with other religions.

From its earliest proclamations, Christianity emphasized the importance of belief in Jesus. While not discounting practice, Christianity has defined itself primarily by a creed—an expression of what is *believed*. The core of the Christian creed focuses on Jesus as Son of God. For much of the history of Christianity, the creed has served as the touchstone of orthodoxy, providing a shared world for Christians, whatever the range of diversity beyond the creed that might be permitted. But the creed has provoked sharp controversy, both in the early centuries of its formation and in the modern period, as various groups within Christianity challenged some point of its declaration. The modern debates focus particularly on the status of Jesus, the very core of the creed. The sides are sharply divided, with no likely resolution in sight.

The second challenge facing Christianity is its relationship to other religions. Closely associated with the spread of western culture since the

1500s was the dramatically successful establishment of Christianity in areas far from its European center, making Christianity into the dominant religion in the world. But such a triumphal march into territories and cultures that had been long claimed by others offends modern sensibilities, which promote an environment of religious and cultural pluralism. It remains to be seen how missionary religions such as Christianity will resolve their profound sense of obligation to spread their message while at the same time nurturing genuinely respectful relationships with other religions. A related issue for large sectors of the Christian community is how to express the essence of Christianity in non-western voices. This is becoming increasingly important as the majority of Christians are no longer of western European or Mediterranean background.

| CHAPTER FIVE | Islam |

HISTORY

The Historical Context

Islam arose in a region of the west-central side of the Arabian Peninsula, primarily in the two main populated areas, Mecca in the south and Yathrib (later renamed Medina), almost three hundred miles to the north. Mecca lay at the crossroads of major trade routes connecting Africa, the Mediterranean, and Central Asia through the Arabian peninsula.

Many semi-nomadic peoples moved to Mecca to take advantage of the opportunities of this growing urban center. Such change, however, created stresses on the traditional social system and the safety nets of a tribal society. Further, warfare sometimes disrupted or altered trade routes, as happened in the 500s and 600s, when the Christian Byzantine Empire of the eastern Mediterranean clashed with the Sasanids, who had conquered and reestablished Zoroastrianism as the state religion of Mesopotamia in the third century C.E.

The economic picture for Arabia, while not entirely clear, suggests a degree of disruption. Some Arabs gained; others lost. In particular, Mecca and its chief tribe, the Quraysh, prospered. But others suffered in the new urban setting and disrupted economic structures, subject to the booms and busts of commerce. The rich turned from some of their obligations; the poor lost some of the protections tribal society had afforded. It was in this context of economic inequity and stress that Islam arose.

Mecca, the city where Muhammad, the founder of Islam, spent his first fifty years, was the main urban center of the area. Although Mecca held no overarching authority over the Arabian tribes, it held some sway as a center for the trade caravans. As well, Mecca was by far the most important religious center of the Arabian Peninsula. Its sacred space housed various sacred objects, such as the Kaba and the Black Stone, and it served as home to 360 gods, and to the chief god, who was known as Allah (lit., "the God"). Thus, long before Mecca became a religious center and pilgrimage destination under Islam, it had served as a center for Arab religious pilgrimage.

Muhammad (ca. 570-632 C.E.)

Little is known about Muhammad's early life. He was a member of one of the lesser clans of the Quraysh, a tribe that had come to control Mecca and its commerce. Muhammad's father appears to have died before Muhammad was born and his mother died when he was yet a small boy. He was looked after by his grandfather, then adopted by his uncle. Some think that Muhammad's experience as an orphan made him particularly sensitive to the plight of the disadvantaged, a concern that he addressed often in his adult life.

As a young man, Muhammad pursued work in the caravan trade, as many young men of Mecca would have done. His abilities brought him to the attention of a wealthy widow, Khadija, whom he married when he was twenty-five and she somewhat older—forty, according to some sources.

Muhammad was about forty when he began to experience religious trances. At first he doubted the nature of his experiences, but his wife encouraged him to continue his meditation, which he did for some time before he began to have experiences in which he would break out in verse. These utterances were to continue until his death twenty-two years later. This body of material, which Muslims view as recitations by Muhammad of divinely revealed messages, came to constitute the full content of the Quran, Islam's holy book.

Muhammad's message stressed the coming judgment of God, proclaimed one true God in face of Arab polytheism, condemned idols, and demanded justice for the oppressed and the weak. Each element attacked in some way the conduct or interests of the leaders in Mecca, and at first Muhammad gained enemies far more quickly than he gained converts. Although Muhammad was himself protected by the tribal obligations of his powerful uncle, his followers often lacked such protection. In 615 C.E., Muhammad encouraged some of his followers to move to

Abyssinia (modern Ethiopia), where the Christian government there offered them protection. When Muhammad's wife and uncle died, Muhammad was himself at considerable risk from his powerful enemies in Mecca. He had no choice but to flee secretly, along with his remaining followers. This event, referred as the *hijra* ("emigration"), became the first year of the Islamic calendar, corresponding to year 622 C.E. of the western calendar.

Mecca, which was to become the chief city of Islam, was initially hostile both to early Islam and to Muhammad. A more receptive area was Yathrib, a cluster of agricultural villages about two weeks by camel to the north. The area had a powerful Jewish element—perhaps as much as half of Yathrib's population. Tribes in the area had clashed, and they invited Muhammad to arbitrate, as a neutral outsider. Arbitration was successful, and Muhammad became the key player in the politics of the area. He organized Yathrib around principles of what he considered a model Islamic society, and the area became the first safe environment for the young Islamic community.

But Mecca remained the key center for Arabs, both religiously and economically. Its economic strength made it a serious threat to the security of the young Islamic community in Medina. The religious practices and social abuses that had earlier provoked Muhammad continued. If Arab religion and behavior were to be reformed, Mecca would need to be brought under Muhammad's control.

Fortunately for Muhammad, Medina was not only friendly to Muhammad and his leadership, it was ideally situated along the main caravan route. This allowed Muhammad to repay in kind to the Meccan caravans the ill treatment he and his followers had received from the Meccan elite. Although Muhammad's forces won some battles and lost others, the raids were troublesome enough to the Meccan economy that Mecca submitted to Muhammad, two years before his death. Muhammad died unexpectedly, in 632 C.E., at the age of sixty-two. By this time, most of the Arabian Peninsula had allied with him.

The Companions of the Prophet (632–661 C.E.)

Muhammad appears to have made no provision for the succession in leadership of the Muslim community in the event of his death. In this lies the core of one of the earliest disputes within Islam, a dispute that led to inter-Islamic conflict and division that has persisted to the present. The dispute centered on whether Islam should be led by a close relative of Muhammad or by an early convert to Islam, particularly one who had worked closely with Muhammad during the difficult years in Mecca. These latter individuals were known as "companions" of the prophet and were supported by the main community (the Sunni) who chose to elect pious members of Muhammad's tribe. A smaller group (the Shiites) insisted that leadership must run through Muhammad's family. Muhammad had no surviving son, so the matter of succession through his family line was not without its problems, although those who argued for such succession were satisfied with Ali, Muhammad's cousin and son-in-law, who had married Muhammad's daughter, Fatima.

The Shiites also developed the view that not only was the family of Ali to hold the office of caliph, every valid caliph, whom they called *imams*, would be empowered with the same spirit that had empowered Muhammad, and they could speak authoritatively to new situations. By contrast, in Sunni Islam, the caliph was the upholder of the tradition; he had no power to innovate.

A further problem was that with either choice, the leadership would be in the hands of people whose tribal roots were in Mecca. Cut out completely were natives of Medina, who had welcomed Muhammad and other emigrants from Mecca, and whose acceptance helped to assure the survival of the persecuted and fledgling Muslim community. The people of Medina had battled the armies of Mecca in support of Islam, and many had died in support of Muhammad's cause. The door to leadership, however, was closed to them.

It was one of the companions, Abu Bakr, who was chosen as *caliph* (lit., "successor"). He was Muhammad's father-in-law. Further, he had the support of leaders of the Quraysh tribe. Although the tribe had long opposed Muhammad and had only recently converted to Islam, it remained powerful and extended that power within the young Islamic community, to the resentment of many. Bakr's short reign of two years was involved in putting down various challenges to his leadership, including revolts among various bedouin ("desert dwellers") tribes, who refused to pay taxes after Muhammad's death. Bakr's greatest accomplishment was the organization of an army to attack Syria, but he died before the surprising military successes there were realized.

Bakr was followed in succession by three other companions of Muhammad: Umar (Muhammad's father-in-law), Uthman (Muhammad's son-in-law), and finally Ali (Muhammad's son-in-law and cousin). Ali had been favored by some since the death of Muhammad as the proper claimant to lead the Muslim community. All four were originally from Mecca; all four were from Muhammad's tribe, the Quraysh.

Under the capable leadership of Umar, the Arabs poured out of Arabia, conquering the Sasanid Empire and the eastern Mediterranean, most notably Egypt, within a decade. When Umar was murdered by a servant, Uthman became caliph. He, too, was from Muhammad's tribe, but he was a member of the previously long-dominant clan within that tribe, the Umayyads. That clan, when first threatened by the expanding interest in Muhammad's religion, had rendered the stiffest opposition to the fledgling Islamic movement. Although Islam continued its rapid expansion and Uthman was regarded as very religious, his caliphate was tainted by charges of nepotism and scandal. His selection of relatives for key posts made it appear to many that the Umayyads were back in control as they had been prior to Muhammad. Uthman was assassinated by dissident Egyptians. Ali then became caliph. But there were other claimants, thus Ali

MAJOR EMPIRES

Umayyad: (661-750). The first Muslim empire, lasting for ninety years. It arose after the death of the fourth "rightly-guided" caliph. Its capital was Damascus. After defeat by the Abbasids, the Umayyads developed a significant Muslim culture in Spain.

Abbasid: (750-1258). The 500-year Muslim empire that overthrew the Umayyads. Its capital was Baghdad. Led by descendents of Muhammad's uncle al-Abbas, the new dynasty provided opportunities for non-Arabs in the Muslim community, and came to reflect Persian and other non-Arab influences. Its golden age was in its first hundred years, after which it declined as states broke away and its leaders became the puppets of the palace guard. Initially it had the support of the Shiites.

Fatimid: (909-1171). A Shiite dynasty in Egypt, claiming descent from Muhammad's daughter Fatima.

Mongol: (1206-1481). The largest world empire prior to the Soviet Union. It rapidly expanded in the 1200s, overthrowing most nations from the Pacific to the Danube, including the Abbasid Empire.

Mughal: (1526-1857). The Muslim empire in India. Its name is the Persian form of the word "Mongol," and the founders were descendants of Mongol and Turkish leaders.

Ottoman: (1300-1922). The Turkish-based empire. It captured Constantinople in 1453. In the 1500s and 1600s it was the world's leading empire. It held the caliphate from 1515-1917.

came to his rule without the full support of the Muslim community. Some even charged that Ali had had a passive role in the assassination of Uthman. Ali was forced to fight rival claimants. While preparing to challenge one of the other claimants in battle, Ali agreed to submit the matter of leadership to arbitration. This disillusioned many of his most faithful supporters, especially a group that came to be known as the Kharijites ("dissenters" or "separatists"). Ali fell out of favor and was assassinated by a former supporter. Thus all but the first of the "rightly-guided caliphs," as these four companions of the prophet came to be known, met a violent end.

During the turbulent period under this early leadership, much of the eastern Mediterranean and Mesopotamian areas fell under Muslim control. The explanations for the remarkable success of the new Muslim armies vary. The two dominant powers in the area, the Byzantine and Sasanid empires, had worn themselves out in a series of wars against each other, and had even alienated some of their old Arab allies. Further, each empire had suppressed populations within their borders, and such peoples (like the Monophysite, Nestorian, and Jewish communities) had little loyalty to the empires that had disadvantaged and mistreated them. Some of these peoples felt that their lot had actually improved under Islamic rule. Some of the swift Muslim success must be attributed to the fiery zeal of the Arab warriors, who knew that success and survival in battle would bring them boundless booty (eighty percent of which they could keep), and who believed that death in battle would bring them something even greater—immediate entry into Paradise.

The Umayyad Empire (661-750)

Muawiya, a relative of the caliph Uthman whom he had appointed to govern Damascus, challenged Ali's claim to the caliphate, and on Ali's death, he was able to secure his claim to the leadership. Muhammad's generation had largely died by this time, and the Umayyads, the leading clan of Mecca, seized the leadership, although not without opposition. Their rule was to last almost ninety years (661-750 C.E.), and was established in the new capital Damascus, rather than in Medina, the traditional center of Muslim government. The Umayyads doubled the size of the Muslim territories, which under them came to stretch from Spain to the borders of India.

The westward expansion of Islam was halted in 732 by Martin of Tours about a hundred miles south of Paris, exactly one hundred years after the death of Muhammad. The Muslim armies then were pushed south of the Pyrenees, the mountain range between France and Spain. A rich Muslim culture developed in Spain, and became the center of the Umayyad dynasty shortly after 750, after the Umayyads lost all their other territories to a new Muslim empire, the Abbasid.

Much had changed during the Umayyad years. Arabs were now the minority in the Muslim community, for a host of conquered peoples outside the Arabian Peninsula had converted to Islam. In spite of that, most of the key positions in the Muslim community were still held by Arabs. Complaints arose that non-Arabs were being treated as second-class Muslims.

The Abbasid Empire (750-1258)

Under Persian influence, opposition to the Umayyad dynasty formed behind one of the descendants of Muhammad's uncle al-Abbas. The new dynasty was initially supported by Shiites, who were violently opposed to Umayyad rule under the Sunnis. The Umayyad dynasty was wiped out, except for one member who escaped to Spain. The new Abbasid Empire established its capital at Baghdad, and from that point forward considerable non-Arab influence was exerted upon Islam, as non-Arabs, particularly the Persians, had access to more opportunities within Islam. The power behind the throne soon shifted its alliance back to the Sunni majority, however. This led to the rise of various Shiite counter movements.

It was during the period of the Abbasid Empire that Islam entered into a creative engagement with philosophy,

MAJOR GROUPS

Sunni: The more traditional form, making up about 85% of Islam. They consider that valid leadership of Islam lies in a caliph of Muhammad's tribe.

Shiite: (lit., "party"). The largest minority, they maintain that valid leadership lies in the *imam*, a direct descendant of Muhammad, through his daughter Fatima and her husband Ali. Most groups of Shiites believe in twelve *imams*, and are sometimes called the "Twelvers." They are a majority only in Iran and Iraq.

Ismaili: Also called "Seveners." A Shiite group, which disagrees with other Shiites about who should have become the seventh *imam*. They consider their leader, the present Aga Khan, to be the forty-ninth *imam*.

Kharijites: (lit., "to go out, leave"). Early puritanical supporters of Ali, who withdrew their loyalty from Ali. The Kharijites argued that the caliph need not be from the prophet's family (the Shiite position) or the prophet's tribe (the Sunni position). Any pious Muslim could lead.

Sufis: Mystical movement of Islam. Their name comes from the plain woolen garment they wore, in contrast to silks and expensive materials. One well-known group of Sufis are the Whirling Dervishes.

Wahhabi: A puritanical Sunni reform movement founded in 1746. They opposed Sufi interest in saints, and rejected as heresy previously accepted interpretations of Islam. Modern Saudi Arabia reflects their influence.

Zaidites: A Shiite movement that follows their own fifth *imam*, Zayd.

particularly as Muslims encountered the ideas of the classical Greek philosophers. Various Muslim schools of interpretation flowered. But some viewed philosophy with suspicion, particularly as it compromised or weakened the nature of revelation in the Quran. Somewhat in reaction to Islamic philosophy, the Sufi movement arose, with its emphasis on mysticism. Al-Ghazali, a leading eleventh-century Muslim intellectual, underwent a religious experience that led him to Sufi mysticism. He wrote many works, attempting to put the intellectual pursuit in its proper place and emphasizing the need for revelation.

Although the Abbasid empire was to last in name for five hundred years (750-1258), its "golden age" was during its first hundred years, a period captured in the stories of the *Arabian Nights*. The Abbasids functioned as a unified empire hardly longer than the previous Umayyad empire had. After that, Islam came to be represented by a variety of powers rather than a single dominant power. During much of the Abbasid reign, serious competition for the leadership of Islam came from the Umayyads of Spain and the Fatimids of Egypt (see below).

Other Muslim Empires

The grand Abbasid Empire quickly began to break apart. A Shiite based Ismaili Fatimid caliphate (or anti-caliphate) came to control North Africa, Egypt and Palestine (909-1171). Seljuk Turks seized land in Syria, Persia, and Iraq during the same period, and Turks came to control the Abbasid court. Christian crusader armies held territory in Palestine during the 1100s and 1200s. Finally, the Mongols swept through, capturing Baghdad in 1250, bringing the Abbasid Empire formally to an end.

The Mongol Empire soon split up, and Mongols who settled in Muslim lands adopted Islam. After the decline of the Mongols, two great Muslim empires arose that would rival the old Muslim Umayyad and Abbasid empires, in cultural accomplishments if not in extent of their territories. These were the Ottoman Empire, centered in Turkey but controlling most of the Middle East, and the Mughal Empire of India. Both reached their height in the 1500s. These empires displayed an opulence that was unmatched by anything in Christian Europe at the time.

Ottomans (1300s-1918). The Ottoman Empire had its roots in Turkey, expanding at the expense of both Christian and Muslim empires. To the south, the Muslim Fatimid dynasty in Egypt fell. The Ottomans conquered most of present-day Turkey, followed by territory in Europe from Greece through the Balkans and to within sixty miles of Vienna. The Christian Byzantine capital, Constantinople, eventually fell in 1453.

(One should note that recent tensions in the Balkans have roots in this conquest, for it brought Muslims and Catholic and Orthodox Christians under one rule.)

Under Suleyman I (1520-66), the Ottomans experienced their golden age. At its height the Ottoman Empire reached from the Persian Gulf through North Africa, almost to the Atlantic Ocean. But by the 1800s, the empire had declined considerably, and this encouraged the rise of nationalist movements. European nations took special interest in the area, often propping up the crumbling Ottoman Empire in order to assure an acceptable balance of power in the region. Following its defeat as an ally of Germany at the end of the First World War, the Ottoman Empire, the last of the great Muslim empires, was finally brought to its end in 1922 by the Turkish secular revolutionary, Ataturk. In an explicit policy of westernization, Ataturk abolished the caliphate in 1924, which the Ottomans had held since 1517; he closed Islamic institutions; banned Sufi (Muslim mystics) groups; and changed the script for the Turkish language from Arabic script to Latin characters.

Mughals (1526-1857). The Mughals rose to power in the 1500s in India. Other Muslim empires had controlled northern India earlier, having arrived there as early as 722 C.E., during the Umayyad Period. The most significant Muslim dynasty prior to the Mughals was the Turkish Sultanate of Delhi (1191-1398). Its policies were pro-Muslim, and a small minority of Hindus converted. The Muhgal dynasty was more tolerant and experimental, however, with one of the leaders, Akbar, attempting to establish a new religion based on elements of various religions. New groups, such as the Sikhs, prospered. But the

---

SYMBOLS

Crescent and Star: The most recognized symbol of Islam in the modern world, though not an official symbol. It was borrowed from Christian Constantinople by the conquering Ottomans.

Allahu akbar: (lit., "God is Greatest"). The audible symbol of Islam, pronounced in daily prayers but also on numerous other occasions, from the serious to the mundane.

Hijab: The scarf or head-covering worn by most Muslim women.

Halal **Certification:** Identification of approved products, like the *kosher* labels used by Jews. Commonly marked by an "M" enclosed in a circle with a crescent.

Minaret: The tower of a mosque from which the call to prayer is made five times each day. Some mosques have several minarets.

Prayer Mat: Used by Muslims at prayer. A design is woven into the mat to point the worshipper in the direction of Mecca.

Prayer Beads / Rosary: In Islam, a string of prayer beads consists of one hundred beads, divided into three sections. They are used for reciting the ninety-nine names of God.

The Color Green: The color most often identified with Islam. It was Muhammad's favorite color (the color of his turban) and is often the color of flags of Muslim nations. Also, garments to be worn in paradise are said to be green.

Calligraphy: When Islam discouraged pictorial art, handwriting became an art, featuring words from the Quran.

tolerance angered the orthodox clerics, who in time were able to shift government policy back to a more conservative Muslim perspective, under which Hindus, Sikhs, and even Muslim Sufis (judged by the clerics to be heretics) were persecuted. This suppression led to revolts by Hindu rajputs, Sikh Gurus, and Muslim sultans, all of whom had controlled their own small territories within the larger empire. Thus weakened, the Muhgal Empire was unable to withstand the British move into India, which had begun in the 1700s.

The importance of the Muhgal Empire and of previous Muslim empires in India is that the India subcontinent (India, Pakistan, and Bangladesh) now is home to the largest population of Muslims in the world. With the partition of India into largely Hindu (India) and Muslim (Pakistan and Bangladesh) nations and the deadly conflicts that stemmed from such partition, radical forms of Islam developed, particularly in Pakistan. In India, the tensions between Hindu and Muslim populations sometimes explode, most recently over the sensitive religious issue of which religion has rightful ownership of numerous disputed holy sites.

Western Influence

In the late 1400s, European monarchs and adventurers began to seek a way around the Arab middlemen who controlled the spice trade. Portugal sought a way south around the Horn of Africa to India; other European countries sailed westward to find what they hoped would be an even shorter and less dangerous passage to India. The ventures were more successful than the Europeans could have imagined. Not only did they discover a route around the middlemen to India and its spices, they found new sources of supply in China and other lands of the East Asia, and a unimagined bonus: a new continent dripping, it seemed, with gold. With such sources of wealth and secure trade routes, European nations came to be the dominant world powers, setting up trading posts wherever they wished, and disregarding or replacing the Muslim rulers and merchants.

This weakened situation for Islam was to last until the 1900s. Two things changed the modern fortunes of Muslim countries: the huge Ottoman Empire collapsed and European colonial rule came to an end. But there was to be no return to the age of the great Muslim empires of the past. Independence in India did not restore the Muslim Mughal Empire that the British had abolished in 1857; rather, it divided the area into hostile nations: India (largely Hindu) and the much smaller Pakistan and Bangladesh (largely Muslim). Following World War I, the Ottoman Empire, labeled the "sick man of Europe," died a slow death as various peoples, some Muslim and some Christian, rebelled and set up their own states. In 1922, Turkey, the very heart of the Ottoman Empire, declared itself a secular republic and abolished the caliphate. Remaining territories of the old Ottoman Empire came under special mandates from the League of Nations, as Europe decided how to reshape the Middle East, often creating for Bedouin loyalists entirely new states that lacked any historical legitimacy. In some of these states, however, a recent rise in Muslim fundamentalism has removed many of the vestiges of the European presence.

As early as the 1700s, the puritanical Wahhabi movement in the Arabian Peninsula waged war on the Ottomans

> **PRAYER**
> **Al-Fatihah:** (lit., "The Opening"). The first *surah* of the Quran is used as a common prayer by Muslims, being repeated at least seventeen times a day.
>
> In the name of Allah,
> the Beneficent, the Merciful.
> Praise be to Allah,
> Lord of the Worlds,
> The Beneficent, the Merciful.
> Master of the Day of Judgment.
> You (alone) we worship;
> You (alone) we ask for help.
> Show us the straight path,
> The path of those whom You have favored;
> Not the (path) of those who earn Your anger nor of those who go astray.

and all other forms of Islam in the area. Through an alliance with a sheik of the Arab Saud tribe, the movement experienced a mixed series of successes and defeats, but with the weakening and final collapse of the Ottoman Empire, the Wahhabi / Saud alliance finally was able to gain control over most of the Arabian Peninsula. By 1932 they had established the nation of Saudi Arabia, whose government was dedicated to the strict Wahhabi application of Islam law. Because of its control over the holy places of Islam, Mecca, and Medina, the Wahhabi perspective has been exported out of the Arabian Peninsula and has colored numerous groups within modern Islam with a strong religious conservatism. Countering this are those who reject the Wahhabi influence as unrepresentative of the spirit of Islam. They view the Wahhabi rejection of all other interpretations of Islam as heretical and contrary to the practice of Islam for a thousand years, during which four major schools of Islamic law were all treated as orthodox and their interpretations of law respected as valid.

Wahhabi fundamentalism is of a Sunni variety. Islamic fundamentalism of a Shiite variety came to its fullest expression in the Iranian Revolution of 1979.

Today Islam faces a major crisis of definition and direction as the voice of fundamentalist Islam becomes more pronounced. Few political or religious pundits have a confident enough grasp of these tensions to predict what the outcome of the renewed vigor of fundamentalist Islam will be.

BELIEFS

The Various Influences

Islam sees itself standing in line with the major religious traditions within its early setting. Elements of Judaism, Christianity, and pre-Islamic Arab beliefs and practices are incorporated into Islam, with one reservation–Muslims contend that all previous revelation has been corrupted to some degree by those to whom it had been given. Jewish and Christian practices, beliefs, and stories that appear to be borrowed by Islam often have some differences in detail in their new Muslim context. Muslims view such parallels not as borrowings but as restorations of traditions that had become corrupted or as replacements (abrogations) of previous revelation that was of a provisional character.

Of the three traditions mentioned, Christianity, in both orthodox and heretical forms, contributes the least to Islam, though that contribution is not insubstantial. Jesus (Isa) is mentioned often in the Quran (twenty-seven references by name, and further references to the Messiah). A host of other characters from the Christian texts are also mentioned (Mary, John the Baptist, and the Apostles). Moreover, the Christian Gospel is elevated to the status of divine revelation, along with the Torah of Judaism and the Islamic Quran itself. Muslim speculation about the end of the world has substantial Christian (and Jewish) parallels, with such features in common as the resurrection of the dead, the final judgment, and heaven and hell. Features of Christian monasticism are reflected in the mystical Sufi movement of Islam.

But considerable tension is reflected between Islam and Christianity as well, particularly regarding the Christian belief in the Trinity and the description of Jesus as the "Son of God"–an affront to the central Islamic belief in stark monotheism. Wherever the Christian Gospels make such claims, there Muslims see evidence of the corruption of the Christian text. Otherwise, the claims in the Gospels are respected: Mary was a virgin; Jesus is the Messiah, though not in the full-blown Christian view; he resides in heaven with God and will return at the end of the world to defeat the forces of evil. The story of the crucifixion, death, and resurrection of Jesus are rejected however.

Islam shares more with Judaism. Much the same as Christianity had done, Islam borrows substantially from the Hebrew Bible for their own background. Key heroic figures of the Hebrew story are mentioned in the Quran: Adam, Noah, Abraham, Isaac and Ishmael, Jacob and the tribes of Israel, David, Solomon, and the prophets. Moses is especially featured, being mentioned more than 200 times. Where Islam both draws most closely to Judaism and departs most sharply from it is in the story of Abraham. Jews and Muslims both claim Abraham as the physical forefather of their nation and the literal founder of their faith. Both claim that God selected Abraham for a special relationship and confirmed that relationship with a covenant.

But at this point agreement ends. To which of Abraham's sons did God intend his special covenant to be transferred and maintained? Jews claim it was to Isaac (the son of Abraham and Sarah, Abraham's wife); Muslims claim it was to Ishmael (the oldest son of Abraham, whose mother, Hagar, was Sarah's maid). The Hebrew Bible notes the tension between the two claimants and comes down solidly on the side of Isaac. The Quran comes down solidly on the side of Ishmael. It is not Isaac, but Ishmael, who was almost sacrificed by Abraham at God's command, according to Muslims. Indeed, many of the activities of the Muslim pilgrimage to Mecca recall the life and struggles of Abraham and Ishmael. Abraham, on a visit to his exiled son Ishmael, is said to have built the Kaba, the house of God. There is some evidence that even before Muhammad, the Arabs traced their ancestry to Abraham, a link that Muhammad sought to highlight.

A third cluster of borrowing comes from the pre-Muslim religion of the Arabs: reverence for Mecca and the Kaba as a holy site, the importance of the Black Stone, the practice of pilgrimage to Mecca, and some traditions about Abraham. Further, Arab attitudes of manliness,

The 99 Names of God

Various translations of the ninety-nine name of Allah exist. The names describe God's attributes.

God; The Compassionate; The Merciful; The King; The Holy; The Source of Peace; The Guardian; The Protector; The Strong; The Compeller; The Majestic; The Creator; The Maker; The Fashioner; The Forgiver; The Subduer; The Bestower; The Provider; The Opener; The Knower; The Constrictor; The Enlarger; The Abaser; The Exalter; The Honorer; The Humiliator; The Hearer; The Seer; The Judge; The Just; The Subtle; The Aware; The Gentle; The Mighty; The Forgiving; The Grateful; The High; The Great; The Preserver; The Sustainer; The Reckoner; The Sublime; The Generous; The Watcher; The Responder; The All-Embracing; The Wise; The Loving; The Glorious; The Resurrector; The Witness; The Truth; The Trustee; The Strong; The Firm; The Friend; The Praiseworthy; The Counter; The Originator; The Reproducer; The Restorer; The Life-Giver; The Death-Giver; The Living; The Self-Subsisting; The Finder; The Noble; The Unique; The Eternal; The Able; The Dominant; The Promoter; The Retarder; The First; The Last; The Manifest; The Hidden; The Governor; The Exalted; The Righteous; The Relenting; The Forgiver; The Avenger; The Compassionate; The Ruler; The Lord of Majesty and Bounty; The Equitable; The Gatherer; The Self-Sufficient; The Enricher; The Withholder; The Propitious; The Distresser; The Light; The Guide; The Everlasting; The Inheritor; The Rightly Guided; The Patient.

hospitality, and honor were retained and reshaped. Around the time of Muhammad, various Arab poets, called *hanifs* (lit., "pious"), preached reform and reflected monotheistic tendencies, perhaps from Jewish and Christian influences in the area. Such poets were similar enough in tone to Muhammad that he was often identified as one, and some of their ideas are similar to ideas in the Quran.

God

The central declaration of Islam is that that there is only one God. The assertion of the unity or oneness of God is called *tawhid.* This conviction lies at the heart of Muhammad's zeal to cleanse Mecca of its vast array of deities.

It is the view of the divine that places Islam most sharply at odds with Christianity. A number of times the Quran states that God has no son, a direct challenge to the Christian teachings about Jesus and the Trinity. God is one; there is no other, Muslims affirm.

To associate any divine power or to attribute divine qualities to anyone or anything other than to God or to contend that there are gods besides Allah is condemned as *shirk.* But there are degrees of *shirk:* to associate some divine attribute or power to a person (e.g., saint worship) or thing (e.g., regard for omens and sacred objects) is different from blatant polytheism, where various gods are treated as real and are worshiped. Sometimes, puritanical reform movements have rejected all degrees of *shirk,* even destroying Muslim holy sites or preventing pilgrimage to such sites.

Non-Muslims sometimes think that the word "Allah" is the personal name of the Muslim god. But the word "Allah" is simply the transliteration of the Arabic word meaning "the God." Wherever the word "Allah" appears in Arabic documents, the word "God" could be used in English translations. Muslims consider themselves to worship the same God as Jews and Christians, the same God who sent down the Torah to the Jews and the Gospel to the Christians. For that reason, Muslims refer to Jews and Christians as "people of the Book," and generally have tolerated their religious practices, while suppressing polytheism with vigor.

Muslims use a number of epithets for God. God is most frequently referred to as "the Merciful, the Compassionate." Such is the opening line of all but one *surah,* or chapter, of the Quran. Also of frequent use are descriptions of God as "Master of the World" and as "Creator and Sustainer." Muslims have a stock of ninety-nine epithets, or "Excellent Names," by which they can express some characteristic of God. A common saying among Muslims is *"Allahu akbar"* ("God is greater"), expressing the sense that nothing is God's equal and that nothing should be placed beside him.

On the esoteric side of Islam, particularly among some of the small Shiite groups, various beliefs about the divinity of early Muslim leaders have been espoused. These beliefs are at the extreme end of Islamic views of the divine. At the opposite end is the view that nothing can be associated with God. In the middle, expressions of Islam can include saint veneration and belief that Muhammad will act as an intercessor at the last judgment.

The World (Visible and Invisible)

The Visible World. The Quran does not start with a story of origins, as the Hebrew Bible does, but it assumes the basic details of the biblical story: God is the creator of the world; Adam and Eve are placed in the Garden of Eden; and there is a crisis stemming from the eating of forbidden fruit. But, according to Islamic teaching, Adam quickly repents of his sin and is forgiven, leaving no scar on the human condition or on creation. Indeed, Adam becomes the first in a long line of God's prophets, which culminates with Muhammad. Thus the world is God-given and good. It remains a rich creation, to be used by the faithful followers of God, who act as God's regents in the world.

The Invisible World. In addition to the visible world, there is an unseen world, in which angels, *jinn* (spirits), and other of God's creation operate. Angels have particularly important roles for human

---

PLACES

Mecca: The pre-Islamic center of trade and religion for Arabs, which Muhammad reformed into a center of monotheism. Muslims who are able are expected to make a pilgrimage there at least once during their lifetime.

Medina: Originally called Yathrib, this settlement was later renamed Medina to honor Muhammad, who established his first Islamic government there (622 C.E.). Medina means "city."

Jerusalem: The third most holy city of Islam. The Dome of the Rock, a mosque built in 692 on the site of the Jewish temple, is particularly special. Muslims believe that it was here that Abraham offered Ishmael as a sacrifice and that Muhammad ascended to heaven.

Kaba: (lit., "cube"). A pre-Islamic cube-shaped building in Mecca, rebuilt several times. Believed by Muslims to have been built by Abraham. The Black Stone (meteorite) is imbedded in it. It is the center of the Muslim pilgrimage and the place toward which one prays.

Blue Mosque: A mosque, built in the 1600s in the heart of Istanbul, represents a high point of Ottoman achievement.

mosque: (lit., "place of prostration"). The center of Muslim community and religious life. Its most distinctive architectural feature is the *minaret* ("tower"), from which the call to prayer is made.

Taj Mahal: A mausoleum in Agra, India, reflecting Muslim and Indian architecture. It is considered one of the most beautiful buildings in the world.

well-being, from the angel Gabriel conveying the Quran to Muhammad to angels who provide personal attention for individuals. Muslims believe, for example, that two angels are assigned to each individual: one records the good deeds; the other the bad deeds. In addition to the angels, who are viewed as obedient servants of God, there are the *jinn* (sing. *jinni*), whose reputation is slightly more arbitrary and disquieting. They can deceive and cause harm. Such beings have made their way, somewhat rehabilitated, into the popular imagination as genies, from stories of Aladdin and his magic lamp. The chief of the *jinn* is Iblis, the personal name of the devil or Satan. He is the chief tempter. His refusal to bow before Adam at God's command resulted in his expulsion from God's presence, and he has held no goodwill for humans since then.

The Human Condition

Humans are basically ignorant of God's will. God has from time to time sought to remedy that state by sending messengers who speak God's word faithfully and clearly. Muslims respect various collections of these divine messages, particularly the Torah of the Jews and the Gospel of the Christians.

The problem, according to Muslims, is that God's clear message was often corrupted by the human agents to whom the message had been entrusted. Thus the Bible of the Jews and that of the Christians do not always give a clear message or untainted instruction. Such corruption of the message necessitated another "sending down" of God's word, this time to the Arabs. This Arabic message was to be the final message, which had been given many times before. Muhammad, the person chosen to receive the message, would thus be the final prophet. The message itself would be clear, and its text would need to be faithfully preserved to the end of time. With this new revelation, uncorrupted and clear, individuals now were without excuse. They knew what God's will was; they needed now to choose to do it.

Predestination

The sovereignty of God over his creation is strongly emphasized in Islam, so much so that for centuries a kind of fatalism marked Muslim engagement with the world. In this, Islam faces the dilemma of many religious traditions that emphasize that human actions are done in accordance with the will of God (predestination), for how then does one assert human responsibility and accountability for individual conduct?

The theological schools within Islam have debated the matter much, offering various attempts to balance God's control and direction over all of life with human responsibility and choice. God's will is rarely compromised or heavily qualified in these debates. The Muslim sense is that all of life, both the good and the bad, happens according to the will of God. This attitude is reflected in a common Muslim saying: "*insha Allah*" ("if Allah wills").

Death and Afterlife

Death is not the end of one's existence, according to Islam. The dead face a final judgment, at which time their eternal destiny will be announced. Even in the grave, the dead will be questioned regarding their belief in Allah and his messenger Muhammad, and for this reason the words of the Muslim confession of belief are whispered in the ears of the dying. At the end of the age, all the dead will be resurrected and judged. The judgment will be based on deeds done during life: those with a multitude of good deeds will enter paradise; those with a heavier weight of bad deeds will descend to hell. Some intercession by Muhammad may help, although the matter is debated. The judgment, once made, is permanent.

Of the western religious traditions, Islam offers the most detailed description of the afterlife, where a beautiful paradise awaits the righteous and a hideous hell imprisons and punishes the wicked. Some of the language is taken

MAJOR TEXTS

Quran / Koran: (lit., "recitation"). The Islamic Scripture, consisting of 114 chapters (*surahs*) of material that Muhammad "recited" during twenty-two years of religious experiences. Muslims understand this Arabic material to be the reliable revelation of God, replacing the corrupted texts that Jews and Christians had received (the Torah and the Gospel). The Quran is about one-fifth shorter than the Christian New Testament.

Hadith: Stories of what Muhammad did or said. These have become the second manual of authority for Muslims. Each story has a chain of tradition attached, identifying the persons who transmitted the story. That chain serves as the basis for a judgment about the reliability of the story, which can range from sound, good, or weak, to fabricated. Various collections of *hadiths* appeared. About two centuries after Muhammad's death, a serious effort was made to determine which stories were trustworthy. Six collections won general approval.

The Revival of the Religious Sciences: A book by Al-Ghazali, which helped to renew Islam by emphasizing the necessity of religious experience, in contrast to what the author judged to be a legalism and intellectualism of the religious schools.

Thousand and One Nights: Also known as the *Arabian Nights*. A vast collection of secular and esoteric tales about life and fantasy in medieval Islam. Best known to English readers from tales of Aladdin and his magic lamp.

from the rich apocalyptic literature of Jews and Christians, but it is heightened in the intensity of its description. For example, those in hell who beg for water will be given molten lead to drink. Those in Paradise enjoy a garden of luxury, with every good thing, from cool water, lush vegetation, delightful food and drink, to servants and beautiful virgins to do one's bidding. The sensual nature of Paradise has caused some to think that the descriptions are intended to be figurative, or at least to have a figurative dimension, as well as a literal.

Holy War / Jihad

Perhaps the most thorny feature of Muslim belief for non-Muslims is the concept of *jihad*, particularly given the rise of Islamic fundamentalism and the choice of the word *jihad* as the mark of identity of some Muslim terrorist groups. Muslims rightly point out that the word *jihad* means simply "struggle," and that the great *jihad* is the inner personal struggle.

The lesser *jihad* is the point of contention. This *jihad* is what is more popularly called "holy war," and it features a call to arms against adherents of other religions who will not convert to Islam or who stand in the way of the extension of Islam.

The debate within Islam is whether this lesser *jihad* is defensive only, or whether it can have an aggressive side too. A further debate is whether it can be considered genuine submission to God if one is forced to convert to Islam.

Law

The Law (*Shariah*) is a fundamental part of the Muslim consciousness. It is by knowing what God commands and by doing it that one is assured a life in paradise. Muslim law is broad, taking in all aspects of the regulation of behavior, whether religious or secular, whether personal or communal, from the gravely immoral to simple matters of etiquette and personal hygiene. In other words, all behavior falls under the Islamic law.

In the western world, law is usually viewed as commanding or prohibiting ("do" or "don't do"). In addition to these, Islam specifies behavior under three other categories: the discouraged, the recommended, and the permitted or neutral.

Islamic law, then, has a complex and comprehensive scope. One might think that given the centrality of law in Islamic thought, the Quran would be largely a book of legislation—a law book. But it is not. Only a couple hundred of the 6,000 verses in the Quran seem to have such character. Much of the Quran is sermonic, visionary, and anecdotal—hardly the stuff of legislation.

Various schools of interpretation of the *Shariah* have developed. Four legal schools have gained status as orthodox in Sunni Islam. Each is considered to offer a valid interpretation of the *Shariah*. But these are not competing systems. Each has come to operate as the valid interpretation of the Quran within a specific geographical area. In this way, debates over law among the schools do not have significant ramifications for the practical exercise of law in any local context. The most serious challenge to this tolerance of diversity has come from the Wahhabi movement, which has dismissed all interpretations except its own as heretical.

The Sources of Islamic Law

One of the great debates within Islam is the sources upon which the *Shariah* can be established. All Muslims agree that the Quran, as God's revelation, is a valid source for law. In theory, it is the primary source. But since the Quran is not essentially a law book and since it does not address more than a few aspects of behavior, it cannot be the only source.

Muslims view the Quran as the final revelation from God to humans. With Muhammad's death, the revelation was complete. But Muhammad left more than

> **DUTIES & ETHICS**
>
> *Although Islam does not have a formal list of regulations like the Ten Commandments in Judaism,* Surah 17:22-39 *provides one list of expected behavior. The following is a summary.*
>
> - Do not have any other god but Allah.
> - Show kindness to parents.
> - Give to relatives what is their due. Give to the poor and the wayfarer. If you don't have money to give, speak a kind word.
> - Don't waste your wealth.
> - Don't be a miser.
> - Don't kill your children. Provide for them.
> - Don't commit adultery.
> - Don't kill, except as allowed. (Revenge killing is permitted, but controlled.)
> - Don't steal the property of orphans that is in your trust.
> - Use honest weights and measures.
> - Don't act arrogantly.
>
> **The Five Pillars:** The main duties of a Muslim. [See box "The Five Pillars"]
>
> **Shirk:** (lit., "making a partner"). The most dangerous offence in Islam is to associate other gods with the one God (polytheism) or to associate divine qualities to things that are not divine.

his recitation of God's message; he left, as well, the example of his life—the *sunnah* or the way of the prophet. Stories (*hadith*) of what Muhammad did, said, or approved provide a record of the *sunnah* of the prophet. This constitutes the second source of Islamic law. A problem arises in that the quantity of *hadiths* had become enormous by the time the *hadith* collectors started their work some two hundred years after Muhammad's death. It was recognized that a number of inauthentic *hadiths* were in circulation, and if *hadith* was to be a sound source for Islamic law, some method had to be applied by which the collectors could distinguish between authentic and inauthentic traditions. The principle generally agreed on was an examination of the chain of transmission of the *hadith* to determine the reliability of each person involved: the more reliable the transmitters of the *hadith* and the more unbroken the chain, the more reliable the *hadith*. Using this method, six approved multi-volume collections came into circulation, and the number of accepted *hadiths* was reduced to about 6,000 from several hundred thousand that had been in circulation. Associated with this effort was the creation of collections of biographies of the transmitters of the *hadith* tradition.

The Quran and the *hadith* might have served as adequate sources for Islamic law had Islam remained a religion of Arabs and Arabia. But Islam expanded rapidly, encountering wide ranges of life foreign to the experience of Arabia or to the first generation of Muslims. This required some means by which to extend the Quran and *hadith* to these new situations. Two further principles of law were established, though these are more subject to debate. They are analogy (*qiyas*) and consensus (*ijma*). The use of analogy involves finding a passage in the Quran or the *hadith* of sufficient parallel to address a new situation. The prohibition on consumption of alcohol and drugs, for example, is established by analogy: the Quran prohibits a common Arabian intoxicant; by analogy, all alcoholic drinks are banned. The fourth principle is the appeal to consensus of the earliest generations of the Islamic movement. There is a conviction that Allah would not have allowed his community to live long in error, therefore practices of the older Muslim community are considered valid.

Fine points of debate over each of these principles highlight Muslim debate about law.

Leadership

Islam claims that there have been 124,000 prophets, from Adam to Muhammad. Twenty-six are mentioned by name in the Quran. Of these, almost all are characters from the Hebrew Bible; John the Baptist and Jesus are New Testament figures. Five of these prophets are judged to have been messengers *par excellence*: Noah, Abraham, Moses, Jesus, and Muhammad. Muhammad is considered the final prophet, the "seal" of the prophets.

Muhammad was the first leader of the Muslim community, but his influence has continued through every generation of Muslims to the present. Muslims are guided by Muhammad's example, as preserved in the *hadith*. For example, although Muslim men are not required to grow a beard, many do, solely out of respect of the example of Muhammad. Or we could observe the practice of pious Muslims putting on clothes (right foot or arm first) or going through doors (right foot first) or going into restrooms (left foot first); each action follows the practice of Muhammad as recorded in a *hadith*. Popular piety has sometimes made Muhammad into a wonderworker and a figure of devotion. While such views go beyond the orthodox portrait of Muhammad, most Muslims show considerable reverence for Muhammad: routinely when Muslims mention the name of Muhammad, they will immediately follow the name with the comment "peace be upon him," often abbreviated in English as PBUH.

Images

Muhammad declared that only one God existed. Anything that challenged that view, whether in word or in image, was a dangerous distraction, with the power to draw one away from God. Muhammad's first action when Mecca fell to him was to purify the Kaba, destroying all the religious images, which represented 360 gods housed there. This negative view of religious images is called *iconoclasm* (lit., "image breaking").

FESTIVALS / SACRED TIME

The festivals are listed in chronological order. Islam uses a lunar calendar.

New Year's Day: This celebrates the flight (*hijra*) of Muhammad from Mecca to Medina in 622 C.E. It marks the beginning of the Muslim calendar.

Muhammad's Birthday (Mawlid): The celebration of Muhammad's birthday.

Night Journey (Miraj): A celebration of Muhammad's journey (ascension) to heaven from Jerusalem.

Night of Power: The celebration of the beginning of the revelatory experiences of Muhammad that came to comprise the Quran.

Id al-Fitr: "The Festival of Fast Breaking" or the "Small Feast." A two- or three-day event marking the end of the month-long fast of Ramadan.

Id al-Adha: "The Feast of the Sacrifice" or the "Great Feast." It marks the end of the pilgrimage to Mecca. Muslims offer a sacrifice on this occasion, commemorating Abraham's "sacrifice" of Ishmael.

Friday Noon Prayer: Although Muslims do not have a weekly holy day, such as the Jewish Sabbath or the Christian Sunday, Muslims try to attend Friday noon prayers in the mosque.

Even images of people and animals were prohibited, according to an early *hadith*. Such reservation about the depiction of living beings shifted artistic energies to geometrical designs and calligraphy, the latter which took as its subject matter verses of the Quran. Where representational art has been allowed, Muhammad and members of his family appear veiled, and Muhammad is often surrounded by a flame.

The iconoclastic tendency is a feature of the puritanical Wahhabi movement that arose in the 1700s in the Arabian Peninsula. The Wahhabis destroyed tombs of Muslim saints to prevent their veneration. Such views came to influence Muslim areas outside of Arabia. In the spring of 2001, the Taliban in Afghanistan destroyed two Buddha statues (the largest in the world), which had been carved into a mountainside in the 400s C.E. Most Muslim groups condemned the destruction, as did the worldwide community.

Revelation

Muslims hold the Quran (lit., "recitation") to be the most recent revelation from God to humans. It is God's very word, which Muhammad merely "recited." More importantly, it is the final revelation. As the last revelation that God will give to humans, it must not be corrupted, and most Muslims assert that the text of the Quran has remained unchanged from Muhammad's time to the present.

About ninety of the 114 *surahs* are from Muhammad's years in Mecca (604–622); the other twenty-four are from the ten years in Medina. In the twenty years following Muhammad's death, several collections of the *surahs* were made. Of these collections, the caliph Uthman authorized only one; the others disappeared. In the authorized collection, the *surahs* were arranged largely in terms of length, which coincidently seems to have placed the later *surahs* first.

The Quran recognizes two kinds of passages that comprise its corpus: the clear and the ambiguous. Shiites and Sufis have found a fairly rich mine of quite diverse ideas in the ambiguous parts. The Sunni regard only the unambiguous passages to be of primary importance.

Abrogation. The Quran is based on twenty-three years of Muhammad's religious experiences. Some of Muhammad's contemporaries pointed out changes or contradictions within the developing body of Quranic material. For example, Muslims were originally instructed to pray in the direction of Jerusalem; a later Quranic passage changes that direction to Mecca. Passages in the Quran itself respond to these charges of inconsistencies. In Surah 16.101, the Quran notes that some have charged Muhammad with deception, but that when God exchanges one verse for another, God knows what he is doing. In similar vein, Surah 2.106 states that whatever verse God abrogates and casts into oblivion, he provides a better or similar verse in its place. Muslim scholars debate this matter, attempting to decide what Quranic verses may have been abrogated (replaced or removed), and how the process works (e.g., whether something in a *hadith* might abrogate something in the Quran). Chronology is an important consideration in the matter, since the more recent abrogates the earlier.

The Satanic Verses. In 1989, Salman Rushdie, an Indian author, published a novel titled *The Satanic Verses.* It was widely condemned in the Muslim community for its portrayal of Muhammad, provoking such outrage that clerics in Iran placed a multi-million dollar reward on Rushdie's head. The book took as its title a phrase that had been used to identify the most controversial passage associated with the Quran. The short passage supposedly mentioned three Arabian goddesses, daughters of Allah, and recommended their worship. According to one widely received story, the passage had once been part of the Quran, but it was removed after Allah informed Muhammad that the words actually had come from Satan. Some scholars see in this some evidence for an accommodation to some forms of Arabic belief in the earliest days of Islam. The Quran itself denies any such early command in favor of these deities (53:20-3).

Sufism: The Mystical Tradition

The mystical tradition in Islam is both profound and diverse; its origins are early but uncertain. Some of its inspiration can be traced back to the mystical encounters of Muhammad himself. The emphasis on asceticism that marks much of Muslim mysticism is thought to have been a reaction to the opulent lifestyles adopted by the Muslim leadership as wealth flowed into the treasuries from the early conquests.

Muslims were surrounded by various ascetic traditions among the peoples they conquered. Both Christian monasticism

---

THE FIVE PILLARS

The following practices are common to all Muslims.

Creed / Profession of Faith (Shahadah): (lit., "bearing witness"). The confession: "I bear witness that there is no God but God and Muhammad is the Prophet of God." The sincere repetition of this makes one a Muslim.

Prayer (Salat): Ritual prayer offered at five specific times of the day: dawn, noon, afternoon, sunset, and nightfall. Worshippers pray wherever they are, though Muslims try to attend the mosque for the noon prayer on Friday. Muslims pray facing Mecca. Prayer is preceded by ritual washing and a formal call to prayer.

Alms (Zakat): A tax on possessions and various levels of taxes on agriculture produce. The tax is used for poor relief and religious purposes, such as education and building of mosques.

Fasting (Sawm): For the entire month of Ramadan, Muslims fast from dawn to dusk. A few exceptions are allowed (young, elderly, the ill, pregnant or nursing mothers, travelers). The fast involves abstinence from food, drink and sexual relations.

Pilgrimage (Hajj): Once in one's lifetime, Muslims are expected to journey to Mecca, if they are able. The pilgrimage occurs over a six-day period in the last month of the year, and involves a complex set of rituals around Mecca, recalling stories of Abraham and Ishmael. After completing the pilgrimage, the pilgrim bears the honorific title of *hajji* (for males) or *hajjah* (for women).

and Hindu asceticism exercised some influence on the developing mystical traditions of Islam. In turn, the mystical traditions within Islam, through
their missionary efforts, came to exercise considerable influence broadly
on Islam, illustrated by the fact that between half and two-thirds of Muslim
men are thought to have been attached to a mystical order, or brotherhood,
in the 1700s and 1800s.

Although considerable diversity exists, it is common to speak of Muslim mysticism simply as Sufism. The term is derived from the Arabic word
for "wool," appropriate because of the ascetic woolen garments worn by
Sufi disciples, in contrast to the rich silks of the Muslim leadership.

At the core of religious mysticism is a devotion to God and a quest to
be lost in or absorbed by the divine fullness, coming into a union of some
kind with God. Often the path to this experience is marked by the gaining
of esoteric knowledge or by the mastering of specific disciplines. The
best-known Sufi behavior is the dance of the Whirling Dervishes, a group
of Sufis who enter a mystical trance state by means of a whirling dance.
Other Sufi groups are marked by various distinctive behaviors, such as the
Weeping Dervishes. The word dervish comes from the Persian word
meaning "poor," and this captures the ascetic focus of the Sufi disciples.

Sufis tend to regard their leaders as having elevated status, and their
masters, or *shaykhs*, are considered an essential element in the sufi's successful quest for union with God. From this focus on the leader, a strong
tradition of saint veneration developed in Islam.

Sufism was a powerful missionary force in Islam, but it has met considerable opposition from some of the ultra-conservative reform groups of
modern Islam. In particular, the Wahhabi movement took as one of its
main goals the suppression of the Sufi movement and its many popular
practices, such as saint veneration and pilgrimages to tombs.

Relations with other Religions

Islam has incorporated elements from a variety of religious traditions. In the first years of the movement, Muhammad was particularly
sympathetic to Jews and Christians, whom he considered "people of the
Book" and fellow monotheists. But when these peoples were largely unre-
ceptive to Muhammad's claims about his revelations and his status as the
spokesman of God, Muhammad's attitude hardened. Many Jews and
some Arab tribes that had previously converted to Judaism lived in the
area of Medina and their resistance to and open mockery of Muhammad's claims presented a serious challenge to the survival of the new
Muslim experiment. The opposing Jews were exiled or slaughtered; their

wives, children, and goods claimed as booty. After that, the policy of Islam generally has been to allow Jews and Christians to live and practice their religion under Muslim governments as *dhimma* ("protected"), upon payment of a tax. They must not, however, attempt to convert Muslims to their religion. Zoroastrians were tolerated under the same rules in Persia. Otherwise, the expectation is that conquered people will convert to Islam or be put to the sword. There is no place in Muslim rule for atheists, idolaters (i.e., polytheists), or apostates (Muslims who leave their faith).

PRACTICES

Islam has absorbed many cultures in its expansion, and it has adopted a range of native customs in its local expressions. In the discussion below, the "Five Pillars" are the most uniform of Muslim customs; in the other matters discussed, greater variety of practice is found.

The Five Pillars

The most defining elements of Muslim practice comprise what is called the "Five Pillars." These are: Confession, Worship/Prayer, Alms, Fasting, and Pilgrimage. Some are daily rites, some annual, some at least once in a lifetime (if one is able), and some, as the occasion permits. All Muslims follow these rituals and actions, although slight difference in interpretation may hold for different groups.

Confession (Shahadah). The most condensed summary of Islamic belief is two short statements: one bearing witness that there is one God, the other bearing witness that Muhammad is God's messenger. These statements provided adequate marks of identity for the early Muslim

RITUALS / RITES

Muslims have few rituals, and since Islam does not have priests, the rituals are carried out by the individual, not preformed by the clergy.

Prayer: Prayer is ritualized in Islam, with five set times of prayer and with prescribed words and physical movements (prostration, bowing, and standing). Each cycle of movements is called a *rakah*, performed in the direction of Mecca. Careful ritual washing is required, as is a prayer mat. Prayer can be made anywhere, though the Friday noon prayer is to be done collectively in the mosque. One of the Five Pillars.

Fasting: A day-time fast during the month of Ramadan. One of the Five Pillars.

Circumcision: Practices vary, but male children are circumcised from four years old or older. Although not commanded in the Quran, it copies the practice of Muhammad. Female circumcision is also practiced in some Muslim cultures.

Pilgrimage: The high point in the life of a Muslim is a pilgrimage to Mecca. The pilgrims clothe themselves in simple dress, they visit particular sites associated with Abraham and Ishmael, and they circle the Kaba seven times. This is one of the Five Pillars.

community: the confession of one God separated the monotheistic Arabs (Muslims) from other Arabs, who were generally polytheistic; the reference to Muhammad separated Muslim monotheists from other monotheists, such as Jews and Christians. Repeating that confession once, sincerely and preferably in the company of witnesses, makes one a Muslim.

Prayer/Worship (Salat). Ritual prayer is the most distinctive visible mark of the Muslim. Five times a day, Muslims follow carefully prescribed patterns of physical movements (prostration, bowing, and standing), while reciting prescribed prayers. Each cycle of movements is called a *rakah*, and each prayer time consists of two to five cycles. Prayer is performed in the direction of Mecca, the sacred center, and the one praying is expected to have prepared a sacred state and a sacred space from which to conduct those prayers. Careful ritual washing of specified areas of the body (from head to feet) creates a sacred, or pure, state; removing one's shoes and using a prayer mat creates a sacred space. Prayer can be made anywhere, though the Friday noon prayer routinely is done communally at the mosque (lit., "place of prostration"). In Muslim countries, often all other activity comes to a halt at prayer time, and the most memorable sound for visitors to Muslim countries is likely to be the call to prayer, often boomed out over loudspeakers from the minaret ("tower") of the mosque, at dawn, noon, mid-afternoon, dusk, and late evening.

Alms (Zakat). Muhammad's first observations about life in Mecca reflected his concern about inequity. Whether this concern was rooted in his own experience as an orphan is unclear; what is clear is that he often challenged social ills and his message first attracted the disadvantaged in Mecca. Muhammad attempted to address such inequities by imposing a tax on all believers. The tax was set at a varying rate on specific goods, and in the initial years of Islam, that tax sufficed to meet the various needs of the community, from poor relief to the building of mosques. In addition, voluntary charity was encouraged. Unlike Christianity, which encouraged asceticism and voluntary poverty, Islam restricted charitable giving to a maximum of one-third of one's possessions. Normal family life in society was to be maintained; the monastic impulse largely checked. In the modern world, few Muslim countries have an official *zakat* tax; it is more often a voluntary contribution to support the poor, pilgrims, debtors, and volunteers in *jihad*, as well as the collectors themselves.

Fasting (Sawm). Muslims are expected to fast during the month of Ramadan. Ramadan is regarded as auspicious, being the month in which Muhammad received the first Quranic revelation. The fast is strict: no food, drink, or sensual pleasures during the daylight hours (marked off by whether there is adequate light to distinguish between a black thread and a white thread). Children, the aged, the ill, pregnant women, and travelers are exempt, although one is expected to perform a delayed fast later, when one is able. During the month, a heavier emphasis is placed on pious reflection, attendance at special mosque events, and the reading of the Quran. The fast ends with the great "Feast of the Fast-Breaking."

Pilgrimage (Hajj). To Muslims, Mecca is the sacred center. It is the home of Adam and Eve, of Abraham and his son Ishmael, and of Muhammad, the final prophet. As the sacred center, not only is it the destination for Muslim pilgrimage, it is a forbidden city to all non-Muslims, as is Medina. The pilgrimage, in the last month of the Muslim calendar, involves a six-day regimen that each pilgrim must follow while in the area of Mecca. Many of the features go back to Arab religious practice prior to Muhammad. But the activities have taken on specifically Islamic meaning. Mecca is still the center of pilgrimage; the Black Stone is still the sacred object and the Kaba its sacred house around which pilgrims still circle, as in pre-Islamic times. But each activity is now associated with events in the lives of Abraham and Ishmael, from Hagar's frantic search for water to save her son Ishmael to the stoning of Satan.

For most of Muslim history, a pilgrimage to Mecca involved great cost, time, and danger. Some individuals spent years on the pilgrimage, and thousands died on the way. Considerable respect was paid to one who had completed the pilgrimage, and pilgrims were permitted to affix the title *hajji* to their name.

OFFICES

Caliph: (lit., "successor"). The leaders of the Islamic community after Muhammad. These were not considered divinely inspired individuals, for Muhammad was the last of the prophets. Their role was religious and political.

Caliphate: The succession of caliphs, leaders of Sunni Islam. The institution was terminated by the Turkish Republic in 1924, and attempts by various states to revive it have not been successful. Often, an anti-caliphate challenged the legitimacy of the governing caliphate.

Imam: (lit., "he who stands before"). The leader of the Shiite community, comparable to the caliph of the Sunnis. In its more specific use, the term is applied to the leader who is a descendent of Ali and who has supernatural powers to interpret Law.

Mahdi: In Shiite tradition, the hidden *imam* who will return at the end of the world (cf. Jewish and Christian "Messiah").

Ayatollah: (lit., "sign of Allah"). In Shiite tradition, a few very pious and learned men have the authority of the *Imam*.

Dervish: (lit., "poor"). Derived from the Persian word "Darwish," which is a translation of the Arabic "Fakir." Initiates into the ascetic lifestyle of the Sufi brotherhood.

Mullah: A scholar of one of the schools of law.

Muezzin: (lit., "crier"). One who formally calls Muslims to prayer five times daily from the minaret.

Sultan: (lit., "ruler"). First used for semi-autonomous rulers under the Abbasids. Later became a term for a ruler of many Islamic states.

From the mid-1900s to the present, modern, fast, and relatively inexpensive means of transportation have caused the number of pilgrims to swell, from about 30,000 to over two million. This has put considerable pressures on the pilgrimage sites.

In some Muslim reform movements, the idea of pilgrimage came under attack. Initially, the Wahhabis considered pilgrims to be idolaters, and they destroyed the tombs of Muhammad and the saints, which had become places of devotion for the pilgrims.

Rites of Passage

Rites vary from area to area and from group to group. The following are fairly common rites, although the details can vary from culture to culture.

Birth. The child is named seven days after birth. The name chosen must express something positive and good. Sometimes a hyphenated name is used: the first name Abdul ("servant") is often connected to some epithet of God. The hair of the child's first haircut is weighed, and an equivalent weight in silver or coin is given to the poor.

Circumcision. Although the Quran does not mention circumcision, Islam promotes the practice on the basis of the second source of Islamic law, the *sunnah* of the prophet. Muhammad was circumcised—a custom already practiced in Arabia before the rise of Islam. Islam continues that tradition. The *Shariah* recommends that Muslim males be circumcised, and this has in practice been treated as a requirement. There is no specified time for the ceremony, as there is in Judaism, but often it is done after the child is four years or older. Female circumcision is not required, but it is widely practiced. Converts to Islam need not be circumcised.

Marriage. Multiple marriages are acceptable among Muslims; more specifically, polygyny (multiple wives) is acceptable, since only men are permitted multiple marriage partners. Men are permitted up to four wives, if they treat each equally, though in reality few Muslim men have more than one wife, and in many countries multiple marriages are simply not permitted. Muslim men may marry Christian or Jewish women; Muslim women must marry a Muslim man. Divorce is permitted, and the divorced are allowed to remarry after a brief period. Sexual relations outside of marriage are prohibited, and in areas where Quranic law is interpreted literally, violators are subjected to harsh penalties: one hundred lashes or execution by stoning. The matter is complicated because the Quran specifies lashings or house arrest only;

execution by stoning is legislated only in the *hadith*. Muslim scholars debate which punishment was prescribed first, for the later legislation could annul (or abrogate) the earlier legislation. Execution by stoning for prohibited sexual relations is carried out in a number of Muslim countries today. In 2002, several contestants withdrew from the Miss World Contest scheduled for Nigeria because Muslim clerics there had passed such sentences.

Temporary marriages, contracted for a limited, specified period, are permitted in the Shiite Twelver tradition. Such temporary marriages are thought to have developed because Arab warriors were often away from their families for long periods; this concession allowed children born to temporary unions to be counted as legitimate. The practice continues, often used by individuals away from home for female companionship, although it is rejected by all other branches of Islam as an improper sexual arrangement.

Death and Funerals. Similar to Judaism, Islam emphasizes swiftness and simplicity in funerals. The body is to be buried on the day of death, if possible, after proper ritual washing of the corpse and prayers. The shroud-wrapped body is placed in the grave without a coffin, and positioned on its right side, facing Mecca, or the head is slightly tilted in the direction of Mecca. The grave may be marked with a stone, but no inscriptions are permitted, nor should any monument be built over the grave, though in actual practice local customs often make a Muslim cemetery little different from cemeteries of other religions about them.

A brief three-day period of mourning is allowed, although a longer period is permitted for the death of a spouse. Mourning should not involve wailing or tearing of the clothes. Death is God's doing; the faithful should be careful not to question God's will.

TERMINOLOGY

Dar al-Islam: (lit., "The Abode of Islam"). Those lands in which Islam is dominant and Muslim law prevails. See "*ummah.*"

Dhimmis: (lit., "protected persons"). In Islamic countries, Jews and Christians are permitted to practice their religion as *dhimmis,* after paying a special tax.

Fatwa: A legal opinion by a qualified jurist, clarifying a disputed point of law. In practice, a *fatwa* is treated as having the force of law.

Islam: (see SLM) (lit., "surrender"). The term for the religion of Muslims.

Jihad: (lit., "struggle"). The personal struggle of a Muslim in the way of piety, or the militant struggle to defend and extend Islam. The latter is commonly called "Holy War."

Muslim: (see SLM) (lit., "one who surrenders"). The term for an adherent to Islam.

SLM: The letters of the consonantal root upon which the words "Islam" and "Muslim" are built. Its primary meaning for Muslims is "surrender."

Ummah: The People; the Community. Used by Muslims to identify the community of Islam, ideally undivided, although from the earliest days the *ummah* has been split.

Food Taboos

Muslims use the term *halal* for whatever in life is permitted and *haram* for whatever is prohibited, though the more prominent use of the terms is associated with Muslim food laws. The basic prohibitions somewhat follow the food taboos of the Hebrew Bible: pork, blood, meat offered to idols, birds of prey, and improperly killed animals are prohibited, although Muslims have a wider range of acceptable animals. The most distinctive difference between Muslim and Jewish food taboos is the prohibition against alcohol: the Quran prohibits a common intoxicating Arabic drink, which Muslims have generally extended to include all alcoholic drinks. In Judaism, wine is a common drink featured in many Jewish rituals.

In the United States, *halal* products are approved primarily by The Islamic Food and Nutrition Council of America (IFANCA). Their symbol, a crescent in a circle with an "M," is found on products in many countries. Various other Muslim agencies also certify food products. Since Jewish *kosher* certification is much more widespread, Muslims often eat Jewish *kosher* foods, for these normally would meet the conditions of *halal*.

Religious Officials

Islam has no priesthood. Generally any pious Muslim may lead community prayers, the main group activity in Islam. But Islam does have a range of religious figures of recognized status and function.

The prophet is the primary religious figure in Islam, and a series of twenty-six such figures, from Adam to Muhammad, are referred to in the Quran. Muhammad, believed by Muslims to be the last of the prophets, left no instructions about the leadership of the *ummah*, the Muslim community. Such structures have developed as the need arose.

Caliphs. The primary leadership is associated with the office of caliph (lit., "successor"), established in the reorganization of the Muslim community following Muhammad's death. The first four caliphs had all been early converts to Islam and were related by marriage or blood to Muhammad's family, though the importance of the family connection became a principle only for the Shiites. The caliph was responsible for guiding the community according to the principles of Islamic Law (*shariah*). The caliphate generally moved with the center of the dominant Muslim power. It last had force under the Ottoman Turks. Dissident Muslim groups have sometimes established an anti-caliphate or counter caliphate. Under the secular Turkish revolution, the caliphate was abolished in

1924. No successful effort to reestablish the caliphate has been made since then, even though traditionally there has been a sense within Sunni Islamic tradition that the "House of Islam" should have one leader, rather than many.

Imam. The *imam* (lit., "leader") can be any pious Muslim who leads the assembly in the communal prayers, although frequently it is a formally trained religious official who functions in this role. In Shiite Islam, the *imam* had a position almost parallel to the caliph in Sunni Islam, but superior in that the *imam* was viewed as having received secret knowledge and direct divine guidance. Shiites debate among themselves as to how many *imams* there have been: the primary dispute is whether there were seven or twelve. There is, as well, a debate regarding whether there is a "Hidden *Imam*," waiting to be revealed at the end of the age.

Ayatollah. The term *ayatollah* (lit., "sign of God") was used for leading Islamic jurists, but in the Iranian Revolution of 1979 the title came to be particularly linked to Khomeini, the Muslim cleric behind the revolution. Although the word of an *ayatollah* traditionally did not have the force of law, it has gained that authority among various groups. Many religious leaders in the Shia community now bear the title.

Mullah. The term *mullah* (lit., "lord") has had a variety of uses, politically and socially, but in its religious use, it generally specifies someone trained in one of the schools of law. Often a *mullah* will lead in the communal prayers.

Sultan. The term sultan means leader. It was a term used of semi- and fully autonomous rulers under the Abbasid Empire, and became a common title for the leader of Islamic nations.

Shaykh (Sheik). The term *shaykh* (lit., "chief," "old man") is used in a variety of contexts in Muslim countries. As a religious term, frequently it is used to identify the leader of a Muslim religious community. In Sufism, the term has the fullest meaning. The *shaykh* is not only a leader; he is the essential spiritual guide under whom the life of a Sufi mystic is to develop; without such a guide, the path is difficult or impossible.

Muslim Divisions

Sunni vs. Shia. Numerous divisions mark Islam. The major division developed in the first generation of Islam, drawing lines that still serve as the primary line of demarcation among Muslims. On the one hand are the Sunni; they make up between 85% to 90% of Muslims. The remainder are Shia (Shiites), so-called because they were of the "party" (or *Shia*) of Ali.

The initial difference stemmed from disputes about proper succession when Muhammad died. The Shiites insisted that succession should be through Muhammad's family; the Sunni thought that leadership could be held by any pious member of Muhammad's tribe.

The Kharijites. The Kharijites (lit., "seceders") formed the first schism within Islam. They had been strong supporters of Ali. When Ali submitted the matter of leadership to arbitration, some of his most loyal followers deserted him, coming to be known as the Kharijites. They viewed any pious Muslim as qualified for leadership of the Islamic community. Since they regarded the rest of Islam as apostate, they had no reservation about attacks on other Muslim communities. Ali took action against the Kharijites, defeating them two years after he became caliph and driving them underground. Three years later, Ali was assassinated by a Kharijite. Their puritanical vision of Islam became the state religion in a few small Muslim states, and it is still the religion of Oman.

Shiite Divisions

Among the Shiites, numerous divisions have developed. The primary ground for division has been dispute over the rightful successor to the office of *Imam,* the primary leader in Shiite tradition. At first, the assumption was that the *imam* had to be a descendant of Ali and Fatima, Muhammad's favorite daughter. Some came to dispute the necessity of descent from Fatima; most radical were those who questioned the necessity of descent from Ali. The majority of Shias required descent of the *imam* from the Ali-Fatima line.

Zaydis. About eighty years after the death of Ali, a group called the Zaydis formed, following a different line of succession of *imams* from the majority. They argued that the proper fifth *imam* was Zayd, great-grandson of Ali, who had led an unsuccessful revolt against the Umayyads. Their main center was in northern Yemen, where an *imam* ruled until a revolution in 1962 established a republic.

Ismailis (Seveners). Another major break among the Shiites occurred about twenty-five years after the Zaydi break. The issue was over who was the proper seventh *imam.* Ismail, the first-born son of the sixth *imam,* died before his father. His father then appointed the oldest surviving brother of Ismail as successor. Some felt that succession should have gone through Ismail's family, and they formed a new party around the descendants of Ismail. Their group came to be known as the "Seveners" or the "Ismailis." At times, the movement exercised considerable influence, particularly under the Fatimid caliphs of Egypt. Much of the time, however, they survived as an obscure and splintered sect, characterized by esoteric doctrines. They came into prominence again when they moved their center from Iran to India in the 1800s. Under their leaders, known as the Aga Khan, the Ismailis have emerged onto the modern stage as a wealthy, socially conscious, and liberal expression of Islam. The adherents of the main Ismaili branch number about 20 million.

Druzes. The Druzes are a sub-group of the Ismailis, having broken from the main movement in the early eleventh century. They believe that their leader was a manifestation of God. When he disappeared, the Druzes maintained that he had entered occultation (a hidden state), but would return at the end of time. They also maintain that souls are immediately reincarnated. They survive today in small numbers in Lebanon, Syria, and Israel.

Imami (Twelvers). The main group of Shiites is the Imami, who follow a succession of twelve *imams*. The twelfth *imam* disappeared into occultation at age four. He will return, the Twelvers contend, at the end of time, along with Jesus. Of the Shiites, the Imami are most close to the Sunni. One main difference is that they extend the concept of the authoritative *sunnah* not just to Muhammad, but to all twelve *imams*, covering some three hundred years. The largest Imami group is in Iran, where they have been the dominant religious force since the 1500s.

Major Feasts

Muslims celebrate two major annual feasts, each concluding a period of intense religious endeavor. The greater is "The Feast of the Sacrifice," which is also called the "Great Feast" (Id al-Adha). It marks the end of the pilgrimage to Mecca, and recalls Abraham's sacrifice of Ishmael. Muslims, whether on pilgrimage or at home, offer a sacrifice for this occasion, and part of the meat is given to the poor. The second feast is a two- or three-day event called "The Festival of Fast Breaking" or the "Small Feast" (Id al-Fitr); this marks the end of the month-long fast of Ramadan.

Celebrations Associated with Muhammad's Life. Most of the feasts of Islam focus on some event in the life of Muhammad. The Muslim calendar begins in the year 622 C.E., when Muhammad fled from Mecca to the safety of Medina, where he was able to establish the first Muslim society. Muslims mark their New Year with a celebration of Muhammad's flight (*hijra*). Muhammad's birthday is celebrated in the third month; Muhammad's miraculous journey to Jerusalem and ascension to heaven ("Night

Journey") is celebrated in the seventh; and Muhammad's first revelation ("The Night of Power") in the ninth.

Shiite Memorials. The Shiites have additional memorials, related to the martyrdom of Ali and particularly of his son Hussain. The New Year is marked by a ten-day period of mourning, accompanied by reenactments of the suffering and death of Hussain, who, along with his entire family, was killed by Umayyad troops when Hussain tried to gain support for his claim to the caliphate.

CONCLUSION

As the second largest and fastest growing religion in the world, Islam will be a force of considerable influence in years to come.

Internally, Islam is faced with struggles over the essence of its character, particularly as a renewed conservatism gains visibility and influence. The influence of the puritanical Wahhabi perspective, particularly with its rejection of alternative visions of Islam, stands in contrast to the more diversified Islamic experience throughout most of Muslim history. It is difficult to predict to what degree religious uniformity and narrowly defined orthodoxy will dominate the tone of the internal dialogue of Islam.

Equally difficult to predict is the future of the alliance between fundamentalist expressions of Islam and terrorist groups, as in the Taliban and Al-Quaeda alliance in Afghanistan and in the religious zeal behind the suicidal attacks on the World Trade Center and the Pentagon in 2001, and the London subway bombings in 2005. Many Muslims and non-Muslims have attempted to dissociate authentic Islam from terrorism. Whether the alliance between elements of conservative Islam and terrorism is but a chapter in the long history of Islam or whether it represents a pronounced shift in the character of the Islam of the future has yet to be determined.

Eastern Religions

CHAPTER SIX   Hinduism

HISTORY

Origins: Religious and Social Context

Unlike religious traditions that have developed from a singular source (e.g., a founder or an authoritative set of teachings), Hinduism is rooted in a highly varied array of beliefs and practices. "Hindu" and "India" are related, and derive from the Sanskrit word *sindhu*, meaning "river," the modern-day Indus. The Persians pronounced the word "Hindhu," the Greeks made it "Indos," and the Romans called the land around and beyond that great river "India." The term "Hindu" was coined by Muslim rulers of India in the medieval period to refer to all non-Muslim inhabitants of the Indian subcontinent, irrespective of their actual religious affiliations. Even the term "Hinduism" is a construction of the last few centuries, initially used by the British rulers of India to designate the religion of the vast majority of Indians who were not obviously classifiable as Muslims, Jains, Sikhs, Christians, Buddhists, or Parsis. Although we shall use the terms "Hindu" and "Hinduism" because they have widespread currency in the study of religions, it is important to note that most Hindus do not typically identify themselves or their religion as such. When talking about their religion, Hindus are likely to refer to the particular constellation of practices in which they engage, the deities they worship, or their philosophical perspectives on the world and the human condition. They are likely to identify themselves through their caste, their family lineage, their home village, or with some communal or sectarian association.

The Hindu traditions of today are a composite of the indigenous religions of the Indian subcontinent and those of the groups that entered the region over the last four thousand years. The most significant immigrant influence is undoubtedly that of the Aryans ("the noble ones"), an Indo-European people believed by many scholars to have entered the subcontinent before 1200 B.C.E. The religion of the Aryans provided Hinduism with much of those foundations that have subsequently come to be regarded as authoritative. For instance, the cardinal literary compositions of the Aryans, the Vedas, hold a privileged status, since they are regarded by the Hindu priestly class, the *brahmins*, as *shruti* ("divinely revealed"). The indigenous religions include those of the ancient Indus Valley Civilization and tribal folk traditions. While the Aryans left behind a valuable literary record of their religious life through compositions in their sacred language, Sanskrit, scholars face challenges when trying to surmise the exact nature of the non-Aryan, indigenous religious traditions. They must rely primarily upon archeological evidence for the Indus Valley Civilization and more contemporary anthropological observations for the nature of folk religious practices. It is certain, however, that the changes that took place in the Aryan religious forms and practices, as evidenced in their literature in the centuries after their arrival on the Indian subcontinent, were shaped and influenced by their non-Aryan co-habitants.

The Indus Valley (Harappan) Civilization

It was only in the 1920s that archeological excavations began to reveal the existence of a vast civilization that flourished along the Indus river valley between 3300 B.C.E. and 1300 B.C.E. This Indus Valley Civilization is now known as the Harappan civilization, after one of its largest excavated cities, Harappa, and appears to have covered an extensive region well beyond the Indus River, including much of north-western India and modern-day Pakistan. In fact it was larger than the other three great urban civilizations of the time: Egypt, Mesopotamia, and China. Mohenjo-daro, another of the civilization's large cities, along with many of the over one thousand sites discovered thus far, display remarkable similarities to Harappa. Pottery, brickwork, architecture, and writing suggest a unified civilization that developed independently from local village cultures, and not as an outgrowth of influences from the great mid-Eastern civilizations. Although the Harappans had developed a pictographic written script, the specimens that survive are short inscriptions with only a few characters and it has not yet been deciphered. Harappan religion thus needs to be inferred through an examination of the material culture unearthed so far.

An intriguing feature in Mohenjo-daro is a large rectangular pool, designated the Great Bath, which resembles the bathing tanks found in Hindu temples. Its design and location suggest that ritual bathing may have played an important part in Harappan culture. A large number of terra-cotta figurines of females with distinctive headdresses suggest votive rites to goddesses. Especially tantalizing artifacts are thousands of rectangular seals and amulets found in Harappan sites. The surfaces of these seals are often inscribed with Harappan script that may refer to the accompanying pictorial motifs, which are mostly of animals, although there are a few with human figures. Among these seals there are depictions of a figure often referred to by some scholars as the "proto-Shiva." The figure, who wears a horned headdress, appears to be naked, seated in a yogic posture with the soles of the feet pressed together, and is surrounded by animals. In certain seals it appears that the figure has an erect penis. Since the Hindu deity, Shiva, called the Lord of Beasts (Pashupati), is worshipped in the form of a phallic symbol, the *linga*, and is associated with yoga, it suggests that the seals depict an early form of the deity. However, this, and most other suggestions about the nature of Harappan religion are naturally speculative. The

> **TEXTS**
>
> **The Vedas:** The most revered texts in Hinduism, possessing the status of *shruti*, divinely revealed teachings. There are four Vedic sets of texts, known as the *Rig, Sama, Yajur,* and *Atharva Vedas.*
>
> **The Upanishads:** The last portion of each of the Vedic sets of texts. The Upanishads contain philosophical speculation about the nature of reality, the relationship between the Atman and Brahman, and the notion of liberation (*moksha*).
>
> **The Epics:** The two great epics, the *Ramayana* and the *Mahabharata*, provide important information (e.g., social, geographical) not found in the Vedas. The *Ramayana* recounts the exploits of the prince Rama, Vishnu's seventh incarnation. The *Mahabharata* recounts the adventures of the Pandavas, five heroic brothers who fight to regain their kingdom.
>
> **The *Bhagavad Gita:*** "The Song of the Lord." A portion of the *Mahabharata*, consisting of a conversation between Krishna, a human incarnation of Vishnu, and the warrior Arjuna about the purpose of existence.
>
> **The Puranas:** Large, often sectarian, pseudo-historical compendiums, containing mythological accounts of the creation, favorite post-Vedic deities, royal dynasties, and holy places.
>
> **The Tantras:** A vast assortment of texts, often written as teachings of a deity such as Shiva or the Devi, emphasizing ritual, spiritual practice, and the feminine Divine. They criticize orthodox Hindu practices as inferior or elementary.

suggestive affinities to later Hinduism cannot be ignored, but only substantive discoveries, such as the deciphering of the Harappan script, will enable us to make definitive claims about the religious lives of the Indus Valley inhabitants.

The Aryans and Vedic Religion

The prevailing theory among western scholars is that around the time of the demise of the Harappan Civilization, Indo-European settlers began a series of migrations into the Indian subcontinent. They called themselves the Aryans ("the noble ones"), and possessed superior technology to the peoples of the lands they colonized. Their language, which developed into Sanskrit, is the classical tongue of subsequent Hindu literature. Among the peoples they overran were the descendants of the Harappan civilization, some of whom they pushed further south. Hinduism developed from the religious traditions of these non-Aryan cultures, often collectively referred to as "Dravidians" ("Southerners"), their Aryan colonizers, and tribal groups on the subcontinent. Less accepted are propositions that the Aryans developed from the Harappan culture itself, and that the "Dravidians" were other civilizations further to the south.

The interaction between the dominant Aryans and the colonized non-Aryans led to the development of a class system. The three upper classes, consisting of the priestly class or *brahmins*, the ruling class or *kshatriyas*, and the mercantile class or *vaishyas*, were referred to as twice-born. They enjoyed the privilege of participating in a special rite in which they were given a looped sacred thread to wear over a shoulder and across the torso. The ritual was a type of spiritual rebirth, and distinguished these classes from the *shudras*, the servant class. The distinction between the twice-born classes and the *shudras* probably served to separate the Aryans from those they subjugated. It also was a mechanism to keep the Aryans from intermarriage with others, for the class system developed rigid rules inhibiting marriage across classes. This system of four classes, and a more complex subsystem of thousands of occupational subgroups, collectively known as the caste system, is still an enduring feature of Hindu social organization.

Scholars discern changes in Aryan religion in the centuries following the composition of the *Rig Veda Samhita*, the first and oldest of the four collections of Vedic hymns. They speculate that many of these changes were due to the influence of the religion of the non-Aryan indigenous people of the Indian subcontinent. For instance, the *Atharva Veda Samhita*, the fourth Vedic hymn collection, contains assortments of incantations and magical rites (such as instructions on creating a talisman), quite different in style and scope from the *Rig Veda Samhita*, which was composed earlier. Similarly, the Aranyakas and Upanishads, later Vedic texts also regarded as *shruti*, offer a religious view that is substantively different from the sacrificial religion of the Samhitas and Brahmanas. The Aranyakas, or forest texts, emphasize the value of renouncing social life by retreating to the forest to live close to nature. They also offer the option of meditative visualizations by individuals, to replace and accrue the benefits of *yajna*, or sacrifice, thus foregoing the need for a priest. By the late Vedic period, the time of the composition of the Upanishads, in about the seventh century B.C.E., the religious climate in India had changed considerably. There was social and intellectual foment in which traditional structures and beliefs, such as in the class system, the authority of the brahmin class, the *shruti* status of the Vedas, and the true nature of reality were under sustained critical examination.

The Epic Period

The Hindu tradition has two extremely influential epics, composed during a period from about 400 B.C.E. to 400 C.E. These are the *Ramayana (The Story of Rama)* and the *Mahabharata (Great Epic of India)*. The *Mahabharata* contains the *Bhagavad-Gita*, a scripture that is highly revered by Hindus. Although they do not belong to the category of *shruti*, to most Hindus the content of these stories is far better known than the Vedas. In fact, the actions of the characters in the epics and the teachings they convey influence the moral values of Hindus much more explicitly than do the Vedas. Serialized

---

DEITIES

The following became popular in the post-Vedic period and are widely worshiped today.

Shiva: In early theology, identified with the destructive principle of the cosmos. To devotees of Shiva, he is the supreme deity who reconciles the seeming polarities of creation and destruction. Shiva is worshiped in the form of a symbolic erect phallus (*linga*).

Vishnu: All-pervading, and often depicted blue like the sky. Vishnu, through his incarnations (*avatara*), preserves righteousness when forces of chaos and unrighteousness threaten the cosmic order. Vishnu is generally portrayed as a cosmic king, resting on an endless serpent.

Devi: The Great Goddess, also called Durga, the source and summation of all female deities, and the power (Shakti) that animates the entire cosmos. She embodies both a fierce and a benign nature.

Ganesha: Popular, elephant-headed, potbellied deity; leader of Shiva's forces who presides over obstacles.

Krishna: Eighth incarnation of Vishnu; featured in the epic *Mahabharata.*

Lakshmi: The goddess of prosperity and good fortune is often linked with her consort Vishnu. Also known as Shri, she is depicted as a beautiful woman seated upon a lotus.

Kali: Dark, fierce goddess, who symbolizes time and destruction. Kali is often depicted naked, with disheveled hair and a garland of skulls.

Hanuman: The monkey god; he is often worshiped as a protector.

versions of these epics broadcast in the late 1980s attracted the largest audiences for an Indian television show, affirming the influence those ancient religious texts continue to have on Hindus today. The epics mark the rise of many of the deities of classical Hinduism, in particular Vishnu and his incarnations as Rama and Krishna.

An influential seventeenth-century poetic version of the *Ramayana*, written by the poet Tulsidas in a vernacular dialect of Hindi, emphasized Rama's divinity and revitalized the value of devotion (*bhakti*) to him. In tandem with the recent television serial, the persona of Rama and the ideal of his righteous rulership (*Ram-rajya*) have seized the Hindu public imagination, and Rama has become a potent symbol in the Indian political landscape. In the early 1990s, a Muslim mosque, believed to have been built on the site of Rama's birthplace, was destroyed by enraged Hindu activists, and there are pressures by various Hindu organizations to reconstruct a temple on the site. This Ayodhya temple movement is one of the more serious flashpoints in the tensions between Hindus and Muslims in India. It reiterates the abiding potency of the religious epics in the moral, social, and political life of Hindus today.

Philosophical Schools and Hindu Law Books

As early as the first centuries of the Common Era, Hindu literature had expanded to include treatises on philosophy and moral duty. Various schools of philosophy, later classified as orthodox or unorthodox, had developed from the speculative spirit first evidenced in the Upanishadic period. Orthodox Hindu philosophies were those that did not explicitly dismiss the *shruti* status of the Vedas, or the rigid structure of the caste system. Buddhism and Jainism, on the other hand, philosophical schools that questioned the validity of any scripturally "revealed" truths and rejected the attribution of social status based on birth, were categorized as unorthodox.

Interpretation of the teachings of the *Bhagavad-Gita* and the Upanishads forms the basis of Vedanta, one of the most acclaimed schools of Hindu philosophy. Another enduring philosophical school is Yoga, which focuses on psycho-physical disciplines for the attainment of Self-realization. An influential treatise on the subject, known as the *Yoga-sutra*, was written by the philosopher Patanjali in about the second century C.E. There have been numerous commentaries written on Patanjali's system, known as Raja Yoga ("Royal Yoga"), which still forms the foundation of yogas that are currently popular in the West.

The compendiums on social structure and moral duty are called the Dharma Shastras. Composed by brahmin males, these texts reflect social values of the period. Rather than being strict formulations for the exercise of justice, the "laws" in the Shastras are more akin to prescriptions. Sometimes the category of *smriti* ("that which is remembered"), which is discussed below, is used to refer to them alone. The most famous of these Dharma Shastras is the *Laws of Manu*, which presents an idealized set of values that were probably never fully obeyed. It is in these Law Books that the class system is more thoroughly defined. There are prescriptions on the ways in which men and women of the various classes should conduct their lives. They include such details as what values people should hold, whom they should marry, what they should eat, and how and when they should perform life-cycle rites. It is here that the notions of the four stages of life and the four goals of life are developed (discussed later).

GROWTH AND SELF-DEFINITION

Classical Hinduism

PLACES

There are dozens of places that are highly revered by Hindus. These are a few important ones.

Varanasi (Banaras): Located on the river Ganga (Ganges), it is an ancient city, renowned as a center of Vedic learning. It contains temples to many deities, but is regarded as particularly dedicated to the god Shiva.

Badrinath: One of four pilgrimage sites at a source of the river Ganga, and the location of a temple dedicated to Vishnu.

Prayag (Allahabad): Located on the river Ganga, where millions of Hindu pilgrims gather for a purifying bath during the Kumbha Mela.

Kanchipuram: One of the most influential monastic centers of Hindu orthodoxy, reputedly established by Shankara.

Ayodhya: Birthplace and capital city of the mythic god-king Rama.

Hardwar: One of the seven sacred cities of the Hindus. It lies at the foothills of the Himalayas, where the Ganga descends to the plains. About thirty miles upstream lies Rishikesh, another city popular for its many yoga and meditation retreat centers (*ashrams*).

Shrirangam: Great south Indian temple complex dedicated to Vishnu. It is a center of qualified non-dualistic Vedanta philosophy.

Hinduism developed in tandem with rival religious philosophies, such as those of the Jains and Buddhists. These latter groups often received royal patronage, but it was during the period of the Gupta Empire (ca. 320-540 C.E.) that Hinduism flourished in what has come to be known as the Classical period. There were great advances in mathematics and science, and astronomy, architecture, and the arts received imperial support. Sculptures of Hindu deities, temple architecture, and religious dramas reached high standards of sophistication. Shiva and Vishnu grew in prominence as the most venerated gods in Hinduism, while the popularity of the Vedic deities began to recede. Hindu kingdoms expanded their influence beyond the Indian subcontinent into neighboring areas of Southeast Asia, such as modern-day Myanmar (Burma), Thailand, Cambodia, Vietnam, and Indonesia.

Puranic Hinduism and Tantra

A century or so after the Gupta Period, we note the rise of the conception of a Great Goddess, the Mahadevi or Devi. The Devi is envisioned as the amalgamation of all goddesses, and the supreme power that animates the cosmos. She is therefore also called Shakti (Power), and her followers are Shaktas. Followers of Shiva are known as Shaivas, while those who choose Vishnu, or one of his incarnations, as their primary deity are known as Vaishnavas. Mythological tales of Shiva, Vishnu, or the Devi are often contained in a large corpus of writings with a Shaiva, Vaishnava, or Shakta slant. These are known as the Puranas ("ancient writings"). The most important Puranas were composed between 400 and 1000 C.E. although many of the stories they contain belong to much earlier periods. The Puranas reflect the rise of *bhakti* traditions in Hinduism, and strive to resolve the tension between life as an integral member of the social world versus the renunciation of normative social roles and obligations.

Another development in Hinduism after the eighth century is the emergence of hundreds of texts known as Tantras. They reflect a rejection of the social constraints of orthodox brahminism, and likely developed from indigenous oral traditions much older than the dates of the written texts would suggest. Tantra, as the teachings promoted by these texts are called, is characterized by secrecy, and its oral teachings were traditionally passed from teacher to student through a series of graded initiations. Even the texts that promulgate Tantric philosophy are often coded in a symbolic language that needs to be deciphered with the aid of an initiated expert.

Hindu Tantra aims the disciple in the direction of Self-realization, through a unitive encounter with Absolute Reality. Absolute Reality, however, is often conceived of as feminine and also typically formulated as the union of male and female cosmic principles. These principles are respectively called Shiva and Shakti by Shaiva Tantrics. By mapping the microcosm of the human body upon the macrocosm of the universe, and with the aid of esoteric techniques such as Kundalini Yoga, Tantrics seek to invert the process of creation. In this yoga, a psychic energy, believed to lay dormant within one's body, is awakened and manipulated. Sacred utterances (*mantra*), sacred gestures (*mudra*), and richly elaborate symbolic constructions (e.g., *yantras, mandalas*), may be used as meditative aids. Tantrics embrace the acquisition of supernormal powers (*siddhi*), and a wide range of ritual techniques may be used in order to attain these. Tantrics further distinguish themselves into followers of the right-hand or left-hand path. Tantrics on the left-hand path perform rites that invert orthodox notions of purity and pollution, which are of such crucial importance in Hinduism. To the dismay of orthodox brahmins, the consumption of taboo foods and illicit forms of sexual union may play a part in the religious rituals of left-hand Tantrics. Tantrics see these rites as effectively moving the practitioner from a dualistic worldview, composed of bipolar categories, such as pure and polluted, to a holistic, all-embracing reality, in which all of creation is sacred.

Islamic Rule

Islam reached India in the seventh century, but it was only in the twelfth century that it made notable territorial conquests in North India. For several centuries this region was ruled by various Muslim dynasties of Turko-Afghan origin, with their capital in the region of Delhi. In the sixteenth century, Babar, a descendant of the Mongol ruler, Genghis Khan, won a decisive battle over the Muslim rulers in Delhi, initiating two centuries of Mughal rule. The Mughals (from "Mongol") were also Muslims and continued the process of extending Islam further into India. Powerful Mughal rulers such as Akbar conquered and united large portions of south India with the north. The Mughal emperor Aurangzeb, a zealous Muslim, is renowned for his destruction of hundreds of Hindu temples and other forms of persecution. While some Hindus converted to Islam during this period, the majority did not. Syncretic traditions, such as Sikhism, which strove to fuse certain Hindu ideas with Muslim beliefs and practices did develop at this time.

OFFICES

Priest: One who presides over the performance of religious rituals. Priests conduct rituals in shrines and temples, but also at rites such as marriage and death. Priests are mainly brahmin males, but on rare occasions lower caste women perform priestly roles in the worship of certain goddesses.

Guru: One's teacher. Generally used to designate the most important guide and mentor in one's spiritual development.

Yogi: A person who is wholly committed to the discipline of *yoga*, a philosophy promulgating the complete integration of oneself with the Absolute, through specific, often austere, psycho-physical practices.

Swami: A title bestowed on those who have become renouncers through particular organizations, such as the orders founded by Shankara or Chaitanya.

Sadhu: A generic term used to designate any Hindu holy man. These include members of monastic institutions and itinerant ascetics.

Personal forms of religious devotion, such as *bhakti*, and secret rites as promulgated by Tantra, which could be conducted discreetly, naturally gained favor.

Modern Hinduism

Mughal power in India eventually fell to the British who arrived in 1600 C.E. The British came to rule the entire subcontinent from the eighteenth century until Indian independence in 1947. The Christian values of the English rulers, together with the general critique of tradition ushered in by the industrial age, led to the rise of reform movements and the revitalization of Hinduism. For instance, Ram Mohan Roy (1772–1833), a Bengali brahmin, created the Brahmo Samaj, a society to promote the monotheistic values he saw both in Christianity and the Upanishads. The society also fought to abolish certain Hindu practices such as *sati*, the expectation that a pious and devoted wife would voluntarily have herself cremated on the funeral pyre of her deceased husband. The spirit behind such movements was to demonstrate that Hinduism possessed a heritage that was ennobling, offered teachings that were adaptable to modernity and rationality, and held values that were not dissonant with the highest principles of Western religious traditions.

Mahatma Gandhi, who fought relentlessly for the fair treatment of Indians by the British, and eventually for Indian independence from Britain, drew much of his inspiration from traditional Hindu values such as non-violence (*ahimsa*) and religious tolerance. In texts such as the *Bhagavad-Gita*, he found teachings that could be adapted and utilized in the social and political struggles he faced. Gandhi's successful use of *satyagraha* ("the force of truth"), which entailed active, but non-violent resistance to oppression, demonstrated the resilience of Hinduism in the face of centuries of religious subordination, and its capacity to provide guidance that was relevant to the demands of modernity.

Recently, however, the religious tolerance that was the hallmark of post-Independence India has experienced a backlash. Political parties that promulgate fundamentalist interpretations of Hindu values over secular democracy have been garnering greater support. The Bharatiya Janata Party (BJP) rose to power in India on precisely such a pro-Hindu platform. Its religious wing, the Vishwa Hindu Parishad (VHP), is working toward restoring the Hindu temples that were destroyed and replaced by Muslim mosques centuries earlier. A particularly controversial example is the movement to rebuild a temple to the god-king Rama in the city of Ayodhya on the former site of the Babari Masjid, a mosque built by the Mughal emperor Babar in the six-teenth century. The Babari Masjid, built on the site of a Hindu temple believed to mark Rama's birthplace, was demolished by an enraged Hindu mob in 1992.

Another relatively new development is the expansion of Hindu teachings far beyond the confines of South and Southeast Asia. Not only have the Diaspora of Hindus abroad taken their religion with them to all parts of the globe, but the last century has seen a growing interest in Hindu philosophy and psycho-physical spiritual techniques, such as *yoga*. An important figure in the early stages of this process was Swami Vivekananda, a dynamic and articulate religious teacher who attended the World Parliament of Religions in Chicago in 1893. Vivekananda spearheaded Western interest in Hindu mythology and Vedanta philosophy, in particular. Since then, a steady stream of Hindu religious teachers have made their way to the West. Both they and their teachings have been met with a mixture of reverence, amusement, and suspicion by various segments of the populace.

A few decades ago, Maharishi Mahesh Yogi gained widespread media attention when the musical pop group, The Beatles, chose him as their religious mentor or *guru*. His teaching, known as Transcendental Meditation (TM), requires the student to repeat a *mantra* twice daily for a twenty-minute period. The mental tranquility and emotional equilibrium that this practice is reputed to bring has generally made the once alien notion of meditation and its benefits common-place. While Maharishi Mahesh Yogi's TM has conveyed a single yogic technique of

GROUPS / DIVISIONS

Hindu society is divided into over 3,000 castes (jati), social groups into which one is born and within which one is expected to marry. The castes are distributed within four major classes (varna), the first three of which are regarded as "twice-born" (dvija). The political and economic meaning of caste is changing, but traditional values continue to influence Hindu social interactions.

1. Brahmin: The priestly class. They retain and closely guard their authority to learn and teach the Vedas. Generally respected due to their association with religious knowledge and spiritual purity.

2. *Kshatriya:* The ruling class. Members of this group of kings, warriors, and landlords held the power to rule and govern. Their duty was to protect the land and its people. They were entitled to learn the Vedas, but not teach it.

3. *Vaishya:* The mercantile class. They, too, were entitled to study but not teach the Vedas. They raised cattle, farmed, and traded. They constituted the economic backbone of the society.

4. *Shudra:* The servant class. Their duty was to serve the other classes. Since they were not one of the "twice-born" classes, they were not entitled to study the Vedas. They owned little, if any, wealth or property.

5. Untouchables: The classless or "outcaste" group. They consisted of outsiders and lowest caste individuals, generally holding the most inferior and defiling occupations. They are believed capable of spiritually polluting the "twice-born."

mantra meditation to the West, other *gurus* have promoted far more traditional forms of Hinduism, complete with Indian cultural trappings. Swami A.C. Bhaktivedanta Prabhupada, for instance, formed the International Society for Krishna Consciousness (ISKCON) after his arrival in New York in 1965. Members of this Hare Krishna movement, as it is popularly called, publically dance, clash small cymbals, and chant a *mantra* to the god Krishna, as a form of devotional practice (*bhakti*). This practice, together with their traditional garb of Hindu monks which includes shaved heads and saffron colored robes, has made them a highly visible group. Although media attention has focused on scandals in the recruitment practices or in methods of fundraising, these organizations have managed to attract hundreds of thousands of disciples worldwide.

BELIEFS

The Cosmos

Hindus believe that the universe undergoes cyclical processes of creation, preservation, and destruction. Thus the current manifestation of the cosmos is just one of innumerable universes that have preceded it, and that will succeed it. Since antiquity, the Hindus have had a sense of the vastness of cosmic time, and thus each manifestation of the universe is measured in periods of immense duration. It is believed that we currently live in the Kali Yuga, the most degenerate period within a group of four *yugas* known as a Mahayuga. The quality of life and human virtue progressively decline throughout a Mahayuga, which lasts 4,320,000 years. The Kali Yuga lasts for 432,000 years, and only recently began, its onset marked by the great war of the *Mahabharata* in about 3000 B.C.E. A thousand Mahayugas constitute a Kalpa, which is also called a day of Brahma. This is followed by a night of Brahma, of similar duration. One hundred such years (360 days) of Brahma constitute a single manifestation of the cosmos.

The cosmos is made up of many realms, but the basic subdivision is often called the *tri-loka*, or triple world system. These are the heavenly, earthly, and subterranean worlds, each of which contains many subdivisions. A wide assortment of beings occupies these realms. The heavens are the abode of the gods (*deva*), goddesses (*devi*), powerful demons, and other semi-divine beings, such as *apsaras* (angelic-like damsels). The subterranean realms are the abode of lesser demons, ghosts, and a host of other, often malevolent, beings. These beings are not restricted to these realms, for in myth and folklore, human beings in the earthly realm often have encounters with the beings from other realms.

Religious Texts

The oldest extant literary compositions of the Aryans are the Vedas, which consist of four collections, each of which is divided into four parts. The four collections, beginning with the oldest, are the *Rig, Sama, Yajur,* and *Atharva Vedas.* The four parts of each of the Vedas, also beginning with the oldest, are the: (1) Samhitas, hymns of awe and praise of various deities, (2) Brahmanas, texts describing the method of performing sacrificial rituals, (3) Aranyakas, dealing with meditative visualizations, and (4) Upanishads, texts of speculative philosophy on the nature of ultimate reality.

The oldest portion of the Vedic literary corpus is thus the *Rig Veda Samhita,* which contains over a thousand hymns to the many gods (*devas*) and a few goddesses (*devis*) of the Vedic pantheon. The most prominent of the ancient Vedic deities is Agni, the god of fire, who functioned as a messenger conveying sacrificial offerings to the heavenly realms. Other gods, most of whom are personified aspects of the natural world, include Surya (the Sun), Vayu (the Wind), and the goddess Ushas (the Dawn). Prominence, however, does not imply a rigid hierarchy, for the nature of the hymns display what has been termed "henotheism." This is the tendency, in a polytheistic system of many gods, to raise whichever one is being adored to the highest position.

LEADERS

Shankara: Eighth-ninth century, South Indian renouncer, known for his Vedanta philosophy of radical non-dualism (*advaita*). Brahman, which has no attributes, is regarded as the absolute and only reality. The apparent diversity in creation is the result of *maya*, the power of illusion. Shankara is also credited with creating the first Hindu monastic system.

Ramanuja: (ca. 1017-1137). Proponent of Qualified Non-dualistic Vedanta, in which Brahman is the only reality, but possesses attributes (*saguna*), such as compassion and grace. Manifest reality is not an illusion but reflects Brahman's glory.

Madhva: (ca. 1199-1278). Taught a dualistic (*dvaita*) Vedanta, in which Brahman is different from human souls and the creation.

Chaitanya: (1486-1533). Bengali saint who popularized public dance and chanting as a form of devotion to Krishna. The Hare Krishna movement, founded in 1966 by A.C. Bhaktivedanta, developed from Chaitanya's organization.

Ram Mohan Roy: (1772-1833). Founder of the Brahmo Samaj, an organization that emphasized rationalism, humanism, and social reform. Fought against practices such as widow burning (*sati*).

Swami Vivekananda: (1862-1902). Founder of the Ramakrishna movement. Influenced the West's knowledge of Hinduism.

Mahatma Gandhi: (1869-1948). Proponent of active, but non-violent resistance to oppression, used in the struggle for Indian independence from British rule.

Another prominent Vedic deity is Indra, a warrior god associated with thunder and lightening. Indra often battles other cosmic powers, sometimes under the influence of the mysterious hallucinogenic plant, Soma, which is also venerated as a deity. Soma, which some scholars speculate may have been a hallucinogenic mushroom, was consumed by the *rishis*, "seers," who are believed to have discerned the divinely created hymns of the Vedas, and subsequently transmitted them to their disciples. The non-human origin of all the Vedas, from the Samhitas to the Upanishads, confers on them a special status, referred to as *shruti* ("that which is [divinely] heard"). In fact, these texts were for thousands of years mainly transmitted orally from teacher to student, since the act of writing them would have compromised their sacredness. A scriptural justification for the origin of the four classes is found in a Vedic creation hymn, in which a primordial deity, known as Purusha, is sacrificially dismembered by the gods. From his mouth the priestly class was created; from his arms, the ruling class; from his legs, the merchants; and from his feet, the servant class. Orthodox Hindu belief in the divinely inspired origin of the Vedas confers the status of unshakeable truth to assertions such as the class system that are found within it. All other Hindu scripture is regarded as *smriti* ("that which is remembered"), and holds less prestige and authority than *shruti.*

The *Ramayana,* one of Hinduism's influential epics, tells the story of prince Rama, born in Ayodhya, the capital of a north Indian kingdom. Heroic and righteous, Rama proves his valor and wins the hand of the beautiful princess, Sita. Immediately before his coronation, as a result of palace intrigue, Rama is exiled to the forest for fourteen years. He is accompanied by Sita and his half-brother, Lakshmana, both of whom endure the hardships of forest life with him out of love and loyalty. In the last year of their exile, Sita is abducted by a powerful demon, Ravana, and carried to the southern kingdom of Lanka. There, the demon tries to win her love, failing which, he intends to kill her. Rama and Lakshmana search relentlessly for Sita. Finally, with the aid of Hanuman, the general of the monkey kingdom, and his armies, they find and rescue Sita. Rama slays Ravana. Sita proves that she has remained chaste while in the clutches of Ravana by undergoing a fire ordeal. The heroes return triumphantly to Ayodhya where Rama is finally crowned king and rules righteously.

Many of the *Ramayana's* characters come to be regarded as deities, and serve as models upon which many Hindus pattern their lives and values. Rama is seen as the ideal ruler and husband, who exhibits righteousness (*dharma*) in all his actions. He is understood to be a human incarnation of the god Vishnu. Sita is viewed as an ideal wife, who loves her husband, endures hardship and offers him support through life's travails, and who remains loyal to him, even when confronted by fear or temptation. She is associated with the goddess Lakshmi, Vishnu's eternal consort. Hanuman is regarded as the ideal devotee, willing to serve Rama unstintingly in his quest. Some people think of Hanuman as a manifestation of the god Shiva.

> ## THE FOUR GOALS OR AIMS
> *Regarded as the most worthwhile objectives in life.*
> **1. Dharma:** One is expected to understand the meaning of duty or righteousness, and apply it in one's life.
> **2. Kama:** Knowledge of love, sexual and sensual pleasure, joy, and happiness.
> **3. Artha:** The pursuit of wealth, power, and attainments through the development of one's potential.
> **4. Moksha:** Liberation from the bondage to worldly existence, and the cycles of reincarnation, through Self-realization.

Hinduism's second epic, the *Mahabharata*, is held by many to be the world's longest poem. In some 100,000 verses, it tells of the clash between princes of a north Indian kingdom, five heroic brothers, the virtuous Pandavas, and their not-so-virtuous cousins, the Kauravas. Deceit and greed by the Kauravas lead the cousins to a portentous battle, in which the forces of good and evil stand in the balance. Although outnumbered, one of the Pandavas is the nearly invincible warrior, Arjuna, whose charioteer and friend is the god Krishna. Krishna, regarded as a human incarnation of the god Vishnu, has agreed to join the Pandavas in their battle, but in a non-combatant role. Through the defeat of the Kauravas, Krishna seeks to tip the cosmic balance in favor of righteousness.

Arjuna and Krishna survey the armies arrayed on the eve of the battle, and in a crisis of conscience, seeing among his enemies the ranks of relatives, friends, and teachers—people he loves and respects—Arjuna decides not to fight. Krishna strives to convince Arjuna to fight, because without his martial prowess, the Pandavas face certain defeat. The conversation that takes place between them in the dramatic setting of the battlefield is known as the *Bhagavad Gita* (*Song of the Lord*). It is a book of eighteen small chapters contained within the *Mahabharata*, and is one of Hinduism's most cherished scriptures. In the two millennia since its composition, the *Gita*, as it is often called, has served as a source of inspiration for countless numbers, from Hindu philosophers and politicians such as Shankara and Mahatma Gandhi, to Western authors and poets such as Henry David Thoreau and T. S. Eliot.

Among the teachings that Krishna gives to Arjuna, which succeed in convincing him to fight and defeat the Kauravas, are three paths to Self-realization or liberation. These paths, also known as *yogas*, are means through which one can come to know the true nature of the Self. By so doing, it teaches, one is freed from the kinds of conflict that Arjuna faced, which arise from misunderstanding the nature of the Self and God. In the *Gita's* context, the supreme manifestation of God is Krishna, although the text actually acknowledges innumerable forms of the Divine and pathways to knowing God. Arjuna's conflict is seen as a metaphor for every person's struggle for meaning and value in the face of life's apparent meaninglessness. The *Bhagavad Gita's* three cardinal paths or *yogas* teach the individual how to know (*jnana*) the Self and God, how to love (*bhakti*) them, and how to act (*karma*) in any and all circumstances in a way that will lead to Ultimate Truth. The *Gita* is perhaps the earliest Hindu text to promulgate the path of *bhakti* or the Yoga of Loving Devotion. In subsequent centuries, *bhakti* grew in popularity. It developed characteristic acts of worship, and has become the dominant approach used by Hindus today. As one of the most loved and studied books in Hinduism, the *Gita's* status among Hindus is akin to *shruti*, although as part of the epics, it belongs to the category of *smriti*. We shall return to the teachings of the *Gita* shortly.

Hindu Deities

The Hindu tradition boasts a wide assortment of deities, both male and female, who are the objects of devotion (*bhakti*). Myths that recount the origin and major exploits of the gods and goddesses are found in the Epics and the Puranas. Devotional hymns, in the regional, vernacular languages of India, also sing the praises of these divine beings, who are worshipped in homes, temples, and a variety of shrines.

Vishnu is one of the two great gods of Hinduism. Initially he was a god worshipped in the Vedic period, whose popularity grew through his association with Krishna and devotional Hinduism, as evidenced in the *Bhagavad Gita* and Puranic writings. Vishnu is believed to incarnate or descend from his heavenly abode in the form of various *avataras* to reestablish the cosmic balance when the forces of non-righteousness (*adharma*) and chaos threaten to overthrow righteousness (*dharma*) and order. He thus fulfils the role of cosmic preservation in the Hindu trinity of creation, preservation, and destruction. Over time, a standard system of ten *avataras* developed. Rama, the manifestation to defeat Ravana, is regarded as Vishnu's seventh *avatara*. Krishna, who defeated the adharmic Kauravas, is Vishnu's eighth *avatara*. The tenth *avatara* in this cosmic eon is thought to be Kalki, identified with a "white horse," who will rectify the final cosmic unbalance. Vishnu is typically portrayed as a youthful, cosmic king, with four arms, signs of his divine attributes. In his arms he wields a conch shell, a club, a discus, and a lotus flower. He may also be shown reclining on an unending cosmic serpent, symbolizing his activity in the preservation of the process of cosmic cycles from one series of dissolutions to the next. His mount is Garuda, the king of birds.

Krishna is one of the most highly venerated incarnate forms of Vishnu, and is regarded by many as the supreme form of divinity in his own right. Krishna is associated with the pastoral life of cowherders, and has enormous appeal to the rural segment of India's population. He offers devotees a range of forms through which he may be approached, from the adorable baby Krishna of Puranic myths, to the spiritual advisor and political ally and king known through the *Mahabharata* epic. He is also known and worshipped as an irresistible lover through his amorous exploits with the cowgirls (*gopi*) of his pastoral youth. Krishna's dalliance with the *gopis* exemplifies the notion of *lila*, or divine play, which provides a rationale for divine action in the world. The actions of God are not motivated by divine or human needs, but by spontaneous, exuberant playfulness.

Shiva is the other of Hinduism's two great gods. His worship may have originated among the peoples of the Harappan civilization, and he is associated with the god Rudra in the Vedas. He is often seen as the destroyer in the scheme of the Hindu trinity, but his persona extends beyond destruction. His abode is believed to be Mount Kailasa, in the Himalayas, where he dwells with his consort, the goddess Parvati. In appearance, Shiva resembles yogis and ascetics, for

FESTIVALS

There are dozens of festivals celebrated by Hindus with many regional variations. Dates follow a lunar calendar and thus vary each year. The following are a few that are pan-Indian.

Divali: A festival of lights celebrated on the new moon between mid-October and mid-November. Homes are painted and decorated with lamps, firecrackers are set off, and people buy new clothes and feast. The festival marks the victory of light over darkness, and begins the new year for many communities.

Navaratra: A nine-night festival beginning on the new moon between mid-September and mid-October. It is dedicated to the Devi, who is worshiped in a variety of forms, especially as Durga.

Holi: Celebrated in February/March, it commemorates the defeat of the demoness Holika. Exuberant throwing of colored water and powder marks this festival in which the restrictions on gender and inter-caste interactions are partially suspended.

Mahashivaratri: Celebrated in honor of Shiva. Devotees fast during the day and worship Shiva *lingas* throughout the night with offerings of milk and Ganga water.

Kumbha Mela: Every twelve years, Hindus may make a pilgrimage to bathe in a specific part of a sacred river such as the Ganga. The Kumbha Mela held at Allahabad (Prayag) is the largest gathering of people in the world, attracting over fifteen million, who seek purification by ritual bathing.

he is regarded as the renouncer of social norms, *par excellence,* and the embodiment of the transcendental wisdom associated with renunciation. Naked, or clad in animal skins, his body smeared with ashes from the cremation grounds, and with long matted hair tied in a top-knot, he strikes a formidable appearance. Due to his practice of yoga and his sexual continence, he is reputed to possess enormous sexual powers, evident in the erect phallus, the primary symbolic form in which he is worshipped. His mount is the bull, also a symbol of virility. Another widespread portrayal of Shiva is in his form as Lord of the Dance. Sporting four arms, one of which holds the fire that will destroy the cosmos at the end of time, he dances the universe to destruction.

We know little about the goddess worship evident in the Harappan civilization, and goddess worship was not central in the Vedic hymns of the Aryans. But by the sixth century Hinduism developed the notion of a Great Goddess (Devi), who is the summation of all goddesses, and amalgamates all the powers of the male gods. As such, she is the overwhelming power, or Shakti, that animates the creation, and is often referred to as Ma, or Mother. In some measure, the Devi assumes the creative faculty of the Hindu trinity originally associated with Brahma, the Vedic creator god, whose worship is now marginal in contemporary Hinduism. As the formidable goddess Durga, one of the Devi's most common forms, she is depicted as an irresistibly beautiful woman whose numerous arms wield the weapons of the male gods. She rides a great lion, and like Vishnu, battles and destroys various demons to restore the cosmic balance. As the combination of all goddesses, the Devi combines both the qualities of benevolent goddesses, such as Lakshmi and Parvati, and destructive goddesses, such as Kali.

Ganesha, another popular Hindu deity, is depicted with the rotund belly and body of a young boy, and the head of an elephant. He presides over obstacles, removing them if propitiated. He is thus worshipped at the start of religious rituals to ensure that there will be no unexpected problems in the midst of the rite. He is regarded as the son of Shiva and Parvati, and his image is frequently placed above doorways where he acts as a guardian figure.

Hanuman, the monkey general of the *Ramayana* epic, is worshipped as a deity in his own right. He, too, serves as a guardian figure, and some consider him to be a manifestation of Shiva. Because of his unswerving devotion to Rama, he is regarded as the definitive *bhakta,* or devotee, and is a model for all worshippers.

There are numerous goddesses worshipped by Hindus. Three of the most widely worshipped are Lakshmi, Sarasvati, and Kali. Lakshmi is regarded as the goddess of good fortune and associated with the preserver god Vishnu. She wears a red sari, and has money flowing from her fingertips. She stands atop a lotus flower and elephants shower her with water from their trunks, in a symbol of royal consecration. Sarasvati is associated with the creator god Brahma, and is the goddess of creativity and learning. She carries a lute and a book (the Vedas), symbols of her patronage of music, the arts, and education. Kali is a dark, naked, fearsome goddess, with disheveled hair and a lolling tongue that drips blood. She wields a bloody cleaver and holds a decapitated human head in one of her hands. She is associated with Shiva and the principle of destruction. She symbolizes Time, which brings an end to all things. Although these goddesses (*devi*) are often called "wives" or "consorts" of the male gods, they may be viewed as feminine conceptions of the principles with which their male counterparts are associated.

> **THE FOUR STAGES OF LIFE**
>
> *Traditionally prescribed for "twice-born" males.*
>
> **1. Student** [*shishya*]: Originally a period of formal Vedic education with a spiritual mentor (*guru*). Also known as *brahmacharya*, since the student was supposed to lead a pure, austere lifestyle and remain celibate.
>
> **2. Householder** [*grihastha*]: Married life during which one is expected to conduct the household rituals, contribute to society, and raise children, particularly a male heir.
>
> **3. Forest-dweller** [*vanaprastha*]: Option prescribed for grandparents. It involves retiring to the forest to live a simple life dedicated to religious study.
>
> **4. Renouncer** [*samnyasin*]: Highly esteemed option. It requires one to conduct their own death rituals, abandon spouse and society, and live entirely off the alms given by others.

The Human Condition

Hindus believe that the creation operates in an orderly fashion, and is subject to laws that govern its functioning. The principles that operate within the macrocosm are mirrored at the microcosmic level, within smaller portions of the universe. Therefore, like the cosmos, Hindus hold that human beings, and all other living entities, are subject to the cycles of birth, death, and rebirth. This process of repeated rebirth, commonly called reincarnation, is known to Hindus as *samsara. Samsara*, or worldly existence, consists of rebirth in any realm in the triple world system as any life-form. Humans, therefore, are merely one type of creature that happens to inhabit the earthly realm.

All creatures, in the grip of samsaric existence, are subject to the law of *karma*, which is a moral principle of action and causality. Just as a seed may be regarded as the *cause* of a fruit, which is in turn the *effect* of the seed, *karma* is thought to operate on all actions like a seed and its fruit. All actions, including thoughts and feelings, sow karmic seeds. Actions are judged as either good or evil, based on the kinds of karmic fruit they bear. The law of *karma* thus circumscribes the Hindu conception of morality, for it is *karma* that dictates the outcome of a person's every deed. Hinduism does not hold a high god to be the ultimate judge of human actions, for even the gods are subject to *karma*, which is a principle within the very fabric of the creation. Thus the circumstances of a person's life are the result of past *karma*, and it is one's actions in this life that will dictate the circumstances of one's future, in this life and in lives to come. Karmic seeds may lay dormant for many lifetimes before bearing fruit. One's social status (the class into which one is born), gender, fortune, and even the relationships and chance encounters one may have with others, are all held to be the result of *karma*. *Karma* dictates whether or not one is born as a human being, a god, or as some lesser creature. However, all karmic actions, whether good or evil, bind one to samsaric reality, for they generate the causal seeds that will produce future effects. The highest goal in Hinduism is to gain freedom from samsaric existence, and the effects of *karma*.

The Goal and the Path

In the earliest Vedic writings, the goal of human beings appeared to be centered on the performance of beneficial karmic actions, such as the ritual worship of the gods, in order to attain rebirth in the heaven of the creator god, Brahma. By the time of the Upanishads, however, this notion yields to the belief that all rebirths are of a finite duration, and although rebirths in the realms of the gods are of inordinately long durations, they too will eventually end. Thus although rebirth in a heavenly realm is desirable, it is not the ultimate goal. The highest goal in Hinduism is the attainment of Absolute Truth, knowing who one really is and the true nature of reality. This knowledge of the true Self (Atman) is thought to provide liberation from the bondage to *samsara* and *karma*. The term most commonly used for the liberation that accompanies Self-knowledge is *moksha*. Hindus acknowledge that there are numerous ways through which one may attain *moksha*. The paths that one chooses to follow are called *yogas*. The word *yoga* means "union," and could be thought of as a uniting of one's seemingly separate self with one's true Self.

Brahman and Atman

The Upanishads reflect some of the metaphysical thoughts of the late-Vedic period. They mark a fertile beginning to a crucial and enduring aspect of Hindu religion, namely, its speculative, philosophical dimension. A characteristic concern of the Upanishads is the nature of reality and the individual. In the Upanishads, the many deities of the early Vedic period are surmised to be parts of a greater whole, a vast singular power that encompasses and embodies all of creation. This expansive, overarching power, which is both the mysterious source of all creation, as well as the creation itself, is called Brahman (Supreme Being or Absolute Reality). The Upanishads dwell at length on how the apparent diversity of the natural world and the cosmos, including the deities of the early Vedic pantheon, is pervaded by the single, invisible essence that is Brahman. As one Upanishad puts it, although a river may appear to be a separate entity, like all other rivers its source, substance, and end is the ocean, which is just water. So, too, the manifold creation has its source, substance, and end in Brahman. Extending this reasoning further, the individual's essential nature (Atman) is thus intimately grounded in Brahman.

Beyond attempting to establish that Brahman is all there is, the Upanishads emphasize that the nature of Brahman is elusive and hidden from us. Even the self that we traditionally perceive, and with which we identify, is not our real Self (Atman) but the coarse manifestation of our egos, shaped through identification with aspects of the external world and thus subject to continual change. The quest to come upon our true Self (Atman) is an arduous one, often best accomplished through withdrawal from the world and

RITES / RITUALS
Birth and Early Childhood: There is an assortment of Hindu pre-natal rites: some to enhance the chances of producing male offspring; others to enhance the mother's fertility or the safety of childbirth. One rite designates the exact time of birth, for horoscopic purposes. Others, such as the first tonsure, demarcate stages in the child's development.
Sacred Thread: Males of the "twice-born" classes, particularly brahmins, traditionally between ages eight to thirteen, are given a sacred utterance (*mantra*) to repeat, and a loop of sacred thread to wear over their left shoulders. This introduces the student stage of life and the study of the Vedas.
Marriage: Generally arranged by parents, often involving horoscopic consultations. Marriage formally initiates men and women into the householder stage of life, enabling them to fulfill their societal obligations by raising children.
Death: Regarded as the final sacrifice in a person's life. Death rites transform the deceased's spirit from the state of a ghost (*preta*) to that of an ancestor, and restore the family to spiritual purity. Bodies are generally cremated, and the ashes strewn into a sacred body of water.
Renunciation: An optional rite of passage prescribed for people in their old age. A renouncer (*samnyasin*) must perform their own death rituals, and strive to be detached from family and material desires. Renouncers often wear ochre-colored robes, and depend on almsgiving for their livelihood.

a regimen of intense meditative practice. These practices, which may include both bodily and psychological disciplines, are collectively known as *yoga*. If successfully practiced, they may lead individuals to the realization of the true Self (Atman), which is none other than Brahman. In a renowned phrase uttered in one of the Upanishads, a father repeatedly instructs this lesson to his son by saying, "*Tat tvam asi*" ("You are That!"). Since Brahman's characteristics are eternal existence (*sat*), absolute consciousness (*chit*), and unbounded bliss (*ananda*), Self-realization confers one with these immutable attributes. This state is known as *moksha* (liberation), and its attainment comes to be regarded as the ultimate purpose of human existence and the highest religious goal in Hinduism.

Raja Yoga

In the second century, the Hindu sage Patanjali compiled the *Yogasutra*, a treatise that concisely and systematically described the then-current teachings on yogic philosophy and practice. His system has come to be called Raja Yoga ("Royal Yoga"). Patanjali defines yoga as the controlled stopping of all mental and emotional activity, for it is only through this that the true Self may be known. He outlines procedures though which one can bring about this control and the seemingly supernormal powers that one may attain along the way. Yogic practice is built upon a firm moral foundation that requires the practitioner to avoid coveting, stealing, lying, and harming any living thing. Sexual abstinence is also held in high regard in the yogic path. Physical exercises (*asana*) and breath control are important intermediary practices to develop the fortitude for the yogic quest. These have received much attention in the West, where the emphasis is often on the attainment of physical fitness and the removal of stress and its related disorders. Ultimately, however, Raja Yoga is centered on the development of concentration and expertise in meditation (*dhyana*). The attainment of the highest state of contemplative absorption, known as *samadhi*, culminates in yogic Self-realization.

Jnana Yoga

Krishna, in the *Bhagavad-Gita*, offered Arjuna the three paths of *jnana*, *karma*, and *bhakti yoga*. They are often said to reflect the kind of emphasis individuals are likely to place on an approach to Self-realization that suits their varying personal temperaments. Jnana Yoga is the Path of Transcendental Knowledge, and it emphasizes a mental and meditative approach to Self-realization. According to Shankara, the renowned eighth-century

Vedanta philosopher, Jnana Yoga is the best path. Shankara stressed the importance of meditation in penetrating the veil of ignorance (*maya*) that separates us from Absolute Truth. To Shankara, Absolute Truth is Brahman, which is the only reality. Thus Shankara's Vedanta is known as Advaita, which means non-dualistic or monistic. In Shankara's Advaita Vedanta, the sole reality that is Brahman is mistakenly viewed as a multiplicity of forms and entities, due to the power of *maya*. When seeking our Atman through Jnana Yoga, we move beyond the pluralism generated by *maya*'s effects on our consciousness, to discover that the only reality is Brahman. Our Atman is thus none other than Brahman, mistakenly perceived as a separate entity when under the sway of *maya*, but correctly perceived as Brahman when liberated. Attributing qualities to Brahman reduces its true nature, which is beyond attributes. Thus it is called Nirguna Brahman (Brahman beyond qualities). For the conceptual needs of the worshipper or yogic practitioner when thinking about the Absolute, Shankara offers the concept of Saguna Brahman (Brahman with attributes). Among the qualities the mind affixes to Brahman are *sat* (being, existence), *chit* (consciousness), and *ananda* (bliss). Brahman is Being itself. Brahman is the seat of all consciousness. And Brahman is the blissful purified consciousness that has transcended the dualities of joy and sorrow.

SYMBOLS

Om/Aum: Perhaps the most sacred syllable or utterance (*mantra*) in Hinduism. It embodies Absolute Reality, and is the sound that encapsulates all sound. It is chanted in meditation, and precedes most Vedic prayers.

The Cow: Symbol of fecundity and prosperity, it is venerated by Hindus who will not kill or eat it. It is symbolically linked with Krishna, the cowherd deity.

Divine Images: Hinduism abounds with images (*murti*) of deities whose extraordinary appearance immediately conveys their trans-human nature. Multiple arms wielding weapons or other items, symbolize the deity's powers, while specific postures and gestures (*mudra*) convey messages about the deity's nature, mythological acts, or teachings.

Linga: Cylindrical stone effigy of the male reproductive organ and symbol of Shiva.

Yoni: Stone receptacle into which a *linga* is often placed. Effigy of the female procreative organ and symbol of the Devi, it is regarded as the source from which creation emerges. The *linga/yoni* conveys that the Absolute embodies, yet transcends, male and female principles.

Svastika: An ancient symbol of well-being (*svasti*) and auspiciousness. Often used to decorate entrances of homes and temples, or inscribed on sacred objects.

Karma Yoga

The approach offered by Karma Yoga reconciles tensions that emerged between Vedic ritual religion and meditative renunciation. *Karma* refers to acts, classified as either good or evil, that determined one's present condition, and dictate one's future circumstances. The regular performance of Vedic rites was prescribed as a means of acquiring good *karma*, leading to progressively more desirable rebirths. Since the meditative traditions promoted *moksha*, total freedom from the inexorable workings of *karma*, they did not have a place for social action or the performance of rituals. The *Bhagavad Gita's* teachings on Karma Yoga brought a new perspective to how the path of *karma* may indeed be used to attain liberation. The *Gita* prescribes that actions should be performed without attachment to their results. Such detached action frees one from the personal sense of being the actor, and cultivates recognition that all actions emanate from the Absolute. Eventually the individual self detaches fully from the chain of cause and effect that is *karma*. Karma Yoga allows one to engage in the full roster of activities that constitute a traditional life "in the world," such as assuming the responsibilities of family life, community service, and the performance of conventional religious rites. However, if these are done in the spirit of renunciation, by surrendering all acts to the greater power of the Absolute, *karma* is thought not to accrue.

Mohandas "Mahatma" Gandhi (1869–1948) used the principle of Karma Yoga in his approach to active, but non-violent opposition to oppression. He stressed the value of doing the right thing in the struggle for justice by holding fast to the truth, without attachment to the anticipated effectiveness of the actions. In this manner, he believed, the force inherent in truth (*satya*) and non-violence (*ahimsa*), which is the power of the Absolute, would bring about the appropriate outcome. Gandhi's approach was used effectively in India's struggle for independence from British rule, and has been adopted by numerous groups since then, such as factions within the civil rights movement in the United States and the anti-apartheid movement in South Africa.

The notion of selfless action has also developed into other forms of socially responsible activity. Karma Yoga is often viewed as voluntary service at temples, in religious hermitages (*ashram*), and in the community. The Hindu saint Sri Ramakrishna initiated a movement that has established hospitals, medical dispensaries, orphanages, and other charitable missions. These provide opportunities for people to provide service to others, not as an end in itself but as a means for the volunteers to approach God through detached action.

Bhakti Yoga

Bhakti Yoga is the most widely applied approach among contemporary Hindus. This is because Bhakti Yoga, the path of loving devotion, is said to lend itself most easily to human nature. The *Bhagavad-Gita* appears to hold this approach in the highest regard. It also states that Bhakti Yoga is not only open to males and the upper classes of Hindu society. Anyone, including women, *shudras*, and even those outside the caste system are capable of using loving devotion to a deity as a means of achieving Self-realization. Since Jnana Yoga is directed at an intuitive insight into the nature of the highly abstract notion of Nirguna Brahman (Brahman beyond conceptual qualities), and Karma Yoga involves both ritual and self-less action, these paths involve salvation primarily through human effort. Bhakti Yoga, by contrast, elicits the aid of a deity in the attainment of liberation.

By demonstrating love and devotion to a god or goddess of one's choice, devotees invoke the aid of that deity to help them achieve their goals. The spirit behind *bhakti*, however, is to express a self-less love for the divine, without expectation of anything in return. The *Gita* promoted Krishna as the Supreme personalized form of Godhead, equivalent to the Absolute Brahman. In contrast to Shankara's notion of Nirguna Brahman, other Vedanta philosophers, such as Ra-

Defining the Hindu:

While scholars have been hard-pressed to find suitable definitions for what it means to be a Hindu, the Indian Supreme Court has produced the following set of workable criteria.

1. The Vedas should be accepted and revered as the foundation of Hindu philosophy.
2. One should have a spirit of tolerance, and recognizing that truth has many sides, be willing to understand and appreciate the viewpoints of others.
3. One accepts belief in recurring cosmic cycles of creation, preservation, and dissolution spanning vast amounts of time.
4. One accepts belief in reincarnation.
5. One recognizes that there are numerous paths to truth and salvation.
6. One recognizes that although the worship of idols may be deemed unnecessary, there may be many deities (gods and goddesses) worthy of worship.
7. In distinction from followers of other religions, one does not believe in a specific set of theological or philosophical conceptions.

manuja and Madhva, later developed theologies promoting a vision of Saguna Brahman, an Absolute with personalized attributes (*saguna*), who could be identified with the god Vishnu. In the centuries after the composition of the *Bhagavad-Gita*, a host of other Hindu deities, such as Shiva and the Devi, had already become objects of devotion. Hinduism also developed formalized methods of demonstrating loving devotion, such as worship at temples and home shrines, devotional singing, and performing pilgrimages.

Although Jnana, Karma, and Bhakti Yogas are highlighted in the *Bhagavad-Gita*, they are not the only approaches to liberation. Most people utilize a mixture of knowledge, action, and love in their spiritual life, emphasizing one or the other of these elements based on their temperament.

The *Bhagavad-Gita* makes it clear that, whatever the methods used and the forms of the divine venerated, sincerity in the quest will lead to salvation. This openness to variation, as opposed to rigid adherence to specific dogmas and doctrines, becomes another hallmark of Hinduism.

PRACTICES

Community Structure

The vast majority of Indians live in villages of a few hundred to several thousand inhabitants. Especially in these rural settings, caste still plays an important role in the social structure of Hindu communities. Hindus in villages mostly work in traditional hereditary occupations, such as in agriculture or as artisans, while members of the priestly class (brahmins) still conduct religious rites. The effects of modernization and the political changes in post-Independence India on the caste system are more evident in urban settings and in the Hindu Diaspora. Although many Hindus in these locales may no longer pursue hereditary occupations, caste still functions strongly in decisions regarding marriage.

Sacrifice

Vedic religion included the performance of sacrificial rituals, some extremely elaborate, which centered on animal or vegetable offerings into the sacred fire. While many of these rites, collectively known as *yajna*, are no longer practiced, the method of performing them, described in the Brahmanas, are still known to certain members of the brahmin class. Hindu patrons, even today, commission brahmin priests to perform certain types of *yajnas* on special occasions. The exact utterance of various Vedic verses, known as *mantras*, accompanies the priest's ritual actions during *yajna*. *Yajna* is believed to be the mechanism through which the gods are nourished with the offerings made into the sacred fire. In return, the gods reciprocate by bringing the rains, or providing the patron with offspring, generally ceding to the patrons their desires for social and natural order. Since the priests are the only persons with the knowledge of the sacred Sanskrit *mantras* and the capacity to utter them correctly, they are the indispensable actors in the performance of *yajnas*.

The Religious Specialists and Institutions

Members of the brahmin class are the primary functionaries in religious education and the performance of religious rites. Learned members of the brahmin class may specialize in reading and teaching Sanskrit grammar and scripture, while others may be commissioned to conduct recitations of the Vedas or other Sanskrit scriptures. Yet others may work as temple priests, or be commissioned to preside over communal or private religious rituals, including rites of passage.

The Priest. The temple priest is a functionary, generally male, whose occupation is to care for and conduct the worship rites for a temple deity. The Hindu temple is an abode where the deity is believed to reside. Often through specific rituals of invocation, but also because the presence of a deity has been discerned in a particular locale, a shrine develops around the god or goddess abiding there. The image of the deity may be a stone or metal statue, or some discernable symbolic form, such as a *linga* of Shiva. Goddess shrines often have a cloth-draped image with prominent eyes. Hindu temples/ shrines may be as small as a cupboard or as large as a small city. The great South Indian temple to Vishnu at Shrirangam has some 50,000 inhabitants and functionaries on its premises. Large temples may have dozens, or hundreds, of smaller shrines to lesser deities on their premises.

The henotheistic principle found in the hymns of the Vedas is also evident in Hindu temples. Each temple places a particular deity in the supreme position, with the other gods and goddesses serving as minor officials in a monarch's palace. Hindus may worship at several temples through the course of the year, month, week, or even in a single day, thus, for example, giving Ganesha the preeminent

YOGAS

Yogas are paths of physical and psychological practices whose goal is liberation (moksha). There are numerous types of Yoga in Hindu practice. These are some of the most well-known.

Karma Yoga: A path of selfless action described in the *Bhagavad-Gita*. It emphasizes detachment from the outcome of all actions, which should be performed in a spirit of sacrifice to the divine.

Jnana Yoga: A path that centers on the intellect and regarded as difficult. Scriptural study, inquiry into the question, "Who am I?" and meditation may be regarded as belonging to this quest for transcendental knowledge (*jnana*).

Bhakti Yoga: The *Bhagavad-Gita* introduces this approach, which calls for loving devotion (*bhakti*) to a deity. Devotional worship (*puja*) is the most common way in which loving devotion is expressed, although it may take other forms, such as prayer, song, and pilgrimage.

Raja Yoga: Royal Yoga, which centers on stopping the "turnings of thought" and offers eight aspects (limbs) that need to be developed in order to perfect it.

Kundalini Yoga: The yoga of the "coiled" (*kundalini*) energy, envisioned as a dormant serpent. In Hindu Tantrism, this awakened energy is understood to convey supernatural powers.

Hatha Yoga: A yoga emphasizing posture (*asana*) and breath work. It is popular in the west, since the focus is on physical and psychological health.

place of worship at his temple, and the Devi preeminence at her abode. The temple priest's actions parallel those of a dedicated royal servant, but are directed to the deity, who is regarded as a divine monarch. Thus the priest may awaken early, and after performing his own ablutions, proceed to wake up, dress, and feed the deity with appropriate rituals. He will perform regular formal ritual worship (*puja*) to the deity, as well as for the benefit of visiting devotees through the day, and may even put the god or goddess to bed at night.

Guru. In the distant past, male members of the twice-born classes would receive formal education in Sanskrit scriptures from a brahmin teacher, known as a *guru*. The *guru* would educate each person in their specific class duties. Over time, the knowledge of Sanskrit receded primarily to the brahmin class, and the formal system of residential school with a brahmin *guru* has yielded to the public education system. Nevertheless, there are still families who send their children for religious education with brahmin *gurus*. Others opt for such studies when they are older. The term *guru*, although now applied to all sorts of teachers, has not lost its spiritual significance. In theory, in the spirit of the Upanishads, whether one is teaching grammar, music, or wrestling, the *guru* is expected to teach the student deeper religious truths through the vehicle of their particular discipline. Ultimately, the mastery of music, language, or any skill is believed to derive from grasping the essence of Absolute Reality, the true source of all creative endeavor. Thus Self-realization is the goal and end of all learning. Here, too, the *Gita's yogas* of learning and doing with love and devotion, find application.

The Renouncer. Some of the most visually arresting religious specialists in the Hindu tradition are those who have opted for the path of renunciation. Attempting to detach themselves from the conventions of society, many renouncers revert to various states of naturalness, rejecting the dictates of fashion and socio-cultural convention. Some of these renouncers may have long, matted hair and beards, and don simple clothes, while others may eschew clothing entirely. Some emulate the lifestyles of other renowned renouncers, or engage in rigorous psycho-physical practices to discipline the mind and gain liberation. Those who practice physical or mental forms of *yoga* are called *yogis*, although the term is often applied loosely to any spiritual seeker. Certain renouncers may emulate the mythic life of the great god Shiva, who is regarded as a *yogi, par excellence.* Like Shiva, they may frequent the cremation grounds, smear their near naked bodies with ashes, live off alms provided by householders, and engage in severe forms of asceticism. They may smoke cannabis to enhance their visionary capacities, and undertake formidable pilgrimages to various holy sites in India, and in the Himalayas, an abode of the gods.

A Hindu may choose a path of renunciation at any time, but the Dharma Shastras prescribe it for a later stage in one's life. Those who choose to undergo a formal rite of renunciation, with the trappings of a particular institution, may be recognized by the type of clothing they wear, their accoutrements (such as a begging bowl and staff), sect marks (applied with sandalwood paste or ash to the forehead), or their new names. For instance, the Vedanta philosopher, Shankara, reputedly initiated a monastic system for renunciation. In a public rite with several others, would-be renouncers shave their heads, perform their death rituals, and don ochre-colored robes. They are given the title of *Swami*, and are expected to live pious lives of poverty and chastity, while engaged in their search for liberation. Such *Swamis* are more likely to be found engaged in a type of retreat at various monastic centers (*ashram*) throughout India, such as at Kanchipuram or Haridwar, where they spend their time in reading, teaching, and contemplation.

The Religious Cycle

Hinduism is a religious tradition often characterized by its emphasis on ritual life. In Vedic times, *yajna* sacrificial rites formed the backbone of religious life. In the modern period, too, Hindu life is orchestrated by religious ritual prescriptions throughout one's life. These include life cycle rites, daily religious practices, and calendrical festivals.

The Dharma Shastras sought to reconcile the tension between the external, ritual worship of deities and internal, meditative practices. They recommended that twice-born males should demarcate their lives into periods,

TERMINOLOGY

Shruti: (lit., "divinely heard"). This category is applied exclusively by orthodox Hindus to the Vedic Samhitas, the Brahmanas, the Aranyakas, and the Upanishads. The divine origin attributed to these texts gives them a status akin to the "revealed scriptures" of other traditions.

Smriti: (lit., "remembered"). This category of Hindu sacred writings includes all that is not *shruti*. It includes the Epics, the Puranas, and the Tantras, although it is particularly applied to the Dharma Shastras, which are sometimes collectively called *smriti*. Certain *smriti* texts, such as the *Bhagavad-Gita*, although not classified as *shruti* by Hindu orthodoxy, are treated by many Hindus as divinely revealed.

Self: Numerous Sanskrit terms are used to describe one's inner spirit or soul (e.g., *jiva, atman, purusha*). However, because of the pervasive influence of non-dualistic Vedanta philosophies, the term Atman is most often translated as "Self." This Self is generally distinguished from the idea of a personal soul, because it is often regarded as trans-personal, even being equated with Absolute Reality (i.e., Brahman).

Brahman: (lit., "the Expansive"). Several Hindu words derive from the Sanskrit verbal root, "brih," to expand. For instance, *Brahman* refers to the all-encompassing, Absolute Reality. The Brahmanas are Vedic ritual texts. The brahmins are members of the priestly class, while Brahma is the name of the Hindu creator god.

fulfilling each stage to the best of their abilities, before progressing to the next state. The prescribed Four Stages of Life were: Student, Householder, Forest-Dweller, and Renouncer. Each stage is characterized by particular activities that aid in the development of the Four Aims or Goals of Life. These are: Dharma, Kama, Artha, and Moksha.

There are a number of rituals that mark the early years of childhood, from birth, naming, to the first eating of solid food, and even the first haircut, in which the hair is completely shorn. Each rite sanctifies an important juncture in life, moves the child towards a greater sense of individual identity, and often mimics the motif of renunciation that leads to liberation. This is well evidenced in the Investiture with the Sacred Thread ritual, traditionally prescribed for twice-born boys between the ages of eleven and thirteen. With head shorn, the boy receives his last mouthful of food from his mother's hand, and he takes up the saffron robe, staff, and begging bowl of the renouncer. He is given a sacred loop of string to drape across his torso and over his left shoulder. The ceremony marks a sort of formal rebirth into the spiritual life and a beginning of the Four Stages of Life.

Traditionally, the first stage, the student life, involved residence with a brahmin *guru*, where one learned literacy. In particular, this was a time where the *guru* instructed the student in the *dharma* of their particular caste. Thus a *brahmin* child would learn the *dharmic* obligations and behaviors appropriate to brahmins; a *kshatriya* child would learn about politics and warfare; and a *vaishya* child would learn the *dharma* of business practices. The instruction of these virtues has now shifted to the public education system and to the family. Public education has also opened the doors to women and the lower classes. Sexual continence was traditionally prescribed during student life, and the prevalent cultural characteristic among Hindus even today is to remain celibate during one's stage as a student.

Entry to the householder stage was marked by the rite of marriage. Hindu marriages, even today, are generally arranged by the parents or older relatives of the prospective partners, often in consultation with an astrologer, to determine the couple's compatibility. Marriages are conventionally arranged within classes, and there are strong traditions against women marrying beneath their class. Tradition also prescribes that a woman's highest spiritual practice is dedication to her husband, whom she is to regard as her spiritual teacher (*guru*), and even a god. Marriage sets the partners on the journey of building a family, in which at least one male child is still a strong preference for Hindu couples. Sons generally carry on the lineage, and a son is believed to be indispensable in the performance of the death rites for his parents. Although women appear to have enjoyed an honored status in the early Vedic period, their position in Hindu society deteriorated subsequently. In most Hindu social groups, daughters involve a financial burden, since they are expected to bring a dowry with them on marriage, even though the practice has been legally abolished in India. Furthermore, old religious texts, such as some Dharma Shastras, frequently portray women as fickle, vain, and sensual, and thus in need of constant control by the male members of the family. Notable exceptions are Tantric texts, many of which elevate women to the status of divinity.

It is during the householder stage that the goals of *kama* and *artha* are pursued with vigor. *Artha* refers to the development of skills and the know-how to provide for one's family. Traditionally, for men this meant successfully earning a livelihood, while for women it meant managing the affairs of the household. The householder stage also marks a Hindu's entry into sexual life. *Kama*, the legitimate pursuit of love and pleasure, in all forms, is prescribed for this stage.

When a man and woman are grandparents, the Shastras prescribe that they move to the next stage. The forest-dweller stage is a sort of retirement from material and sensual acquisitions. After passing on their inheritance to their children, a man and his wife may retire to a humbler, more isolated abode, and begin their contemplation of the fourth and highest goal, *moksha*. While in ancient times a hut in the forest was prescribed, nowadays the devout might retire to a holy city such as Varanasi or Rishikesh. The final stage, which is rarely embraced, is that of the *samnyasin*, or renouncer. Here a man (and it is mainly men who become renouncers) performs his own death rituals, and takes up the ochre robe, the begging bowl, and staff. He is expected to wander the world, not depending on or clinging to anyone or anything, but engaged fully in the pursuit of liberation. When a renouncer dies, he may be entombed or have his body delivered to a sacred body of water, such as the river Ganga (Ganges). For others, death is followed by cremation, and a series of rites are performed to insure that the soul does not end up as a disembodied ghost. Cremation reiterates the procedures of Vedic *yajna*, and may be regarded as a Hindu's last sacrificial rite.

The Religious Calendar

The Hindu religious calendar comprises a complex network of rites that occur daily, weekly, monthly, yearly, and even during longer cycles of time. For instance, there are the bathing and water oblation rituals that are to be performed thrice daily by members of the twice-born classes. Only devout members of the upper classes still adhere to these prescriptions. Hindus may visit temples daily or weekly, based on pledges they have made, although there is no formal expectation that they do so. Religious rites may follow either the solar or lunar calendar, and it is not uncommon for a rite to begin, for instance, at moon-rise on the fifth day of the waxing fortnight of a particular lunar month. There are days of the week that are ruled by pernicious planets, such as Mars or Saturn, and temple visits with appropriate rites are prescribed to ward off their effects.

Every deity enjoys a particular festival period in the year, and particular regions of India are renowned for their celebrations in honor of certain deities. For instance, Hindus in the state of Maharashtra celebrate the festival of Ganesha with great exuberance, while the Bengalis are known for their worship of the Great Goddess, Durga. In both festivals, colorful life-size clay images of Ganesha and Durga, respectively, are fabricated by artisans and worshipped for several days in homes and community settings. At the festival end, the images are delivered into a sacred body of water. The goddess Lakshmi is worshipped during the Festival of Lights, called Divali, when Hindus decorate their homes with lamps, and set off fireworks. The lights are believed to attract good fortune into the home. On the festival of Holi, societal boundaries are dissolved as young and old, teacher and student, brahmin and *shudra*, men and women, exuberantly splash colored water and powders on each other. The carnivalesque atmosphere of Holi offers a temporary catharsis from the otherwise rigid constraints of the class and social system. Krishna's birthday is another popular holy day, as is the Great Night of Shiva (Mahashivaratri). Most Hindus are likely to participate in the festivals to the great gods and goddesses every year. However, there are innumerable regional and minor deities that only receive worship by select groups of devotees on specific occasions.

Hindus often go on pilgrimages to renowned sacred sites. Four holy temples in the high Himalayas, located by tributary sources of the Ganga, and a Brahma temple by the sacred lake of Pushkar are examples of such places, although there are hundreds throughout the Indian subcontinent. There is a pilgrimage circuit around holy city of Banaras, and a few Hindus even perform pilgrimages around the river Ganga, or the mountain abode of Shiva, Mount Kailasa. One of the most dramatic gatherings takes place once every twelve years, when Hindu pilgrims flock to the confluence of the Ganga and Yamuna rivers. There, pilgrims seek to bathe in the rivers at a specific astrological conjunction when the waters are believed to be transformed into a spiritually-purifying nectar. The Kumbha Mela, as this festival is called, is the largest gathering of humanity, attracting over fifteen million people.

CONCLUSION

Because of its liberal attitude to its adherents' conceptions about the nature of divinity, and their methods of approaching, encountering, or even uniting with divinity, the Hindu tradition encompasses a richly complex assortment of scriptures, rituals, and patterns of belief. At one level of discourse, there is little in any human being's religious life that a Hindu would deem non-Hindu. And yet, historical and cultural forces have given Hinduism a particular set of characteristics that stand in tension with the aforementioned spirit of openness. Thus orthodox Hindus see the Vedas as sacrosanct and the caste system as divinely dictated. There are innumerable prescriptions for men and women, of each class, at every stage of their lives, to keep them aligned with what is dharmically appropriate. When conjoined with its notions of purity and pollution, auspiciousness and inauspiciousness, its large number of deities, festivals, and other calendrical observances, the Hindu tradition provides its followers with a worldview that thoroughly governs their lives. One might even find the system oppressive in its rigidity. And yet, as a complement to this highly structured system, one notes that the most highly regarded religious pursuit is to step outside of this system. Renunciation entails a detachment from all social structures, including the religious ones. Thus Hinduism upholds that all of humanity's religious and social forms, even the ones that Hinduism itself promotes and holds in highest regard, are ultimately merely conceptual frameworks that human beings have created, often to provide life with a moral order and social stability. The renouncer detaches from all these conceptual frameworks, in search of the highest truth. Seeking this highest Truth, which transcends mere human worldviews, is the Hindu's noblest religious pursuit. And Hindus regard the attainment of Absolute Truth as a human being's highest achievement, bestowing with it realization, immortality, genuine freedom, and everlasting peace.

CHAPTER SEVEN

Buddhism

The Buddhist tradition is based upon the teachings of Siddhartha Gautama, a sage born in a Himalayan foothill kingdom and who taught in the area of the Ganges/Ganga river valley. He is reputed to have attained the highest state of insight into the nature of reality and hence came to be called the Buddha, or the Awakened One. His teachings eventually spread throughout the Indian subcontinent and beyond, into most parts of South, Southeast, and East Asia, undergoing philosophical elaboration and culturally moderated changes along the way. Although some of the later forms of Buddhism may appear quite different from its earlier forms, they share common beliefs and values regarding the goal of Buddhahood.

HISTORY

Origins

The story of Buddhism begins earlier than the life of Siddhartha Gautama, for he was born in a time when the search for Truth had become commonplace. Like the Sophists in ancient Greece, Asia too had numerous wandering philosophers known as *shramanas*. In India, *shramanas* wandered the subcontinent, questioning and discussing the meaning of human existence with other philosophers, or debating those with whom they disagreed. Certain *shramanas* gained sizeable numbers of disciples, which led to the development of religio-philosophical schools based on their perspective on life. The Sanskrit term *darshana* refers to one's worldview, and the teachings of various *shramana* schools came to be regarded as representative of a particular *darshana*. Thus the teaching of the Upanishadic sages on the nature of Atman and Brahman was viewed as encapsulating a particular *darshana*, later given the general name of Vedanta. Similarly, the teachings of the sage Mahavira developed into the *darshana* known as Jainism. A *darshana*, it should be emphasized, is both religion and philosophy, since these categories were not separated from each other in India, as came to be the case in the West. It was into this milieu of religio-philosophical speculative investigation that Siddhartha was born in about 500 B.C.E.

Life of Siddhartha Gautama

The exact dates of Siddhartha Gautama's birth and death are still debated by scholars, but all Buddhist texts acknowledge that he lived to the age of eighty. Some scholars, dating backward from the known dates of the rule of the emperor Ashoka, who patronized Buddhism and left behind inscriptions, place Gautama's death as recently as 267 B.C.E. Others, based on information in the chronicles of the island kingdom of Sri Lanka, and from other archeological and textual evidence, date his birth at 563 B.C.E. Most Buddhists are familiar with an extensive number of stories about Siddhartha Gautama's birth and teaching life, but scholarly investigations highlight that the historical accuracy of these stories is questionable, for they were recounted in scriptures written centuries after his death.

Early scriptural sources tell us that Siddhartha was born in the Gautama family of the Shakya clan. The Shakyas inhabited a region in the foothills of the Himalayas, and Siddhartha was born in the town of Lumbini in present-day Nepal, close to Kapilavastu, the city governed by his father. Although raised in a warrior caste, he is believed to have renounced his governing birthright and joined the *shramana* way of life at the age of twenty-nine. After experimenting with arduous asceticism, which was commonly believed by many *shramana* groups to be necessary for the discovery of Absolute Truth, he devised a path that mediated between self-mortification and sensual indulgence. This contemplative approach led him to the attainment of *nirvana*, the apex of meditative insight, at the age of thirty-five. Thenceforth he was known as the Buddha, the Awakened One. "The Buddha" is thus a title, not a name, and may be applied to any being that has attained the highest state of awakening. As an enlightened sage (*muni*) from the Shakya kingdom, Gautama was and still is often referred to as Shakyamuni Buddha.

The Buddha spent the next forty-five years wandering the area of the kingdoms of Koshala and Magadha in the Gangetic river plain, attracting disciples through his teachings. He formed a monastic organization known as the Sangha, or community, based on virtue, moderation, and meditative practice, and managed to attract some royal patronage during his lifetime. Through this patronage certain areas of forest land were granted to him and his monks as resting places. In time, monasteries, known as *viharas*, developed in these and other places, where monks could take shelter from their wanderings, particularly during the rainy season. These *viharas* also provided access to the Buddha and other monks for people who were drawn to Buddhist teachings, but unable to join the Sangha.

Growth and Self-Definition

The Buddhist Councils and the Tripi-taka. It was not long after the Buddha's death that disputations arose about the exact nature of his teachings. Buddhist writings indicate that such conflicts even arose during the Buddha's own lifetime, but that he was generally able to mend rifts by clarifying his teachings for the benefit of the disputants. A common source of difficulty was the interpretation and application of monastic rules, since certain factions of the Sangha leant towards greater laxity, while others wanted more disciplinary rigor. Traditional accounts hold that at the first rainy season retreat after his death, a First Council was held in the city of Rajagriha to codify the Buddha's teachings. Five hundred monks, all Arhats, "worthy ones" (those who had attained *nirvana*), gathered to recite all of the teachings. Two such standardized collections, known as Pitakas, literally "baskets," were prepared. These were the *Sutra Pitaka,* a collection of

GROUPS / DIVISIONS

Theravada: "Doctrine of the Elders." The only surviving branch of the non-Mahayana Buddhist groups. It is the dominant form of Buddhism in Sri Lanka, Myanmar (Burma), Thailand, and other parts of Southeast Asia. It is characterized by the pursuit of *nirvana*.

Mahayana: "Great Vehicle." Form of Buddhism that emerged in the first century and spread from north India to China and Japan. It is characterized by the ideal of the *bodhisattva*, one who strives to bring all beings to *nirvana*.

Vajrayana: "Diamond or Thunderbolt Vehicle." Form of Buddhism characterized by Tantric practices, which became dominant in Tibet, and later spread to Mongolia and India.

Zen: Known as Chan/Ch'an in China, it is a Mahayana Buddhist tradition that emphasizes meditation in the attainment of *nirvana*. In Japan, two main schools of Zen emerged, the Rinzai and the Soto.

Pure Land: A school of Mahayana Buddhism characterized by faith in the compassion of the Buddha Amitabha. Adherents hope to be reborn in Amitabha's Pure Land, also known as the Western Paradise.

the Buddha's discourses, and the *Vinaya Pitaka*, a collection primarily of teachings on monastic discipline. A third basket, the *Abhidharma Pitaka*, consisting of philosophical arguments developing the Buddha's teachings, was composed later. These three Pitakas, known as Tripitaka, constitute the Canon for some Buddhist schools, and are included by virtually all Buddhist groups in their larger collections of canonical materials. Scholars question the complete authenticity of the events of the First Council as they are recounted in the Buddhist texts, and see in these stories an attempt by the Sangha to consolidate the community and legitimate a particular collection of teachings.

About a hundred years after the First Council, disputes on matters of monastic discipline led to the convening of a Second Council at Vaishali. Unfortunately, the Second Council was not able to resolve the tensions, and soon after the Sangha split into two groups. One group was known as the Sthaviravada, or The Doctrine of the Elders, and the other was called the Mahasanghika, or Great Community. Subsequent centuries saw the splitting away of several other groups from the Sthaviravada, and the formation of another important Buddhist movement known as the Mahayana, or Great Vehicle. Most of these divisions and developments were based on variations in philosophical interpretations on the nature of the self, and the constitution of reality, Buddhahood, and its attainment. However, a Third Council that was convened by the emperor Ashoka around 250 B.C.E. primarily concerned itself with issues of monastic discipline. It was also in this period that the *Abhidharma Pitaka* ("Basket of Further Teachings") was taking on its most developed form.

Emperor Ashoka

Ashoka, of the Mauryan dynasty, inherited a vast empire in 268 B.C.E. with its capital at Pataliputra (modern-day Patna). After suppressing a rebellion in the southern kingdom of the Kalingas, in which over a hundred thousand people lost their lives, Ashoka felt enormous remorse for the suffering he had inflicted, and committed himself to the teachings of Buddhism. He erected stone pillars throughout his empire with inscriptions telling of his conversion to a more non-violent approach to governing his territory. Ashoka's empire encompassed much of today's India, including regions in present-day Pakistan and Afghanistan. His patronage and promotion of Buddhism extended to his sending missionaries as emissaries to neighboring lands and thereby spreading the religion beyond the Indian subcontinent. The semi-historical Buddhist chronicles of Sri Lanka tell how Ashoka's own son and daughter, a monk and a nun respectively, came to that island nation and converted all the inhabitants. It was the Theravada school of Buddhism that was most patronized by Ashoka, although he supported Buddhism generally and many other religions, such as Jainism, as well. Ashoka is also reputed to have opened up the ten original *stupas*, funerary mounds in which the Buddha's cremated remains were entombed, and distributed these into thousands of *stupas* throughout his empire. Not only did these *stupas* provide Buddhism with a highly visible profile far and wide, they likely served as focal points for a burgeoning cult of devotion to the Buddha.

The Development of Mahayana and Non-Mahayana Schools

Traditional accounts suggest that some eighteen Buddhist schools—although there were likely others—developed from the original Sangha as splits occurred due to differing interpretations of Abhidharma doctrine. One of these schools, which got established in Sri Lanka through the patronage of Ashoka, took the name Theravada, which in the Pali language, like the Sanskrit Sthavira-vada, also means the Doctrine of the Elders. The schools that developed from the Sthavira-vada, including the Theravada, were distinguished from the other major branch of Buddhism known as the Mahayana. The Mahayana developed in conjunction with the Maha-sanghikas, the group that broke with the Sthavira-vada during the first split in the Sangha shortly after the Second Council. The manner through which the Mahayana arose is still unclear to

LEADERS
Shakyamuni: "Sage of the Shakya Clan." Title used by Buddhists to refer to Siddhartha Gautama, the historical Buddha. He lived between the sixth and third centuries B.C.E., attained *nirvana* at the age of thirty-five, and preached until his death at the age of eighty.
Ashoka: King of the Mauryan dynasty who ruled much of the Indian subcontinent from 273-236 B.C.E. After a bloody campaign for which he felt great remorse, he converted to Buddhism, helped to establish it throughout his empire, and to spread it to neighboring countries such as Sri Lanka.
Nagarjuna: Second/third century C.E. Buddhist philosopher and founder of the Madhyamika ("Middle Way") school. He taught that the ultimate characteristic of all things is Emptiness (*shunyata*).
Asanga: Fifth/sixth century Buddhist philosopher, who together with his brother, Vasubandhu, is credited with founding the Mahayana school of Yogachara Buddhism.
Padmasambhava: Eighth century missionary. Schooled in the Tantras, he emphasized elaborate rituals and magical practices, establishing the Vajrayana form of Buddhism in Tibet.
Bodhidharma: A semi-legendary Indian meditation master, who founded the Chan school of Buddhism in China in the sixth century. Connected in legend to the martial art, kung-fu.
XIVth Dalai Lama: Most widely known contemporary Buddhist leader, Tenzin Gyatso, a Nobel laureate for peace and head of the Tibetan government in exile.

scholars, although its relationship to the Maha-sanghikas is evident. Certain Maha-sanghika texts contain rudimentary Mahayana ideas, such as the tendency to emphasize the divine rather than the human nature of the Buddha, and its enhanced participation of the laity in the Buddhist experience. The Mahayana designated itself as the Great Vehicle (Mahayana) and referred to all other schools, somewhat pejoratively, as belonging to the Hina-yana or Lesser Vehicle. The Mahayana promulgated the *bodhisattva* ideal, which accentuated the character of the individual being (*sattva*) who embarks on the journey to the highest form of enlightenment (*bodhi*).

The earliest Mahayana texts, known as the *Perfection of Wisdom Sutras*, appeared in the first century B.C.E. and continued to be composed until the seventh or eighth century. They emphasized the importance of perfecting various qualities on the journey to Buddhahood, and held the perfection of wisdom (*prajna*) as the highest attainment. Two major schools developed within the Mahayana tradition. These are Madhyamika (Middle Way) and the Yogachara (Practice of Yoga) schools. The first was founded by the philosopher Nagarjuna in about 200 C.E. Nagarjuna used dialectical logic to develop the concept of Emptiness. He argued that conceptualization (ideas, subsequently articulated in words) is often at the root of erroneous perspectives on Truth. The Ultimate Truth (i.e., the way things really are), which is realized upon the attainment of *nirvana*, is beyond all concepts, and thus beyond the capacity of human beings to articulate. The origin of the Yogachara school is attributed to the half-brothers Asanga and Vasubandhu in the fifth century C.E. Its emphasis is on the means of refining one's defiled consciousness so that the Truth may be apprehended. The yogic practices that give the school its name refer mainly to meditative techniques meant to enable one to penetrate through various levels of perception that are conditioned by ignorance and delusion, in order to reach the highest state of undistorted perception.

Another important development in Buddhism was the influence of Tantra, which entered Buddhism via Hindu Tantrism by the fifth or sixth century C.E. Tantrism emphasizes the use of secret initiations and transmissions of knowledge, complex rituals, and meditative practices. It often utilizes conceptions of male and female principles to envision every aspect of creation, and seeks to unite these polarities to achieve the highest spiritual states. Its origins may lie in the indigenous religious cults of the Indian subcontinent that pre-dated the Aryans. These cults, involved with control over agricultural and human fertility, may have given Tantra its sexual imagery and concern with the acquisition of supernormal powers over the forces of nature. Buddhist Tantra is often called Vajra-yana (The Diamond/ Thunderbolt Vehicle). Although once widespread in the Buddhist world, it is now mainly evident in the Buddhism of Tibet and in the Shingon Buddhist school of Japan.

Later Developments and the Expansion of Buddhism

Buddhism in India. Within five centuries of the Buddha's life, Buddhism had sprouted a large number of philosophical schools and practices. There was the Mahayana wing and the numerous non-Mahayana (or Abhidharma) schools. Additionally, there were numerous rival philosophies (*darshanas*), such as those of the Jains and the Ajivikas (who promulgated a form of determinism), not to mention Hindu *darshanas* such as Sankhya and Vedanta. Monasteries that specialized in training Buddhist monks to learn about and debate these competing religio-philosophical systems developed into Buddhist universities. One of the greatest of these was Nalanda, formed in about the second century C.E., not far from Bodh-gaya, the city where the Buddha is believed to have attained *nirvana*. These universities became great centers of learning, holding vast repositories of books, housing thousands of monks, and teaching a broad range of subjects such as science and music. Nagarjuna, the founder of Madhyamika Buddhism, Asanga, the founder of Yogachara Buddhism, and Naropa, who educated important Tibetan Buddhist masters, are reputed to have taught at Nalanda. It was visited by the Chinese pilgrim Xuanzang/Hsuang-tsang in the seventh century. The influential movement of Buddhist logic developed here beginning in the fifth century. Even Tantra entered the curriculum of these universities, although those

TEXTS

Tripitaka: "Three Baskets." Collection of early Buddhist writings, written in Pali, and forming the canon for Theravada Buddhists. The *Sutra* section contains teachings attributed to the Buddha, the *Vinaya* contains rules of monastic discipline, and the *Abhidharma* contains philosophical and doctrinal arguments.

Buddhacarita: The first complete life story of the Buddha, composed in verse by Ashvaghosha, in the second century C.E.

Lotus Sutra: A Mahayana text, dating from the third century, forms the basis of Tiantai and Nichiren Buddhism. It promulgates doctrines on the value of faith and the possibility of universal liberation, because all beings share in the Buddha nature, which is transcendental.

Kanjur/Tanjur: The canon of Tibetan Buddhism. The *Kanjur* consists of ninety-two volumes containing teachings attributed to the Buddha. The *Tanjur* fills 226 volumes of commentary on the *Kanjur*.

Bardo Thodol: A Vajrayana text, also known as the *Tibetan Book of the Dead*. It contains instructions about the after-death stage, prior to rebirth. Individuals familiar with its teachings may, even after death, attain liberation, which is thought to be possible right up to the moment of rebirth.

practices that involved the ritualized transgression of certain moral precepts, such as sexual acts and the use of intoxicants, were restricted to
mental visualization. These monasteries also served as training grounds
for highly effective missionaries, and attracted students from all parts of
the Buddhist world.

With the rise and spread of devotional Hinduism from South India
in the sixth century (which garnered monetary support from the laity)
and the arrival of invading Muslim armies from the north in the eighth
century, the presence of Buddhism began to erode in India. Muslim armies pillaged the north Indian university centers. Nalanda was destroyed in the twelfth/thirteenth century. Buddhist monks from the
south fled to Sri Lanka. Without the support of the laity, and with its monastic infrastructure in ruins, Buddhism was virtually extinguished in
India. It is only in the last century, when the XIVth Dalai Lama of Tibet
was forced into exile in India, that Buddhism has begun its revival there.
A hundred thousand Tibetan Buddhists subsequently fled to India and
have reestablished monasteries and Buddhist communities throughout
the subcontinent. B. R. Ambedkar, a leader in the Indian Independence
movement, converted to Buddhism in protest against the Hindu caste
system, and was joined by tens of thousands of his supporters. They now
number in the millions.

The Southern Spread of Buddhism. Both Mahayana and non-Mahayana
wings of Buddhism coexisted with each other for centuries. However,
over time, due to various factors such as religious persecution or royal patronage, certain schools died out, while others ended up becoming the
dominant form of Buddhism in a particular region. For instance, in Sri
Lanka, where Theravada first established itself, the school found itself in
coexistence and competition with the Mahayana tradition, which had arrived later. The Theravada monks in Sri Lanka committed the originally
oral Tripitaka canon to writing in the Pali language during the first century B.C.E. to the fifth century C.E. When the Hindu Tamils conquered the
island early in the eleventh century the lineage for monastic ordination
was disrupted and Buddhism in Sri Lanka suffered badly. By the late eleventh century, Buddhism and the ordination lines were reestablished with
the help of Burma (Myanmar), which by this time was a Theravada Buddhist kingdom. Unfortunately, the ordination line for Buddhist nuns was
not reestablished and died out in Sri Lanka. In similar manner, Theravada
Buddhism became the dominant form of Buddhism in Sri Lanka, Burma
and Thailand, a role it continues to hold to the present day. In fact, as Buddhism experienced the cadences of time, all other non-Mahayana Buddhist
schools eventually died out, except for the Theravada.

Buddhism had also spread into other parts of Southeast Asia, such as Cambodia, Laos, and the islands of Sumatra and Java. Syncretistic religious forms developed as it fused with Hinduism and the indigenous religions of the regions. The ruins of one of the world's largest Buddhist monuments, Borobudur, is found on the island of Java, testament to the status of Buddhism there in the ninth century. The great Hindu temples in the city of Angkor in the Khmer (Cambodian) Empire were progressively transformed into Buddhist sites as conversion took place from the twelfth to the fourteenth centuries, by which time Buddhism became the state religion of Cambodia. The Buddhist influence in Vietnam came via China. Thus unlike Cambodia and Laos, where Theravada Buddhism is also dominant, Vietnamese Buddhism is characterized by forms adopted from Chinese Mahayana.

The Northern Spread of Buddhism. The emperor Ashoka is reputed to have also sent Buddhist emissaries to kingdoms to the north and west of his empire. It is difficult to know what success Ashoka's and later groups of Buddhist missionaries to the West actually had, for there is little evidence of Buddhist culture beyond modern-day Afghanistan. By the first century C.E., the Kushana Empire ruled the area of central Asia and north India around and including Afghanistan. After members of the dynasty converted to Buddhism, they promoted Buddhism, particularly Mahayana and Sarvastivada (one of the eighteen non-Mahayana schools) throughout their empire. Giant Buddha images from the monastery complexes at Bamiyan dating to the fifth century C.E. stood as testament to the former success of Buddhism in this region until

DEITIES / ELEVATED BEINGS

Shakyamuni Buddha: The historical Buddha, Siddhartha Gautama. In most Buddhist traditions, he is not the first and only Buddha, but is regarded as the teaching Buddha of the current epoch.

Bodhisattva: ("Enlightenment Being"). In Theravada, one who is committed to the attainment of Buddhahood. In Mahayana, one who strives for the fullest form of Buddhahood, and for the liberation of all beings. *Bodhisattvas* may be earthly or transcendent.

Arhat ("worthy ones"): In Theravada, one who has attained the ideal of spiritual perfection. In Mahayana, still regarded as an inferior attainment to the Buddhahood for which the *bodhisattva* strives

Amitabha/Amida: ("Boundless Light"). A Buddha of the Mahayana pantheon, he presides over the Western Paradise, and is worshipped by Pure Land Buddhists. Calling his name with sincerity at the hour of death is sufficient to be reborn in the Pure Land.

Maitreya: ("Loving One"). The next teaching Buddha to appear in this world system, generally depicted as a heroic figure in a stately seated posture. In China, he began to be depicted in the form of the monk Budai/Pu-tai, a bald, fat, and jolly figure often referred to as the Laughing Buddha.

Guanyin/Kuan-yin: ("One who Regards the Call"). Chinese form of the Mahayana transcendent Bodhisattva of Compassion, Avalokiteshvara. The Dalai Lamas of Tibet are regarded as living incarnations of Avalokiteshvara.

the coming of Islam. These images were recently destroyed by the Taliban Muslim rulers of Afghanistan. The Kushana Empire occupied vast areas of the Silk Road, which was a major overland trading route from India into China, and from China to Persia and the West. It was along these routes that merchant caravans, from as early as the first century B.C.E., propagated Buddhism from India to China and beyond.

Buddhism in East Asia. By the first century C.E., Buddhism had made its way to the Chinese capital, where the Buddha was regarded as a sort of deity. Buddhism encountered tensions with both Confucianism and Daoism, the two religious traditions that were dominant in China at the time. Confucian ethics stressed the importance of family and larger social relationships, which were at odds with the Buddhist spirit of renunciation. However, the Confucian emphasis on the acquisition of wisdom and the cultivation of human-heartedness meshed well with the *bodhisattva* ideal of Mahayana Buddhism. Daoism's notion of the mysterious Dao, and its high regard for the sage's harmonious relationship with nature resonated with Buddhist ideas of Emptiness and the monastic preference for remote natural abodes. In time, many Daoist conceptual terms were also used to translate Buddhist terminology into Chinese.

These meeting points between Confucianism, Daoism, and Buddhism enabled Buddhism to make inroads into China after the collapse of the Han Dynasty in the early third century C.E. By the sixth century, during the Sui dynasty, China was ruled by a Buddhist emperor. Buddhism reached its zenith in China during the subsequent Tang Dynasty from the seventh to the early tenth centuries. Xuanzang (602–664), a famous Chinese pilgrim-monk, traveled to India via Central Asia and brought back scores of Indian Buddhist *sutras*, many of which he subsequently translated. He also left a record of his long journey that serves as an invaluable reference for the state of Buddhism in India at that time. Numerous Buddhist schools developed in China, some with a distinctly Chinese character. Among these are the Tiantai/T'ien-t'ai ("Mount Heavenly Terrace"), Huayan/Hua Yen ("Flower Garland"), Chan/Ch'an ("Meditation"), and Jingtu/Ch'ing-tu ("Pure Land") schools.

By the Sung Dynasty, which followed the Tang/T'ang, Buddhism began its decline in China. The rise of Neo-Confucian philosophy clearly contributed to this process. Neo-Confucian philosophers such as Zhu Xi/Chu Hsi drew upon Confucianism, Daoism, and Buddhism to construct a syncretic teaching that emphasized social responsibility and evoked China's pre-Buddhist intellectual heritage. Neo-Confucianism was adopted as the national philosophy in social service examinations, leading fewer young members of the educated classes to join the Sangha. Chan, the meditation-centered school of Buddhism, founded by the Indian sage, Bodhidharma, and Pure Land Buddhism, which is centered on devotion, gained in prominence over the other schools. Buddhism continued its decline despite imperial support in subsequent centuries. During the partly Christian-inspired Taiping/T'ai-p'ing Rebellion (1851–1865) thousands of Buddhist temples in China were destroyed. The final blow to Buddhism came with the rise of communism in 1949. In the Cultural Revolution that followed, monasteries were destroyed, and the monks were forced to take up secular work. Chinese Buddhism retreated to Taiwan, where it now flourishes.

Buddhism spread from China into Korea and from there to Japan by the sixth century. In Korea, it reached its zenith during the Koryo Dynasty (tenth to fourteenth centuries). A version of the Korean Tripitaka containing 1,512 books on more than eighty thousand carved wooden blocks was fashioned in 1251 and is preserved at Haein-sa Monastery. Neo-Confucian teachings were adopted by the subsequent Choson Dynasty, and Buddhism was repressed from the fifteenth to the early twentieth centuries. With the rise of communism in North Korea, Buddhism met a similar fate to the one it suffered in China, although little is known about the actual state of the religion there. In South Korea, Buddhism is dominated by the Chogye Order which oversees both the Son (Chan) and Pure Land monastic traditions.

It was during the reign of Prince Shotoku (574–622 C.E.) that Buddhism became firmly established in Japan. Shotoku exhorted all his subjects to take up the Three Refuges (in the Buddha, Dharma, and Sangha), which essentially makes one a Buddhist. There were, of course, tensions with the indigenous religious traditions of Japan, in which spirits known as *kami* were worshipped through priestly rites.

Buddhism, which brought the high civilization of China, along with a rich ritual life that resonated with *kami* worship rites (collectively called Shinto), appealed to the ruling classes. The various forms of Buddhism that were present in China made their way into Japan, although these

OFFICES

Bhikshu: (Pali: *Bhikkhu*). A fully ordained Buddhist monk and member of the Sangha. Monks conduct their lives in accord with the rules laid out in the *Vinaya Pitaka*.

Bhikshuni: A fully ordained Buddhist nun. Nuns, whose numbers are extremely small compared to monks, are subject to stricter regulations than monks.

Lama: A religious master. The term is often used as a polite form of address for any Tibetan monk. The honorific title, *Rimpoche* ("highly precious"), is applied to highly attained teachers or monks.

Dalai Lama: ("Ocean [of Wisdom] Lama"). Title and rulership of Tibet bestowed on the head of the Gelug Order of Tibetan Buddhism in the sixteenth century. The current Dalai Lama, who was selected as a child through a complicated search and testing procedure, is regarded as the fourteenth incarnation.

were initially state-sponsored and controlled. During the Heian Period (794-1185), when the capital moved from Nara to Heian (Kyoto), two distinctly Japanese schools developed. These were the Tendai and Shingon schools. Tendai was based on Chinese Tiantai, but had notable differences due to contributions by its founder, the monk Saicho. Another monk, Kukai, carried the lineage of a form of Chinese Tantric Buddhism to Japan, and founded the Shingon Buddhist school. As individual monks whose monastic schools grew in reputation, Saicho and Kukai broke Japan's state domination of Buddhism.

In subsequent centuries, Zen (Chan) and devotional Buddhism (Pure Land) made major inroads into Japan. Japan was ruled by feudal warlords known as shoguns, while the imperial court remained powerless in Kyoto. A new form of devotional Buddhism based on homage to the *Lotus Sutra*, an influential scripture throughout Buddhist East Asia, was developed by the monk Nichiren. The Tokugawa Period (1603-1867) saw the rise of Neo-Confucianism as a unifying philosophy for a newly unified and progressively secular Japan. The political influence that Buddhism had wielded for centuries ended. In 1868, when the emperor Meiji was restored to power, Shinto was made the national religion. Buddhism and Shinto, which had been fused for centuries, with Buddhist monks often serving in Shinto shrines, separated. Buddhist monks were permitted to marry, and today most are married. Zen and devotional Buddhist schools are currently the most popular in Japan, and these have begun to gain influence in the West.

Buddhism in Tibet. Buddhism entered Tibet on the invitation of its king Songsten Gampo in the seventh century. It was a Buddhist Tantric master, Padmasambhava, who was successful in quelling the initial resistance that the religion faced from the Bon religion that was established there. Bon was an animistic religious tradition in which a host of deities were worshipped with a rich array of rituals including sacrifice and spirit possession. Padmasambhava's school, known as the Nyingma-pa ("Ancient School"), continues to survive, along with several others that developed over the centuries. The most notable of these schools is the Gelug-pa ("Virtuous School"), to which the Dalai Lamas, the political and spiritual leaders of Tibet, belong.

By the thirteenth/fourteenth century, the Tibetans had compiled a voluminous canon. It consists of hundreds of volumes in two parts. The *Kanjur* is made up of "Teachings" and includes Vinaya, *Perfection of Wisdom* scriptures, and Tantric texts. The larger *Tanjur* (*Translation of Treatises*) contains commentaries on the *Kanjur* texts that have been translated from the Indian Sanskrit sources, and which were also written by Tibetan Buddhist scholars. With the destruction of the Indian Buddhist universities' rich treasury of texts, such Tibetan scriptural sources have provided the world with an invaluable collection of material once thought to have been irretrievably lost. Unfortunately, the Chinese communist occupation of Tibet has resulted in the death of over a million Tibetans and the destruction of almost all of its over six thousand monasteries. The fourteenth Dalai Lama escaped to India in 1959 at the age of twenty-four in the face of imminent assassination. He received the Nobel Peace Prize in 1989 for his efforts to find a solution to the plight of the Tibetan people through peaceful negotiation. Although the Dalai Lama is probably the most recognized figurehead of Buddhism and has raised the profile of Tibetan Buddhism among people around the world, there are few signs of any religious revival in Tibet today.

BELIEFS

The Legendary Life of the Buddha

The story of the Buddha's life, in various versions and recensions, is told in books such as the *Lalitavistara* (*Delightful Description*) and the *Buddhacarita* (*Acts of the Buddha*) composed in the first and second centuries C.E., respectively. Episodes of his life are also recounted in portions of the Pali Canon, the Tripitaka. It is evident that the story has been embellished, making it difficult to separate historical fact from mythic accretions.

SYMBOLS

Three Refuges/Jewels: Buddhists take refuge in the Three Jewels: the Buddha, the Dharma (the Buddha's teachings), and the Sangha (the Buddhist community of ordained men and women, but in its broader connotations may also include laypersons).

Dharma Chakra: ("The Wheel of the Law"). A wheel with eight spokes, used to symbolize aspects of the Buddha's teachings, such as the Four Noble Truths, and the Noble Eightfold Path. The wheel also symbolizes the spread and development of Buddhist teachings through time.

Buddha Images: Often following fixed iconographic prescriptions, the Buddha is arguably the most depicted human being in the world. In statues and paintings, he is often portrayed atop a lotus flower in a variety of traditional poses or gestures (*mudra*).

Lotus: A kind of water-lily. Symbol of the Buddha-nature within all beings, which emerges undefiled from the muddy depths of worldly existence (*samsara*). In inconographic depictions, it is frequently used as the seat or throne of the Buddha.

Stupa: Originally funerary mounds, these structures contain relics, sacred texts, or are purely symbolic representations of states of consciousness and the awakened mind. They serve as focal points for veneration or meditation.

Mandala: Intricate two or three dimensional constructions representing realms of consciousness. Used as a focus in Mahayana or Vajrayana meditation.

According to these sources, the Buddha was born to Queen Maya and King Shuddhodana who ruled the princely kingdom of Shakya. His birth took place in the forest grove of Lumbini, not far from Kapilavastu, the capital of the Shakya kingdom. The prince was named Siddhartha (he who has achieved his goal), and a venerable hermit, upon examining the child, predicted that he would become a great spiritual teacher. A week after his birth, Siddhartha's mother, Maya, died. King Shuddhodana married her younger sister, Mahaprajapati, who raised Siddhartha like her own son. Siddhartha grew up in aristocratic luxury, sheltered from the harsh realities of the world. He was virtually imprisoned in a palace of sensual delights by his father who wished him to become a great emperor, rather than the religious teacher he was predicted to become. Siddhartha did indeed excel in the princely arts, and when he reached adulthood was married to the princess Yashodara. In time they gave birth to a son, named Rahula.

Siddhartha, however, grew restless to see the world and experience life beyond the confines of his sheltered existence. On subsequent chariot rides beyond the palace walls, he witnessed the "Four Sights" that changed his life. He saw a man, withered with age, and was awakened to the transient nature of youth, vitality, and beauty. Next he saw someone horribly diseased, and was awakened to the happenstance nature of suffering that can afflict anyone at any time. The third sight was a corpse. This awakened Siddhartha to the transience of life itself, for death was a reality no one would escape. The fourth sight was a religious mendicant, a *shramana*, whom he was told had renounced the preoccupations of social life, in order to find the truth about existence, and therein find freedom from the apparently dismal human condition. Siddhartha returned to the palace determined to attain this goal of the liberating realization.

In what is known as the Great Renunciation, Siddhartha took one last look at his wife, Yashodara, and young son, Rahula, and at the age of twenty-nine left Kapilavastu. He cut his hair and took on the ragged robes of a renouncer. Initially he studied with various *shramana* masters, perfecting the highest meditative states possible in their systems, but still did not feel satisfied with his achievements. He finally joined a group of ascetics and practiced severe asceticism, fasting and mortifying his body to near death in the quest for an insight into Truth. He did have an insight, which revealed to him that the extremes of self-mortification were as damaging to the pursuit of realization as the life of sensual indulgence he formerly enjoyed. He therefore embarked on "the Middle Way" between these extremes. Seating himself under a *pippal* tree, his strength and mental equilibrium regained after eating, he entered into deep meditation.

Pushing through progressively higher contemplative states, he finally attained the pivotal liberating insight that he had sought for some seven years. This was *nirvana*, a realization that extinguished all illusions about reality. While he, like all other human beings, had been in a sort of waking dream, *nirvana* was akin to an awakening from that dream. He was now the Awakened One, the Buddha. The place where his awakening took place is known as Bodh-gaya. And the type of tree under which he attained enlightenment is now referred to as a Bodhi ("enlightenment") tree.

The Buddha, as he was now called, walked to Sarnath, near the holy city of Banaras, where he met up with the group of five ascetics with whom he had previously practiced. Thinking he had given up on his quest, they had deserted him when he abandoned the rigorous austerities in which they had all engaged. But upon seeing and conversing with him, they too were soon convinced of his achievement, and became his disciples. His teaching to them is referred to as the First Sermon. Since the Buddha's teachings are referred to as the Dharma, the First Sermon is said to have set in motion the "Wheel of the Dharma." The First Sermon consisted of teachings of the Four Noble Truths, which include the Noble Eightfold Path. These serve as the source of the most common symbol of Buddhism, the *dharma chakra*, the eight-spoked Wheel of the Dharma. The discipleship of the first five ascetics is regarded as the origin of the Sangha, the Buddha's monastic community.

According to tradition, hundreds of men joined the Sangha during the forty-five years of the Buddha's teaching career. Among these was Ananda, who served as his attendant, and was reputed to have the best recollection of the Buddha's teachings. After some persuasion, the Buddha also approved of an order of nuns five years after the male monastic

PLACES

There are many Buddhist sites of great historical, architectural, or cultural significance. However, the following are traditionally regarded as the four holy places of Buddhism.

Lumbini: In present-day Nepal; the traditional birthplace of Siddhartha Gautama and marked by a stone column erected by the emperor Ashoka. Near Kapilavastu, capital of the Shakya Kingdom.

Bodh-gaya: In the state of Bihar, India. The Mahabodhi temple located there, reputedly marks the spot where Siddhartha Gautama attained Buddhahood. A descendent of the Bodhi tree under which he meditated is the focal point of pilgrimage.

Sarnath: Located near the sacred Hindu city of Banaras. A large *stupa* marks the spot where the Buddha delivered his First Sermon, an event traditionally referred to as "Setting in motion the wheel of the Dharma."

Kushinagara: Present-day Kasia, in the state of Uttar Pradesh, India. Place where the Buddha entered *parinirvana*. Once a great pilgrimage site, the *stupa* reputed to have held his remains was destroyed before the seventh century.

order was formed. Queen Mahaprajapati, his step-mother, was the first ordained nun. In its acceptance of women and men from all classes into the Sangha, including those who were from the classless (i.e., untouchable) segment of society, and in its teaching that everyone was capable of attaining *nirvana* in this lifetime, without having to be reborn as an upper class (i.e., brahmin) male, Buddhism offered a trenchant criticism of orthodox Hindu teachings. There were soon many lay (i.e., non-monastic) supporters of the Sangha, a crucial necessity in Buddhism, because the monastic communities depend on the laity for their sustenance. The Buddha is reputed to have urged his monks to travel and spread the Dharma far and wide. This initiated the missionary spirit within Buddhism.

The Buddha entered a state known as *parinirvana* ("Further Nirvana") at the age of eighty in Kushinagara. Since *nirvana* is regarded as a state beyond birth and death, for someone who has attained it, the final release of the physical body is not regarded as death but a further manifestation of the nirvanic state. According to the *Sutra Pitaka* the Buddha's last words were: "All conditioned things are transient. Work on your own liberation with diligence." They underline the spirit of self-reliance that is characteristic of most forms of Buddhism. The Buddhist tradition generally fosters a healthy scepticism of all teachings, especially those that are promoted as revealed scriptures, such as the Vedas, urging its disciples to question and verify beliefs through personal experience. Here, too, it parted ways with orthodox Hinduism, and came to be regarded as an unorthodox *darshana*.

The Buddhist Worldview and the Human Condition

The Buddha is reputed to have avoided answering questions about the origin and destiny of the cosmos, and other such questions of a speculative metaphysical nature. He once offered as an answer a parable of a man shot with a poisoned arrow who wanted to know endless details about the arrow and the man who shot it, before his wound was treated. Just as such a man would die before he was cured, the Buddha explained that the human condition is as if we were shot with the poisoned arrow of ignorance and suffering. Speculative discussions would not bring an end to the suffering of existence, and thus the focus of his teaching was on the attainment of the liberating insight of *nirvana*. As a result, by default, the Buddhist worldview and cosmology derives quite substantially from perspectives that were commonplace in India at the time. This included the idea of the triple world system of heavenly realms populated by gods, goddesses, and powerful demons, earthly realms where humans and animals dwell, and the hellish realms, where ghosts and lesser demons reside and beings suffer terribly. Of all these, Buddhists regard the human incarnation as possessing the consciousness that is optimally suited for the attainment of *nirvana*. In some measure, it is because human beings exist in a zone between the pleasures of heaven and the sufferings of hell. Buddhists, too, accept a law of *karma*, in which intentional actions have consequences, and affect the nature of one's rebirth. However, Buddhists do not acknowledge the existence of an unchanging and eternal soul that transmigrates from one incarnation to the next. Nevertheless, rebirth is affected by intentional actions, which influence the subsequent form of one's consciousness.

The ultimate goal in Buddhism is not the attainment of rebirth in a heavenly realm, but complete liberation from the cycle of rebirth (*samsara*) altogether. In this it parallels the Hindu goal of *moksha*. However, there is a subtle, but cogent, distinction between how Buddhists and Hindus view the nature of the innermost self that is revealed upon the attainment of liberation (see The Anatman Doctrine and Dependent Arising below). *Nirvana*, like *moksha*, delivers one from samsaric existence, and moves one beyond the inexorable grip of the law of *karma*. Once Buddhahood has been attained, there is no more rebirth in any realm.

The Four Noble Truths

A succinct presentation of the Buddha's teachings is found in the Four Noble

FESTIVALS

Vesak: (Vaishakha). Celebrated in Theravada countries on the full moon day in May. It was inaugurated by Ashoka to commemorate the Buddha's birth, enlightenment, and *parinirvana*. Monks perform special *pujas*, and present teachings on Dharma to large crowds.

Buddhist New Year: Three-day celebration in Theravada countries beginning on the first full moon in April. Tibetan Buddhists celebrate it in February, and Chinese, Koreans, and Vietnamese celebrate it on the second new moon after the winter solstice.

Sangha Day: Celebrated on the full moon of Magh (February/March), it commemorates a spontaneous gathering of the Sangha to receive the Buddha's teachings. The laity gather for processions at Buddhist monasteries and listen to talks on the Dharma to gain merit.

Kathina Ceremony: A ritual in which the laity presents new robes and other necessities to members of the Sangha; held near the end of the rainy season retreat.

Ulambana: Also called Ancestor Day; offerings are made to departed ancestors. In Mahayana Buddhist countries, food offerings are made to alleviate the suffering of the ghosts who normally inhabit the lower, hellish realms, but briefly visit the human realm around this time.

Guanyin's Birthday: Commemorates the goddess who embodies the compassion of the *bodhisattva* Avalokiteshvara. Devotees make pilgrimages to Guanyin/Kuan-yin's shrines.

Truths which constitutes part of his First Sermon. Like a doctor of the human spirit, the Four Noble Truths appraise the problem, diagnose its cause, propose a cure, and prescribe a treatment. It is especially important to adhere to the prescription.

1. *Duhkha (Pali: Dukkha)*. Literally, sorrow or suffering. The First Noble Truth states that all living, sentient (i.e., feeling, sense-possessing) beings experience suffering. This condition is rooted in the physical realities of old age, sickness, and death, emotional feelings of sadness and despondency, and in a host of other personal feelings of dissatisfaction with the nature of existence.

2. *Origin/Cause*. It is our insatiable craving, desire, or thirst for sensual gratification that is a major cause of *duhkha*. Unfortunately, due to the impermanent and transient nature of the world, our sensual gratifications pass, and we find ourselves once again in the grip of craving. Craving also takes the form of pursuing an identity through the acquisition of such things as wealth, power, prosperity, self-image and so on, while avoiding that which is regarded as unpleasant and undesirable. This craving, which is grounded in an erroneous view of the self, is one of the engines of our suffering.

3. *Cessation/Ending*. The means of ending our *duhkha* is by ending the craving that causes it. This cessation of craving, which is an ending of the ignorance at its root, is called *nirvana*.

4. *Path (marga)*. This is often called the Noble Eightfold Path and it is prescribed in Buddhism as the means of attaining the goal of *nirvana*. It is important to emphasize that since *nirvana* is regarded as an unconditioned state, beyond the principle of cause and effect, the actions of the Eightfold Path do not cause *nirvana*. They aid in the realization of the state that is *nirvana*, the state that is free from all craving and delusions about the nature of the self and reality. The Noble Eightfold Path is so-called because it consists of eight aspects or dimensions that need to be cultivated. The terms are prefaced with the adjective "right" (*samyak*), which should be thought of as "full," "skilfull," or "intelligently appropriate." These are:

i. *Right Worldview/Understanding (darshana)*: in essence, this involves developing the philosophical perspective that enables one to penetrate through one's deluded conceptions of reality.

ii. *Right Intention/Commitment*: this involves developing a sincere commitment to embark upon the path to liberation with determination and diligence.

iii. *Right Speech/Communication:* to use language and communication for the transmission of Truth, and to refrain from speech that adds to the suffering of the world.

iv. *Right Action:* following the Five Precepts, Buddhism's moral code, of not-harming, not-stealing, not-lying, avoiding intoxicants, and avoiding sexual misconduct. It also refers to putting into practice the actions that lead one to the attainment of liberation.

v. *Right Livelihood:* work that is not injurious to other sentient beings and conducive to the attainment of liberation.

vi. *Right Effort:* the development of one's consciousness so that it is free from craving requires perseverance, the sustained effort to release consciousness from its unwholesome mental states, while cultivating wholesome states of mind.

vii. *Right Mindfulness:* the practice of meditative awareness so that the processes through which thoughts and feelings, the attendant cravings, and ego-constructing activities may be discerned with clarity.

viii. *Right Contemplative Absorption* (*samadhi*): the deepening of Mindfulness leads to focused states of consciousness, akin to deep concentration, in which both tranquillity and penetrating insight may be obtained.

The Anatman Doctrine and Dependent Arising

Two of the most conceptually challenging notions in Buddhism are the *anatman* doctrine and the process of Dependent Arising. In a way, to apprehend them fully is to have attained Buddhahood. Conceptually, Dependent Arising is a psychological process that occurs in the consciousness of all sentient beings. It is described as a series of psychological phenomena

RITES / RITUALS

Buddhism did not develop childhood or marriage rites of passage. Buddhists generally follow traditional procedures based on local cultural traditions.

Ordination: Ceremony in which one is officially accepted into the Sangha. In the lower ordination one first becomes a novice, and through the higher ordination one become a full-fledged monk or nun. Mahayana Buddhism includes a further ordination, in which one takes the *bodhisattva* vow.

Almsgiving: Traditional early morning procession by the Sangha to seek food. Laypersons are expected to put edible food in the alms bowls of the Sangha members. Such charitable almsgiving (*dana*) provides the laity with an opportunity to gain merit (*punya*). In turn, the Sangha members chant prayers of blessing.

Uposatha: One of the most important observances in Theravada Buddhism. On every quarter moon lay Buddhists may gather at a monastery, listen to religious discourses, and spend the day in fasting and meditation. They may reaffirm their adherence to various rules of moral discipline (*shila*). On full and new moon days, the Sangha gathers to hear the recitation of the monastic disciplinary code (*pratimoksha*) and confess their faults.

Death Rituals: In Theravada countries, Buddhist monks are asked to preside over cremation rites. They chant from Buddhist scriptures and transfer merit to the deceased. In Vajrayana Buddhism, the *Tibetan Book of the Dead* is read aloud.

that form a sort of cyclical chain of causes and effects that give rise to and condition our identities. Our perceptions are mediated by past experiences, and these in turn cause us to crave certain things and avoid others. One's sense of identity becomes contingent on that which is desired. This identity, self, or ego-construction, like all aspects of reality, is therefore conditioned/dependent. That is to say, it is the result of, or depends on, a network of causes and supporting factors. Since these causes and factors are impermanent, the self that has been constructed (i.e., arisen) also grows old, decays, and dies. With this process of decay comes sorrow, which serves as a factor that conditions the "arising" of the next ego-construction.

A somewhat oversimplified illustration is found in the kinds of self-images certain companies market to us through advertising campaigns. We may see a sports or entertainment celebrity using or promoting a particular product, or the product being used in a desirable situation. The perception of those images is conditioned by many other previous (i.e., karmic) ideas provided by our society and culture. Subsequent to seeing the advertisement we may "unconsciously" identify with the person, group, or lifestyle that is connected to the product, and may even buy it, or buy into its promise. Eventually, as that particular identity or lifestyle identification begins to wane, we begin to experience sorrow. However, by this time, to ameliorate our suffering and loss of identity, we may have already begun to move onto another identification that was partially mediated and conditioned by our previous experience. The selves that are constructed through the effects of blatant advertising gimmickry are, of course, much more easily discernable, and often less painfully disposed of, than those that we adopt unconsciously through the course of our lives. These generally encapsulate our deepest values, and bear the imprint of our most significant life experiences. From the Buddhist perspective, we therefore cling tenaciously to our identification with these selves, experiencing sorrow (duhkha) all the more profoundly as they decay.

Although Hindu Vedanta philosophy essentially affirms a similar truth, it postulates that beyond the many contingent, conditioned, ego-generated false selves, there is a true Self. This Self is called the Atman. The Buddhist position is referred to as the Anatman Doctrine because it does not put forward the notion of an Absolute, true Self. Buddhism acknowledges the existence of an empirical self (knowable to the senses), a body-mind complex. So the Anatman or No-Self Doctrine should not be mistakenly thought to be a doctrine that nothing exists, or that the body-mind complex is an illusion. Rather, in Buddhist teachings, the empirical self is made up of impermanent constituents, and there is nothing akin to a permanent, unchanging soul, or greater Self to be found anywhere within (or outside of) its constitution. Reality is a sort of dynamic process with a constantly changing play of interacting elements, none of which is permanent. The self is like a candle-flame or an ocean wave, appearing to be a separate entity, but which in fact is something that is constantly changing and impermanent. Just as the candle-flame is a dynamic interplay of such items as wax, wick, air, and a spark, and the ocean wave, an interplay of water, wind, and so on, the self is the result of a combination of factors (e.g., matter, feelings, thoughts, perceptions) and will vanish as these, which are themselves composed of other impermanent components, disintegrate.

Emptiness (Shunyata)

The same notion that there is no permanent, independently existing "thing" or entity in existence is further developed in Mahayana Buddhism. There, it is often referred to as Emptiness (*shunyata*). A common misunderstanding is that the Buddhist teaching of *shunyata* is a nihilistic doctrine that "nothing really exists." Instead, the doctrine suggests that no thing exists permanently or independently. It points particularly to such things as the Self or Atman, but also to notions of Absolute Divinity, such as Brahman or God, to which people commonly cede these attributes. The Buddhist philosopher Nagarjuna developed a keen sensitivity to the relational connection between concepts (that is, the ideas we have about things), which often tend to be given a similar, absolute, self-existent status. Thus even the idea of *nirvana* (not *nirvana* itself), he pointed out, does not make sense without the concept of *samsara* (deluded worldly-existence), and thus it, too, is relationally conditioned.

THE FOUR NOBLE TRUTHS

1. Duhkha (*Pali: Dukkha*): Literally, sorrow or suffering. All living, sentient beings experience suffering, a condition rooted in the physical realities of old age, sickness, and death and in emotional feelings of sadness and despondency.

2. Origin/Cause: The major cause of Duhkha is the insatiable craving, desire, or thirst for sensual gratification. But due to the impermanent and transient nature of the world, our sensual gratifications pass, and we find ourselves once again in the grip of craving.

3. Cessation/Ending: The means of ending our Duhkha is by ending the craving that causes it. This ending of craving, which is an ending of the ignorance at its root, is described as *nirvana*.

4. Path (marga): This is often called the Noble Eightfold Path and it is prescribed in Buddhism as the means of attaining the goal of *nirvana*. The Noble Eightfold Path is so-called because it consists of eight aspects or dimensions that need to be cultivated.

The Bodhisattva Ideal

A core distinction between the Mahayana and non-Mahayana wings of Buddhism centers on the "*bodhisattva* ideal," the way of the *bodhisattva*.

In fact, the Mahayana sometimes refers to itself as the Bodhisattva-yana. Since the Indian worldview at the Buddha's time included the notion of rebirth, it was natural for people to wonder about the previous lives of the Buddha. The Tripitaka tells of a certain young man named Sumedha who eons earlier had been inspired by a previous Buddha, and took up the vow to become a Buddha himself. After innumerable lifetimes, sometimes as a king, but even as animals such as a monkey or a deer, Sumedha eventually was reborn as Siddhartha Gautama, and became the Buddha. Hundreds of stories of the Buddha's previous lives are contained in a collection known as the *Jatakas* ("Birth Stories"). The *bodhisattva* ideal is grounded in the vision of a being (*sattva*), like Sumedha, who strives with determination and tireless commitment over eons and countless lifetimes to achieve the highest state of Buddhahood, liberating not just him or herself, but all sentient beings along the way.

Thus, the vehicle (*yana*) that the *bodhisattva* embarks upon is not intended merely to take him or her to the "far shore of liberation," but is intended as a raft to save all beings. The imagery of a boatman who ferries people across the perilous waters of life to liberation on the other shore is common in Buddhism. Herman Hesse used it effectively in his contemporary classic *Siddhartha*, a fictitious tale of a young man, whose life runs parallel to and is contemporaneous with that of the Buddha. It is sometimes stated that *bodhisattvas* take on the vow to liberate all beings before they themselves leave the samsaric wheel of existence. By taking on rebirth repeatedly, in various realms, as varied sentient beings with various forms of consciousness, *bodhisattvas* strive to grow in wisdom (*prajna*) and compassion (*karuna*), the two cardinal qualities of the awakened consciousness. The maturing of these qualities enhances the skills of the *bodhisattva* to further alleviate the sorrow of sentient beings and lead them to Buddhahood. The Mahayana holds that the *bodhisattva* path leads to a state of Buddhahood surpassing that achieved by non-Mahayana approaches. They refer to those who have attained *nirvana* by following non-Mahayana teachings of the Buddha as *arhats*.

Buddhas and Bodhisattvas

In Buddhist scriptures as early as the Pali Tripitaka, one finds references to the existence of other Buddhas, such as Dipankara, the Buddha who inspired the young Sumedha to pursue the *bodhisattva* path to Buddhahood. The notion of previous Buddhas, who taught the Dharma in past eons, parallelled Jainism, whose historical founder, Mahavira, roughly contemporaneous with Gautama Buddha, is regarded not as the first but the twenty-fourth in a series of great teachers. The Mahayana tradition developed a larger array of Buddhas, and Buddha-like *bodhisattvas*, some of whom represent particular qualities of Buddhahood. For instance, the *bodhisattva* Avalokiteshvara ("The Lord who Looks down from Above") is an embodiment of the compassionate nature of awakened consciousness, and Manjushri ("Sweet Splendor") embodies the wisdom of the Buddha-mind. Japanese Shingon Buddhism is centered on the Buddha Mahavairochana with whom the practitioner strives to identify. Pure Land Buddhists offer homage to the Buddha Amitabha/Amida in the hopes of gaining his paradise. The historical Buddha is reputed to have taught that the Dharma, which is a perennial truth, tends to get distorted and misunderstood over time. There periodically arise Buddhas like himself, who both awaken to the Dharma and decide to teach it, thus reviving it for sentient beings of a particular epoch. Thus the notion of Maitreya ("the Loving One"), the next Buddha to come, who will revive the Dharma when it has reached a state of serious deterioration, also developed in Buddhist scriptures. Buddhists often refer to the historical founder of Buddhism as Gautama Buddha, or Shakyamuni Buddha in order to distinguish him from these various *bodhisattvas* and Buddhas, some of whom may actually receive the greater part of their religious attention.

BUDDHA IMAGES

Since the fashioning of Buddha and divine bodhisattva images is regarded as spiritually meritorious, the Buddhist world abounds with depictions of these figures. Buddha images often conform to specific prescriptions, such as possessing some of the physical signs reputed to be characteristic of an extraordinary being. Furthermore, the figures are generally portrayed in particular postures known as mudras. Since iconography attempts to comply with some of these characteristics, Buddha images often have a trans-human appearance.

The Thirty-two Major Signs: These were likely derived from preexisting notions of auspicious physical attributes that characterized a deity or an extraordinary person, and were applied to the Buddha. They include: an erect posture, even fingers and toes that are webbed, long arms descending to below the knees, a thousand-spoked wheel on the footprint, a protuberance on the crown of the head, and a curl between the eyebrows. In addition, texts sometimes mention eighty minor signs.

Earth-touching posture: In these images the Buddha is seated cross-legged with his left hand in his lap and the right hand reaching down to touch the earth. It represents the episode in his quest for enlightenment when he defeats the temptations of the demon Mara, in which he reached down to ask the earth to testify to his victory.

PRACTICES

The Three Refuges or Jewels

The Pali scriptures indicate that the Buddha initially merely invited people to join the community of monks, and if they accepted his invitation, they became members of the Sangha. Soon, however, the process required one to take the Three Refuges. Eventually, as the numbers of rules and regulations for the monastic community grew, the ordination procedures for monks and nuns became more complex and the Three Refuges have since become the means of formal induction into the non-monastic (i.e., lay) community of Buddhists. In the presence of members of the Sangha, one states: "I take refuge in the Buddha. I take refuge in the Dharma. I take refuge in the Sangha." Due to the precious nature of these three entities, the Refuges are also known as the Three Jewels. For Buddhists with a devotional temperament, the Three Refuges are a reverential homage to the historical Buddha, his canonical teachings, and his monastic community, which serve as a source of help and protection. They relate to the Buddha, the Dharma, and the Sangha much as members of other theistic traditions might to their religion's deity, its scriptures, and its organization of religious specialists. Other Buddhists may regard the Three Refuges as representative of the awakened state of mind, any teachings that emanate from and lead to that state, and the community of all those who seek that attainment.

The Five Precepts

Lay Buddhists are expected to try to follow the Five Precepts, which serve as a basic moral code for all Buddhists. These are: 1) to refrain from taking life, 2) to refrain from taking what is not given (i.e., stealing), 3) to refrain from sexual intercourse, 4) to refrain from lying, and 5) to refrain from intoxicating drinks, which result in heedlessness. Since it is thought to be extremely difficult to live in worldly society and adhere to these principles, the monastic life is regarded as virtually indispensable for the most committed practice of Buddhism. For most lay Buddhists, and for married monks in certain Buddhist orders, the precept of celibacy is generally modified to "refraining from sexual misconduct."

The Sangha

The Buddha stipulated for the Sangha a number of rules for ethical conduct, for a simple life, free from excessive material attachments, and for dignified deportment. A number of "lesser rules" also developed through the course of his teaching career. Shortly after his death, at the First Buddhist Council, the Sangha decided to maintain and adhere to all of the monastic disciplinary precepts, major and minor. These are collected in the *Vinaya Pitaka* or *Basket of Monastic Discipline*. They outline some 227 rules for monks and 311 for nuns. The additional rules for nuns places them in a subordinate position in the monastic social order, but also offers them a measure of protection and dignity. In contrast to the prevalent thinking of his day, the Buddha acknowledged the equal capacity of women to attain spiritual enlightenment, and approved that their instruction be in no way inferior to that offered men.

A Buddhist monk is known as a *bhikshu* (Pali: *bhikkhu*), which literally means "beggar," although it has developed the honorific meaning of a religious renouncer "who depends on alms." Nuns are known as *bhikshunis* (Pali: *bhikkhuni*). Full ordination into the monastic community can only take place when one is an adult, after serving for a number of years as a novice. In certain countries, such as Thailand, it is fairly common for young men before entering their married and working life to spend from two weeks to several months as novices. Novices follow an additional five precepts to those followed by the laity. The responsibility of adhering to the entire disciplinary code is only incumbent on fully ordained monks.

If there is a sufficiently large community of monks in a particular place, they are expected to gather fortnightly and recite the Code of Discipline known as the Pratimoksha. At this time monks and nuns who have broken the disciplinary rules are expected to make a public confession. Minor infractions require only confession; others earn a reprimand or probation. The most serious offences lead to permanent expulsion from the Sangha. These are intentional sexual intercourse, theft of something substantial, murder, and making false claims about one's meditative attainments.

BUDDHA IMAGES (continued)

Setting in Motion the Wheel of the Dharma: In this *mudra*, the Buddha's index finger and thumb of each hand touch at their tips to form two circles. It symbolizes his teaching of the Four Noble Truths during the First Sermon at Sarnath, which began the turning of the Wheel (*chakra*) of his Teachings (*dharma*).

Meditation (*dhyana*) Posture: In this the Buddha is generally seated cross-legged with one or both hands in his lap, palms facing upward. The right palm is generally placed above the left. On occasion, particularly with images of Amitabha Buddha, the palms may curl and meet at the knuckles and thumbtips.

Other Postures: Two other common postures are the fear-not and boon-granting postures. In the former, with a bent elbow and fingertips pointing upward, the outward facing palm is held up at shoulder level as if say, "stop." It is a call to bring an end to fear and the sources of unskillful action. In the latter, the open palm faces forward with fingertips downward as if offering devotees some form of charitable giving (*dana*).

The daily routine of monks varies with their particular communities. Sangha members are expected to go on an almsround in the morning and humbly accept the food offerings placed in their bowls by supportive members of the lay community. They often wake early and eat only twice a day, with the last meal eaten before noon. Afternoons may be spent in study, meditation, or in the chanting of Buddhist scriptures. In certain Tibetan Buddhist communities, monks may learn various ritual arts, such as sacred dances and the construction of elaborate symbolic paintings known as *mandalas*. Others specialize in the art of debate on subtle nuances of Buddhist metaphysical doctrines. In certain schools of Chan/Ch'an (Zen) Buddhism, monks may occasionally engage in intensive periods of meditation, seated motionless for virtually every hour of the day for a week or more at a time.

Monks may also be called upon by the lay community to preside at certain occasions, such as at death rituals. Their activities at such times may involve chanting Buddhist scriptures known as *sutras*, the hearing of which is believed to be beneficial. Activities may also involve teaching the Dharma. In the Tibetan Buddhist tradition, immediately after a person's death a monk may be asked to recite the *Bardo Thodol* in the presence of the deceased. The *Bardo Thodol* (*Tibetan Book of the Dead*) is a text that serves as a sort of guide to the disembodied spirit of the deceased. It is believed that by hearing its teachings, the deceased may still have a chance to attain enlightenment, before taking rebirth in another bodily form.

There is an inseparable link between the lay and monastic communities in Buddhism. The Sangha needs the laity for its sustenance, since monks are not permitted to earn or even handle money, and should depend on offerings by others. The alms provided confer spiritual merit (*punya*) on the laity, since it inculcates in them the value of charitable giving. The Sangha, in return, provides the laity the most precious gift of all, teachings of the Dharma, which can lead to the most valuable attainment, *nirvana*. Even without providing any teachings, the Sangha stands for the community's highest values and aspirations. It embodies a sacred congregation that is a reservoir and even a sort of center for channeling merit and protection. When merit accrues to members of the Sangha, they are expected to transfer it mentally to needy sentient beings throughout the cosmos. In such a fashion the monastic and lay communities work together towards undermining the human tendency towards ego-centric actions while nurturing selflessness and purity of spirit.

Meditation

A crucial characteristic of Buddhism is its emphasis on the attainment of a pivotal insight into the nature of reality, which constitutes the attainment of *nirvana*. This insight is not believed to be attainable merely through a moral lifestyle, nor through the intellectual understanding of the Dharma. The last two items in the Noble Eightfold Path point to the necessity of developing Right Mindfulness (*smrti*) and Right Contemplative Absorption (*samadhi*), beyond the moral injunctions of Right Speech, Action, and Livelihood, and the intellectual orientation of Right Understanding and Intention/Commitment. Over the millennia since its origin, the Buddhist tradition developed many forms of meditation. Two major wings of the meditative process involve the development of mental calmness (*shamatha*) and insight (*vipashyana*). *Shamatha* develops as one watches the often turbulent activities of the body-mind complex. The practice of adopting a still posture and focussing one's awareness on the senses and the movements of thoughts and emotions is said to cleanse consciousness of its defilements. *Shamatha* meditation is intended to produce tranquillity, metaphorically calming the winds that churn up waves on what should be the smooth surface of the ocean of one's consciousness. Only with the surface calmed, can one gaze into its depths of the ocean of consciousness. *Vipashyana* practice enables one to observe the patterned relationships within physical and psychological processes. Uncovering these processes leads to insights into the nature of the mind, and is said to give the practitioner greater wisdom. Small insights may lead one to notice, for instance, the connection between certain perceptions and the arising of craving or revulsion. Insight into the complete

TERMINOLOGY

Pagoda: Term used to designate Buddhist *stupas* or temples in East and Southeast Asia. The word derives from *dagoba*, the Sri Lankan term for a *stupa*. *Pagodas* in Myanmar may be either solid structures housing relics, or temples for Buddhist deities. In China and Japan they are characterized by multiple tiers of roofs, which developed from the honorific motif of placing umbrellas atop most *stupas*.

Vihara: A Buddhist residence for monks. In Sri Lanka and Thailand it refers to a large prayer or meditation hall that houses a Buddha image. The Indian state Bihar derives its name from *vihara*.

Mantra: A sacred utterance. It is a syllable, word, or phrase used as an aid in meditation or in ritual activities. A well-known *mantra* in Tibetan Buddhism is *Om Mani Padme Hum* in which the *Om* and *Hum* correspond to cosmic vibrations and *Mani Padme* (*The Jewel in the Lotus*), may refer to the combination of wisdom and compassion that characterizes Buddha consciousness.

Smriti: Mindfulness, the main form of Buddhist meditation. Proper mindfulness is one of the items of the Noble Eightfold Path. *Smriti* is based on developing an unbroken awareness of sensory perceptions and the processes within consciousness. Deep calm (*shamatha*) and penetrating insight (*vipashyana*) may thus be developed.

Punya: Spiritual merit. Wholesome *karma* generated through generosity, virtue, and meditative realizations, it is believed to result in better rebirths, and may also be mentally transferred to other beings in need.

workings of the process of Dependent Arising is tantamount to the perfection of wisdom and the attainment of *nirvana*.

The two major schools of Zen Buddhism that developed in Japan emphasize meditative approaches that are suggestive of the *shamatha* and *vipashyana* practices. The Japanese word *zen*, from the Chinese *chan*, is derived from the Sanskrit word *dhyana*, which means "meditation." Zen Buddhism is thus centrally Meditation Buddhism. In the Soto school of Zen, the practice of calm, sitting meditation, known as *zazen*, is the central practice. In the Rinzai school, a characteristic practice is the pondering of an enigmatic question, known as a *koan*, such as the well-known example, "What is the sound of one hand clapping?" As the thinking mind struggles with this intellectually unanswerable question, a profound insight into the mechanics of thought and the thinking self is a possible outcome.

Devotional Buddhist Practice

In the Pure Land Buddhist schools, such as the Chinese Jingtu/ Ching-t'u and Japanese Jodo Shinshu, devotion is directed to the Buddha Amitabha (Chinese: Amituo Fo; Japanese: Amida). A Buddhist scripture from about the second century C.E. told of a *bodhisattva* named Dharmakara who, after extraordinary resolve and practice, created a heavenly realm known as the Pure Land or the Western Paradise, over which he presides as Amitabha Buddha (The Buddha of Boundless Radiance). The text teaches that anyone who expresses genuine faith in Amitabha and calls upon him with sincere desire will be reborn in his paradise. This has led to the practice of repeating the sacred utterance (*mantra*), "Nanmu Amituofo" ("Homage to Amida Buddha") repeatedly. In Nichiren Buddhism, another devotional form that developed in Japan by the teacher whose name it bears, devotion is expressed to the *Lotus Sutra*, rather than to a specific Buddha. Although these devotional practices appear to deviate from the goal of insight leading to *nirvana*, since they focus on personal moral development and depend on salvation from a divine source rather than through one's diligent effort, mantric repetition has been a perennial form of meditative practice in Asia dating to antiquity.

Other forms of devotional practice include addressing prayers to various savior *bodhisattvas*. Avalokiteshvara, the Bodhisattva of Compassion, often depicted with many arms to symbolize his capacity to help innumerable beings, progressively transformed into a female goddess as his cult moved through China and Japan. There he/she is worshiped as the compassionate goddess Guanyin/Kuan-yin (Japanese: Kannon), Cry Receiver. Another female *bodhisattva*/Buddha who is called upon for salvation, particularly in Tibet, is Tara, whose name means Savioress.

Tantric Practice

The Tantric approach in Buddhism centers on the use of esoteric (i.e., secret, hidden) teachings passed from teacher (*guru*) to disciple through graded initiations. The teachings and practices often involve the use of elaborate rituals whose ultimate purpose is to enable practitioners to realize their innate Buddhahood. Since *nirvana* is described as neither a place nor an effect brought about by a cause, but a penetrating realization into the truth about reality, the capacity for Buddhahood is within the grasp of all beings. Put another way, the Buddha nature is intrinsically present in all beings, but obscured by ignorance. Tantra regards itself as the most effective means of achieving Buddhahood.

Among Tantra's many practices are taking refuge in the spiritual teacher (*guru*), the use of sacred utterances (*mantra*), gestures (*mudra*), and diagrams (*mandala*), and elaborate meditative visualizations. Due to the emphasis that Tantra places on initiations, lineages of teachings have developed based on the transmitted teachings of particular *gurus*, known in Tibetan as *lamas*. For instance, the Dalai (Ocean [of Wisdom]) Lama of Tibet belongs to the Gelug-pa school whose teachings emanate from its founder Tsongkha-pa. The Nyingma-pa school traces it lineage back to the revered Tantric master, Padmasambhava. Tantra's secret transmissions may involve learning how to use particular *mantras*, which when repeated or uttered in the proper manner and context are believed to awaken dormant regions of consciousness, or even to unleash supernormal powers. A widely disseminated *mantra* is that of Avalokiteshvara, the Bodhisattva of Compassion: "*Om Mani Padme Hum*" (Om! The Jewel in the Lotus! Hum!). *Om* and *Hum* are sounds that cannot be translated, but are said to resonate with a primordial cosmic vibration. The Jewel is the symbol of the diamond-like (or thunderbolt) purity and indestructible nature of the wisdom of a Buddha-consciousness. This is why the Tibetan Tantric path is often called the Vajrayana or Thunderbolt Vehicle. The Lotus is another widespread symbol in Buddhism, representing the flowering of compassion of the Buddha-mind. Buddhas, like many Hindu deities, are often shown seated atop a lotus flower, which serves as a throne for the deity, who like a monarch presides over the flowering of the entire creation. The "Jewel in the Lotus" thus conveys the combination of wisdom (*prajna*) and compassion (*karuna*), the attributes of a fully awakened consciousness. It is often stated that they are one and the same, for the apex of wisdom is to be compassionately disposed towards all sentient beings, while to know true compassion for all beings is the highest wisdom.

The distinctive uses of meditative visualizations in Tantric Buddhism may have the practitioner meticulously visualize the image of a particular Buddha or *bodhisattva*. Avalokiteshvara, Manjushri, or Tara may be among the figures chosen, but there are countless others. *Mandalas*, elaborate sacred diagrams that depict the realm over which that Buddha presides, may be drawn, painted, or painstakingly constructed from colored grain or sand. *Mantras* may then be uttered while the practitioners also adopt bodily gestures known as *mudras*, to aid in forging an alignment with the visualized embodiment of enlightenment. Unlike devotional practices, in such Tantric practices one is not praying to the visualized Buddha or *bodhisattva*, but attempting to become one with it. In Japanese Shingon Buddhism, for instance, which is Tantric, *mudras, mantras,* and *mandalas* are the three elements used to fuse the body, speech, and mind of practitioners with that of the Buddha Mahavairocana (The Great Enlightener).

The Religious Cycle

Buddhism did not develop an elaborate festival cycle in many of the countries to which it migrated. The most widespread and important Buddhist festival day is Wesak/Vesak (Sanskrit: Vaishakha), which takes place on the full moon of the lunar month of Vaishakha (generally in May). It commemorates the Buddha's birth, his enlightenment, and his *parinirvana*. The inauguration of the festival is attributed to the emperor Ashoka. On this day members of the Sangha chant *sutras*, perform special *puja* ("ritual worship") rites, and give talks on the Dharma. Lay devotees visit monasteries, make donations to monks, attend Dharma talks, and perform devotional worship at Buddhist shrines. They may circumambulate *stupas*, light candles, offer flowers, burn incense, and recite prayers.

Such activities also take place throughout the year, but especially during Uposatha, which falls on full and new moon days. This is the time when the Sangha gathers to recite the Pratimoksha, and the laity use the opportunity to avail themselves of the community of monks. Lay members are also present when a person decides to join the Sangha, especially for ordination as a novice. Part of the rite has the novice monks receiving food that is placed into their alms bowl by members of their family. The almsround is the most common daily activity for Buddhists. Monks are expected to walk to the residences of lay persons and with a humble downcast gaze await food offerings. If none are offered, they should move on, monitoring their feelings. They are expected to display neither joy nor disapproval at whatever is placed in their bowls. For the Buddhist laity, this is an opportunity to demonstrate generosity, and in Buddhist countries it is not leftovers, but a portion of the family's own meal that is shared with the monks. Buddhist monks who reside in monasteries (*vihara*) may find that lay persons bring food offerings to the *viharas* for the monks as a gesture of charitable giving.

Although there are no mandatory requirements to go on pilgrimages, Buddhists are often attracted to sacred sites such as renowned temples, monasteries, and *stupas*. The four most important sites for Buddhists are Lumbini, where the Buddha was born, Bodh-gaya, where he attained *nirvana*, Sarnath, where he preached the First Sermon, and Kushinagara, where he entered *parinirvana*.

CONCLUSION

The twentieth century has seen a number of notable changes in the fortunes of Buddhism around the world. The rise of communist political philosophies in Asia led to the virtual destruction of Buddhism in the Soviet Union, China, Tibet, and parts of Southeast Asia. During the rule of the Khmer Rouge in Cambodia from 1975-1979 all but about three thousand of its fifty thousand monks were killed and all of its 3,600 temples were destroyed. It has only recently begun its revival there. The communist regime in Vietnam keeps Buddhist organizations under vigilant control. Thich Nhat Hanh, a Vietnamese Thien (Zen) monk whose spiritual maturation was forged during the turbulent period of the Vietnam War, has become one of the most well-known voices of Buddhism in the West.

While Chinese communism has had devastating effects on Buddhism in mainland China and Tibet, Buddhism in Taiwan is experiencing a marked revival with hundreds of new temples and thousands of newly ordained members of the Sangha in that country. Notably, the majority of the monastic community's members in Taiwan are now women.

The Chinese occupation of Tibet, while continuing to have an adverse effect on the people and on Buddhism in the region, has had beneficial side effects. After the XIVth Dalai Lama's exile to India, tens of thousands of Tibetans have joined him as refugees. This has contributed to a revival of Buddhism in India, the country of its birth, but from where it had virtually disappeared for many centuries. The Beat and counterculture movement in the 1950s and 60s contributed to the West's awakening to Buddhism, as has the plight of Tibet, the experiences of Americans during and after the Vietnam war, increased immigration from Asian countries, and the arrival of Buddhist teachers. Zen, Tibetan, and devotional forms of Buddhism are growing rapidly. Many are also attracted to intense insight (*vipashyana*) meditation retreats, of much shorter duration than commitment to the full monastic experience, since these mesh well with Western attitudes and lifestyles. The interest in Buddhism by women in the West is leading to fresh examinations of the tradition's attitudes to women and their potential place in the Sangha, where in some traditions, such as the Theravada, the lineage for the ordination of nuns has been wiped out.

Buddhism's inroads into the West have also led to its encounter with Western religious traditions. Thomas Merton, a monk from the Benedictine order, spearheaded interfaith dialogue between Christians and Buddhists, and similar interreligious engagement now occurs between Buddhists and many other faiths. In what is sometimes called "engaged Buddhism," certain Buddhist groups have applied the *bodhisattva*'s spirit of compassionate action to social inequities and injustices, and to tackle ecological and environmental issues that threaten all life. Such activities, along with developing socio-political philosophies that are informed by Buddhist values, reflect the ongoing transformation of Buddhism as it moves beyond the eastern hemisphere, its home for over two millennia, to engage sentient beings throughout the world.

Jainism is a religion characterized by the high value it places on non-violence (*ahimsa*). Most scholars attribute the establishment of the religion to the religious teacher Vardhamana Mahavira. Most Jains, however, regard Mahavira as the last in a line of twenty-four illustrious teachers known as Tirthankaras. Although there are about four million Jains in India and elsewhere in the worldwide Diaspora, most people know little about this ancient religion.

HISTORY

Vardhamana Mahavira

Although it is difficult to ascertain exactly when Mahavira ("Great Hero") lived, he is generally regarded as a contemporary of the Buddha. Most sources cite that he was born in 599 B.C.E. in Kundagrama, near Patna in northern India. Legendary accretions and variations in the textual narratives of his life make it difficult to extract fact from fiction. The story of Mahavira's life parallels that of the Buddha in so many ways that scholars wonder if the Jains borrowed their versions from the Buddhists or vice versa. Mahavira is reputed to have been born a prince in the royal family of king Siddhartha and queen Trishala. In some versions of the story he marries a woman named Yashoda and has a daughter named Priyadarshana. After the death of his parents, at about the age of thirty, he renounced his family and worldly life and embarked on a journey of self-discovery. He tore the hair off his head and beard as a symbol of his renunciation and joined a group of ascetics.

Mahavira's form of asceticism was intense. It included nudity, and begging for leftovers for one's food. He did not bathe, and did not ward off the attacks of animals. After a dozen or so years of such self-mortification, Mahavira attained what he regarded as *nirvana*, the highest state of enlightenment. He had become the Jina ("The Conqueror"), victorious over the effects of *karma* and the cycle of birth, death, and rebirth. Mahavira preached his doctrine of salvation for about thirty years, and died at the age of seventy-two. Some sources place his death at 527 B.C.E. Others claim he died in 467 B.C.E., and hold that he was born seventy-two years earlier. During his time as a teacher Mahavira attracted a number of disciples and formed a monastic community made up of monks, nuns, laymen, and laywomen. They are known as Jainas or Jains ("Followers of the Conqueror").

Sects

There were occasional disagreements among members of the community even during Mahavira's life. A renowned disciple, Goshala Maskariputra, broke away and founded his own tradition, known as the Ajivakas. The Ajivakas, whose deterministic belief system was based on the overarching power of "fate," flourished for many centuries. However, by the 14th century, they had vanished completely. About 200 years after Mahavira's passing, a First Council was held in Pataliputra (modern-day Patna), in northern India to consolidate the teachings. Around this time a group of Jains is reputed to have migrated to avoid a famine, but on their return discovered that the books that had been compiled and considered canonical disagreed with their own understanding of the teachings. This story offers a rationale for the division, and whatever the actual factors behind the first major division may have been, divisive disagreements appear to have certainly been evident by the first century C.E.

The two major sectarian divisions among the Jains are the Digambaras and the Shvetambaras, whose names reflect one major source of disagreement. The Digambaras ("Sky-clad") are the sect that insists on nakedness for true renouncers. They believe that Mahavira was naked and that any form of possession, including a simple garment, is a sign of vanity, modesty, or shame, and of attachment to material things. Hence clothing or ornamentation of any kind is a mark that one is not liberated. Shvetambara monks wear a simple white cloth, and hold that this is appropriate for life in society. Other differences between these sects will be discussed later.

Scriptures

There are substantial differences between what the Digambaras and Shvetambaras regard as sacred. Both groups agree that their earliest religious texts, known as the *purvas*, have now disappeared. The *purvas* are believed to have been teachings preached by each of the twenty-four Tirthankaras. The teachings of Mahavira were transmitted orally for several generations by successions of disciples. The Digambaras believe that Mahavira, after his enlightenment, only made a sacred mantric sound, which was not understood by anyone but his most advanced disciple, Indrabhuti. The Shvetambaras believe that Mahavira taught his disciples in the vernacular language, Ardhamagadhi. The earliest teachings, known as *sutras*, are placed in collections called *agama* or *agama sutras*, which are composed in Ardhamagadhi. Other texts, composed later but also held to be sacred, are found in languages such as Tamil and Sanskrit.

The Shvetambaras maintain that their canonical literature was preserved and compiled during various councils in the centuries after Mahavira's death. The first was held in Pataliputra, about 160–200 years after Mahavira's death. The second set of councils was held in the mid-fifth century C.E. at Mathura and Valabhi. It was at the third, the Council of Valabhi in the early sixth century, that the canon is held to have taken on its final form. The Shvetambara *agama* collection now consists of up to forty-five *sutras* divided into twelve groups known as *angas*. In addition there are numerous

LEADERS

Mahavira: The last of the twenty-four great Jain teachers. Legends state that he was a prince, named Vardhamana, from a northern Indian kingdom, who lived between the fourth and the seventh centuries B.C.E. He is said to have renounced worldly life at the age of thirty, and attained enlightenment at forty-two. He was then called "The Conqueror" (*jina*), a term from which his followers get the name, Jains. He attained final *nirvana*, leaving his physical body at the age of seventy-two.

Rishabha: The first of the twenty-four Jain spiritual teachers known as *tirthankaras*, or "ford-makers." He is believed to have lived on the India subcontinent eons ago, and established the current world order, with his son Bharata, the first emperor of India. His teachings are said to have been identical to those of Mahavira. He is also known as Adinatha.

Parshva: Said to have lived in Banaras, India and preached 250 years before Mahavira. There is some evidence that he was a historical figure.

Bahubali: Also known as Gotameshvara. Believed to be a son of Adinatha and brother of the legendary King Bharata. Bahubali renounced his throne and performed severe austerities. A megalithic statue of him is located in Shravanabelagola, a spiritual center for the Digambara Jain sect.

other works, also held in high regard but classified as "outside the *angas*" (*anga bahya*).

The Digambaras believe that much of the *agama sutra* collection was lost by the time of the First Council, and the rest of it by the middle of the second century C.E. They thus hold other texts, written by Jain scholars, as sacred. The two most highly regarded of these later compositions are Dharasena's *Shatkhanda agama* (actually written by two of his disciples) and Gunabhadra's *Kashayaprabhrita*. Some twenty other texts, grouped into four Anuyogas, round out their collection.

The Spread of Jainism

Mahavira's area of influence was in the region of the kingdom of Magadha (the north-east state of Bihar in modern India). Jain scriptures tell of missionaries to the regions of Kashmir and Nepal. An inscription dated to the second or third century B.C.E. recounts that King Kharavela of Kalinga (modern day Orissa), a kingdom to the south of Magadha, was a convert and disciple. Among the Mauryan rulers of Magadha, Ashoka's grandfather, the great emperor Chandragupta (ca. 300 B.C.E.), was reputedly a Jain, as was one of Ashoka's grandsons. Due to our sketchy knowledge of early Indian history, it is difficult to reconstruct the early diffusion of Jainism. However, it is clear that it managed to spread to southern India and westward to Rajasthan and Gujarat. The Digambaras believe that the disciple Badrabahu, who was the most knowledgeable of the original Jain teachers, took many of his followers south to avoid the effects of a famine in northern India. We also know that since the second and third councils were held at Valabhi, in Gujarat, that northwest Indian region must have had a substantial Jain community.

A Chinese pilgrim in the seventh century refers to a sizeable community of Digambara Jains in India, who appear to have outnumbered the Shvetambaras. Under royal patronage, the Digambaras flourished in southern India. The scholar-monk Jinasena, author of the *Adi-purana*, and his pupil Gunabhadra, composed books in the ninth century that are revered by Digambara Jains. A seventy-foot tall colossal statue of the saint Gomateshvara, sculpted from a single granite rock, suggests the vibrancy of the Jain community at Shravanabelagola (in the southern Indian state of Karnataka) in the tenth century. Meanwhile, Shvetambara numbers were increasing in the northern states of Gujarat and Rajasthan. In the eleventh century, king Kumarapala patronized the Jain scholar-monk Hemachandra, who authored treatises on Jain philosophy, music, grammar, and morality.

These developments were not un-hindered. The Jains found themselves challenged by rival religious groups such as the Buddhists and the Ajivakas. Their strong stance regarding non-violence initially put them in conflict with Hindu sects that promoted animal sacrifice. However, with the rise of devotional Hinduism in southern India, and the progressive rejection of blood offerings, particularly among Vishnu-worshipping Hindus, Jainism began to experience a weakening of patronage as Hindu sects gained royal converts. By the thirteenth century, when Islam began its ascendency in north India, Jain temples were often destroyed. Numbers declined. The influence of Islam on Jainism is perhaps evident in an offshoot of the Shvetambaras, the Sthanakvasi Jains, whose origin can be traced to the fifteenth century. Unlike the Murtipujaks, who perform devotional worship (*puja*) of images (*murti*) in temples, the Sthanakvasis reject image worship, preferring meditation halls as gathering places.

GROUPS/DIVISIONS

Shvetambaras: "White Clad." Sect that interprets Jain teachings more liberally. They permit monks to wear a white garment, and cover temple images of *jinas* with clothes. Women may be ordained as nuns and are regarded as capable of attaining liberation.

Digambaras: "Sky Clad." Conservative sect that emerged during the main major division in the first century. Monks do not wear clothes, and clothed images are regarded as unfit for worship. Women are thought to be incapable of attaining liberation. They also hold that those who have attained liberation have no further involvements with worldly activities.

Sthanakvasi: One of the sects of the Shvetambaras, which separated in the 1600s. They oppose the use of temples and images for worship.

The Modern Period

Since the Jains do not actively proselytize, their numbers have not grown dramatically, and their geographical spread has primarily been on the Indian subcontinent. Nevertheless, due to the immigration of families during the last few centuries, there are Jain communities throughout the world, with some numbering in the tens of thousands in Britain, the United States, and Canada. Due to their strong emphasis on non-violence, Jains have mostly gravitated towards professions in business and law. As a result, some have become financially prosperous. This prosperity has resulted in philanthropic acts, such as temple building and donations to the needy. Some Jains have made notable academic contributions, and Jainism is beginning to gain the attention of scholars. Jain values, which may have once seemed extreme, have begun to be revisited and embraced by people who perceive a growing culture of violence in the

modern world. For instance, Srimad Rajchandra, a Jain teacher, is believed to have inspired Mahatma Gandhi's high regard for non-violence.
The enormous influence that Gandhi, although he was not a Jain, has subsequently had on non-violent approaches to confronting injustice and oppression, may be seen as rooted in Jain teachings. Modern Jains, particularly
in the Diaspora, have begun to interpret and apply the principles of non-
violence more broadly. They have become involved in issues of social justice,
civil rights, nuclear proliferation, and animal rights, along with their traditional concerns with vegetarianism and asceticism.

BELIEFS

Tirthankaras *and the Cycles of Time*

Jainism conceives of itself as an everlasting religion that is taught at
various periods in the course of the cycles of time. The eras of time are lik-
ened to the turnings of a wheel in which the upward motion signifies a
vast period of positive growth in the condition of beings. However the
downward motion marks the progressive degeneration of existence. The
wheel's downward half cycle is envisioned as consisting of six spokes, or
eras. It is toward the end of the third era that the first great Jain teacher appears. He is Rishabha, who besides initiating the teachings of Jainism is
credited with the acts of a culture hero, bringing to humankind the
knowledge of fire, raising crops, and so on. Rishabha, also known as Adinatha (First Master), is the first of twenty-four such masters, known as
fordmakers (*tirthankara*), since they activate a teaching that bridges communities of renouncers and lay followers creating a ford (*tirtha*) across the
perilous waters of worldly existence.

The life stories of the Tirthankaras are very similar, as are their
teachings, since it is held that there is a singular truth that is realized
and enunciated again and again. However, the lifespans of the early
Tirthankaras are long, as are the time intervals between the arrival of
each. Thus Rishabha is believed to have lived for more than seventy tril-
lion years and stood three thousand feet tall. The life spans, physical stat-
ure, and intervals between their arrivals progressively diminish until the
arrival of Mahavira, the last in this cycle of Tirthankaras, near the end of
the era marked by the fourth spoke of the wheel. We are regarded as currently living in the era of the fifth spoke, which, like the sixth era, has a duration of some 21,000 years. The twenty-third Tirthankara, Parshva,
arguably a historical figure who was born and taught in the sacred city of

Banaras, is believed to have lived two and a half centuries before Mahavira. Little is written about the other Tirthankaras, and in iconographic depictions it is difficult to differentiate one from another. Each is generally associated with a particular emblem that is often placed on their chests or on their seats. Rishabha's emblem is the bull, Parshva's is the snake, and Mahavira's is the lion. Shvetambara Jains regard the nineteenth Tirthankara, Malli, to have been a woman. Digambara Jains consider him male, since they do not believe that enlightenment is possible while one is incarnated as a woman.

The Jain Worldview and the Human Condition

An influential text, accepted by both Shvetambara and Digambara sects, which summarizes and systematizes much of the metaphysical and ethical dimensions of Jain teachings, is the *Tattvartha Sutra*. It was composed in about the fifth century C.E. in Sanskrit by Umasvati. This text along with commentaries written on it in subsequent centuries provide the basis of the Jain worldview.

The Jains accept the notion of a triple world system (*tri-loka*), which is where the cycles of rebirth occur. The divisions within these worlds (*loka*) are complex and relate to the varying states of consciousness of the beings that may inhabit them. Rebirth in these realms is determined by the action of *karma*. Simply put, the triple world system consists of upper or heavenly realms inhabited by the gods, the middle realms where human beings exist, and the lower, hellish realms, where beings suffer terribly. Rebirth in any of these regions is fundamentally unsatisfactory and although a life spent there may be of a very long duration, it is nevertheless temporary. At the

TEXTS

Purvas: A collection of fourteen texts, which constitute the earliest teachings. Both Shvetambaras and Digambaras hold that these were lost long ago.

Agamas: The principal scriptural collection of the Shvetambaras, composed of some forty-five sacred texts grouped into *angas* ("limbs") and the *anga bahya*. There are twelve *angas*, the twelfth of which supposedly contained the *purvas*, but is now lost. Some texts appear to date from the 400s B.C.E.

Anga bahya: ("Outside the *angas*"). Subsidiary texts including works on monastic law. The Digambaras claim that both the *angas* and *anga bahya* collections were lost by the second century. Instead, they hold certain later compositions in reverence.

Kalpasutra: A Jain text, deriving from the *anga bahya* collection, composed in the second century B.C.E. It is recited during the Paryushan festival.

Epic poetry: Jain moral values are conveyed in such texts as the *Cilappatikaram* (*The Story of the Anklet*) and the *Manimekalai* (*The Jeweled Girdle*), composed in the fifth century by a Jain prince who became a Jain monk.

Adi purana: Ninth-century poem, composed by Jinasena, recounting stories of the lives of the early Tirthankaras, and other Jain heroes.

very top of the triple world system, depicted like an umbrella, is the Ishatpragbhara, which is the abode of liberated souls who have been completely freed from the cycles of transmigration.

The material of the world is composed of souls (*jiva*) and non-souls (*ajiva*). Souls are fundamentally pure, endowed with bliss, consciousness, energy, and omniscience. However, due to the effects of *karma*, they are embodied and entrapped. *Karma*, in Jain belief, is not merely a moral principle of cause and effect, as is the case in other Asian religious systems, but is a fine material substance that adheres to the soul, obscuring its intrinsic purity. The passions are particularly powerful attractors of karmic particles. However, *karma* is drawn to every one of a being's thoughts or actions, both intentional and unintentional. There are many types of *karma*, which negatively affect the soul's capacities of perception, energy, and consciousness in various ways resulting in ignorance and suffering. After death, the disembodied soul transmigrates to another body, carrying with it the sheath of *karma* from its previous life.

Liberation of the soul, which is the ultimate goal of Jainism, is only possible when one is free from the effects of *karma*. This is possible by engaging in a life of moral sobriety that inhibits the acquisition of new *karma*. However, rigorous austerities performed with strict discipline are essential to destroy the effects of previous *karma*. When the soul is nearly freed from its karmic bondage it may still be embodied, as was the case with the Tirthankaras, but no new *karma* of much consequence is acquired in that state. When the physical body is released, the *jiva* travels to the Ishatpragbhara, where it joins an infinite number of liberated souls, and enjoys perfect bliss and consciousness. Among the characteristics of a liberated soul is omniscience, understood not merely as the complete realization of the nature of the self or soul, but as the full possession of all knowledge.

Since without liberation the soul's capacities for full knowledge is flawed, the Jains have a high regard for relativity in philosophical assertions about the nature of reality. Their epistemological attitude, that is, their perspective on the manner in which we come to know what we do, is characterized by multi-valence (*anekanta*) and qualifications (*syad*). Since all things are constantly undergoing changes, however subtle, it is not possible for any statement to encompass comprehensively the nature of any item within reality. A suitable illustration, attributed to the Jains, is the story of the blind men who upon touching parts of an elephant, such as its tail or leg, assert that it is a rope or a pillar, since they are unable to apprehend the full nature of the creature. Similarly, a person may be a father, a son, a husband, and so on, depending on the perspective of the person who is observing and commenting upon him. This epistemological doctrine is therefore known as *syadvada*, or the Doctrine of Maybe (*syad*). Any statement attempting to assert a truth about the world cannot be accepted as fully true. It is subject to a range of uncertainties and qualifications.

Symbols

The Jain symbol, recently adopted during the 2,500th anniversary celebrations of Mahavira's *nirvana*, consists of a number of important symbols placed together. The symbol's outline is an octagonal shape that represents the cosmos, with the hellish realms at the bottom and the heavenly realms near the top. In the lower trapezoidal-shaped portion of the symbol, there is a human hand, its palm facing outward. It signifies a call to halt. Inscribed on the palm is a wheel within which is the word *ahimsa* or nonharming. Thus the symbol of the upraised hand is a call to non-violence. Above the hand, in the hexagonal portion of the outline is the *svastika*, an ancient symbol whose Sanskrit name translates as "well-being." To the Jains the *svastika* symbolizes the cycles of rebirth or *samsara*. Its four spokes refer to the four types of rebirth as heavenly beings, as humans, as animals or plants, and as beings who inhabit the hellish realms. Its four spokes may also evoke the four-fold community of monks, nuns, laymen, and laywomen.

Placed above the *svastika* are three dots, which stand for the Three Jewels of Jainism; Right Faith/Viewpoint, Right Knowledge, and Right Conduct. A semicircular arc above these dots, at the very top of the symbol represents the Ishatpragbhara, the abode of liberated souls. The liberated soul, or *siddha*, is symbolized by a dot within the space bounded by the arc and uppermost edge of the octagon. A Sanskrit phrase below the diagram reads, "*Parasparopagraho jivanam*." It translates as, "Living beings render service to one another."

SYMBOLS

Svastika: "Well-being." A sacred symbol whose spinning spokes signify the stages of existence on the wheel of worldly existence (*samsara*). They may also signify the four realms of possible rebirth: divine, human, animal, or hellish.

Open Palm: This is the symbol of the Jain principle of non-violence (*ahimsa*).

Cosmological Symbol: An eight-sided polygon resembling a giant being, which contains the open palm and the *svastika*. The *svastika* is topped with three dots, which symbolize the three jewels of right viewpoint, right knowledge, and right behavior. These are further topped with a crescent and dot, which represent the dwelling place of the perfected ones, or *siddhas*.

Images: The Tirthankaras and other Jain heroes are often depicted in immobile seated or standing positions. The Tirthankaras are all naked, and can only be distinguished from each other by a symbol upon their chests and their seats.

PRACTICES

The Jain community is composed of monks (*muni, sadhu*), nuns (*sadhvi*), laymen, and laywomen. Although the monks and nuns enjoy a higher status for their religious commitment, the laity are vital members of the community because of the support they provide for those who have renounced the householder lifestyle. Entrance into the renouncer's life requires a special initiation (*diksha*), which is often preceded by a preparatory period that may last for several years. Ancient prescriptions required initiates to tear out their hair in handfuls in the presence of their preceptor. In certain Shvetambara rites much of the hair on their head may be shaved, reducing the quantity that is actually pulled out. The renouncer accepts a robe (if Shvetambara), or abandons clothing (if Digambara), and receives a fly-whisk to brush away insects, a water-pot, and a new name. Renouncers also commit themselves to the Five Mahavratas (Great Ascetic Observances), which will define the nature of their asceticism. In significant ways the Five Mahavratas characterize Jainism, and rigorous adherence to them is believed to confer spiritual power on the ascetic. Lay Jains follow the *anuvratas*, or lesser ascetic observances, which are modifications of these great vows.

The Five Mahavratas

Of the five Mahavratas, it is the first that has given Jainism its most distinguishing value. This is *ahimsa*, or non-harming. It consists of rigorously avoiding practices (i.e., thought, word, or deed) that would inflict harm on any living creature. Jain ascetics thus watch where they walk to avoid stepping on small insects indiscriminately. Certain ascetics may carry a broom with which they sweep the ground before them to remove creatures that might inadvertently be harmed by their footsteps. The ground is also swept before sitting. Terapanthi and Sthanakvasi Jains wear a mask that covers nose and mouth to prevent the accidental inhalation of small organisms. Water is strained before drinking, and many ascetics do not bathe to avoid harming tiny creatures on the body or in the water. Naturally, because of the importance of the precept of non-harming, all Jains are vegetarians. However, since plants are also a life form, the very act of eating is fundamentally an act of *himsa*, or violence. Thus long and frequent periods of complete fasting are prescribed for ascetics. Naturally, for lay Jains, occupations that involve harming life should also be avoided. This has meant that Jains have not taken up professions such as hunting and fishing, and many have gravitated to professions in business, law, and education. This has resulted in economic prosperity for the community. Although the Jains differentiate between the degree of *karma* that results from intentional acts of violence versus unintentional ones, both types of action generate *karma*. Accidental harming is therefore also to be avoided.

The second Mahavrata is to adhere to a principle of truthfulness (*satya*). Jains are enjoined to tell the truth at all times, unless this would result in harm to another. In such cases, silence is preferred to telling a lie. This principle of truthfulness should extend to all of a lay Jain's activities including business and legal transactions. The third Mahavrata is the principle of not-stealing (*asteya*), more often described as not taking what is not given. The fourth Mahavrata is the vow of sexual purity. For renouncers it entails refraining from all sexual activity, while for lay persons it means adhering to the acceptable norms of sexual life, while striving for total celibacy. Sexual ejaculation is held to cause the death of countless life-forms. The fifth Mahavrata is non-attachment. This principle extends beyond the human propensity to acquire material objects. Jains are encouraged to give away material possessions, such as

---

FESTIVALS

Paryushan: A ten-day sacred period in September, celebrated by Shvetambaras, who recite the *Kalpasutra*. On the final day, they perform a ritual confession of their faults and seek forgiveness from family and associates. Digambaras celebrate a similar festival, known as Dasha Lakshana Parvan ("Period of Ten Signs"), which occurs shortly after Paryushan.

Dipavali: (lit., "row of lights"). The Hindu festival of lights is celebrated by Jains who regard it as the day Mahavira attained *nirvana*. They also worship the goddess of prosperity and good fortune, Lakshmi. Since many Jains are business people, they open new account books on this day, which also marks their new year.

Mahavira's Birthday: Celebrated on the thirteenth day following the new moon between mid-March and mid-April.

Akshaya Tritiya: Celebrated on the third day after the new moon between mid-April and mid-May. It commemorates an event in which the first Tirthankara, Rishabha, was given juice to break a long fast. Both Digambaras and Shvetambaras celebrate this act of generosity by undertaking fasts themselves.

---

clothing and jewelry, and even to limit the amount and types of food ingested. One should also be unattached to the cravings of the other senses, such as for visual and auditory stimulation. Occasionally added to this list is the injunction against eating after dark, which is regarded as unhealthy and potentially destructive to life-forms that may be attracted to lamp-flames.

It is thought to be extremely challenging for a person to maintain such principles while engaged in normal social life. This is why the renouncer's lifestyle is regarded as preferable or even indispensable for the attainment of liberation. Lay Jains normally adhere to modified forms

of the Five Mahavratas, and may only attempt to embrace all of them during short retreat periods. Many hope that in a future incarnation they will
have the capacity to take up the path of renunciation.

The Three Jewels

The Five Mahavratas constitute a portion of the principle of right
conduct, which is one of the Three Jewels of Jainism. The other two are
right views/faith, and right knowledge. Right views involves apprehend-
ing the perspectives that lead to the realization of Truth, and that the
teachings of Jainism embody the path to it. This produces a steadfast faith
in the Jain path of purification. Through the earnest application of the rigors of right conduct one progressively frees oneself from the defilements
of karma and enhances the acquisition of right knowledge.

The Six Obligatory Actions

There are six obligatory acts that are expected to be performed by
Jains sequentially as a single rite twice daily. However, since the proper
procedure for a single performance can take several hours, it is mostly incumbent on monks and nuns. Even these may opt to perform it less frequently, and lay Jains may do so only once in a year. The first obligatory
action is equanimity, which is at the heart of ascetic practice. It is a purification of oneself through meditative calm and thoughts of benevolence to
all souls. One should stand motionless for forty-eight minutes during this
procedure. The second action is to show reverence to the ford-makers.
This is normally done by reciting a twenty-four-verse hymn of praise to
the Tirthankaras. The third action is adoration of the community of
monks and nuns, especially one's own teacher.

The fourth obligatory act, known as pratikramana (repentance), is
central to the entire process. This is because the obligatory acts are
grounded in an attitude wherein one realizes that day-to-day existence in-
evitably brings one into injurious contact with other living beings. Thus
one needs to take stock of the damage that has been caused, seek forgiveness, and resolve to engage in the precepts of non-violence with renewed
determination. Among the assortment of vows reaffirmed during this
portion, the ascetic utters the statement: "I ask forgiveness from all souls.
May they all forgive me. May I have affection for all beings and enmity to
none." The fifth obligatory act is a meditation on the liberation of the jiva
from its material confines. In a motionless position, standing or sitting,
that mirrors the depictions of Tirthankaras, one meditates on the process

of abandoning the body. In the sixth act, one vows to renounce a long list of actions and to take upon various types of food restrictions. The completion of this rite is said to leave the devotee spiritually invigorated.

Sallekhana

One of the most highly regarded acts in Jainism, which is often perplexing to outsiders, is *sallekhana*, a religious fast resulting in death. The concept of *sallekhana* grows naturally from Jain metaphysical doctrines, as well as its ethical sensibilities. Restlessness and passion in thought, word, and deed leads to the accumulation of *karma*. Thus liberation necessitates the elimination of all previously acquired *karma*, and stopping the acquisition of new *karma*. When one intensifies the application of Jain ethical principles, which are grounded in nonviolence and equanimity, dispassion towards physical life is believed to grow. One is able to remain motionless for progressively longer periods of time, and even the drive for food and drink to sustain the needs of the body diminishes. As meditation deepens, one draws further inward, until finally one is able to release oneself consciously from the fetters of physical existence.

Thus *sallekhana* is not regarded as a suicide, but a religious death. Suicide is generally an act of desperation and emotional upheaval, grounded in violence towards oneself and an escape from suffering. By contrast, *sallekhana* is viewed as a heroic and dispassionate act, performed in a lucid mental and emotional state. Originally performed by renouncers at the peak of their religious practice, it was later prescribed for the devout in the last stages of their lives. Although its occurrence these days is rare, there are numerous literary accounts of *sallekhana* in the past, and hundreds of memorial markers have been unearthed for those who chose it as a form of death.

RITES/RITUALS

Pratikramana: "Going back." A ritual confession of one's transgressions and repentance for these actions. Although it is prescribed to be performed twice daily, it is mandatory once a year, on the last day of Paryushan.

Fasting: Most Jains partake in periodic fasting, either privately or in public communal form. Some involve total abstention from food and water, while in other fasts only certain items are avoided. The austerity of fasting is thought to purify the soul.

Charitable giving: Jains hold elaborate ceremonies during which portions of their wealth are given away. This is done to enhance their attitude of nonpossessiveness.

Caturmas: "Four months." The retreat period for wandering monks during the monsoon rains. Lay people frequent their institutions to listen to religious talks and frequently undertake fasts.

Puja: The veneration of images of deities and Tirthankaras with offerings of flowers, food, and an honorific flame.

Jain Puja

Although Jainism promotes an ascetic ideal, the fabrication of images of Mahavira for the purposes of worship seems to have been evident a few centuries after his death. In the centuries that followed, the tradition of worshipping the Tirthankaras was established. Eventually each Tirthankara was paired with a male (*yaksha*) and female attendant (*yakshi*). This, together with the worship of other deities, such as the goddess of wealth, Lakshmi, and the goddess of learning, Sarasvati, expanded the Jain pantheon considerably. At Shravanabelagola, the center for Digambara Jains, a megalithic statue of Adinatha/Rishabha's son, Bahubali (Gotameshvara) is the focus of a special consecration rite. The statue, which is almost seventy feet tall and hewn from a single rock, depicts the naked Bahubali standing in an intense meditation of such duration that his body is overgrown with vines. Every twelve years, the image is bathed in milk and other liquids, and showered with flowers and fruit in a gesture of devotion.

Devotion to the Tirthankaras, other Jinas, deities, teachers, and so on, is encouraged by senior members of the Jain community. The typical Jain devotional rite or *puja* consists of eight parts. After a respectful circumambulation (walking around) of the image, it is bathed, anointed with a fragrant paste, and garlanded with flowers. Incense and a lamp flame are passed before it, and it is offered rice, then sweets, and finally fruit. Such devotion is held to be conducive to one's personal spiritual advancement, because unlike deity *puja* in Hinduism, the Tirthankaras neither need adoration nor intervene to fulfil a votary's desires.

Annual Rites

An important period in the yearly cycle occurs during the four months of the rainy season known as *caturmas*. Because the rains impeded the wandering life for ascetics, who could also trample on freshly germinated seedlings and other life forms, the season developed into a period for more stationary religious pursuits such as prayer and meditation. An eight-day period during *caturmas*, known as Paryushan (Abiding), is dedicated to the recitation of *sutras* and the confession of sins. Shvetambara monks recite the *Kalpasutra*, a text that tells the stories of Mahavira and the other Tirthankaras, while Digambara Jains read from the *Tattva-artha Sutra*. The last day of the festival is particularly important. Jains make stringent efforts to prevent the taking of life, sometimes contacting community groups such as slaughterhouses with a plea, or with funds, to stop the killing of animals on that day. They participate in a communal confession of sins, and even send letters to friends and acquaintances asking forgiveness for any harm they may have caused.

The Hindu festival of lights, Dipavali/Divali, is celebrated by Jains in honor of Mahavira's liberation. It takes place in the month of Kartika (October/November) and marks the beginning of the Jain New Year. Merchants close their annual accounts, and purchase new account books for the year ahead. The goddess of fortune, Lakshmi, is worshipped, as are other objects that are symbols of wealth and prosperity.

On the full moon of the month of Kartika, Jains celebrate the end of the rainy season, and monks and nuns once again take up their role of wandering, which had ceased during the monsoons. Jains may now eat green vegetables, and some embark on a pilgrimage to Palitana, in Gujarat. Palitana is the village beside Mount Shatrunjaya, one of Jainism's most holy places because renowned figures in Jain mythology are reputed to have attained liberation there. There are over 850 shrines in the temple complex.

There are also festivals to commemorate the important events in the lives of the Tirthankaras. The most celebrated of these is Mahavira Jayanti, in honor of Mahavira's birth in the month of Chaitra (March/April).

HISTORY

Neither Hindu Nor Muslim

When we think of India, we tend to think of its Hindu character. But for at least a thousand years, Muslims had considerable influence there. In a succession of diverse empires, Muslims usually held the reins of power in the northern part of the vast lands, and often in the central and southern areas. Sikhism developed in that mixed environment, where a Muslim elite and a native Hindu majority wrestled in various ways with their uneasy relationship.

In this cultural and religious mix, some tried to create a religious synthesis, incorporating ideas from both Hindu and Muslim religious speculation. The success of such attempts was hindered by sharp core differences. Muslims rejected images; these were central to Hindu religious life. Muslims were unwavering monotheists; Hindu religion teemed with gods and goddesses. Muslims stressed the equality of all believers before God and rejected priesthood; Hinduism was defined and divided in all areas of life by the caste system, and one caste had exclusive rights and honors as priests.

Sikhism was but one of many attempts to fuse this unlikely coupling. Even with Sikhism—the most successful of these efforts—the fusion was one-sided, for Hinduism had the stronger influence. Indeed, Sikhs were

often identified as Hindus in the first four hundred years of their movement, while other groups that made up the cultural mix in India, such
as Muslims, Buddhists, Parsis, and Jains, were never confused with or
counted as Hindus. In the later part of the 1800s and early 1900s, however, Sikhs made a determined effort to distinguish themselves fully from
Hinduism. Hindu images were removed from local Sikh buildings and
from the famous Golden Temple, and greater distinctions between Sikh
and Hindu rituals were introduced.

In recognizing the influence of the mixed cultural environment in
which Sikhism took its shape, we should not dismiss the originality and
genius in the distinctive Sikh message. From a Sikh perspective, their religion is a revelation from God to their Gurus, not a synthesis of Hindu and
Muslim belief and practice.

Muslim India Prior to the Rise of Sikhism

Nanak, the founder of Sikhism, was born in the Punjab, a region that
lies partly in northwestern India and partly over the border in Pakistan.
Nanak's hometown lies within Pakistan, as do some other sites significant
to the Sikhs. Most Sikhs now live in the Indian area of the Punjab, having
fled there in 1947 in the violence that marked the independence and
partition of India and Pakistan.

Some Muslim influence had been felt in the area of the Punjab from
712, when the Arabs conquered Sind, the northwest coastal gateway into
India. But it was not until the arrival of the Turks, themselves recent converts to Islam, that Islam's forceful presence was felt throughout the north
of India. The Turks annexed the Punjab in 1022; in the same year they
founded Lahore, the first Muslim Indian capital. By the early 1200s, the
Turks controlled most of northern India, and some of the central part,
under what was called the Turkish Sultanate, with a new capital at Delhi.
The Turks were keen religious zealots, and they destroyed many cherished Hindu temples and images, the presence of which offended Muslim
monotheistic sensibilities. During this period, many Hindus converted to
Islam: some converted for tax breaks or improvement of their low caste
status, others because of the religious appeal of Islam. Various groups
arose, too, that espoused a mixture of Hindu and Muslim beliefs and
practices.

Much of the known world fell to the Mongols in the early 1200s.
India, however, escaped. The Delhi Sultanate was able to defend the
northern Himalayan mountain passes, causing the Mongols to bypass

India in their sweep westward, where they brought the Muslim Abbasid Empire, centered in Baghdad, to an end in 1258. The Mongol advance was checked shortly after that, and its empire split apart. Mongols who settled in the western territories intermarried with the local elite and adopted Islam.

Timur, the Lame (sometimes called Tamerlane), was from this mix, being of Mongol and Turkish ancestry. In the later part of the 1300s, he entered India and destroyed the Delhi Sultanate, but he left no stable government in place as he focused on other areas in his scheme of empire. This left northern India largely desolate, with Delhi in ruins. Rival Muslim sultans and Hindu warlords (*rajputs*) squabbled and fought each other throughout the 1400s, until a new Turko-Mongol ruler, Babar (the "Tiger") descended into northern India.

By this time, Islam had been a formidable religious and political force in northern India for 500 years. During this period, Muslim rulers generally had showed little tolerance of Hinduism. Babar and the early successors in his Mughal (Mogul) dynasty changed that, removing the legal restrictions on non-Muslim religions and taking an active interest in vigorous theological debate and exchange among all religions for which he could find representatives. This early Mughal period is the most important religious and political setting for understanding the foundation and growth of Sikhism, for it was in this tolerant environment that Sikhism established itself. Later, however, conditions deteriorated; Sikhism was suppressed and forced to develop a militaristic character.

EMPIRES IN INDIA

Turkish Sultanate of Delhi: (1206-1526). A Turkish Muslim empire, of various dynasties, generally repressive of Hinduism. Extended rule into central India.

Mughal: (1526-1857). Founded by Babar, these Turko-Mongol rulers initially were tolerant of religious diversity. Sikhism flourished initially under the Mughals until a more conservative Muslim influence arose. The Mughals ruled India until 1857, though in the latter years as puppets of the British.

British Raj: (1757-1947). Great Britain started its conquest of India in 1757, but did not formally depose the Muslim sultan until 1858. Its social and political policies led to unrest and rebellion, though the Sikhs came to prosper under British rule.

MAJOR LEADERS

Ten successive Sikh Gurus led the movement during its first two centuries. We list the three most significant.

Nanak: (1469-1539). The founder of Sikhism and author of almost one thousand of the hymns in the 6,000-hymn *Adi Granth*.

Arjan: Fifth Guru and first martyred Sikh leader. Led the Sikhs from 1581-1606, during a time of considerable success. He built the Golden Temple and established the Sikh canon. He composed over one-third of the hymns.

Gobind Singh: Tenth and last Guru. Led the community from 1675-1708. Under him, the militant *khalsa* movement was established, along with the distinctive "Five Ks" of Sikhism.

Kabir and the Sant Tradition

Although Nanak (1460-1539) is considered the founder of Sikhism, he was profoundly influenced by the ideas of Kabir (1440-1518), an older contemporary. Kabir and others in this Sant ("saint") tradition were influenced by both Hindu and Muslim ideas: from Hinduism, they drew from the *bhakti* tradition; from Islam, they drew from the Sufi tradition. Both emphasized the oneness of God and the need for loving devotion to God as the highest duty of humans. Such devotion was the means by which one would attain the highest religious goal—a union with God and, in Hindu terms, freedom from *karma* and rebirth. The Hindu *bhakti* movement in North India, which emphasized monotheism and rejected much of the ceremonial and priestly side of Hindu religion, had itself been shaped under the devotional influences of Islam.

Kabir had rejected the standard cherished texts of his contemporaries—both the Quran of the Muslims and the Vedas and Upanishads of the Hindus. Loving devotion to God and the repetition of God's name were more powerful than priest, sacrifice, or ceremony. Kabir expressed many of these ideas in poetry, and Nanak copied that technique to spread his message. So closely parallel were the ideas of Nanak and Kabir that almost 300 of Kabir's hymns were incorporated into the Sikh canon. Kabir is still regarded as a sage and saint in Sikhism, Hinduism, and elements of Islam.

Nanak

Nanak was born in 1469 C.E. to Hindu parents in the Punjab. He became a herdsman, and later a civil servant; he married, and fathered two sons. Some stories report that he gained a reputation in his community for miraculous powers and exceptional religious devotion, while still a youngster. More important to the Sikh tradition, however, was a religious experience he had at about the age of thirty. He sensed that he had been ushered into the divine presence, where God was revealed to him as the "True Name." From this experience, he believed he had been commissioned to spread the message of the one God, a sentiment that the first line of the first hymn in the Sikh canon expresses: "There is one God." Nanak concluded from this insight that the religious distinctions and identities maintained by his contemporaries were irrelevant or nonessential. "There is," he said, "no Hindu or Muslim."

After his initial experience, Nanak left on a twenty-year mission throughout India, accompanied by his faithful friend and musician,

Mardana, a Muslim. Reflecting his new perception of the unimportance of religious boundaries that marked the world about him, Nanak wore a mixture of Hindu and Muslim clothing (his lower garments were Hindu, his upper garment and headdress Muslim). He and Mardana visited religious sites of importance to both traditions. Some legends have Nanak journeying even to Mecca and Medina, chief Muslim centers, where, according to the story, he violated Muslim custom by sleeping with his feet pointing toward the Kaba. When challenged, he inquired as to which direction he could place his feet so that they did not point to God, since God was everywhere. Whatever the historical worth of the story, it does capture the spirit of Nanak. Similar stories show him questioning Hindu sensibilities as well. During his travels, Nanak composed numerous hymns, which he sang to Mardana's accompaniment, as he attempted to spread the news about the "True Name." Out of these verses came the core of the Sikh holy book, the *Adi Granth*.

Growing older and becoming ill, Nanak returned to the Punjab with disciples (lit., *Sikhs*) he had made. They settled in Kartarpur, the first town in which a Sikh way of life was instituted. It was in this area that Nanak's message had its greatest success. Over time, most of the Punjab was converted to Sikhism. This gave Sikhism a distinctly Punjabi culture and ethnic character. There, against the claims and counter-claims of Hindus and Muslims, Nanak adopted new forms of community behavior. In particular, Nanak's followers, met regularly at a communal kitchen (*langar*) where all ate together, regardless of caste

---

MAJOR TEXTS

Adi Granth: (also called "*Granth Sahib*"). *Granth* means "book;" *Adi* means "first," distinguishing it from a later supplement. This holy book of the Sikhs is the focus of Sikh devotional life. It contains about 6,000 hymns, mainly from the first five Sikh Gurus, but some from Hindu and Sufi mystics.

Dasam Granth: (lit., "tenth book"). Hymns of Gobind Singh, the tenth Guru.

Janamsakhis: (lit., "birth stories"). Prose works (in contrast to the poetry of the *Adi Granth*), compiled in the 1600s, some time after the death of Nanak. These recount Nanak's birth and life.

MAIN FESTIVALS

Sikhs modify and celebrate the main Hindu festivals of northern India, in addition to their own special days, which are associated with one of the Gurus.

Vaisakhi (Baisakhi): The Sikh (and Hindu) New Year celebration (April 14). Sikhs recall the founding of the Khalsa. The complete text of the *Adi Granth* is read and the Sikh flag is replaced with a new one.

Divali: The four- to five-day Indian festival of lights, held in late autumn. Sikhs decorate their *gurdwaras* with lights. Sikhs commemorate the freeing of the sixth Guru, calling the event "Day of Freedom from Imprisonment" (*Bandi Chhorh Diwas*).

Gurpurbs: Celebrations of some event associated with one of the Gurus, such as birth or martyrdom.

distinctions. Normally caste boundaries would have prevented that kind of close social interaction. The communal meal is still a highlight of the Sikh's week.

Before his death at about seventy, Nanak appointed Agnad, one of his followers, as the community's leader, or Guru. For whatever reason, he did not select one of his sons, though the office of Guru was soon to become hereditary within the Sikh movement.

Growth and Self-Definition

Sikhism began during a time of dramatic political change. The Mughal emperor Babar had started his conquest of northern India shortly before Nanak settled his followers in the Punjab. The new Muslim rulers, established mainly in Delhi and the Punjab, were sensitive to the Hindu religion of the native peoples. During the reign of Akbar, Babar's grandson, who came to the throne only fifteen years after Nanak's death, Hindus, as well as Muslims, could reach high office in the Muslim court.

Akbar (1556-1605) eliminated special taxes on non-Muslims and permitted the construction of Hindu temples. Sikhs, being viewed largely as Hindus, flourished under such tolerance and religious experimentation. By the time of the fourth Sikh Guru, Ram Das (1534-1581), Sikhism had become wealthy, in large part from imperial favor. Ram Das used Sikh wealth to support missions throughout the land, which increased the Sikh reputation and appeal. The Sikhs established a capital in the new town of Amritsar (lit., "pool of immortality"), named for a large manmade water pool dug there.

Sikhism attracted even more converts under the fifth Guru, Arjan (1563-1606), when he undertook relief efforts during a famine that hit the Punjab. Under his leadership, two distinctive features of Sikh religion were established. The Sikh temple was built in Amristar, being completed in 1601. In 1604, the first authorized canon was finalized, over one-third of which consisted of Arjan's own compositions. This was the high point of Sikh creativity and consolidation as a religion.

But the Muslim elite quickly came to regard Akbar's generally tolerant treatment of Hindus as a threat to their own privileges. Further, Akbar's favors to Hindus raised suspicions about the adequacy of Akbar's own Muslim faith among his fellow Muslims. Against mounting opposition from Muslim traditionalists, Akbar declared himself the final interpreter of the Quran, and in 1582 he established a new religion, the "Divine Faith" (*Din Ilahi*). In spite of opposition from Muslim clerics, Akbar was able to expand his empire throughout much of India, increasing its wealth and splendor beyond that of any empire in the world at the time. Art and literature flourished; religious toleration was court policy.

The considerable success of the Sikh movement brought suspicion and reaction from the Muslim government in Delhi and its provincial administration at Lahore in the Punjab, where the Sikhs were clustered. The Sikhs had become more than an interesting and novel sect; their success had made them into a political force. Given that the Mughals already faced threats from the older dynasties of Muslim sultans and from Hindu princes, new opposition could not be treated lightly. Further, the emperor was beginning to feel pressure from conservative Muslim clergy, who opposed the Mughal policy of religious toleration. When Guru Arjan unwisely sided with a son of the emperor Jahangir (ruled 1605-1628) in a revolt against the emperor, Jahangir put down the revolt and had Arjan executed, along with others. Relations between the Sikhs and Mughals were to remain strained from then until the collapse of the Muhgul Empire over two hundred years later.

Under the next emperor, Shah Jahan (ruled 1628-1658), best known for the construction of the Taj Mahal, the court became more rigorously Muslim. Hindus suffered extensive loss of rights, as did Muslim "heretics," and new groups, such as the Sikhs. Many Hindu temples were destroyed, including the ones believed to mark the birthplace of Krishna and Rama. On these spots, mosques were built. (Incidently, in 1992, one of these mosque was destroyed by Hindu fundamentalists, and riots and mounting deaths

PRINCIPAL SYMBOLS

The "Five Ks": Symbols of the Khalsa. (See box below.)

Turban: Although now a distinctive feature of Sikh male dress, it was the common Muslim headdress, still used in various Muslim areas.

Nishan Sahib: The triangular yellow or saffron Sikh flag, always flown from the *gurdwara*. It bears the *khanda* symbol.

Khanda: The primary symbol of Sikhism. It consists of a two-edged sword surrounded by two daggers, with a circle at the center.

Ik Onkar: A term used for the one God, formed by the figure "1" and the "O" sound in the Gurmukhi script. The "O" sound is the same as that featured in the OM sound.

THE "FIVE Ks"

Symbols of the Khalsa. They represent a militant commitment to the defence of Sikhism. All five terms start with the "K" sound in Punjabi.

Kes (uncut hair): This includes hair on the head and the beard. The turban helps keep the hair tidy, and the long beard is often combed up under the turban.

Kangha (comb): Given the obligation not to cut one's hair, a comb is an essential tool for grooming.

Kirpan (sword, now ceremonial and small, like a knife): The military nature is clear.

Karha (steel bracelet): Generally this is worn on the right hand.

Kachha (long shorts): Now a garment of underwear. It was originally designed for solders and military action.

over the matter continue, as Hindus fight for the right to built a temple to Rama on the spot.)

Guru Arjan's son Hargobind (1595-1645) became the sixth Guru at the age of nine. During his reign, the Sikhs took more active defensive measures against the Mughals. The Sikhs moved from the Punjabi plains to the foothills of the Himalayas, and started training in the arts of war. Further, they built a fort in Amritsar to defend the Sikh Temple. For much of the 1700s, the Sikhs were clustered in these foothills.

The Khalsa Brotherhood

Gobind Singh (1675-1708), the last of the Sikh Gurus, led the community throughout most of the reign of the Mughal emperor Aurangzeb (1658-1707). Mughal policy shifted sharply back to orthodox and conservative Islam, reimposing many of the restrictions under which non-Muslims had lived prior to the more tolerant reign of the earlier Mughals. On Baisakhi, the Hindu New Year's Day, in 1699, Gobind called upon Sikhs to become part of a new association of soldier-saints, called the Khalsa (the "pure"). This group took as its mandate the establishment of God's kingdom as a political as well as a religious reality.

The new brotherhood consciously rejected caste concerns, which had remained part of the Sikh consciousness, in spite of Nanak's efforts to minimize such distinctions. The brotherhood was to be the caste of the initiates. Many low caste men and untouchables joined the movement, empowered by the new dignity they gained within the brotherhood.

Initially, the Khalsa movement had mixed military results. Gobind Singh's sons were killed in battle or captured and executed. Sikhs were pushed from the plains of the Punjab, and hundreds of Sikhs were executed. But the Muslim elite had setbacks too. The Sikhs wiped out most of the Muslim landowners in the Punjab during the conflict. Further, the Mughal Empire itself soon began to weaken, and the Sikhs were able to reestablish themselves firmly in the Punjab in the latter half of the 1700s, inspired by the vision of the Punjab as their Holy Land. They built a line of defensive forts, and settlements in the area paid them money for protection. Under Ranjit Singh (1780-1839), a powerful Sikh nation arose in the early 1800s. On Ranjit's death, however, his heirs engaged in a number of dynastic plots and assassinations, leaving their nation weakened.

British Rule and Post-Colonial India

By 1757, Britain had begun its century-long conquest of India. Sikhs fought losing but determined wars against the British (1845–1846 and 1848–1849). When the British annexed the Punjab, the Sikhs surrendered and adjusted to the new political reality. Sikhs quickly proved themselves valuable allies of the British, particularly in the Indian Mutiny ("Sepoy Rebellion") only eight years later, when they sided with the British against their enemy of long-standing, the Muslims. Having become loyal British subjects, Sikhs were recruited to serve as police and soldiers throughout the widespread colonial territories. In the British army, Sikhs gained a worldwide reputation as an elite fighting force. They still constitute a considerable minority in the Indian army, though they represent only about two percent of the Indian population.

The hope of an independent Sikh homeland was frustrated when British colonial rule ended in 1947. Sikhs failed to gain their own nation in the restructuring of India, which resulted in a Muslim Pakistan and a largely Hindu India. Worse, the Sikh homeland (and holy land), the Punjab, was divided between Pakistan and India. In what became a violent period of resettlement, Sikhs in the Pakistan-held areas of the Punjab fled to the Indian-controlled area, ejecting and displacing Muslims, who then fled westward into Pakistan. Most Sikhs now live in the Indian area of the Punjab, the "bread-basket" of India, a highly productive agricultural area, watered by the "five rivers" (which is what Punjab means) that feed the Indus River.

After the Indo-Pakistan War of 1965, India created a Punjabi-speaking province in the Punjab, in which Sikhs constituted the majority.

MAIN PRAYER

Japji: The first passage in the *Adi Granth*, recited each morning by faithful Sikhs.

There is but one God
Whose name is True,
The Creator,
Devoid of fear and enmity,
Immortal, unborn, self-existent,
Great and bountiful.
The True One was in the beginning,
The True One was in the primal age.
The True One is, was, O Nanak, and the True One also shall be.
(MacAuliffe, *The Sikh Religion* [1909], p. 35)

MAIN RITUALS

Baptism of the Sword: Initiation into the Khalsa involves members stirring sugar water in a bowl with a sword, and then sprinkling that water over the head and the eyes of the new member.

Taking the Hukam: On various occasions, the *Adi Granth* is opened at random and the first passage on the opened page provides guidance for the circumstances. In naming ceremonies, the first letter of the passage determines the first letter of the child's name.

Path: A reading of the entire *Adi Granth*. Normally this involves continuous reading, taking about forty-eight hours. This is called the Akhand Path. The Sahaj Path, conducted after death, is not continuous, but made to stretch over the ten-day mourning period.

Although most Sikhs have accommodated themselves to their present political realities in India, a militant element still seeks independence for a Sikh homeland, which they call Khalistan ("land of the pure"). India's Prime Minister, Indira Gandhi, ordered an attack on the Golden Temple in 1984 and was assassinated by two of her Sikh bodyguards later that year. These events sharpened nationalist tensions, both in India and in countries to which Sikhs have immigrated.

BELIEFS

The Sikh religion came to birth in a land largely populated by Hindus and governed by Muslims. It is not surprising, then, to find beliefs of both traditions absorbed into the worldview of the Sikhs. A quick scan of their primary beliefs suggests that ideas of God are most informed by Muslim views, ideas of humans and their dilemma are most informed by Hindu beliefs, and ideas of the solution to the human plight are informed by both. But the Sikh borrowings from Islam and Hinduism are more nuanced than any quick glimpse can grasp. For one thing, some Muslim ideas had already influenced Hinduism prior to the rise of the Sikh movement. For another, there is the Sikh genius in shaping diverse elements into a viable religious system.

God

The oneness of God is foundational to Sikhism. God is the creator, and it is to him, and to him alone, that everyone owes worship and obedience. Broadly, this perspective is similar to the general Islamic view of God. More specifically, Sikh beliefs about God share most with the Sufis, a particular perspective within Islam, and with elements of Hindi *bhakti* belief. Both of these traditions had profound impact on Nanak, and on his model, Kabir.

Sikhs do not provide a specific name for God. The main term by which Nanak spoke of God was simply the "True Name." Like Muslims, Sikhs use hundreds of adjectives to describe God. Most of these modifiers reflect some aspect of God's mercy or his justice.

In line with Islamic thought, Sikhs reject any effort to portray God. But Sikhism did show respect to the images of Hindu deities, even housing such images in the Golden Temple until a vigorous reform movement in the late 1800s and early 1900s erased most of the visible links Sikhs had to their Hindu roots.

The World

As in monotheistic systems generally, the world is seen as a work of God, and thus good, according to Sikhs. But the world is not an end in itself, nor is it the ultimate reality in which humans are to find their fulfillment. In line with Hindu thought, the world is part of *maya* or illusion. The world is transitory. Nothing but God has an eternal character.

Humans

Human existence is the highest stage in the cycle of *samsara*, a system of reincarnation based on the forces of *karma*. As in Hinduism, it is only at this stage that one can gain liberation from the cycle.

Sikhs stress the equality of all humans. That is done in a variety of ways. The caste system, which starkly separates one human from another, was rejected, even though in practice it still has some influence within the Sikh community. Women, traditionally subordinate in both the Hindu and Muslim traditions, were treated with greater regard. They can regularly participate in the activities in Sikh assemblies, though they generally are excluded from the governing councils of the *gurdwaras*.

Karma

Sikhs retain many of the primary elements of Hindu speculation. Humans live in a world that at its core is not the ultimate reality, but it is a reality of a kind, which humans are held to by the law of *karma*. Thus the inequities of the world are explained and human responsibility maintained. Good deeds are rewarded; bad deeds are punished. The cycle of rebirths ensures that "one reaps what one sows."

ETHICAL CONCERNS

Rehat Maryada: The Sikh code of conduct and conventions, containing twenty-seven articles. It was compiled in 1931 and has helped make Sikh practice more uniform.

The Five Virtues: Chastity, Patience, Contentment, Detachment, and Humility.

The Five Vices: Lust, Anger, Greed, Worldly Attachment, and Pride.

Four Prohibitions of the Khalsa: (1) cutting hair, (2) eating Muslim *halal* meat (like Jewish *kosher* meat), (3) adultery, and (4) using intoxicants, drugs, and tobacco.

SACRED SITES

Sikhs reject the idea of sacred places and the pilgrimages often associated with such places. The following are important, if not sacred, places.

The Golden Temple: (also called *Har Mandir* ["Temple of God"]). Built under the fifth Sikh Guru, Arjan, the temple sits on an island in a large artificial pool in Amritsar. Destroyed and rebuilt several times. Called "golden" because of gold overlay provided by Ranjit Singh in the early 1800s.

Amritsar: (lit., "pool of immortality"). The Sikh holy city, situated in the Punjab. Site of the Golden Temple.

Khalistan: The ideal and anticipated independent Sikh state in the Punjab.

Gurdwara (*gurudwara*): The Sikh community center. A weekly meal is shared there, and a copy of the *Adi Granth* is centrally featured.

Human Dilemma and the Religious Goal

The primary problem for humans is that their focus is self-centered rather than God-centered. In order to move from self-centered focus, one must see the world moving according to God's plan, with God as judge of his vast creation and individuals a small part of that vastness.

Humans are challenged to provide to God what is substantial and essential: loving devotion, shown most clearly in the repetition of the Name and in moral conduct. Sikhs reject religious rituals and images, and they dismiss extreme asceticism. Life is to be lived in the world, fulfilling one's duties.

The goal is to break from the cycle of reincarnation and to be united with God. This liberation takes place not by removing oneself from the daily flow of life, as Hindu ascetics do, but by living selflessly in the world, doing one's duty, and providing service and charity to others.

Relation to Other Religions

Nanak's first statement after his initial religious experience was that there was neither Hindu nor Muslim. That concern reflects Nanak's context, where these two religions dominated. Had there been other significant religions in the area, Nanak no doubt would have listed these too. The import of Nanak's statement is that no religion has the advantage; in God's eyes what distinguishes one religion from another does not count.

That message is reinforced in other ways within the Sikh religion. Nanak wore mixed clothing, of Hindu and Muslim garb. Nanak's best friend and musician for his hymns was a Muslim. Accounts have Nanak challenging various aspects of the worship of both religions, yet the Sikh canon incorporates hymns from both Hindu and Muslim mystics, whose vision reached beyond the confines of their own traditions. Clearly Sikhism challenged traditional religious boundaries.

PRACTICES

General

Nanak showed little regard for ritual, which he tended to regard as superstitious. He criticized the multitudes of rituals of Hinduism and even attacked the few rituals that Islam had developed. Yet a large number of Hindu practices did become customary in Sikhism, hardly unexpected since most of the converts to Sikhism had previously been Hindus. A reform movement in the latter part of the 1800s rejected many of the traits of Hinduism still visible in Sikhism. Today, many of the rules of Sikh life are primarily rules that prohibit some practice that had ritualistic or magical character in Hinduism or Islam, such as wearing a sacred thread or an amulet or going on pilgrimages. Sikhs are even forbidden to eat *halal* meat because it is connected with unnecessary ritual.

At the same time, Sikh celebrations generally correspond to the major Hindu festivals in northern India, modified to reflect Sikh history and interests. In 1999, Sikhs revised their calendar to bring it in line with the length of the Gregorian calendar. This year was counted as year 531 from the birth date of Guru Nanak.

Having rejected much of Hindu and Muslim ritual, Sikhs ceremonies tend to be simple.

Rites

Naming Ceremony. Shortly after the birth of a child, the parents and relatives gather at the *gurdwara* to name the child. After appropriate prayers, the *Adi Granth* is opened at random (a practice called "taking the *hukam*"), and the first letter of the first hymn of that page is the initial letter for the child's name. An appropriate name is then chosen.

Baptism. When children of the Khalsa tradition reach puberty, they usually join the Khalsa. This initiation is marked by a rite of baptism. The initiate takes the five symbols of the Khalsa brotherhood (the five "Ks"). Six baptized Sikhs conduct the

---

SIKH DIVISIONS

Khalsa: Originally a military brotherhood within Sikhism, formed by the tenth Guru in 1699. Members are identified by the "Five Ks." A Sikh reform movement in the late 1800s gave the Khalsa increasing influence.

Sahajdharis: (lit., "slow adopters"). The name given by the Khalsa to Sikhs who have not joined the Khalsa. Such Sikhs cut their hair, reject the turban, and appeal to pacifist attitudes that marked early Sikhism.

Udasis: An ascetic group, founded by Siri Chand, elder son of Nanak. Now largely identified as Hindu rather than Sikh.

AUTHORITY

Adi Granth: The Sikh scriptures; the foundational authority.

The Ten Gurus: Sikhs hold the Ten Gurus in special regard. All are considered to stand in a special relationship to Nanak, the first Guru.

Akal Takht: (lit., "Eternal Throne"). This is the chief center of authority in Sikhism. Since 1721, Sikhs have met here to settle disputes. Sometimes the Akal Takht legislated independently and widely in matters of politics and religion. At other times, it had little power at all, though from 1925, it has exercised considerable influence within Sikhism. The building, standing opposite the Golden temple, has been destroyed and rebuilt several times.

Takht: Any center where Sikh legislation is formulated. There are now five Takhts.

ceremony. One reads from the *Adi Granth;* the other five prepare a bowl of nectar (sugared water), stirred by their swords. Some of this is drunk by the initiate; some is sprinkled over the eyes and head of the initiate. The four prohibitions of the Khalsa are read and assumed as duties.

Marriage. Marriage is to be monogamous and divorce is not permitted, though Sikhs may seek civil divorce. Marriage may take place in an establishment other than the *gurdwara* provided that the *Adi Granth* has been properly installed there. The bride and groom are seated before the *Adi Granth* for the ceremony; at specific times they walk around the *Adi Granth.* Verses from the "Wedding Song" are featured, as well as the "Song of Bliss." Both songs are part of the *Adi Granth.*

Path. The Akhand Path is a continuous reading of the *Adi Granth,* from beginning to end, and it takes about forty-eight hours. The text must be read by family members or in the hearing of family members. A similar ceremony, the Sahaj Path, features the intermittent reading of the entire *Adi Granth* over a ten-day period after a death. The completion of the reading ends the period of mourning.

Death. Death is viewed as a normal and necessary part of the cycle of reincarnation. Mourning is discouraged. When death occurs outside of India, the body is cremated; in India, the traditional funeral pyre is used. The ashes are placed into a river or sea. A ten-day period of mourning follows the funeral ceremony.

Taking the Hukam. On a variety of occasions, the *Adi Granth* is opened at random and the first hymn on the page is read. This is called "taking the *hukam.*" A child's name is chosen in this manner, and it is a routine practice at marriages, as well at many other occasions. Such action illustrates the central role the *Adi Granth* plays in the life of a Sikh.

The Canon

Central to Sikh religious and personal life is the Sikh canon, the *Adi Granth.* The fifth Sikh Guru, Arjan, undertook to compile an authorized canon in 1603, completing it a year later. Two factors drove this effort. First, the community had expanded considerably, and a common collection was needed to hold these scattered communities together. Second, Arjan, who was the younger son, had been appointed as Guru at age eighteen by his father, an action that created tensions with Arjan's older brother, who felt he had been bypassed. Arjan's brother and his brother's son continued to compose Sikh hymns under the name of Nanak, as was customary for the Sikh Gurus to do. Arjan rejected this new literature, collecting only the hymns that he had himself composed and those from the previous four Gurus, along with a scattering of hymns by twenty Hindu and Muslim mystics. This resulted in a collection of nearly 6,000 hymns, over one-third of which Arjan had composed.

Although these hymns had always been valued, they gained an even more elevated position in Sikhism at the death of the tenth Guru, Gobind Singh. The four sons of Gobind had been killed in battle or executed. When it came time for Gobind to appoint a successor, he looked not for a qualified man, but chose rather the canon itself as the new, continuing and permanent Guru. Thus the *Adi Granth* is often referred to as *Guru Granth.*

As Guru, the *Adi Granth* is treated in much the same way as a living Guru would have been honored. It is seated in a throned place on honor, draped with costly material, brought out in a ceremony each morning and returned at night. Someone fans the book with a

> **TERMINOLOGY**
> **Amrit:** Sweetened water used in the Khalsa baptism ceremony.
> **Gurmukhi:** A distinctive script of the Punjabi language, developed for the writing of the *Adi Granth.*
> **Jat:** A farming subcaste to which most Sikhs belong.
> **Kaur:** (lit., "princess"). The name taken by a baptized female member of the Khalsa.
> **Langar:** The communal kitchen found in Sikh meeting places (*gurdwaras*). The meal, in which all share as equals, is one of the oldest practices of Sikhs.
> **Panth:** The term for the Sikh community.
> **Sants:** Ascetic holy men. Nanak was inspired by many of their ideas of simplicity and devotionalism, though Sikhism rejects asceticism.
> **Sikh:** (lit., "disciple"). The term used to identify the followers (disciples) of Nanak.
> **Singh:** (lit., "lion"). The name taken by a baptized male member of the Khalsa. Today, some are dropping the name in favor of the older family names.

feather as it is being read, as a living Guru might have been refreshed. One bows in front of the *Adi Granth,* and when one leaves, one backs away, rather than turning one's back to the book. The *Adi Granth* holds the central place at all religious ceremonies, and it is carried in honor at weddings, birthdays, and other special events, much as a living Guru would have been invited and honored. This reverent treatment is displayed both in the main temple at Amritsar and in each local *gurdwara.* Some Sikhs treat the *Granth* in the same way at home, even setting aside a separate room for the book.

Except for a few hymns, the *Granth* is organized into thirty-one sections, with hymns in each section determined by a common melodic scale. Within each section, the hymns are arranged in chronological order of their authors, the first five Gurus. After this follows hymns by Hindu and Muslim saints.

The Golden Temple

What is usually referred to in popular literature as the "Golden Temple" is called by Sikhs the Harimandir Sahib ("House of God"). The term "golden" came to be used after Ranjit Singh repaired the temple and overlaid it with gold in the early 1800s. Unlike many Hindu temples that favor a hilltop site and have only one entrance, the Sikh temple was built on low ground and has doors on all four sides. According to Sikhs, this shows that all castes have free access.

As well, unlike many temples, the Sikh temple is not a place of sacrifice. Its central activity and focus is on the holy book, the *Adi Granth.*

Leadership

The Gurus. The first ten Gurus, along with their major writings collected in the *Adi Granth*, provide the heart of the Sikh understanding of religious authority.

Although the first ten Gurus are almost universally accepted by Sikhs, a few dissenters exist. Part of the reason stems from how successors were appointed. Nanak, according to tradition, appointed a friend, rather than one of his sons, to lead the community after his death. But soon succession became roughly hereditary, though not always from father directly to son. The third to the tenth Gurus were from the same family: the third Guru appointed his son-in-law; after that, sons or grandsons were appointed, even if that meant selecting a very young successor. The sixth Guru was nine when he became leader; the seventh was fourteen; the eighth Guru was five—he died of smallpox at age eight; and the tenth became Guru at age nine. This did not prevent some of these young Gurus from providing outstanding leadership as they matured.

The Sikhs have a sense that their Gurus were inspired by the same divine spirit. Most Gurus wrote under the pseudonym Nanak, reflecting a transfer of this original essence of Nanak from one to the other "as one lamp lights another," as Sikhs have described it.

The Akal Takht. Once the *Adi Granth* became the chief authority, with no living Guru to interpret the text, problems arose as to how the community would settle disputes about the meaning of disputed passages in the canon. This problem arises in any religion that "fixes" or "closes" their authoritative writings. If no new authoritative document is provided to address either new issues confronted by the community or passages of ambiguity in the original documents, how does the community decide the appropriate path?

For Sikhs, such problems of interpretation, or clarification of the canon, are handled by the Akal Takht ("Eternal Throne"). Originally, decisions had been made there at annual or semiannual meetings, in which all Sikhs participated. Decisions had to be unanimous; when they were, they became binding on all Sikhs. Disputes are still sent to the Akal Takht, though sometimes this Punjabi-based group has little understanding of the issues that confront Sikhs outside of the Punjab.

There are five Takhts, all of them in the Punjab. The one directly across from the causeway to the Golden Temple in Amritsar has the primary authority, though the building was destroyed in the attack by Indian troops on the Golden Temple in 1984, after the temple had been taken over by Sikh separatists. Sikhs immediately began the reconstruction of the building.

Divisions within Sikhism

Sikhism consists of a variety of groups, and for much of its history it was not carefully distinguished from Hinduism by outsiders, partly because of the many Hindu customs it had retained. In the later part of the 1800s, a reform movement called Singh Sabha was established, which took as its goal the creation and promotion of a Sikh identity clearly demarcated from Hinduism. Since its vision of authentic Sikhism was shaped under Khalsa influence and since it had the patronage of the governing British, Sikhism came more and more to be expressed in terms of the Khalsa. But not all Sikhs define their identity in terms of the Khalsa. Many remain clean-shaven, do not wear the turban, and reject the militaristic emphasis of the Khalsa in favor of the pacifist attitude that marked Sikhism in its earliest days. Although these Sikhs are referred to as "slow adopters" (sahajdharis) by members of the Khalsa, in terms of historical roots, they are fully Sikh.

Various other groups, all quite small, are associated with Sikhism in some way. Some follow living Gurus. One group, quite extreme in their asceticism, follows the elder son of Nanak, Siri Chand. These are called the Udasis, and they behave much like the Hindu ascetics.

The Khalsa itself is not without division. One modern tension is between innovators and traditionalists, who clash quite sharply over the direction of the movement. One dispute became so sharp in the 1990s that Canadian police had to intervene. In the Fraser Valley of British Columbia, a favorite area for Sikh immigration to Canada, some Sikhs introduced tables and chairs into the gurdwara. Sikhs customarily sat on the floor, even for their common meal, demonstrating that all had the same status before

God. The innovators argued that the same sense could be maintained at a table from which none was excluded. When the matter was referred to the Sikh religious court in India, the innovators lost, and failing to bow to that decision, were excommunicated. To some extent, these conflicts have arisen from the new experiences of Diaspora Sikhs. Although most Sikhs live in the Punjab province of India, about ten percent of Sikhs live outside of India, largely in parts of the old British Empire, where Sikhs were often employed in police forces. Diaspora Sikhs, as minorities in the countries to which they have moved, face adjustments of a different kind from Sikhs who live as members of the majority culture in the Punjab and whose tradition is largely shaped by the Punjabi environment and traditions.

In the Punjab, itself, there are divisions among the Sikhs of the Khalsa. The tension is over the political realities. Should Sikhs fight for an independent homeland, as the Khalsa Dal separatists maintain, with bombs and assassinations, as need be? Or should Sikhs be political moderates, working within the governmental structures to gain concessions for the Sikh Punjab within a diverse India? The 1990s saw a rise in Sikh violence as Sikh separatists pressed their cause.

The Khalsa

In preparation for initiation into the Khalsa, individuals undergo a baptism, and they commit themselves to a stricter code of conduct, which prohibits alcohol and tobacco. Further, they carry five items that remind them of their mission to defend Sikhism: uncut hair (*kes*), comb (*kangha*), sword (*kirpan*), steel bracelet (*karha*), and long shorts (*kachha*). These five items are referred to as the "Five Ks," since each starts with a K sound in the Punjabi language. All items reflected the Khalsa's militant commitment to the defense of the Sikh people and land. Long, *tidy* hair, for which the comb was important, set them apart from the numerous Hindu ascetics, whose unkempt appearance showed they had renounced the world. The iron bracelet represented strength and unity; the short pants the uniform of the soldier; and the sword an obvious symbol of the Sikh's new militaristic intent. Those who became members took the surname Singh, meaning "lion." Later, women were admitted; they took the name Kaur, meaning "princess" or "lionness."

CONCLUSION

Sikhism is small; hardly one percent of the size of traditions such as Hinduism, Buddhism, Christianity, and Islam. But Sikhism often claims that it is the fifth largest religion in the world. It does have more adherents than Judaism or Jainism. But whether it is the fifth largest religion depends on how we define religion and how we define adherents. Confucianism, Taoism, and Shinto have a wider but less defined membership and influence.

Whether Sikhism is a "world religion" is also open to question. Although its initial proclamations reflected insights that could have developed into a universal appeal, even in the days of its founder Sikhism had come to be identified firmly with Punjabi culture and locale, where Sikhism had its greatest success. Most Sikhs today come from one farming subcaste, the Jat; most Sikhs are clustered in the Punjab area of India, Sikhism's home for the last five hundred years; and Sikhs treat the Punjabi language as a sacred language, disapproving of translations of the *Adi Granth* from Punjabi. Whether Sikhism gains a "world" character beyond its Diaspora communities is yet to be determined.

CHAPTER TEN

Chinese Religions

The types of religious beliefs and practices that developed in China and which are discussed here would later spread to other East Asian countries (e.g., Korea, Japan). Although these traditions continued to develop in distinct ways in their new cultural environments, East Asian religious forms and values are strongly influenced by their Chinese heritage. The four main sources of Chinese religion are: 1) the ancient heritage, 2) Confucianism, 3) Daoism, and 4) Buddhism. Like crossroads of a major highway, where lanes of traffic intersect, these four sources merge and mingle with each other, with mutual influences, through the course of Chinese history.

HISTORY

The Ancient Heritage

Chinese history is generally divided into dynastic periods. The earliest unified period for which there is archeological evidence is the Shang

Note: In rendering Chinese words into the Romanized alphabet, the Pinyin system of transliteration is used, since it has been officially adopted by the Chinese government. However, the Wade-Giles system of transliteration was widespread in western scholarship. Therefore many words will often be presented in both Pinyin and Wade-Giles spellings, in that order. Thus we see Xia/Hsia, Qin/Ch'in, or Dao/Tao.

Dynasty (ca. fourteenth to eleventh centuries B.C.E.), which developed along the Yellow River valley. Recent archeological digs reveal the earlier presence of inscribed pottery, animal bones used for divination, stone altars, and clay phallic effigies in sites along the Yellow River basin and other scattered locales, dating as far back as 3000 B.C.E. These discoveries suggest the existence of a pre-Shang Chinese civilization made up of a conglomerate of regional groups with distinct religious practices. Chinese myths do refer to a dynasty known as the Xia/Hsia, which preceded the Shang Dynasty, but it is premature to suggest that the current collection of ancient material remains that have been excavated are certain evidence of the Xia/Hsia Dynasty's existence.

The Shang Dynasty was founded on agriculture and animal husbandry. Its system of writing, consisting of pictograms, ideograms, and phonograms, is evident on large numbers of inscribed animal bones that have been unearthed. These Shang "oracle-bones" bear inscriptions that reveal the widespread practice of divination and a belief in ancestral and nature spirits. Bronze craftsmanship during the period was sophisticated. The lineage of Shang kings, who headed a divine cult to propitiate the divine spirits, enjoyed a privileged courtly life. They ruled much of northeast China and were finally overthrown by the northwestern Zhou/Chou Dynasty.

The Zhou Dynasty (1045-221 B.C.E.) was the longest surviving in Chinese history. It is subdivided into the Western or Early Zhou (1045-771 B.C.E.) and the Eastern or Later Zhou (771-221 B.C.E.). The Zhou Dynasty was loosely organized along feudal lines. Although people hunted and raised animals, the majority farmed for a living. They propitiated nature deities to ensure a good harvest. It was part of the king's duties to ensure that these deities were placated, and his right to rule often depended on the people's agricultural success. The Western Zhou Dynasty was overthrown by nomadic groups from further to the north and west, which would, in times of hardship, routinely raid the settled agricultural communities to the east. The Eastern Zhou Dynasty which followed is further divided into two periods. The first of these, the Spring and Autumn period (722-479 B.C.E.) is named after a book attributed to Confucius (ca. 551-479 B.C.E.), a scholar and tutor, who is reputed to have composed a chronicle of the era. China entered the Iron Age at this time. Iron was a technological advancement that furthered both economic development and warfare. Where there were once as many as two hundred feudatory states, the number had progressively declined to seven. Towards the end of the so-called Warring States Period (479-221 B.C.E.), the leaders of each of these seven states renounced paying tribute to the Zhou king and vied for kingship for themselves. The turbulence of the Warring States Period served as a catalyst for thinkers who proposed theories about human nature and the means of restoring order to society. The era is therefore also known as the Period of the Hundred Philosophies, reflecting the abundance of teachings it provoked.

The leader of Qin/Ch'in, the most powerful of the seven warring states, eventually conquered the others. He unified the country and through further conquests spread his dominion from Mongolia to Vietnam. Named Qin Shi Huangdi/Ch'in Shih Huang Ti, he took the title of First Emperor of China, giving the country both its name and its imperial scope. To inhibit attacks from the northwestern "barbarians," he initiated the construction of a massive wall, which has come to be known as the Great Wall of China. The First Emperor feared the Literati, the scholarly community that had developed during the Later Zhou period. He had many killed and even launched a campaign to destroy all books, except technical treatises. Although the Qin dynasty, due to its extremism, was short-lived (221–207 B.C.E.), it established a centralized bureaucracy in which the country was ruled by appointed officials, and not by aristocrats who had inherited their positions of power and authority. After its collapse, the Qin was followed by the Han Dynasty, a four hundred year period of relatively stable rule (206 B.C.E.–220 C.E.). It was during the Han Dynasty that Confucianism (i.e., the Literati tradition) became officially established in China.

CONFUCIAN PHILOSOPHERS

Confucius: (551?–479 B.C.E.). Latin form of Kongfuzi/K'ung fu-tzu ("Master Kong"). He was a teacher and founder of a school of thought known as Confucianism, or the scholarly or Literati tradition. He promoted tradition but interpreted it in ways that made important reforms in Chinese thought and values. He is associated with the concepts of "filial piety," human-heartedness (ren/jen), and the cultivated person (junzi/chun-tzu).

Mencius: (372–289 B.C.E.). Latin form of Mengzi/Meng-tzu ("Master Meng"). He contributed to what is sometimes called the idealistic wing of Confucian philosophy. He lived during a period of social and political turmoil in China, but built his teachings on the notion that human beings were intrinsically good. He promoted the idea that rulers should be benevolently disposed toward their subjects.

Xunzi/Hsun-tzu: (312–238 B.C.E.). "Master Xun" belonged to the realistic wing of Confucianism, which taught that human nature was intrinsically selfish but could benefit from learning. He thus promoted education, traditional values, and rationality over superstition.

Zhu Xi/Chu Hsi: (1130–1200 C.E.). Most renowned Neo-Confucian. Drawing upon ideas from Daoism and Buddhism, he promoted meditation as a means to a Confucian end (the cultivating of one's moral nature). His interpretation of Neo-Confucianism became the norm in Chinese civil service examinations from the 1300s–1900s.

Confucianism

Although he is perhaps the most influential teacher in Chinese history, our knowledge of the life of Confucius is somewhat sketchy, and rife with legend. We know that he was born in the state of Lu, and was named Kong Qiu/K'ung Ch'iu. Referred to by his students as "Master Kong," (i.e., Kongfuzi/K'ung fu-tzu), his name was Latinized into Confucius by Western scholars. The exact date of his birth is uncertain, and it is nominally placed at 551 B.C.E. As a young man, he held short-lived, minor government positions in the aristocratic houses of the state of Lu. There he is said to have developed his understanding of the injustices inherent in the two-tiered social system that had the aristocracy living off the labor of a heavily burdened peasantry. Confucius lived in a period experiencing the erosion of the central authority of the Zhou leadership, and his teachings center on the rectification of appropriate human relationships in order to regain social harmony. He traveled for many years with his disciples, attempting to find a ruler who would commission him as an advisor and implement his social philosophy, but was unsuccessful. In the later years of his life, he immersed himself in the study of the Chinese classics and in teaching his disciples. A smattering of these teachings is found in a collection of aphorisms and short conversations with disciples known as the *Analects*. Although the editing or authorship of numerous other texts, such as the Five Classics, has been attributed to Confucius, there is little evidence to verify such claims. Confucius certainly did uphold the importance of studying the classics and taught a deep reverence for tradition. Confucius died in 479 B.C.E., without having had significant social or political influence on China during his lifetime.

Confucian teachings developed in the centuries after his death. They grew in response to other rival religious and ethical philosophies, such as Daoism and Mohism. The Mohist school was led by Mozi/Mo-tzu (i.e., "Master Mo") (c. 470–391 B.C.E.) and its teachings are found in a text known as the *Mozi/Mo-tzu*. It promotes a radical philosophy of universal love and religious ritual. Two of the most important followers of the Confucian school were Mencius and Xunzi/Hsun-tzu. The teachings of Mencius (372–289 B.C.E.) or Mengzi/Meng-tzu (i.e., "Master Meng"), are found in the *Book of Mencius*. They systematize Confucian values and articulate them more directly. Since the era in which Mencius lived was torn with political strife, his teachings on benevolence and goodness were regarded as impractical and idealistic. The teachings of Xunzi/Hsun-tzu (i.e., "Master Xun/Hsun") (312–238 B.C.E.) and his disciples are found in a book that bears his name. The *Xunzi/Hsun-tzu* teaches that although human nature is inherently self-serving, it could be refined through education.

Xunzi's form of Confucianism, which was seen as more pragmatic, initially grew more influential than that of Mencius during the Han period and subsequent centuries. The Han rulers had made the mastery of the Five Classics, texts deemed important by Confucian thinkers, vital for all scholar-bureaucrats, thus raising the Confucian/Literati tradition to a pre-eminent position in Chinese society. By now, these Confucian influences were already beginning to be transmitted to Korea (ca. 100 B.C.E.). However, after the fall of the Han Dynasty (220 C.E.), Daoism and Buddhism began to flourish in China. Although these traditions dominated the intellectual movements of the period, scholar-bureaucrats continued to develop Confucian philosophy through, for instance, commentaries on the Five Classics. By the sixth century, Confucianism, along with Buddhism, had been transmitted to Japan, via Korea. Eventually, through the rise of Neo-Confucian philosophy after the eleventh century, Mencius's more idealistic form of Confucianism surpassed that of Xunzi/Hsun-tzu.

Neo-Confucianism developed in response to Daoism and Buddhism, which dominated China from the fall of the Han Dynasty (220 C.E.) to the fall of the Tang Dynasty (907 C.E.). The most prominent of the Neo-Confucian philosophers was Zhu Xi/Chu Hsi (1130-1200) who wrote commentaries on four Confucian classics, known as the Four Books. These commentaries were an integral part of the nation's civil service examinations for the next six hundred years, making Zhu Xi's Neo-Confucianism enormously influential in the history of Chinese religio-philosophical thought. Neo-Confucianism also entered Korea during the Korean Yi Dynasty (1392-1910). Although it

DAOIST AND OTHER PHILOSOPHERS

Laozi/Lao-tzu: (sixth century B.C.E.?) "Old Master." Quasi-historical figure, credited with authoring the Daodejing/Tao-te ching, he is the patriarch of Daoist philosophy. His teachings evoke the mysterious nature of the Dao, and the means of harmonizing with it.

Zhuangzi/Chuang-tzu: (fourth century B.C.E.?). "Master Zhuang/Chuang," taught a form of nature mysticism that is characteristic of Daoist philosophy. He used stories and humor to promote a philosophy of freedom from social constraints and conditioning that could lead one back to an original undistorted state of being.

Mozi/Mo-tzu: (ca. 470-391 B.C.E.). "Master Mo," offered a teaching that rivaled Confucianism. He placed great emphasis on Heaven, the hierarchy of divine spirits, and sacrificial rituals. He also was a pacifist who promoted universal love for all human beings.

Han Feizi/Han Fei-tzu: (ca. 280-233 B.C.E.). "Master Han Fei" was the authority on Legalist philosophy, and student of Xunzi/Hsun-tzu. He held that human nature is intrinsically evil and that people act from selfish motives. Thus government should legislate strict laws and rule through generous rewards for those who abide with them while meting out severe punishments for those who do not.

has evolved as it adapts to the challenges of modernity, Neo-Confucianism continues to be influential in Korea even today. In Japan, Neo-Confucianism flourished during the Tokugawa Shogunate (1603–1867). Drawing on the notion of a hierarchical relationship between rulers and subjects, the Japanese developed the ideal of the warrior-intellectual, the *samurai*, whose code of honor included unswerving loyalty to the leader. Since Confucian teachings articulated the relevance of ritualism, they naturally meshed with Japanese Shinto. Shinto possessed an ancient collection of rites and traditions that could now be interpreted with the aid of Confucian conceptual categories.

In 1906 the Manchu (Qing/Ch'ing) Dynasty (1644–1911) attempted to deify Confucius, but their fall shortly thereafter led to a decline in state-supported Confucianism in China. In 1973–1974 during China's Cultural Revolution (1966–1976) headed by Chairman Mao Zedong/Mao Tse-tung, there was even a brief anti-Confucius campaign. Confucianism was perceived as conservative and "backward-looking," in contrast to the progressive ideals of the new Communist state. It is unlikely that a Confucian political philosophy will replace the current system in China in the near future. Nevertheless, Confucian values and morals are still strongly evident in Taiwanese and Korean society, and although challenged by such forces as secularism and egalitarianism, continue to shape and influence life within many East Asian families.

Daoism

Daoism is the term used to designate a cluster of beliefs and practices that developed among Chinese recluses who had a strong affinity for nature. In fact, it is sometimes referred to as a form of "nature mysticism." It derives its name from the word Dao/Tao ("the Way"), which, however, is not exclusive to Daoism and is used in all the major Chinese religio-philosophical traditions. Daoism is often divided into a philosophical wing (Daojia/Tao-chia) and a religious one (Daojiao/Tao-chiao). The two main contributors to classical Daoist philosophy are Laozi/Lao-tzu and Zhuangzi/Chuang-tzu, both of whose lives are cloaked in legend. Actually, it is difficult to say with certainty if either of them really existed. Laozi/Lao-tzu is believed to have been born in the sixth century B.C.E., somewhat earlier than Confucius. However, scholars place the *Daodejing/Tao-te ching*, an enormously influential text attributed to him, anywhere between the sixth and fourth centuries B.C.E. The *Daodejing/Tao-te ching*, also known as the *Laozi/Lao-tzu*, consists of two parts, the first dealing with the Dao (or Way) and the second treating the concept of De/Te (or

Power). Archeological discoveries made in the mid 1970s uncovered manuscripts of the text dating to the second century B.C.E. in which the second part precedes the first. Some scholars thus contend that the practical political dimensions of the philosophy found in the second part were more important to the redactors of those manuscripts (and the political leaders of that period) than the theoretical metaphysics of the section on the Dao.

The *Zhuangzi/Chuang-tzu*, attributed to the sage with the same name, may well have had multiple authorship. Zhuangzi/Chuang-tzu is believed to have lived at the time of Mencius (ca. 300 B.C.E.). Unlike the *Daodejing/Tao-te ching*, his text displays a disdain for politics and the ruler or bureaucrat's application of its philosophy. With considerable use of humor and anecdote, it espouses a renunciation of social conventions and a contemplative lifestyle in order to achieve a fusion with the mysterious principle of nature, the Dao.

Daoist philosophy developed during the subsequent centuries. Between the third and sixth centuries C.E., in particular, in the social upheaval that followed the collapse of the Han Dynasty, a movement designated by scholars as Neo-Daoism emerged. It was characterized by non-conformity and a criticism of the social establishment. Akin to the counterculture movement of the 1960s, various factions in the movement promoted a naturalistic hedonism, with freedom from the constraints in the way one was traditionally expected to speak to each other, dress, or relate to elders and other authorities. Neo-Daoism embraced

BRANCHES

Ancient Beliefs and Practices: Pre-Confucian Chinese forms of religious belief and activities, including a celestial ruler called "Heaven" and numerous other spirits, such as spirits of dead ancestors. Practices included divination, spirit mediumship, shamanism, and sacrifice.

Confucianism: Associated with the sage Confucius, Confucianism emphasized the study of certain literary classics in order to nurture human moral nature. The Confucian ideal is the cultivated person (*junzi/chun-tzu*), who has perfected the quality of human-heartedness (*ren/jen*).

Philosophical Daoism: Associated with the writings of Laozi/Lao-tzu and Zhuangzi/Chuang-tzu, it is a form of nature mysticism. The Daoist ideal is the sage (*sheng*) who contemplates nature in order to return to an original state that is harmonious with the mysterious principle known as the Dao.

Religious Daoism: Developed from Daoist philosophy and older magical and ritual based traditions. It is characterized by a search for bodily immortality, alchemy, and a belief in a pantheon of immortal sages.

Neo-Confucianism: Developed in the eleventh and twelfth centuries. It derived from the interpretation of the Four Books, and influences from Daoism and Buddhism. It views the cosmos as the *Taiji/T'ai Chi* ("Great Ultimate").

Buddhism: Mainly Mahayana forms endured, and distinctly Chinese forms of Buddhism, such as Tiantai/T'ien-t'ai and Huayan/Hua-yen, developed.

creativity in poetry and art, and espoused an appreciation for the unique creations of nature. Its legacy still endures in many aspects of East Asian aesthetics.

What has been designated as Daoist religion (Daojiao/Tao-chiao) has its roots in China's ancient heritage of divination and the worship of nature spirits. However, it is generally identified as developing after classical Daoist philosophy on whose principles it draws. It also combines notions from the Yin/Yang and Five Phases schools in constructing its vision of the world. By the first century C.E., a certain Zhang Daoling/Chang Taoling, one of the first teachers associated with Daoist religion, founded a secret society known as the Celestial Masters Sect. Among its practices was the confession of sins to remove illnesses, and among its claims was that Zhang Daoling had attained immortality. Numerous other schools of religious Daoism developed in the centuries that followed. They often fused a study of the natural world with psycho-physical practices in an effort to attain immortality through a sort of spiritual alchemy. The reputed success in these efforts has led to beliefs in a vast array of meditative practices, recipes for curative elixirs, and heavenly immortals who achieved the desired state. Writings on these themes contributed to the formation of an enormous canon of scriptures numbering over a thousand volumes. Although religious Daoism's influence has declined in the last few centuries, certain sects, including the Celestial Masters Society, still survive. Religious Daoism's legacy also endures in aspects of Chinese traditional medicine, in shamanistic healing practices, and in forms of popular religious practice.

Buddhism

Buddhism entered China around the first century C.E. via the Silk Roads, major trade routes that connected China to Europe and India. Dominant Confucian values during the Han Dynasty, such as familial and other hierarchical social relationships, were initially in tension with Buddhism's spirit of renunciation. The linguistic differences between Chinese and the Sanskritic-based languages of Indian Buddhism were also obstacles to translators. Nevertheless, Buddhism eventually found resonances with Daoism, whose metaphysical terminology proved useful in the translation of abstract Buddhist philosophical concepts. Buddhism gained a foothold in China after the collapse of the Han Dynasty and flourished during the Sui (581–617 C.E.) and Tang (618–907 C.E.) Dynasties, reaching its zenith in the ninth century. Buddhism declined in later centuries in the face of persecutions and the growth of Neo-Confucianism to the dominant position.

During the period of Buddhism's growth, Chinese pilgrims such as Faxian/Fa-hsien (fourth century C.E.) traveled to India in search of original manuscripts. Xuanzang/Hsuan-tsang (602–664 C.E.), the most renowned of the scholar-pilgrims, returned with a host of Buddhist texts and translated seventy-five of them before his death. He is immortalized in a popular Chinese epic folk tale known as *Journey to the West.* These Chinese Buddhist pilgrims also left invaluable records of Buddhist life in India in their travel memoirs.

Both Theravada and Mahayana forms of Buddhism entered China. However, only the Mahayana forms survived. Of the most important Mahayana schools, the Tiantai/T'ien-tai ("Mt. Heavenly Palace") and the Huayan/Hua-yen ("Flower Garland") schools are distinctly Chinese, because they display philosophical and practical developments of Buddhist teachings beyond their Indian scriptural origins. In the Chan/Ch'an ("Meditation") school of Buddhism, the emphasis was on attaining the kind of awakening experience that the Buddha himself had obtained. Other schools stressed a devotional attitude to the salvific power of celestial *bodhisattvas.* All these and other Chinese Mahayana schools eventually spread to Korea and Japan. The Chan and certain devotional Buddhists schools, such as Jingtu/Ch'ing-tu ("Pureland"), which placed special emphasis on the Buddha Amitabha, managed to survive and prosper even after the other schools of Mahayana Buddhism began to decline. These forms of Buddhism are still the most popular in East Asia today.

MAJOR TEXTS

The Analects of Confucius (Lunyu/Lun-yu): A collection of dialogues in twenty chapters between Confucius and his students, probably compiled many decades after his death.

Daedejing/Tao-te Ching: "The Way (Dao/Tao) and its Power (De/Te)." Also known as the *Laozi/Lao-tzu* to whom its composition is attributed. It consists of about 5,000 words arranged in eighty-one chapters. It is the foundational text of Daoist philosophy.

The Book of Zhuangzi/Chuang-tzu: Or simply the *Zhuangzi/Chuang-tzu,* is attributed to that sage, and is the other important text of philosophical Daoism. In contrast to the *Daodejing/Tao-te ching,* which is made up of short chapters in the aphoristic style of proverbial wisdom, the *Zhuangzi/Chuang-tzu* is full of parables and imaginative stories.

Yijing/I-ching: *The Book of Changes* or *The Oracle of Change* is a classic text on divination that dates to pre-Confucian times. It is a collection of sixty-four hexagrams, consisting of six solid (Yang) or broken (Yin) lines, with appended interpretations to each. These offer advice, often in enigmatic symbolic language, that is purported to be appropriate to the place, time, and situation of the person who is consulting the oracle.

Other philosophical texts: The *Book of Mencius,* the *Book of Xunzi/Hsun-tsu,* the *Book of Mozi/Mo-tzu,* and the *Book of Han Feizi/Han Fei-tzu,* are texts attributed to the authors after whom they have been named, and deal with their particular schools of philosophy.

BELIEFS

Beliefs Rooted in Antiquity

Divination. Archeological finds indicate that as early as 4000 B.C.E., people in the region of China practiced divination. Divination is the process through which one seeks to discover a hidden truth by consulting an invisible power through some medium (human and/or mechanical). The procedure often requires the aid of a diviner, who manipulates the media or serves as the medium, and who may then interpret the results of the consultation. For instance, at Delphi, in ancient Greece, a woman served as a human oracle by answering questions put to her at the Temple of Apollo. She did so while in a trance-like state enhanced by chewing on laurel leaves. In hepatoscopy, the liver of an animal may be examined to divine the sought after piece of knowledge. The form of divination that was commonplace in ancient China was scapulimancy, the application of heat to animal bones (e.g., the large, flat shoulder-blades of oxen, or the underside of tortoises), and the interpretation of the patterns of fissures that appeared on them. This form of divination was well-developed during the Shang and Zhou Dynasties, and information such as the question being posed, its answer, and perhaps even the success of the prognostication would be inscribed onto the bones and shells. Fragments of these old inscribed "oracle bones," which were being used as ingredients in traditional Chinese medicine, led archeologists to their sources along the Yellow River.

Divination was used by the aristocracy as well as the commoners. Since diviners were often consulted in matters of grave consequence for the state, such as whether one should wage war, or what might be displeasing the spirits to induce a drought, these specialists commanded considerable power and influence in Chinese society. Not only did they know how to perform the divination, but were held capable of interpreting the results as well. Thus they were often credited with special intuitive abilities. Some also exercised these intuitions in dream analysis, astrology, and in spirit possession. These latter figures could be classified more appropriately as shamanic in character, rather than mere diviners. Shamans are noted for their capacity for "ecstatic" (i.e., out of self) practice. Shamans are believed to be able to move their consciousness beyond normal parameters, and thus commune with other beings such as animal, nature, or disembodied spirits, deities, and so on. They are thus held to be able to diagnose illnesses, discern the wishes of a deceased family member, intuit the desires of a deity and the like.

Although the efficacy of divination began to be questioned more frequently by the late Zhou period, it still endures in a variety of forms in Chinese religion. In the *Yijing/I-ching* (*Book of Changes*), widely consulted in China and even in the West, one finds a codification of solid and broken lines, derived from the ancient fissure patterns of the oracle bone divination practices. Shamanic spirit mediums are still found among Chinese communities, as well as in Korea and Japan (where they are often women).

Deities and Spirits. Inscriptions left on bones reveal that the people of the Shang Dynasty believed in a high god, who ruled over all other deities. They referred to this supreme lord as Di/Ti. This conception changed during the subsequent Zhou Dynasty, when the supreme principle was known as Tian/T'ien. Although it is usually translated as "heaven," Tian refers more to a power or a deity than to an abode. Tian is a heavenly lord,

> **COLLECTIONS OF TEXTS**
> **The Five Classics:** A group of writings regarded by Confucius and other scholars as particularly important. Knowledge of their content was mandatory for civil servants during the Han Dynasty. They were the *Book of Changes*, the *Book of History*, the *Book of Poetry*, the *Classic of Rites*, and the *Spring and Autumn Annals*. A sixth classic, the *Book of Music*, is now lost.
> **The Four Books:** A group of writings that were given importance by Neo-Confucian philosophers such as Zhu Xi/Chu Hsi. They were the *Analects of Confucius*, the *Book of Mencius*, the *Great Learning*, and the *Doctrine of the Mean*.
> **The Three Caverns:** A vast collection of writings including the *Yijing/I-ching*, *Daodejing/Tao-te-ching*, and *Zhuangzi/Chuang-tzu*, and more than 1,400 other texts that constitute the Daoist Canon (Daozang/Tao Tsang).

akin to a powerful ancestor, who looks down from above with a keen personal interest in human affairs. Tian was like a king who controlled an assortment of other divine beings who were often aspects or powers of nature, such as mountains or the wind. Although mostly male, there were also an assortment of female deities worshipped, such as the Queen Mothers of the East and West, possibly associated with the sun and the moon.

There was also an enduring belief in a variety of ancestral spirits and divine culture heroes. The ancestral spirits are ancient forebears of a particular family clan or even a dynasty. The culture heroes are founders of dynasties or figures who have advanced humanity in some crucial fashion. For instance, the sage Yu, one of group known as the Five Emperors, is believed to have founded the Xia/Hsia Dynasty. He is also reputed with saving his subjects from the flooding of the Yellow River. Another group, known as the Three Sovereigns (Sanhuang/San-huang) is associated with domesticating animals, introducing farming, and mastering fire.

The hierarchical ordering of all these deities mirrored social developments in China. What was once a monarchical system presided over by the kingly Lord on High (Tian), yielded to a more bureaucratic conception. Thus the kitchen god, who is still widely worshipped in China and other cultures that have been influenced by this conception, is seen as a sort of proctor who watches over a family's domestic behavior and conveys this information annually to higher deities.

Ancestor Worship. In Chinese belief, among the spirits that inhabit the heavenly realms are those of departed ancestors. Traces of these beliefs are found dating to about 4000 B.C.E. Physical death was not regarded as the end of a person's existence, but merely the end of their earthly, human existence. These spirits continue to watch over the lives of their descendants and lineage, and need to be remembered and propitiated as one would any other family member. If the departed are not cared for, they may turn to tormenting the living. Although the rites for propitiating the ancestors were forbidden in China after the Communist revolution, some form of ancestor veneration is still widespread within Chinese families.

Nature and Human Beings (Yin-Yang and the Dao). Although the ancient Chinese possessed a conception of a supreme deity, Tian is not viewed as the creator of the world. The cosmos was seen as a process that manifested with a measure of discernable orderliness. By the latter part of the Shang Dynasty, Chinese thinkers ascertained that all natural phenomena could be regarded as composed of two opposite, yet complementary principles, yin and yang. The waxing and waning of the moon, the alternation of night and day, the cyclical rhythms of the season, the bipolarity of male and female genders, could all be explained through the yin-yang theory. These polar principles were in a constant movement, interacting with each other, shifting their relationship to each other, and even transforming each other in what was a dynamic, but impersonal creation. The overarching, mysterious power that governed all these forces of nature was not Tian, but the Dao. The Dao is eventually interpreted and utilized in many different ways in the Chinese religio-philosophical thought of subsequent centuries, particularly by Daoist philosophers.

There had also developed the notion that human actions should harmonize with the principles of nature manifesting through the polarities of Heaven and Earth. The king was regarded as a Son of Heaven, whose responsibility included making sure that human society mirrored the cosmic harmony. The king held the Mandate of Heaven, the sanction by Heaven to mediate between the human order and Heaven and Earth. If there was discord in society, and even within an individual, the larger cosmic balance might be disrupted, and chaos could ensue. Heaven could rain down natural disasters such as floods, famine, or epidemics upon the

Earth to the detriment of human beings. It was therefore incumbent upon the king to be cognizant of the state of the cosmic order and insure that he, his ministers, and the citizens were in accord with the Dao. Divinatory techniques, such as the reading of omens, were thus vital aids for rulers and subjects alike to penetrate the otherwise mysterious flow of the Dao.

Confucian Principles

Confucius, or more correctly the Literati tradition that developed his teachings, left an indelible mark on the character of Chinese values. Born in a time of social upheaval, Confucius hoped to educate rulers to be better human beings, and in turn, to enable society to return to a lost golden age. Confucius idealized a particular ancient aristocrat, the Duke of Zhou/Chou, as such a ruler, because he revered Heaven and strove to follow its will. In Confucian teachings, Heaven plays a more central role than the Dao, for it is Heaven that must be understood, propitiated, and obeyed.

To rectify social disorder, Confucius taught the rectification of the "Five Relationships" that are of crucial importance in the constitution of society. These are the relationship of ruler and government official, father and son, husband and wife, elder and younger brother, and friend and friend. He explained each role's responsibilities and prescribed how people in these relationships should behave towards each other. Confucius elaborated upon an ancient principle known as "filial piety," which deals with the respect and honor that a child must show to a parent. Since each of the Five Relationships in Confucian teachings is hierarchical, not horizontal, the government official, son, wife, younger brother, and younger friend should reverentially defer to their respective hierarchical superiors. However, there are also

SYMBOLS

Dao/Tao: Also know as *Taiji/Tai Chi* ("Supreme Ultimate"), or more commonly as Yin-Yang, it is represented by a circle divided into two portions by an S-shaped line, which gives the circle a dynamic, spinning appearance. The two halves are colored black and white, respectively symbolizing the Yin and Yang principles of the creation. Each colored half contains a small circle of the opposite color, suggesting that the seed of Yin is immanent within the Yang principle and vice versa.

Hexagram: Diagram produced when consulting the *Yijing/I-ching* oracle, consisting of six horizontal lines placed one above the other. The lines may either be solid or broken. Solid lines represent the Yang principle, while broken lines represent the Yin principle. The hexagram is also viewed as the interplay of two three-lined trigrams which serve as another Yin-Yang polarity.

Chinese Zodiac: Constellations depicting various animals associated with particular years in twelve-year cycle. These are the rat, ox, tiger, rabbit, dragon, snake, horse, sheep, monkey, cock, dog, and pig. People born in corresponding years are thought to exhibit the characteristics connected with these creatures.

obligations incumbent on the ruler, father, husband, elder brother, and elder friend, for they must care for their hierarchically inferior counterparts as would a parent for a child.

Confucius is also associated with the promotion of propriety (*li*), righteousness (*yi*), and human-heartedness (*ren/jen*). Confucius taught that the proper functioning of society depended on a respect for tradition, and he therefore supported the performance of ritual and ceremony. This was *li*, a complex of social behaviors (such as greeting a guest with a bow) and ceremonial rites (such as making sacrificial offerings for the ancestors), which provided people with a well-worn path for interacting with each other (and the spirits) in a manner appropriate to their social position. *Yi* refers to the sense of righteousness that develops through the practice of *li*. As one applies the external behaviors of propriety (*li*), these become internalized and one begins to understand the rationale behind righteous conduct.

The highest Confucian principle is *ren/jen*, which is grounded in a deep inner feeling of empathy for one's fellow human beings. In a sense it is related to *shu*, the principle of reciprocity, summed up in the Confucian Golden Rule: "Do not do to others what you do not want done to yourself." However, *ren/jen* has a profoundly subtle quality implicit within it, because it goes beyond the external formalities of proper actions, or even the moral righteousness that underpins social propriety. Even surpassing the egalitarian sense of reciprocity, *ren/jen* ("human-heartedness") frees these virtues from being merely the application of rules and conceptualized values. *Ren* is a feeling that is grounded in a fundamental Confucian notion that human beings are intrinsically good, and empathetic towards others. *Ren*, when it is cultivated and developed, is what makes us superior humans. It is the mark of the *junzi/chun-tzu*, literally the "sons of princes," the term that Confucius used for persons who had perfected their moral character.

This Confucian ideal, the *junzi/chun-tzu*, reflects a shift in reverence from hereditary noble status to personal achievement. The true *junzi* was no longer someone who was an aristocrat by birth, but all persons who had educated themselves through nurturing their intrinsic human-heartedness. These ideas are developed by later Confucian scholars, such as Mencius. Mencius suggested that the will of Heaven is evident to all if they looked within their own hearts. Thus Heaven began to assume a greater role in shaping human morality. He also emphasized that rulers should embody high virtues, ruling through their example, rather than by force. A major difference between Mencius and the Confucian philosopher Xunzi/Hsun-tzu lies in their conception of intrinsic human nature.

While Mencius, like Confucius, held that human beings were intrinsically good, Xunzi held that human nature was evil and self-serving. However, Xunzi shared with his fellow Confucians a belief that human goodness can be developed and nurtured through education. He also believed that adherence to traditional rites (*li*) was a crucial element in the cultivation of human character.

Confucian philosophy often developed in response to rival ideas. Two such rival groups were the Mohists and the Legalists. The Mohist teachings of Mozi/Mo-tzu contrasted with Confucianism because he promoted a philosophy of egalitarianism and militant pacifism. He noted that Heaven looked upon all people with an equal eye and accepted sacrifices from everyone equally. Thus it was necessary to love each other as Heaven does, universally and equally. Mencius found this notion too radical, for the Confucian approach was a love that extends outwards, albeit less intensely, from the family center.

> **DEITY GROUPS**
> **The Daoist Trinity:** Originally involving a single high god who personified the manifest form of the Dao, the concept broadened into a trinity with the addition of "August Ruler of the Dao" and "August Old Ruler." Laozi/Lao-tzu was supposed to be an incarnation of the third deity. Many divinized and now immortal humans rank beneath.
> **The Three Sovereigns:** A triad of legendary culture heroes associated with important developments in humanity's evolution. They bear names such as Firemaker, Animal Tamer, and Divine Farmer.
> **The Five Emperors:** Another set of mythical culture-heroes noted for their benevolent contributions to civilization. They include the Yellow Emperor, during whose reign writing and the manufacture of silk took place, and the Emperor Yu, who is the ancestral founder of the first Chinese dynasty, the Xia/Hsia.

Legalism, another rival philosophy, was articulated by Han Feizi/Han Fei-tzu, a student of Xunzi/Hsun-tzu. It advanced the notion that human beings were intrinsically evil and self-serving, and are incapable of being educated into goodness. Thus the most effective way of maintaining social order is through a set of laws that are rigorously enforced. If those who obey are generously rewarded and those who break the law are severely punished, the human propensity for self-interest will result in social harmony. Legalist philosophy was used effectively by the first Emperor of the Qin/Ch'in dynasty, but proved to be too extreme. In many ways, the enduring success of Confucian teachings may lie in their moderation, which strikes a balance between the kinds of absolutes promoted by Mohism and Legalism.

Daoist Ideals

Dao. Daoist philosophy naturally centers more on the notion of the Dao than it does on Heaven. In the *Daodejing/Tao-te ching*, arguably

Daoism's most important foundational text, the Dao is explained as the mystery of mysteries. As such, the nature of the Dao, the mysterious "Way," as it is also termed, cannot be easily explained or understood. Daoist philosophy thus consists of pointing to it, or evoking its presence in a variety of ways, many of which appear paradoxical or enigmatic. The Dao is the source of all things created and uncreated. It is the source of Heaven and Earth. But the Dao that is conceptualized and spoken about is not the deeply enduring Dao.

These ideas are contained in the opening chapter of the *Daodejing/ Tao-te ching*, a book consisting of eighty-one chapters totalling 5,000 words, which despite its innocuous size ranks as the third most translated book in the world after the Bible and the *Bhagavad-gita.* Its authorship is attributed to Laozi/Lao-tzu after whom it is sometimes named. Laozi/Lao-tzu means "Old Master," pressing scholars to wonder if he was a historical or legendary figure. There is no reliable information about his life, although legends state that he received his name because he was born with a flowing white beard, testament to his great wisdom. Legends also hold that he was an archivist of the Zhou Dynasty, who retired from civilized life to live as a recluse. As he was leaving, a border guard begged him to leave behind some of his teachings. In the *Laozi Lao-tzu*, we have a distillation of his wisdom. The *Daodejing/Tao-te ching* contains advice for rulers, but its greatest influence has been in articulating, albeit often in enigmatic verses, the underlying metaphysics of Daoist philosophy. The Dao is the mysterious portal through which all creation emanates and returns. Thus the dualistic principles of Yin and Yang derive from the Dao.

The Human Condition. Both the *Daodejing/Tao-te Ching* and the *Zhuangzi/ Chuang-tzu* articulate a philosophy that human beings have drifted far from their natural condition, and thus far from the Dao at its source. Civilization, as represented in the philosophies of Mozi/Mo-tzu, Confucius, the Legalists, etc., reveals the efforts of philosophical ideas, in tandem with social pressures, to keep human beings living in an orderly manner. But this, the Daoists proclaim, is the very source of human discontent and disorder. All through our lives we strive to be good or are pressured into particular behaviors by our social groups. These efforts and pressures distort our intrinsic natures, causing us to rebel or react violently. Thus our own natures are degraded and perverted. In essence then, the *Zhuangzi/ Chuang-tzu* promotes a philosophy of freedom from the world constructed by human conventions and strictures. The Daoist ideal is the sage (*sheng*), persons who have returned to their original nature, and thus abide with, or have actually become one with, the Dao.

East Asian Buddhist Beliefs

It is the Mahayana wing of Buddhism that endured in East Asia. Most of the major schools of Indian Mahayana Buddhism entered China and were represented there. However, China also developed its own schools of Buddhism, often derived from a particularly influential Sanskrit scripture. The Tiantai/T'ien-t'ai school of Buddhism, for instance, was based on the *Lotus Sutra*, which came to be regarded as the quintessence of the Buddha's teachings. Tiantai/T'ien-t'ai Buddhism, named after a mountain in Zheijiang/Chekiang on the coast of southeast China, where it originated, attempted to reconcile the variations and seeming contradictions within the various forms of Buddhism that had entered China. It did so by promulgating the notion that the Buddha had taught all these forms at various points in his post-enlightenment teaching life to different groups of disciples, each with different needs and capacities. The *Lotus Sutra* was held to contain his teachings explaining the unity within the seeming diversity, and thus became regarded as the acme of Buddhist teachings. When it spread to Japan early in the ninth century, it was known as Tendai.

The Huayan/Hua-yen ("Flower Garland") school of Chinese Buddhism is based on the teachings of the *Avatamsaka Sutra*. Its teachings center on the interpenetration of each aspect of reality with every other aspect. This fundamental interconnectedness of all things points to the presence of the Buddha nature everywhere, fully contained in each of its apparent parts.

Jingtu/Ching-t'u Buddhism derives from the *Sukhavati-vyuha*, a Sanskrit text in praise of the Buddha Amitabha (Chinese: Amituo) and his paradise (*sukhavati*, "happy land"). Driven by great compassion, the Buddha Amitabha created Jingtu/Ching-t'u ("Pure Land"), a paradise where beings who were devoted to him could be reborn. This school appealed to the masses who found the rigors of self-reliant meditation too demanding. The Chinese had also taken to the concept of *mofa* (Japanese: *mappo*), an end-time wherein those who had not achieved some level of enlightenment could be shut out from the possibility of ever attaining it. This

---

DEITIES

Tian/T'ien: Heaven, developed in the Zhou Dynasty, and perhaps derived from the concept of the Lord on High of the Shang period. Heaven refers to a supreme deity or primordial ancestor, who rules over a large host of nature spirits.

Guanyin/Kuan-yin: "Cry Regarder." Goddess who evolved from the Buddhist Bodhisattva of Compassion, Avalokiteshvara. Receives prayers and devotion from those seeking solace.

Budai/Pu-t'ai: The bald, fat, jolly figure is commonly called the Laughing Buddha. The image is derived from a medieval Chinese Buddhist monk, and he is prayed to for good luck, offspring, and material success. He is a personification of the future Buddha, Lord Maitreya (Mile/Mi-lo).

spurred many to incorporate some measure of Buddhist practice into their lives. Pure Land has grown to be one of the most popular forms of Buddhism in East Asia. In Japan it is known as Jodo, and Amitabha is referred to as Amida.

Unlike the other schools discussed so far, Chan/Ch'an Buddhism did not derive from a particular Sanskrit scripture. In fact, it has a suspicion and disregard for excessive emphasis on scriptures in general. Chan, which derives from the Sanskrit word *dhyana*, means "meditation," which is its primary focus. It is believed to have been introduced to China in the sixth century by the semi-legendary Indian sage Bodhidharma, who is reputed to have meditated in a cave facing a wall for nine years. An even more tenuous claim is his association with the famous Shao-lin monastery, where he introduced East Asia to *k'ung-fu* and other martial arts derived from India. In Japan, Chan came to be known as Zen.

Chinese Buddhism transformed the persona of many figures in Indian Buddhism. Avalokiteshvara, the Bodhisattva of Compassion, became transformed into a female divinity, the goddess Guanyin/Kuan-yin ("Cry Regarder"). Guanyin/Kuan-yin (Japanese: Kannon) is extremely popular as an object of devotion and is often prayed to not particularly to facilitate in the achievement of *nirvana*, but for worldly ends, such as to obtain offspring. In China, the once regal figure of Maitreya, the Buddha-to-come, was associated with Budai/Pu-t'ai ("Hemp Sack"), a pot-bellied, jolly "bag-man," known as the Laughing Buddha. Known as Hotei in Japan, Budai/Pu-t'ai or Mile/Mi-lo is widely worshiped in East Asia, mostly for worldly prosperity. In both these figures, Guanyin/Kuan-yin and Mile/Mi-lo, we note the "this-worldly" concerns of the Chinese shaping and transforming the "other-worldly" character of Indian Buddhism.

PRACTICES

Practices Derived from Antiquity

As previously mentioned, we have ample evidence of the ancient practice of divination. Heated metal rods were applied to flat bones of animals, such as shoulder blades (scapulimancy), and the ensuing fissure patterns were deciphered as oracles. Although there were most likely manuals that decoded these patterns, the process of interpretation involved a substantial intuitive capacity on the part of the diviner. Thus the procedure of divination drew upon supernatural powers that were shamanic in nature. Belief in the capacities to commune with spirits, interpret dreams, consult and interpret oracles, and the like still endure among modern-day shamans in East Asia. The worldview and practices of shamans are often categorized by scholars as "popular" or "folk" religion, although these labels carry their own set of problems. "Popular" may be misunderstood as the opposite of "unpopular," rather than "of the masses/people" as it is intended. Similarly, "folk" sets up a problematic social distinction between upper and lower classes, or between urban and rural groups, because so-called "folk" religious practices may well be found among upper-class, urban folk, not just among the poor in the countryside. At any rate, shamanism is widespread in East Asian societies even today. Mediums (often female) may be consulted to contact the souls of departed ancestors, which they do by entering into trance states.

Although scapulimancy has declined, the ancient use of yarrow stalks in divination endures. The most well-known use is in the consultation of the *Book of Changes* (*Yijing/I-Ching*), which dates to pre-Confucian times. Through an elaborate procedure of dividing and counting the wooden yarrow stalks (nowadays many people opt for a simple procedure of tossing three coins six times), a hexagram composed of solid or broken lines is generated. The solid line corresponds to the Yang principle, which is associated with Heaven, the male, hot, bright, active, and other such attributes. The broken line corresponds to the Yin principle, associated with the Earth, the female, cool, dark, passive, and other such complements to the Yang constituents. There are sixty-four possible combinations of the six Yin and Yang lines in

DYNASTIES

Xia/Hsia: Legendary dynasty of China that pre-dates the Shang. Although archeological materials have been found from a variety of sites that are older than the Shang Dynasty, it is not certain that these belong to Xia Dynasty settlements.

Shang: [ca. fourteenth-eleventh centuries B.C.E.]. Earliest dynasty for which there is archeological evidence. Since it flourished along the eastern part of the Yellow River, it is also known as the Yellow River civilization. Artifacts reveal that it was a bronze age culture that developed writing and practiced divination.

Zhou/Chou: [1045-221 B.C.E.]. The longest lasting of Chinese dynasties, it is subdivided into "early" and "late" periods. Although initially stable, the later period, known as the Eastern Zhou, was one of disunity and civil warfare. Many of China's major philosophical schools, such as Confucianism, Daoism, Mohism, and Legalism developed at this time.

Qin/Ch'in: [221-207 B.C.E.]. Founded by Qin Shi Huangdi/Ch'in Shi-huang-ti, also known as the First Emperor, because he united the various kingdoms into the empire that gives China its name. Legalism was the dominant political philosophy.

Han: [206 B.C.E.-220 C.E.]. Dynasty during which Confucian philosophy became implemented by the state. The selection of government officials was through merit, not based on aristocratic birthright.

Tang/T'ang: [618-906 C.E.]. Buddhism reached it zenith in China in this period.

a hexagram, and the *Book of Changes* provides interpretations for these patterns. This book, also called *The Oracle of Change,* may be consulted to provide advice for any situation. Although the text provides one with a basis for interpretation, advanced practitioners draw upon an intuitive understanding of the line patterns to make prognostications.

It is quite common to find an assortment of divination devices in East Asian temples today. For instance, a container full of wooden sticks may be shaken until a particular stick falls out and the message inscribed upon it is then read. In other places one may even find coin operated machines that provide a paper slip with one's "fortune" written upon it. The technique of *feng-shui,* originally used to select appropriate sites for the burial of ancestors, is now used extensively in many areas of architectural design and layout. A *feng-shui* expert, sometimes with the aid of a compass-like device, can provide advice on everything from the appropriate placement of a skyscraper to furnishings in one's home.

The ancient Chinese performed blood sacrifices to provide food for departed ancestors. Elaborate ceremonies were also performed by the state on behalf of other deities and royal ancestors. In royal sacrifices, special sections of the ancestral temples were allocated for the sacrificial rites. Typically, domesticated animals such as goats and cattle were slaughtered, the internal organs cooked and eaten, and the fat burned in a sacred fire. There is also evidence of human sacrifice in ancient China (as was the case in most ancient cultures). Victims may have been war captives or criminals. The wealthy also buried spouses, attendants, and slaves with the deceased. The first emperor of Qin/Ch'in is reputed to have been buried with all the barren women of his court. Beside his tomb, located near his capital, Xi'an/Ch'ang-an, stands a secondary retinue of thousands of life-sized terracotta soldiers, buried to serve as a surrogate army for him in the afterlife. The grand scale of his burial has not since been duplicated in China, but it reflects the ancient concern with continued existence in the afterlife, which continues even till today.

Ancestor Worship Practices

When a family member dies, tradition dictates that the body be washed and dressed in clean clothes for burial. Ideally, the grave site should be selected through the application of *feng-shui.* The eldest son plays the central role in the funerary rites for the deceased. The family members and mourners dress in white, the color of death, which contrasts with red, the color of life and prosperity, used on other occasions such as marriage. The rites that are performed attempt to keep the Yin pole of the soul, known as the *po/p'o*, which descends into the underworld, from becoming a malevolent ghost. At the same time, the family hopes to receive the blessings of the Yang pole of the soul, the *hun*. The soul may be installed into a wooden tablet and placed on a special altar with other ancestral tablets in the family's home shrine. Great family clans may have separate temples to house all the ancestors' tablets of their lineage. Daoists priests may be commissioned to perform rites, such as burning incense, and Buddhist monks may be asked to chant from the scriptures.

On regular occasions throughout the year, the family members are expected to visit the ancestral tomb or burial site and conduct rites there and at the wooden tablet at the family home shrine. These rites are always accompanied by feasting. Family solidarity is maintained through these practices. It is thus also quite common for Chinese families to keep detailed genealogical records so that important ancestors and their accomplishments can be remembered, acknowledged, and transmitted to future generations. Although the elaborate celebrations of funerary and ancestral rites are prohibited in China today, they are still practiced in rural areas and in Chinese communities outside of the mainland.

The Confucian Legacy

Although Confucius was critical of rituals performed without the cultivation of *ren/jen*, his emphasis on propriety (*li*) led his teachings to be associated

---

CHINESE BUDDHIST TEXTS

The Chinese Buddhist canon contains a large number of texts organized into various sections, a few of which are listed below. Important representative texts are mentioned within their appropriate group.

Agama Sutras: These are essentially equivalent to the Pali Buddhist Canon (associated with the Theravada school), but derived from Sanskrit texts of the Sarvastivada school.

Prajna Sutras: Among the earliest Mahayana Buddhist writings, these pertain to the Perfection of Wisdom (*prajna*) literature, some of whose texts are very lengthy. The most popular of these, in part due to their concise presentation of the essential teachings of this genre, are the *Diamond Sutra* (about 5,000 words) and the *Heart Sutra* (about 250 words). A manuscript of the *Diamond Sutra* (868 C.E.) is arguably the oldest printed book in existence.

Dharma Blossom Sutras: The most influential among these texts is the *Lotus of the True Dharma Sutra*, or simply the *Lotus Sutra*. It forms the basis of Tiantai Buddhism, and serves as inspiration for other works in this group.

Flower Garland Sutras: The *Avatamsaka Sutra* is the most influential in this group of writings. It served as the basis of the Huayan (Flower Garland) School of Buddhism.

Treasure Trove Sutras: Contained within this group are important Pure Land Buddhism texts including the *Sukhavativyuha* (*Treatise on the Land of Bliss*) and others dealing with the Buddha Amitabha.

with the promotion of ceremony and rites. For instance, in an episode in the *Analects* (XVII.21) he acknowledges that although reducing the formal mourning period is permissible, a person of noble bearing would continue with the prescribed three-year period. The ancestor worship rites of the type described above were thus supported by Confucian values. A number of other rituals, such as celebrations of the entry into adulthood and marriage, are found in the *Book of Rites*, one of the Five Confucian Classics. Confucius did not appear whole-heartedly supportive of sacrificial culture without an accompanying inner feeling for the spirits being propitiated. He seems to have been whole-heartedly against human sacrifice even in its symbolic forms. However, a state cult of animal sacrifice to deities developed after his death during the Han Dynasty, and Confucius himself became venerated through sacrificial offerings.

Daoist Practices

Philosophical Daoism emphasized a return to one's original state, sometimes symbolized as an "uncarved block," unshaped by the influences of human conditioning. The would-be sage would likely retreat to an abode close to nature, such as a hut in the woods, or a cave, and there embark on a simple life where meditation and the contemplation of the natural world were the most important activities. Thus the Daoism of Laozi/Lao-tzu and Zhuangzi/Chuang-tzu is a sort of "nature mysticism," through which the sage seeks to become at one with the Dao, the mysterious power within Nature.

Daoist writings sometimes cite water or the willow tree as symbols of the Daoist ideal in the journey back to one's true nature. Water, although soft and weak, can erode away the hardest stone. And the pliant willow tree can survive a tempest, while a massive tree with more rigid branches and trunk might snap. Thus although the sage seeks a harmonious balance between the Yin and Yang principles that constitute the Dao, it is the pliant Yin or yielding path that is favored to lead one there. The world of organized society is excessively Yang. The sage adheres to the natural principle of *wuwei/wu-wei*. Although the term means "non-action," *wuwei* is actually more akin to not acting in a contrived or planned manner. By being unattached to one's actions, and allowing them to occur in a timely and appropriate way, one develops *ziran/tzu-jan*, or spontaneity.

Nature is not only spontaneous, immediately and appropriately responsive to the changes that occur moment to moment, it is uncontrived in its actions. Thus the sage seeks to embody that capacity of the Dao. By so doing, the sage reflects the intrinsic power of the Dao, known as De/Te.

as it is manifest through a person. De can be understood as the intrinsic nature of something, a symbol of which is the specific type of grain in wood. Each aspect of the natural creation has its true nature, its "is-ness," and this is the goal of the sage, who seeks his or her own *de*.

Daoist religion developed its pantheon of deities and deified persons who had apparently achieved immortality. Rituals emerged to propitiate these deities, but the Daoist priesthood also amalgamated with the shamanic and divinatory traditions of antiquity. Thus Daoist priests may be commissioned to diagnose illnesses and perform exorcisms. They perform rituals at seasonal celebrations such as the New Year (lunar) and winter solstice. Around the time of the summer solstice exorcisms of dangerous spirits that will emerge during the ensuing *yin* season (as the nights grow longer) are typical. Daoist priests act as intermediaries between the world of the spirits and humans. They may perform rites to convey the wishes of people to the spirit world. One technique for doing so is, while chanting prayers and after appropriate internal purifications, to burn incense and paper objects that symbolize the worshipper's objects of desire, sending these to the heavens.

The Daoist quest for bodily immortality led to the study of meditative techniques, physical exercises, and the preparation and consumption of special elixirs and dietary supplements. Qigong/Ch'i-kung, for instance, is a fusion of breathing and movement techniques believed to harness the vital energy (*qi/ch'i*), and even to command certain spirits to aid one in the endeavor. In the popular

FESTIVALS

New Year: Based on the lunar cycle, it falls in late January or early February. Businesses usually close and homes are cleaned in preparation for spring. Families gather to worship ancestors and other deities. Firecrackers are ignited and presents are exchanged.

Clear and Bright Festival: Held two weeks after the spring equinox, it is dedicated to the ancestors. Families take purifying baths, and clean and repair ancestral tombs. Picnics are held at the burial sites and food is offered to the ancestors.

Dragon Boat Festival: Held on the fifth day of the fifth moon (June/July), boats decorated to resemble dragons are raced. Rice cakes are eaten, and rituals are performed to ward off evil spirits since the daylight hours will now grow shorter.

Ghost Festival: A Buddhist festival held in late August, dedicated to the suffering souls in lower realms, who are released from their suffering. Food offerings are placed outside the home for these spirits, and families may gather for a feast.

Harvest Festival: on the full moon of the eighth month, a harvest moon festival is celebrated. Round sweet pastries (moon cakes) are eaten to give thanks for the agricultural bounty.

Ancestor and Deity Worship: Traditionally during the tenth full moon, special paper clothes and "money" are burned as offerings to departed family members. Gods and ancestors are worshipped, a family feast is held as the year ends, and the renewal of a New Year begins.

practice of Taijichuan/Tai-chi ch'uan, one notes the combination of meditative practice (Daoist yoga), martial art, and breath work, all believed to be conducive to spiritual enlightenment and bodily health and longevity.

Buddhist Practices

The preeminent practice in Buddhism is meditation, because the majority of Buddhist schools hold the attainment of *nirvana* as the most important goal. This is certainly true in the Chan/Ch'an (Japanese: Zen) schools of Buddhism. Two important techniques utilized by Chan schools are sitting meditation (*zuochan*), and pondering an enigmatic question (*gongan*). The Linji sect of Chinese Chan is associated with *gongan*, and with the possibility of sudden enlightenment, while the Caodong sect focused on gradual awakening through *zuochan* practice.

The most popular forms of Buddhism in China and Japan, in the modern period, are devotional rather than meditative. The Jingtu/Ch'ing-t'u school requires practitioners to chant homage to the Buddha Amitabha repeatedly, with devotion. This technique, known in China as the *nianfo* ("invoking" the name of the Buddha) uses the sacred utterance (*mantra*): "homage to Amituofo" (Amitabha Buddha). Devotional forms of Buddhism have led to the cult of Mile/Mi-lo, the Laughing Buddha, and Guanyin, the Goddess of Mercy. There are celebrations in April/May that honor the Buddha's birth, enlightenment, and death. Buddhist monks chant scriptures and give religious discourses on that day. They may also be commissioned on various occasions throughout the year to perform such activities.

CONCLUSION

Students often remark that the religions of East Asia focus more on ethical behavior, social relationships, and individual self-realization, rather than on such notions as god, sin, and salvation. Although this is certainly true, it does not make East Asian cultures any less "religious" than those in the west. Religion cannot be defined by the worldview and belief of the monotheistic Western traditions, such as Christianity and Islam. It needs to examine the human religious impulse writ large, and see how that yearning manifests in various societies and cultures. From that perspective, China and other East Asian societies clearly have vibrant and well-developed religious cultures. These provide answers for the inexplicable mysteries of existence as well as moral guidelines for living life with a sense of meaning and purpose.

Another noteworthy dimension of East Asian religions is their fusion. It is natural for people to draw upon and thus syncretize the varieties of ideas to which they have been exposed. This was especially easy in East Asia, because the most popular traditions (Confucianism, Daoism, and Buddhism) did not promote exclusivist viewpoints as do Christianity and Islam, which have not as yet had widespread success in East Asia. Furthermore, in such philosophies as Neo-Confucianism one sees a conscious blending of the major traditions and the promotion of this unified religious philosophy for many centuries.

Modern secularism and political ideologies have further affected the nature of Chinese religions and their influence on East Asian societies. In 1949, after the Communist revolution in China, religions were suppressed in favor of Marxist scientific materialism. The situation was exacerbated after 1966 during the Cultural Revolution when there was a direct assault on the religious establishment in China. Monasteries and temples were destroyed and festivals were prohibited. Nevertheless, these types of traditions continue to endure among Chinese communities in rural areas and outside of mainland China where they spread. In such practices as the preference for male offspring, unquestioning respect and obedience for hierarchical superiors, and stern civil punishments, we note continuing strains of Confucian and Legalistic values in some East Asian societies. Currently, as China begins to open up to global influences, there is a slow revival of religion there. Naturally, the forms that emerge will draw upon the ancient heritage, but will also demonstrate creative transformations that offer meaning to the newer generations of adherents.

CHAPTER ELEVEN   Japanese Religions

HISTORY

The Major Religious Traditions

Japanese religion and culture has inspired global fascination with images of Zen Buddhist monks in meditation and the famously photogenic Shinto *torii* ("gateway") that stands majestically in the sea off the shore of Miyajima ("shrine island"). The sense of sacred serenity illustrated by these religious examples contrasts with the equally prevalent perception of Tokyo's pulsing modern technology. Both extremes reinforce ideas, within Japan and from abroad, of Japanese distinctiveness. However, cultural influxes from the Chinese mainland and Korean peninsula have significantly influenced Japanese religion and culture. The two major religious traditions from the beginning of Japan's historical period in the sixth century C.E., Shinto and Buddhism, continue to exhibit East Asian characteristics as well as traits unique to Japan.

Shinto is rooted in the prehistoric practices and beliefs of the Japanese. From these nebulous origins, Shinto has developed its forms, even its name, in conjunction with Buddhism. Moreover, its modern expressions owe much to recent religious and political influences. Shinto has neither a founder nor a central text, but instead consists of a range of ritual, festival, and reverent practices performed to cultivate the symbiotic correspondence between the people and places of Japan and the uncanny spiritual forces, *kami*, understood to permeate the island nation.

Buddhism originated in India and underwent significant transformation in China before arriving in Japan. Although Buddhist schools in Japan's early history closely resembled their Chinese antecedents, the schools that became most popular and influential are more distinctly Japanese. Rather than merely viewing Buddhism in Japan as a foreign tradition transplanted whole into Japanese soil, Japanese Buddhism can be better understood as a hybrid tradition born both from Buddhism and native Japanese culture.

In the section that follows, we will focus largely on the interaction between the two major traditions, Buddhism and Shinto. Other traditions, such as Daoism (Taoism), Confucianism, Neo-Confucianism, Christianity, and a variety of "New Religions" have had lesser degrees of influence at different times.

The Prehistoric Heritage (ca. 10,000 B.C.E.–538 C.E.)

Relative to China's highly developed civilization from ancient times, Japan's early culture and religious traditions are only known indirectly until the introduction of written language and increasingly complex social structures from the middle of the first millennium C.E. In fact, Chinese records provide the few written historical accounts of Japan before this time. Other knowledge of prehistoric Japan comes from archeological finds.

Artifacts from the Jomon Period (ca. 10,000–300 B.C.E.) suggest a hunting and gathering society that had not yet shifted to the rice cultivation for which the subsequent Japanese periods are known. Early evidence of burial—including implements buried with the carefully postured dead—and discoveries of stone phalli and earthenware figurines depicting women with exaggerated breasts, hips, and bellies suggested religious concerns with an afterlife and fertility respectively. The Yayoi Period (ca. 300 B.C.E.–300 C.E.) reflects technological influence from the East Asian mainland. The innovation of cultivating rice in wet rice paddies both allowed for and required more complex social organization. There is much that remains unknown about religious practices. Evidence does point to more communal religious activities, spreading practices of ancestor worship, the use of animal bones and tortoise shells for divination, and belief in *kami*. It is from this period that we can first identify the people and culture that would come to be known as Japanese.

Japan's clan-based society became more centralized at each stage and a head clan—the Yamato ("Sun"), a name synonymous with the area they controlled—consolidated power around 350 C.E. and came to be known as the imperial family of Japan. The account of a Shamanic queen, Himiko or Pimiko, who ruled a century earlier, suggests that women could embody supreme authority, spiritual power, and purity. The myth of the divine descent of the imperial family from the sun goddess, Amaterasu, illustrates this power in the realm of the *kami*, and the role of the chaste imperial princess in caring for Ise Shrine demonstrates purity. These examples are connected as Ise Shrine was built around 300 C.E. to provide a more suitable place to house, worship, and care for this divine ancestor and preeminent *kami*, Amaterasu. Japanese empresses further exemplified religious and political leadership, but their occasional rule fades after the eighth century. Similarly, lead religious roles for women in Shinto seem to have diminished, reflecting the influence of the new Buddhist practices, where monks held most authority. Women did continue to provide some important religious functions, however, such as that of *miko* ("shamaness").

Shinto became more defined only after Buddhism entered the country in the sixth century C.E. There was no need to conceptualize various local practices and beliefs as a unified tradition until confronted by the vast philosophical, religious, material, and cultural totality of Buddhism.

Introduction of Buddhism (538-710 C.E.)

Buddhism originated in India and spread to China in the first century C.E., where it continued to develop and enrich

MAJOR LEADERS (other than founders of Buddhist schools)
Prince Shotoku: (574-622). This ruler incorporated Confucian and Buddhist teachings into his philosophy for the state. He is especially revered for his studies and early promotion of Buddhism on religious and political grounds.
Emperor Shomu: (ruled 724-749). Devout Buddhist Emperor who commissioned the copying and distribution of Buddhist *sutras*, the construction of temples in every province, and a central temple, Todaiji, with its Great Buddha (*daibutsu*) statue of Vairochana, to serve as a unifying and protective force for the nation.
Genshin: (942-1017). Buddhist monk who turned to Pure Land teachings and wrote the *Ojoyoshu*. In this work he emphasized the necessity of Pure Land practice by graphically illustrating both the karmic punishments of various hells and the rewards of Amida's Pure Land in the West.
Hakuin: (1685-1768). Rinzai Zen priest credited with reviving and systematizing Zen practice in the Tokugawa Era.
Motoori Norinaga: (1730-1801). Great scholar of *kokugaku*, "national" or "native" studies. His influence extended beyond close linguistic analysis of the earliest Japanese writings to advocacy of Shinto and native aesthetic principles as superior to Buddhism and Confucianism.
Hirata Atsutane: (1776-1843). *Kokugaku* scholar who borrowed from other traditions in his formulation of Shinto as complete and supreme. He proclaimed Japan, the Land of the Gods, superior to all nations.

China's already impressive civilization. Chinese culture, including religious beliefs and practices, exerted influence throughout East Asia. Buddhism spread from China to Korea in the 300s C.E. and then into Japan. Buddhist materials were sent in 538 as a gift by King Song, one of the rulers on the Korean peninsula who hoped to enlist Japan as an ally. Buddhism's official introduction was political as much as religious. Buddhism was first welcomed primarily for its supposed powers to protect and enrich the country and its ruling clans. This new religion was adopted along with other significant imports from China and Korea, including models of centralized government and the use of Chinese characters to write the Japanese language.

Control and cultivation of Buddhism fell to the powerful Soga clan, a family already involved with Korean politics and culture. The Soga clan sent nuns to study Buddhism in Korea and continued to facilitate an influx of Korean craftsmen, priests, and religious paraphernalia into Japan. Although some clans, most notably the Mononobe and Nakatomi families, resisted Buddhism, the religion continued to gain influence, demonstrated by its official imperial patronage and the construction of Buddhist temples by the end of the sixth century.

Prince Shotoku (574-622) epitomized the early flowering of Buddhism in Japan as he delved deeply into the religious study of Buddhism beyond an allegiance tied merely to politics, clan loyalty, or fascination with the accompanying Buddhist culture. The early seeds of Buddhism had come to fruition in the imperial court and among surrounding aristocratic families by the Nara Period (710-784), which made manifest its Buddhist character through massive Buddhist building projects.

Buddhism and Authority: Nara through Heian (710-1185 C.E.)

Buddhism gained power among the Nara elite of the eighth century, developed new forms of practice and doctrine throughout the Heian era (794-1185), and was progressively permeating all levels of society by the end of this period. Buddhism became solidly established politically, financially, and institutionally in the new capital, Nara, as evidenced by escalating Buddhist building programs. Such mutual support between Buddhism and the state took various forms throughout Japanese history. In general, the state supported Buddhism with land and temples, and Buddhism supported the state by offering the protection of the Dharma through ritual, the recitation of Buddhist *sutras,* and the sheer physical presence of the expanding order of Buddhism in Japan. Emperor Shomu's reign (724-49) exemplifies this support. He ordered that each province make Buddhist statues, erect pagodas, produce and display numerous copies of Buddhist *sutras*, and build separate monasteries for Buddhist monks and nuns. He further sought to unify religious and political authority by ordering the construction of a massive statue of Vairochana Buddha, the cosmic Buddha.

Emperor Kammu had concerns about the state support and growing power and influence of the Buddhist establishment. Just a decade before Kammu's reign, the priest Dokyo had been exiled for trying to usurp the throne through undue influence over the Empress Shotoku. To counter this influence, Emperor Kammu moved the capital away from Nara in 784 and ordered that the major Buddhist temples remain behind.

The Nara schools represented Indian and Chinese philosophical schools of Buddhism with relatively minor changes arising from their move to Japan. Although still based upon forms of Chinese Buddhism, two new schools developed in the Heian era with an emphasis upon practices that increasingly became foundational to distinctively Japanese sects of Buddhism. In contrast to older forms of Buddhism, which were largely patronized by the elite, these later Japanese schools spread widely through the populace.

Saicho (767-822) founded the Japanese school of Tendai Buddhism on Mt. Hiei. Tendai followed the Tiantai school he had encountered in China. It incorporated esoteric teachings, Pure Land practices, seated meditation and doctrinal synthesis of diverse Buddhist texts with particular reverence for the *Lotus Sutra*. Saicho emphasized the Mahayana *bodhisattva*

GROUPS/DIVISIONS

Tendai: Saicho (767-822) founded this sect in Japan based on teachings and practices of Chinese Tiantai Buddhism. Mahayana emphasis of the bodhisattva ideal and esoteric teachings combined with practices of seated meditation, Pure Land recitation, and devotion to the *Lotus Sutra*.

Shingon: Kukai (774-835) founded this sect in Japan based on teachings of esoteric Buddhism (*mikkyo*) that were influential in T'ang China. Shingon means "True Word" and emphasizes enlightenment in this body through the practice of sacred utterances (*mantras*), hand gestures (*mudras*), and cosmic maps (*mandalas*).

Kamakura Schools: The founders of the following schools had trained in Tendai on Mt. Hiei.

Pure Land Schools: Adherents of these sects venerate Amida's name through *nembutsu* recitation with faith that the "other-power" (*tariki*) of Amida Buddha's vow could bring them to the Pure Land. Jodo (Pure Land), founded by Honen (1133-1212), emphasized constant recitation of *nembutsu*. Jodo Shin (True Pure Land), founded by Shinran (1173-1262), emphasized gratitude in response to the conviction (*shinjin*) of Amida's salvation.

Zen Schools: Zen teachings and sole practice of seated zen meditation (*zazen*) were brought back from China by Eisai (1141-1215) in the form of Rinzai Zen and by Dogen (1200-1253) in the form of Soto Zen.

Nichiren: Nichiren (1222-1282) founded this school based on reverence for the *Lotus Sutra*.

ideal of helping all beings attain enlightenment. He outlined a system of training that would yield great monks, dedicated teachers, and servants of the nation. Saicho recognized that the growth and influence of his Tendai school would be severely restricted unless he could convince the imperial court to grant him an ordination platform at Enryakuji on Mt. Hiei, rather than being forced to send would-be monks to Nara, where ordination was traditionally carried out. His wish was granted a week after he died.

Kukai (Kobo Daishi, 774-835), the founder of Shingon Buddhism, provided the other great influence on Japanese religion in the Heian Era. He traveled to China and brought back a wealth of esoteric teachings, texts, and ritual objects. From his monastery on Mt. Koya, away from the capital of Heian (Kyoto), Kukai became known as the master of esoteric Buddhism (mikkyo). He emphasized the necessity of instruction directly from the master, and stipulated—unsuccessfully—that even his rival Saicho must become his student in order to realize the ultimate teachings.

Tendai and Shingon came to dominate Heian Japan as recipients of institutional support and masters of powerful forms of esoteric Buddhism. Although Kukai is the more revered virtuoso of Japanese religions, Saicho's Tendai school came to exert the greatest influence over subsequent religious developments.

Other forms of religious practice continued outside of the imperial court and monastic headquarters. However, it is difficult to determine to what extent Buddhist practice went beyond clerics, aristocrats, and mountain ascetics to reach the masses in the early Heian era. Later in this period, charismatic monks, novices, and wandering holy men (hijiri) embarked on the popular dissemination of Pure Land practices, such as chanting the name of Amida Buddha (nembutsu). This spread of Buddhism beyond the elite accelerated in the tenth century.

Buddhist Proliferation under Samurai Rule (1185-1867)

Genshin and other pioneers of Pure Land Buddhism paved the way for the establishment of distinct schools in the Kamakura period (1185-1333). Jodo ("Pure Land"), Jodo Shin ("True Pure Land"), and Nichiren schools of Buddhism were founded by Honen (1133-1212), Shinran (1173-1262) and Nichiren (1222-1282) respectively. Each of these founders had been a Tendai monk from Mt. Hiei who brought more singular and simple Buddhist teachings to the general population. They opened their practice more widely to all men and women, rich and poor, educated and illiterate. The other two Kamakura schools, Rinzai Zen founded by Eisai (1141-1215) and Soto Zen founded by Dogen

(1200–1253), shared these Tendai roots and focus on one key aspect of Buddhist practice, seated meditation (*zazen*).

Allegiance to one school over another at times fell along class lines. Rinzai Zen quickly became popular among the ruling warlords. The *samurai* elite welcomed Zen's focus on disciplined awareness of the present moment without fear, attachment, or anxiety. The new rulers also appreciated Zen cultural contributions including the direct, simple, immediate, natural, and spontaneous artistic expressions that countered the elaborate, formal aesthetics of the emperor's aristocratic court. Soto Zen, on the other hand, was at times referred to as the Zen of farmers to reflect its more rural base.

The Pure Land schools boasted the devotion of numerous rulers as well as the peasant masses, who welcomed its egalitarian message. The Jodo Shin faith grew rapidly in the late fifteenth century and remains the largest in Japan.

Conflicts erupted among Buddhist factions until the stable Tokugawa period at the beginning of the seventeenth century. Warlords had played religious groups off of each other for military and political ends, and many Buddhist monasteries were destroyed, their resources depleted, and their monks slaughtered. Tokugawa Ieyasu won the final decisive battle for control of Japan in 1600 and in 1603 established a new government in Edo, which later became Tokyo. The ensuing period, known as the Edo or Tokugawa era, lasted for over 250 years with relative peace and stability.

PLACES

Ancient Capitals: The former capitals of Nara and Heian (Kyoto) are especially rich centers of Japanese religious culture. The great Buddhist temples from the 700s still dominate the landscape at Nara. Todaiji remains particularly impressive with its immense *daibutsu* statue of Vairochana/Dainichi. Kyoto has approximately 2,000 temples mixed in with the modern buildings of a major city. The wealth of temples includes the headquarters of the Jodo Shin school of Pure Land Buddhism.

Monastic Complexes: There are also major monasteries in the later capitals of Kamakura and Edo (Tokyo), on mountains, and deep in the countryside. Rinzai Zen monasteries, such as Engakuji in Kamakura, remain vital today and serve as reminders of the power of Rinzai during the Kamakura era. The Tendai monastic complex of Enryakuji still watches over Kyoto from its perch on Mt. Hiei. Shingon temples on Mt. Koya remain the focal point of Japan's esoteric Buddhism. The beautiful monastery of Eiheiji, founded by Dogen far from the capital in the natural tranquility of Fukui, remains a primary training site for Soto Zen.

Pilgrimage Sites: Pilgrims travel to the major Shinto shrines of Ise and Izumo, to the beautiful *torii* and shrine on Miyajima, to Mt. Fuji and other sacred mountains, and to sites associated with religious figures, such as Kukai's eighty-eight-temple pilgrimage circuit on Shikoku.

Despite the end of chaotic conflict and direct attacks on Buddhist institutions, the new era held its own risks for religious traditions. Christianity had come to Japan in 1549 with the arrival of the Jesuit missionary,

Francis Xavier. The shifting allegiances in war-torn Japan played to the advantage of Christian missionaries at first, but soon Christianity came to be deemed a threat as a foreign tradition that called for loyalty to an entity beyond the Japanese nation. The authorities persecuted Christians, kicked the missionaries out of the country, outlawed the religion after a 1637 peasant rebellion that had significant ties to Christianity, and became more isolationist. Furthermore, all Japanese had to register with a Buddhist temple. This *danka* system of temple patronage ensured Buddhist support and weakened Christian allegiances.

Despite its reputation for religious stagnation in its new state role, the Tokugawa scholars advanced Buddhist scholarship. Hakuin (1685-1768), the Rinzai Zen master, also provided much needed revitalization. He systematized the earlier Zen *koans* ("case studies") used in monastic training and added some of his own, such as the famous *koan* concerning "the sound of one hand clapping."

Religious thought in the Tokugawa era included scholars of Ancient Learning (*kogaku*), Neo-Confucianism, National Learning (*kokugaku*), and Shinto. Each perspective arose partly in opposition to Tokugawa Buddhism. The promotion of China as the exemplar of ancient learning and ideal government prompted scholars of national, or native, learning to study Japan's early cultural contributions. Shinto was elevated as the religious ideal along with traits and aesthetic sensibilities most expressive of Japanese character. This attitude was given full expression in the following Meiji Era (1868-1912).

Religion and Nationalism in Modern Japan (1868-1945)

The Meiji Restoration of 1867 marked the fall of Tokugawa rule, returned the emperor as the figurehead of religious and political power, and ushered Japan into a tumultuous period of rapid change to catch up and compete with the modern Western powers. The Tokugawa capital, Edo, was renamed Tokyo and became the new center for imperial reverence and national modernization. The official state role of Buddhism ended with Tokugawa rule, and the new state fueled anti-Buddhist resentments and instituted Shinto as the national religion.

Buddhism faced many challenges, both foreign and domestic. From abroad, Christianity had once again gained entry to Japan in the Meiji era and the Western powers synonymous with Christianity maintained an imperialist grasp over much of Asia. Nevertheless, internal dangers proved more immediate and destructive to Buddhism. The virulent anti-Buddhist persecution of the early Meiji years was prefigured by the rise in national studies and a resurgent—and to an extent invented—"restoration" of supposedly traditional Shinto as separate from and hostile to Buddhism. The ferocity of persecution caught many Japanese off guard and led to speculation that Buddhism would not endure the state-sanctioned "separation of Shinto and Buddhism" (*shinbutsu bunri*).

Buddhism did endure. It began to recover within a decade of its persecution, but it faced ongoing challenges from Christianity and "new religions" as well as criticism from modernizers that Buddhism was a relic of the past and impeded the crucial nation-building project. Critics within Buddhism echoed this concern that their tradition was insufficiently modern. But generally Japanese Buddhists strenuously resisted this interpretation and promoted their Mahayana tradition as the culmination of Buddhist teaching and ideal for the modern era.

The threat from resurgent Christianity arose when the Meiji government rescinded the ban on Christianity in 1873. Communities of "hidden" (*kakure*) Christians then openly embraced their faith, Catholic missionaries returned to Japan, and Protestants initiated their own proselytizing campaign. Although conversion rates were modest and adherents have typically numbered less than one percent of the population, Christianity influenced ideas of modern religious practice from charitable organizations to the Christian wedding ceremony—the form and aesthetics of which have become popular in contemporary Japan.

Modern Japan has witnessed various "new religions" spreading throughout the

OFFICES

Monks: Male members of the monastic community have strongly influenced Japanese arts and aesthetics from literature and poetry to tea ceremony, calligraphy, and landscape gardening. Saicho advocated a shift away from the hundreds of monastic rules, or precepts, of earlier forms of Buddhism, but the strongest challenge to monastic precepts came during the Meiji Era with reforms that attempted to abolish monastic regulations against marrying, eating meat, and growing out one's hair.

Nuns: Female members of the monastic community have played a role in the development of Japanese Buddhism from the Buddhist novices sent to train in Korean monasteries when Buddhism first arrived in Japan up until the present.

Temple Priest: The male Buddhist priesthood has become a primarily hereditary role now that most priests marry and have families. Shinran, the founder of Jodo Shin, married in the thirteenth century and most others followed in the modern period.

Shrine Priest: Male officiants preside over rites at Shinto shrines as well as rituals outside of the shrine connected with various festivals.

Miko: This role encompasses a range of duties conducted by female Shinto participants from that of shaman or medium to assistant to the shrine priest.

Emperor: In addition to their role as divine descendants of Amaterasu in Shinto, many Emperors and Empresses have taken the Buddhist tonsure in retirement and become monks and nuns.

latter half of the nineteenth century, due to social dislocation and cultural change in this tumultuous period. Founders and followers alike were often women, as in the case of Nakayama Miki, who founded the Tenri sect. Tenri, which originated three decades before the Meiji Era and remains popular in contemporary Japan, promised health and wealth like other "new religions."

At the official level, samurai and advocates of kokugaku restored the Meiji emperor as a religious and political figurehead and declared Shinto essential to Japanese identity and fundamental to the national polity (kokutai). In addition to their attempts to separate "native" Shinto from "foreign" Buddhism, they elevated Shinto to the status of state religion. These efforts proved ultimately unsuccessful, leading to the new designation of "State Shinto." State Shinto enforced ideology of the Emperor's sacred status, which was based on the assertion of an unbroken imperial lineage extending back to Amaterasu, as civic duty rather than religious belief. In this way citizens were asked to make sacrifices to advance national campaigns initiated in the emperor's name without contradicting the qualified freedom of religion assured in the 1889 Meiji Constitution.

Nationalistic rhetoric extended beyond Shinto to the other Japanese traditions through the Meiji, Taisho (1912-1926), and first two decades of the Showa (1926-1989) eras. Extreme forms of nationalism, emperor ideology, and ambitions of military expansion contributed to catastrophic destruction in World War II.

New Religions and Post-War Japan (1945-present)

American occupation of Japan led to the disbanding of State Shinto and the renunciation of imperial divinity. Emperor Hirohito's New Year's address in 1946 broadcast his "Declaration of Humanity," which refuted his own divinity and the related ideas of Japanese racial superiority and imperial destiny. The removal of State Shinto, the now unqualified principle of religious freedom, and the societal strain of national rebuilding provided fertile soil for new religions.

Soka Gakkai ("Value Creation Society") is the largest new religion in Japan. It is rooted in Nichiren reverence of the Lotus Sutra, and was originally formed shortly before the war. Soka Gakkai was unusual in its resistance to Japanese militarism. Its founder, Makiguchi Tsunesaburo, and his successor, Toda Josei, were both in prison during the war for their noncooperation. Makiguchi died in prison, but Toda reestablished Soka Gakkai after the war, employed unusually aggressive proselytizing tactics, and witnessed its rapid growth and expanding power. Soka Gakkai even formed a related political party, *Komei*.

Hundreds, if not thousands, of "new-new religions" developed out of the ashes of World War II. One of these, Aum Shinrikyo, is best known for its 1995 deadly release of sarin gas in the Tokyo subway. Such violence is antithetical to most new religions as well as extraordinarily rare within Japanese society and religion more generally. Nonetheless, the group was characteristic of new religions in its leadership by a mystical *guru* and its ability to provide a sense of community and belonging for those who felt alienated in an increasingly fractured and impersonal society.

Conclusion

The violence and apocalyptic prophecies of Aum Shinrikyo, now known as Aleph, has caused great anxiety in Japan and increased government scrutiny of new religions. More established religions, such as Buddhism, face challenges of demonstrating their contemporary relevance for Japanese society. Many young people in Japan seem uninterested in religion and disconnected from much of its related cultural matrix. Fascination with Western culture further threatens tradition. Nonetheless, Japanese religious sites are ubiquitous, festivals are frequent, and the traditions have weathered difficult times of transition in the past. Even globalization holds a silver lining as Japanese religions have attracted significant attention and admiration from abroad.

DEITIES/ELEVATED BEINGS

Izanagi and Izanami: The male and female *kami* create the islands of Japan and many other *kami* in the earliest Shinto mythology. Izanami, the female, dies from giving birth to the *kami* of fire. Izanagi, the male, gives birth to Amaterasu from his left eye during a rite of purification following his mate's death.

Amaterasu: The Sun Goddess is the preeminent Shinto *kami* of the "Land of the Rising Sun." Early Japanese mythology describes her exalted role and status as the divine ancestor of the imperial line. She is venerated at Ise Shrine.

Dainichi/Vairochana: Known in Japan as the "Great Sun" Buddha (Dainichi), the cosmic Buddha (Vairochana) is the central Buddha for Shingon and its *mandalas*. The great Buddha (*daibutsu*) statue at Todaiji depicts him.

Amida/Amitabha: "Boundless Light." Amida Buddha presides over the Western Paradise and is worshipped by Pure Land Buddhists. The vows of Amida promise that calling his name with sincerity at death is sufficient to be reborn in the Pure Land. The Jodo Shin school emphasizes that assurance of rebirth should result in gratitude during this life.

Kannon: Japanese form of the Mahayana Bodhisattva of Compassion, Avalokiteshvara. Like the Chinese form, Guanyin, Kannon is depicted as female.

Jizo: This *bodhisattva* helps beings in all levels of existence including hell. He has become most closely associated with travelers and children, including stillborn and aborted fetuses.

BELIEFS

Beliefs Rooted in Antiquity

Prehistoric. Knowledge of prehistoric religious belief often relies on speculation informed by archeological finds, inferences based on later beliefs and practices in the same culture, and evidence from similar stages in a related culture. These sources of knowledge are heavily dependent on interpretation. As a result, we know little with certainty about beliefs in early Japan. Some of the same beliefs rooted in antiquity of Chinese religions are later evident in Japan, such as divination, ancestor veneration, and ideas about correspondence between nature, human beings, and deities. There is also archeological evidence suggestive of religious beliefs concerning life and death. Themes of fertility and reproduction in the Jomon era are manifest in the artifacts of phallic stones and procreative *dogu*, clay figures featuring female forms with large hips, breasts, and often quite pregnant bellies. In addition to religious interest in fertility and birth, there seems to have been considerable attention focused on death as evidenced by careful burial techniques.

In addition to the later massive burial mounds, tumuli (*kofun*), for which the Kofun period (ca. 250-550 C.E.) is named, excavations of much earlier Jomon graves reveal burial practices of placing the deceased in the fetal position. Although it is difficult to confirm concepts of an afterlife from this evidence, the position may suggest ideas of rebirth or comforting sleep. Moreover, heavy objects placed on the head or stomach of the deceased might have been protective measures to stave off harm from a spirit, an idea consistent with careful religious propitiation of spirits in later periods.

Animism. Animism reflects an understanding that spirits pervade the natural world and that reverence for these nature spirits is necessary both to secure benefits and to avoid wrath. This idea is common to many early societies as their survival was closely tied to natural cycles and resources. This was especially true of Japan, which offered unusually rich bounty from land and sea but also inflicted massive destruction through natural disasters consistent with a volcanic archipelago. Animism found expression throughout Japanese history even into the present in the idea of the *kami*, a term for a range of awe-inspiring forces from anthropomorphic gods to non-corporeal nature spirits. The latter are thought to inhabit the sacred space of Japan, such as impressive mountains and ancient trees. By extension, *kami* could be enticed to enter "approach substitutes" (*yorishiro*), and thereby receive reverence and hear the entreaties of worshipers at Shinto shrines. This same concept extends to the portable shrines (*mikoshi*) that are carried through the streets during Japanese festivals (*matsuri*). Not all spirits are benevolent. *Kami* merit worship for their power, which can bring about destruction or aid. Animistic religious practices such as these typically involve celebrating the forces of nature, appeasing spirits to avoid harm, and propitiating *kami* for health, fortune, natural bounty, and communal survival.

Shamanic Mediation. Shamans provide an important function in animistic societies. They are understood to be able to communicate with spirits and at times influence them through their intercession. The most characteristic shamanic role in Japanese religion has been played by shamanesses, known as *miko*. They often lived separate from ordinary society to maintain purity and reinforce their function as a bridge between human and divine realms. Their activities ranged from local agricultural rituals to serving as oracles for the *kami* in state matters. Queen Himiko is described as a shamaness who remained secluded and ruled Japan through her brother in the first half of the third century C.E. One still encounters *miko* in Japan today, including shrine maidens who function as intermediaries in official rituals and more peripheral blind women who serve as mediums at sacred places thought to afford access to the spirits of the dead.

Creation Mythology and Divine Descent. Cosmogonic myths of the creation of Japan, the *kami*, and the imperial line appear in Japan's earliest written histories, the *Kojiki* (*Record of Ancient Matters*) in 712 C.E. and the *Nihonshoki* (*Chronicles of*

MAJOR TEXTS

Kojiki: This earliest account of Shinto mythology, compiled in 712 C.E., describes the creation of Japan, the *kami* who animate the island nation, and the divine descent of Japan's imperial family from Amaterasu. Shinto scholar Motoori Norinaga dedicated three decades to writing a commentary of this text, which influenced the nineteenth-century rise of Shinto and nationalism.

Engishiki: This early Japanese collection of fifty texts from the late 900s contains instructions for Shinto ceremonies and many of the ritual prayers (*norito*) still used in Shinto rites today.

Lotus Sutra: This most venerated Mahayana text, dating from the 200s C.E., forms the basis of Tendai and Nichiren Buddhism. It promulgates doctrines on the value of faith and the possibility of world transformation and universal liberation, since all beings share in the Buddha nature.

Pure Land Sutras: These Mahayana texts describe the vows made by Amida Buddha, when he was a *bodhisattva*, to create a Pure Land for all sentient beings who called upon him at the time of their death.

Heart Sutra: This concise "Perfection of Wisdom" (*Prajna Paramita*) *sutra* is among the most important and most frequently recited texts in Mahayana Buddhism. It is recited daily in Zen monasteries and at such Buddhist centers as the Shingon sacred sites on Mt. Koya. The entire short text, with its insight, "form is emptiness and emptiness is form," is inscribed on diverse forms from cloths and fans to chopsticks and pilgrims' staffs.

Japan) in 720. Following the Chinese convention of writing an official chronicle, the *Kojiki* was written, in part, as a record of the divine lineages of lead clans and authentication of the Yamato clan's claim to imperial rule. The *Kojiki* describes how the male and female *kami*, Izanagi and Izanami respectively, create the islands of Japan and other deities.

Their anthropomorphic characteristics include human activities of sexuality, reproduction, pollution, purification, and death. Sex is depicted metaphorically in the description of how the first island took shape after these *kami* thrust the sacred spear (or sword) into the waters below. They descended to the island that was created by this act. Further reproduction became more viscerally human as Izanami was burned and died in the process of giving birth to the god of fire. This story suggests that *kami* can die and illustrates the hazards of natural forces. In other details, the story reflects perceived dangers of both the recently deceased and the pollution of death.

Purification rituals ward off this danger, and it was from Izanagi's cleansing in a river that the sun goddess, Amaterasu, was born from his left eye; the moon *kami*, Tsukiyomi, from his right eye and the *kami* of wind, Susanoo, from his nose. Susanoo later upset his sister when he defiled her heavenly realm by polluting her hall with a skinned horse and his own feces. These impurities threatened the nascent world, for the offended sun goddess fled to a cave and locked herself, and the sun's light, away. The other *kami* came to the rescue by luring Amaterasu out. Curious about their revelry, she peeked out and they tied open the door with a great rope (*shimenawa*, subsequently used to demarcate sacred space more generally). Light was restored and life-giving agricultural cycles were maintained.

The sun goddess was not merely a nature god. She came to be known as an anthropomorphic deity and the divine ancestor of the imperial family. The idea of divine descent traces the line of the present emperor back to Amaterasu through her grandson Ninigi, whom she sent from heaven to rule Japan, and Ninigi's great grandson, Jimmu, a quasi-historical figure described within the tradition as the first emperor of Japan in 660 B.C.E. Amaterasu's shrine at Ise remains the principle imperial shrine and a sacred site that inspires nation-wide pilgrimage.

In addition to housing this most revered *kami* in its inner shrine, the Ise shrine complex and its associated rituals illustrate enduring Shinto ideals of purity, vitality, and the fertility and abundance epitomized by agricultural cycles. Whereas minor washing is required to approach any shrine, the inner shrine of Ise demands purity to the extent that only a few priests, priestesses and members of the imperial family are allowed entrance. Vitality is constantly renewed through an exact reconstruction of the shrines with fresh, natural materials every twenty years. The harvest goddess, Toyouke, keeps Amaterasu company from her devotional locus in the outer shrine. As the shrines are renewed, the *kami* are reinvigorated and the prosperity of the nation is constantly replenished.

The very structure of Ise matches more ancient ceramic images of grain storehouses, further reinforcing the links among the prehistoric past, agriculture, worship of the *kami*, and the prosperity of Japan. As the welfare of the nation is tied to rice cultivation, the rice god, Inari, is one of the most popular *kami* in Japan. Inari worship extends to this more general connection with prosperity, which makes him a favorite with artisans as well as those who work in business.

Despite the associations suggested above, it is difficult to determine how far back into Japanese prehistory lie the origins of many Shinto beliefs and practices or to what degree there is continuity between the *kami* worship of early times and Shinto in the present. Although the worship of the *kami* has continued from prehistoric times, the term "Shinto" has only been in regular use during the past two centuries in counter distinction to Buddhism, the way of the Buddha.

Medieval Beliefs

Buddhism. The parameters of "medieval" in Japanese Buddhism are widely disputed. Religious belief in the "middle ages" became inextricable from Japanese culture as Buddhism came to pervade,

KEY DOCTRINES

Rokudo ("six courses"): This Buddhist concept of *karma*, rebirth, and transmigration through six levels of existence was developed in India and formed the worldview of medieval Japan. One's actions dictated the karmic rewards and punishments of this and future lives including movement up or down through the courses identified with gods, humans, *asuras* ("warring demi-gods"), animals, hungry ghosts, and creatures of hell. The order of the second and third levels is reversed in some versions of this Buddhist cosmology.

Hongaku ("original enlightenment"): This important Mahayana philosophical idea critiqued the notion that ultimate realization is dualistically separate from this world, this life, and all sentient beings. This non-dual view stems from early Buddhist notions of interdependence and shaped various religious expressions in Heian and Kamakura schools of Buddhism from Kukai's emphasis on enlightenment in this body (*sokushin jobutsu*) to Dogen's assertion of the "oneness of practice and attainment" (*shusho itto*).

Honji Suijaku ("essence-manifestation"): This doctrine asserts a correspondence between the elevated beings of Buddhism and the Japanese *kami*. The dominant view held the *kami* to be provisional manifestations of the more fundamental Buddhist essence. For example, the sun goddess, Amaterasu, could be considered a manifestation of the cosmic sun Buddha, Mahavairochana (Dainichi).

shape, and unify Japanese culture, texts, arts, symbols, worldview, and intellectual assumptions. The extent and totality of this influence did not form in the immediate aftermath of Buddhism's introduction to Japan and partially unraveled during Confucian and "native learning" pursuits in the Tokugawa Era. Such a definition for "medieval" as corresponding to Buddhist hegemony can extend from approximately the Nara through the Muromachi periods (eighth to sixteenth centuries).

The Buddhist concept of transmigration through the six courses of existence (rokudo) informed the worldview of the Japanese in the medieval era. Buddhist ideas of karma and rebirth took the specific form of a six-level hierarchy of existence where rebirth could lead to realms of gods, humans, warring demigods (asuras), animals, hungry ghosts, and creatures of hell, depending on past actions. This system made sense of the world, and its idea of justice in relation to karmic reward and retribution appears throughout literature and arts, as well as in Buddhist sutras.

Shingon esoteric teachings were expressed through performance of the Three Mysteries (sanmitsu) of body, speech, and mind. As a school in the Tantric, or Vajrayana, branch of Buddhism, Shingon taught that enlightenment was possible in this body during this lifetime. The promise of relatively immediate enlightenment was tempered with the requirement of regimented training under an esoteric master. Both belief and practice were divided into these same sanmitsu categories. Carefully learned bodily gestures (mudras) and properly pronounced chants (mantras) fulfilled body and speech. Dynamic meditation on symbolic representations of the universe (mandalas) transformed mind through identification with the depicted cosmic deities. Tendai shared several of these beliefs and practices along with seated meditation, recitation of Amida's name for rebirth in this Buddha's Pure Land, and special reverence for the Lotus Sutra. Mahayana doctrine, such as the ideal of the bodhisattva, influenced practice along with the individual's personal level of attainment. In Saicho's system for the training of bodhisattva monks, the monks who showed excellent practice and understanding would stay on Mt. Hiei as national treasures while those with good understanding would leave the mountain and teach. Those who showed less understanding would still benefit the country by leaving the mountain and performing various services including manual labor.

Issues of doctrine and related practice divided the Kamakura schools. Most of the schools held some understanding that they lived in a precarious time according to the concept of mappo, the latter days of the Buddhist law. This doctrine describes deteriorating ages of Buddhist teachings. Whereas it would have been relatively easy to achieve enlightenment in

India during the time of the Buddha, it was much more difficult while living in a distant land and a degenerate time. Popular belief held that Japan had entered this age in 1052. Natural disasters, famine, and warfare reinforced this belief for many.

Pure Land teachings provided a solution to the problem posed by *mappo*. Pure Land belief acknowledged that it might be impossible to attain enlightenment through one's own self-power (*jiriki*), and instead depended on the salvific other-power (*tariki*) of Amida Buddha (Amitabha). While still a *bodhisattva*, this Buddhist luminary vowed to help all sentient beings attain salvation. Amida promised to help deliver to a Pure Land those who invoked his name at death.

Buddhist difference of belief is evident even with the apparently similar Jodo shu and Jodo Shin shu Pure Land practice of *nembutsu*, invoking the name of Amida Buddha by reciting "*Namu Amida Butsu.*" Honen and the Jodo school emphasize the constant remembrance of repeated *nembutsu* recitation and the belief that by having your last words invoke Amida Buddha you are more likely to be met by Amida and taken to the Pure Land.

For Jodo Shinshu and Shinran, the question of faith in Amida's salvific power was answered more radically with the doctrine of "one recitation." The belief that one recitation can suffice reflects the concern that delusions of cultivating the right practice through one's own power can be an obstacle to absolute reliance upon other-power for salvation. The focus is instead upon arriving at a pure inner conviction (*shinjin*) that Amida Buddha assures deliverance. At that point, one can understand that Amida's vow has already been realized

SYMBOLS

Rising Sun: The symbolic importance of the sun for Japan encompasses its name, location, gods, imperial family, and flag. Japan's designation as the Land of the Rising Sun is not new. The country's name, Nippon/Nihon consists of the Chinese characters, *kanji*, for sun and origin. The earliest written records concerning this island nation in the far east of Asia make reference to the idea of the sun originating, or first rising, over Japan. The most important *kami*, Amaterasu, is known as the sun goddess and ancestor of the imperial family. Although Japan's flag depicting a red disc sun centered on a field of white was only made the official national flag in 1999, variations of it can be found from the 12th century onward.

Shimenawa: This thick rice straw rope is used to designate any sacred space, from *torii* to shrine structures to natural formations such as encircling an ancient tree or rock. Such a rope appears in an early myth where the *kami* lure the sun goddess out of a cave and use the rope to keep her present. Its function can still be understood as locating the *kami's* power and making it accessible.

Torii: Gateway or series of gates leading to Shinto shrines and marking the entrance to sacred space more generally. Built of various materials and designs, its distinctive shape consists of two horizontal lintels supported by two vertical posts (often made of wood painted orange and black).

and the believer's deliverance into the Pure Land is certain. Performance of *nembutsu* becomes an expression of gratitude.

For Nichiren, the *Lotus Sutra* provided the solution to all religious problems. Nichiren argued that Mahayana *sutras*, the *Lotus Sutra* preeminent among them, were the last taught by the Buddha and superseded earlier teachings that had been provisional, necessary first steps for audiences not ready for the more powerful and direct teachings. In addition to privileging Mahayana *sutras* in general and the *Lotus Sutra* in particular, Nichiren further restricted his designation of Buddha's ultimate teachings to just a few chapters of the *Lotus Sutra*. Practice then became still more narrowly focused on invocation of the title of the *Lotus Sutra* (*daimoku*), which represents the doctrine and power of the entire *sutra*. The *Lotus Sutra* is thereby revered through recitation of the *daimoku*, *Namu Myoho Rengekyo* ("Hail to the Glorious Law of the *Lotus Sutra*") and contemplation of the depiction of the five characters used to write the *daimoku*. These practices were believed capable of facilitating the *Lotus Sutra's* power to transform this world.

Nichiren doctrine includes complex principles from Tendai Buddhism with Nichiren's own spin. Nichiren believed that the present degenerate age, *mappo*, posed a challenge for attaining enlightenment. These tribulations affected all, but did not require rejecting this world for a distant Buddhist paradise, as some Pure Land teachings maintained. Instead, the problems called for resolution in, and transformation of, this very world. In this role, Nichiren identified himself with the Bodhisattva of Supreme Action (Jogyo). Despite the exalted sense of his own importance, his teachings were radically egalitarian with equal access for all regardless of sex, class, or education. Achievement of salvation was open to all, and each individual could help bring about the transformation of society through the multiplying effect of the Tendai principle of *ichinen sanzen* ("one thought equals three thousand worlds").

This idea of transforming society, and Nichiren's concomitant insistence that the ruling powers follow his *Lotus Sutra* practice, differs considerably from Pure Land ideas as well as the self-cultivation through seated meditation characteristic of the Zen schools. However, Zen does share some common ground with both Nichiren and Shingon with regard to an important tenant of belief. All three traditions have an understanding that enlightenment, however conceived, can be attained in this life and in this body (*sokushin jobutsu*). This principle is central to Kukai's teachings and carries over into both the bodily practice manifest in Zen and the Nichiren expectations of transformation here and now. The Pure Land Buddhism of Honen, on the other hand, places enlightenment after death and in the Pure Land, as separate from the realization and place of existence currently experienced by the practitioner. Shinran's Pure Land thought lies somewhat in between as it is more affirming of the here and now due to the practitioner's present assurance of salvation, which arises from the transformative perspective of *shinjin*, the pure heart/mind of faith that appreciatively acknowledges that Amida's vow has already been fulfilled.

These differences in belief relate to fundamental Buddhist philosophical notions of impermanence and dependent co-origination. These ideas are foundational to the general notion of emptiness and non-dualism as well as the specific medieval Buddhist doctrine of original enlightenment. The Buddha's earliest teachings described a radical impermanence and interdependence whereby all things are in constant flux and their transient transformations are inextricably intertwined. Even the idea of a separate enduring Atman (a concept of core selfhood related to ideas of a soul or ego) was denied. Instead, all things, including amalgamations of various perceptions that are mistakenly projected as selfhood, are changing and dependent on each other to the extent that all can be described as "empty" of a stable and separate existence.

Shinto-Buddhism Fusion. In the Heian era a religious development known as Shugendo ("Way of the Mountain") represents a Shinto-Buddhist hybrid tradition that took root in Japan's mountains. Mountains have been seen as especially sacred manifestations of nature's spiritual forces from prehistoric times to the present. The *yamabushi* ("mountain ascetics") of Shugendo exemplify this reverence for mountains and nature along with worship of Buddhist

PRAYERS/CHANTS

Norito: Shinto prayers recited at shrine rites and festival rituals. Some are one thousand years old from sources such as the *Engishiki* and continue to be read in classical Chinese unintelligible to most Japanese.

Nembutsu (*nenbutsu*): recitation of "*Namu Amida Butsu*" ("Praise to Amida Buddha") by practitioners of Pure Land Buddhism.

Daimoku ("great title"): Chant of the title of the *Lotus Sutra* among Nichiren, Soka Gakkai and other Lotus (*Hokke*) schools of Buddhism. The chant, *Namu Myoho Rengekyo* ("Hail to the Glorious Law of the *Lotus Sutra*") is understood to invoke the power of the teachings of this most important *sutra* in Japan.

Sesshin: This period of intensive meditation at a Zen monastery lasts for approximately one week and is typically repeated about every other month with an especially intense version, known as *rohatsu sesshin*, during the first eight days of December. During the *sesshin*, monks dramatically increase their seated meditation and one-on-one meetings with the Zen master (*roshi*) while scaling back or completely forgoing their normal work activities, chanting, begging, and almost all sleep. This period of training is physically and mentally grueling, but is seen as ideal for facilitating a breakthrough realization (*kensho*) of one's true nature or even the complete awakening (*satori*) of a Buddha beyond this initial glimpse of enlightenment.

bodhisattvas and Shinto *kami*—especially those associated with the mountains. Reverence for the *kami* was equally prevalent among Buddhist monks as was belief in Buddhas among Shinto priests. For example, it was common to have a Shinto shrine within a Buddhist monastic complex or to assert that the *kami* of Mt. Koya offered protection to the Shingon temple complex and vice versa.

The doctrinal fusion of Buddhist and Shinto deities is most evident in a correspondence theory known as *honji-suijaku* ("essence-manifestation"). According to the dominant Buddhist interpretation of this relationship, Shinto *kami* can be understood as particular manifestations suited for Japan of essential Buddhas and *bodhisattvas.* The correspondence was often depicted in paintings that showed the Buddhist deities above their *kami* manifestations as if the *kami* were remembering or dreaming of their original Buddhist essence. A less common reverse essence-manifestation theory asserted that the *kami* were primary and the Buddhist deities were merely their manifestations. Yoshida Shinto exemplifies this valorization of Shinto.

Modern

Statements about belief in the modern period become problematic as evaluations of contemporary belief are made without the useful hindsight of historical analysis. Moreover, universal generalizations within a given culture become less reliable due to the very underpinnings of modernity, such as disruption of traditional culture during industrialization, cross-cultural influences leading to more eclectic combinations of beliefs through globalization, fragmentation of beliefs due to social displacement and specialization, and critical questioning of former religious beliefs in the light of science, scholarship, other religious traditions, and competing secular paradigms.

Various beliefs associated with popular religion, including Shinto, remain evident in many of the festivals, rituals, and other practices of Japanese religion. People continue to believe that certain objects ward off bad fortune and appeals to the *kami* may bring benefits in this world. The source of harm and bounty may have shifted but the underlying belief remains. In the modern period many Japanese purchase amulets at shrines thought to protect against an auto accident or appeal to *kami*, such as the *kami* Tenjin at a Tenmangu shrine, for success on the grueling exams that shape one's fate by determining university entrance eligibility. The object of danger or benefit has shifted to cars and exams, but the means to help secure safety and prosperity remain. The new religions similarly emphasize the potential benefits of health, wealth, and general wellbeing.

In the case of Buddhism, the major beliefs remain those rooted in the medieval period. Japan's esteemed academic study of Buddhism can result in a more self-conscious relationship to belief that contextualizes it within a culture and history and compares it with other Buddhist developments. Moreover, some Buddhist thinkers have reconsidered aspects of Buddhist doctrine to better fit a modern worldview.

PRACTICES (SHINTO)

Appealing to the Kami

Basic to Shinto practice are ideas of communicating with the *kami* through prayer and propitiation. A typical visit to a shrine is punctuated by the sound of clapping to get the attention of the *kami* followed by some form of message, voiced, written, or thought, which is directed to the *kami*. This communication could emphasize veneration, appreciation, a prayerful request for favor, or any combination of these appeals. Praise, worship, offerings, and other forms of veneration should precede requests. Such appeals to the benevolence of the *kami* are central to festivals, rituals, and annual observations and rites of passage.

Matsuri (Festivals)

FESTIVALS/HOLIDAYS

New Year's Festival: *Shogatsu Matsuri* celebrations range from cleaning, purifying, rites of renewal, gifts, and congratulatory greetings to the important first shrine visit of the year. This three-day festival now runs annually from January 1-3.

Setsubun: This festival on February 3 or 4 marks the division between winter and spring and beginning of the new year in the ancient luni-solar calendar. Chants of "*fuku wa uchi, oni wa soto*" ("good fortune in, demons out") accompany the throwing of beans as a form of purification, exorcism, and petition for luck.

Peach Blossom Festival: Spring festival; features elaborate displays of dolls from its association with the "Girl's Festival," which is now part of the "Children's Festival."

Children's Festival: Originally Boy's Day, this May festival is marked by flying kites that look like koi (a fish known for its strength) and displaying martial implements, such as a samurai's helmet.

Mid-August Obon: This Buddhist festival for the dead is pegged to the lunar calendar and manifests Shinto influence in the well-known dance (*bon-odori*) for the dead. In order to welcome and honor the dead, the living return to family villages, clean their ancestor's graves, and pray for the deceased.

Matsuri provide the most spectacular forms of communal religious practice in Japan. Spread throughout the year and across the nation, *matsuri* range from small local festivities to major national events. The basic religious purpose mirrors other interactions with *kami*, but on a grander scale. Following rites of purification, the *kami* are praised and thanked for their benevolence, venerated and appeased to avoid malevolence, and petitioned for future favor. Typically, *kami* are enshrined in *mikoshi*, ("portable shrines"), and carried through town as the essential component of the procession. Just as *matsuri* can be austere or wild, the *mikoshi* can be simple or elaborate, even multiple stories high. Many *matsuri* are raucous celebrations with much drinking and shouting by *mikoshi* bearers and crowds alike. The celebratory fervor further fueled by alcoholic spirits can make for a rollicking ride for the enshrined *kami*. The local and communal dimensions of Shinto are everywhere evident as members of the community, rather than specially trained religious officials, work together to parade the venerable *kami* through their neighborhood. Both wild and sober *matsuri* demarcate sacred space and time with an atmosphere separate from mundane existence. Like planting and harvest festivals of earlier times, this serves to bind members together in community as well as to connect them with nature and the *kami*.

Rituals

There are important ritual aspects of the festivals described above as well as distinct ritual ceremonies practiced at shrines and other sacred sites. These typically involve a Shinto priest, often assisted by a *miko*. Rituals for purification are especially prevalent and relate directly to the values and underlying Shinto mythology outlined in the section on beliefs. Purification rituals range from rinsing one's hands before approaching the shrine to immersive ascetic practices, such as standing below an icy waterfall. The latter example illustrates Shinto ascetic practices demonstrative of sincerity as well as purity. Purification, whether from water or the Shinto priest's wand, is preparatory for interacting with the *kami*. Priests read more formal prayers, *norito*, some of which come from collections more than one thousand years old. Official rituals end with communal sharing of food and drink including offerings that had been made to the *kami*.

Annual Religious Practices

Many annual festivals and rituals are rooted in the agricultural cycles that from ancient times were fundamental to religion, community, and survival. Similar themes persist. In keeping with Shinto ideals of vitality, fertility, and renewal, many major annual celebrations coincide with the renewal of the year and the agricultural stages of planting and harvesting. The timing of these annual rites is reckoned variously. A number of festivals occur on the first or fifteenth day (the full moon) of the lunar month while others have been transferred to the Gregorian solar calendar, including the most important annual religious practice, celebrating the New Year. Cleaning and purifying activities in late December prepare for the commencement of the New Year on January 1.

It is a time for celebration as people can congratulate family and friends on the New Year and give gifts of appreciation to superiors and money to children. It is also a time for religious renewal. Homes are restored and their inhabitants revitalized. Shrine paper hanging in the home is burned and replaced so that new protective paper can absorb or ward off evil in the coming year. This special occasion prompts the vast majority of Japanese to visit Shinto shrines. The important first shrine visit of the year (*hatsumode*) seeks favor for the coming year and reinforces family, local and national ties. Families join other members of the local shrine and can further extend communal awareness in time and space through the awareness that a similar scene is playing out across the country as it has through the past and will into the future.

Rites of Passage

Some ritual observations celebrate rites of passage by visiting a Shinto shrine. The first shrine visit for babies (*hatsumiyamairi*) provides an opportunity to present the newborn to the *kami*. The grandmother traditionally petitions the *kami*'s blessing for the infant thirty days after birth. The grandmother may have facilitated this introduction as an older family member known to *kami* and community alike. Moreover, the

---

RITES/RITUALS

Shinto Rites of Passage: Along with going to a shrine at New Year's and other cyclical festival occasions, several visits mark important rites of passage such as the first visit of a newborn and the *shichigosan* ritual for children who are seven, five, or three.

Visiting a Shrine: Approaching the *kami* through a visit to a Shinto shrine is a ritualized activity that begins with purification by rinsing one's hands and mouth. In order to then address the *kami* and make a request or offer thanks, the worshipper stands before the shrine, makes an offering (typically a small amount of money), attracts the *kami*'s attention by clapping twice, and bows with hands pressed together. A final clap after the silent address to the *kami* signals the ritual's end.

Funerals: Funerals continue to be the domain of Buddhism in Japan. In addition to presiding over the funeral ceremony, Buddhist priests grant the deceased a posthumous Buddhist name, *kaimyo*, and perform subsequent memorial rites.

Mizuko Kuyo: Memorial services (*kuyo*) for aborted fetuses and stillborn children (*mizuko*, "water children") have been popular and controversial Buddhist funerary rites in recent decades. In addition to the ritual, small statues of the *bodhisattva* Jizo fulfill a double function of looking after the *mizuko* and being dressed and given gifts as a surrogate for the child who was "sent back."

very young and very old were often viewed as closer to the *kami*, in a certain sense, straddling both worlds.

Another celebratory age for children occurs for boys at age five and for girls at ages three and seven. This festival, *shichigosan* ("seven-five-three"), is held each year in mid-November and again revolves around a visit to the shrine. As the children mature this festival reintroduces them to *kami* and community and fosters their religious growth.

Marriage is another rite of passage addressed by Shinto ceremonies. Although some Japanese have followed Christian wedding practices with the white dress and veil, the appeal is largely aesthetic and expresses a fashionable trend more than a religious substitute. Even in these cases, the couple typically conducts Shinto ceremonies as well. Securing the blessing of the *kami* in marriage is in keeping with Shinto principles of sincerity, purity, fertility, and close communal bonds. Death, on the other hand, has been left almost entirely for Buddhism to ritually address.

Nationalism

The most contentious Shinto practices strike their critics as remnants, or even resurgent instances, of the nationalism and militarism with which Shinto was intertwined in the modern era. Official visits by heads of state to Tokyo's Yasukuni Shrine have been especially inflammatory. This shrine is understood to house the spirits of Japan's war dead from the Meiji Restoration onward (including those tried as war criminals in the aftermath of World War II). These spirits have been deified by the state as heroes in life and protective *kami* in death. Japanese officials promoted fighting and dying in war as both national and religious duties for all citizens with the reward of enshrinement in Yasukuni as compensation. To many critics, Yasukuni remains a symbol of dangerous state support of religion and official validation of Japan's past militant aggression and imperial expansion in the name of the divine emperor.

PRACTICES (BUDDHISM)

Recitation

Forms of religious recitation are found in all Japanese Buddhist sects. The very name of Shingon Buddhism, which means "True Word," recognizes the power of words as an integral part of esoteric rituals. The use of *mantras* (sacred spoken formulas) is accompanied by *mudras* (ritual hand gestures) and the contemplation of *mandalas* (cosmic maps) in the perfection of speech, body, and mind. Similar forms of recitation can be found in esoteric dimensions of Tendai and even mountain religious traditions, such as Shugendo, that were influenced by these forms of Buddhism.

More general ideas of *sutra* recitation are found from earliest Buddhism in Japan to the present. Early forms of recitation were closely tied to the idea that the reading of the *sutra* activated the protective power of the *dharma* ("law/teaching"). During its first millennium in Japan, Buddhism was promoted in terms of its ability to bring protection and prosperity to the country. Practices of copying, displaying, and reciting certain Mahayana *sutras* provided a critical religious service for the nation's rulers. Other forms of *sutra* recitation, including the daily recitation of the *Heart Sutra* in Zen monasteries, have more didactic and meditative connotations. Even in modern monastic and temple practice, the *sutras* can be understood to exert a certain supernatural power. The practice of fanning open and shut a *sutra* written on accordion-style folded paper speaks more to the inscribed magical powers of the Buddhist dharma than to its contemplation.

The most popular recitation practices in Japanese Buddhism involve the short formulas, "*Namu Amida Butsu*" for Pure Land adherents and "*Namu Myoho Rengekyo*" for Nichiren Buddhists. As discussed above, Honen and earlier Pure Land popularizers, such as Kuya, advocated constant *nembutsu* repetition with special emphasis on invoking the name of Amida Buddha at death. For Shinran, *nembutsu* practice emphasized gratitude to Amida. Nichiren practice reveres the *Lotus Sutra* by reciting its title in the form of the *daimoku, Namu Myoho Rengekyo* ("Hail to the Glorious Law of the *Lotus Sutra*"). These recitations have extended beyond Japan as Nichiren adherents have proselytized abroad and marched to promote peace accompanied by chanting and drums.

The principles of practice vary only slightly among Zen schools and practitioners. The use of *koans* to precipitate a break-through experience (*kensho*) is generally associated with Rinzai Zen, traced back to Eisai (1141-1215), rather than the Soto school, traced back to Dogen, (1200-1253), but the practices have never fallen so neatly within sectarian boundaries. Dogen's emphasis, in contrast to *koan* practice, is just sitting still in meditative contemplation (*shikan taza*). The sole focus on seated meditation also carries the sense of focusing on the sitting itself as opposed to thinking about religious attainment. A goal orientation could interfere with one's practice and obscure Dogen's realization of the identity of practice and attainment.

Funerary Practices

The Japanese, like their East Asian neighbors, show deep reverence for their ancestors. Some practices of ancestor veneration take place at home, such as burning incense and setting offerings on a small Buddhist altar before a picture of the deceased. These daily memorials at home supplement the funeral service and related memorial rites performed by Buddhist priests. Buddhism has long been associated with rituals conducted at the time of death and concepts of future rebirths, despite little Buddhist doctrinal concern with death and funerals. The connection in Japan has become ubiquitous as many temples include dense groves of gravestones and much of the temple's income and ritual activity relate directly to memorial rites for the dead. This is a source of criticism and Buddhist institutions appear to be moving away from charging high fees for granting a special Buddhist name (*kaimyo*) to the dead. Nonetheless, considerable sums of money continue to come in as donations for the original funeral service and subsequent memorial rites conducted at set intervals.

CONCLUSION

The Japanese freely participate in a variety of rituals and beliefs without conflict or contradiction. Buddhist and Shinto practices and ideas often blend and in other circumstances perform complementary services, such as Shinto wedding ceremonies and Buddhist funerals. This mix incorporates aspects of popular religions, from shamanic divination to protective amulets and petition for worldly benefits. The synthesis of different practices and beliefs, or syncretism, is characteristic of East Asian religions. Japan's geographic distinctiveness has reinforced perceptions of uniqueness despite these ties. Even as its proximity to the Asian mainland has facilitated the influx of continental influences, its separation has protected it against invasion and fostered highly developed methods to adapt, transform, and integrate foreign ideas and practices into Japanese culture and society.

This strong sense of a distinct, enduring, and unified identity manifests itself from early times in the idea that Japan is the land of the gods ruled by an unbroken imperial lineage descending from the most important *kami*, the sun goddess, Amaterasu. This view became dangerously politicized in the emperor ideology of the modern era, when it was mobilized for militant expansion. In the post-war era, Shinto and Buddhism increasingly face competition from new religions, global influences, and secularization; however, Japanese religion has proved to be highly adaptable to changing times and diverse doctrines.

In a textbook such as ours, decisions had to be made as to what religions to include and what to set aside. We offer brief notes below on some of the traditions we have not included in the main body of the text but which may be encountered by first-year students in their general readings.

BAHAI

The Bahai religion began in Persia in the 1860s. It represents the most successful schism among the Babis, the followers of Siyyid Ali-Muhammad, who had assumed the title Bab (lit., "the Gate") and preached religious reform until his execution in 1850. The Bahais are that branch of the Babis who followed an individual known as Bahaullah, one of the disciples of the Bab. The Bahais see the Bab as the forerunner of Bahaullah, and accept the two as manifestations, or prophets, of the unknowable God, along with Adam, Abraham, Moses, Krishna, Zoroaster, the Buddha, Jesus, and Muhammad. The list of prophets reflects the Bahai conviction that the major religions have a common essence, at least in their origin. More broadly, the Bahai movement is a schism from Shiite Islam, though they see themselves not as a schism but as a new revelation of God. They anticipate one world government under the Bahai faith, and they have made world peace and religious tolerance primary concerns. They have few rituals and no clergy; their holy days are connected to events in the life of the Bab and of Bahaullah. The number of adherents is difficult to determine, but it is usually estimated to be about five or six million. The Bahai scriptures consist of the writings of the Bab, Bahaullah and Abd ul-Baha (the eldest son of Bahaullah). The Bahai headquarters are in Haifa, Israel.

NATIVE AMERICAN RELIGIONS

The term "Native American Religions" includes in its scope the diverse beliefs of hundreds of tribal groups in the Americas, some with considerably complex traditions, such as the Incas and the Aztecs, and others reflecting the religious sensibilities of hunting and gathering societies. The idea of a Great Spirit or Force that undergirds all things, with a host of other forces animating the natural order, is prominent, though details differ from tribe to tribe. When living closely with the physical environment it was important to guarantee as benevolent a natural world as possible. This was done through a variety of rituals designed to address the forces that permeated and controlled the natural world.

Shamans helped the tribe to tap into the resources of the spirit world, and sweat lodges, long fasts, prayers, and dance helped to assure a non-hostile world. Sometimes a sense of a kinship relationship between tribal groups and the spiritual forces was emphasized, and the idea of a guardian spirit for an individual was prominent. In some of the more complex societies in Central and South America, an order of priests replaced the shaman and huge temple complexes became the more visible locus of the divine world. The royal family was viewed as descendants of the divine, and often related to the Sun god. Human sacrifice, especially among the Aztec, was understood to protect the society from malevolent forces. Native religions lost much of their influence as Catholic and Protestant missionaries planted Christian churches in native communities. Today, native traditions are experiencing some renewal, though often adherents retain many of their Christian views too.

NEW AGE MOVEMENT

In the 1980s, a diverse collection of esoteric movements came to be grouped by the media as the "new age movement." The ideologies that sometimes were classed as "new age" ranged from environmentalism, holistic medicine, feminism, self-help explorations, and ventures into the mystical and the magical—from astral travel, astrology, tarot, crystals, channeling, and psychic healing to various western appropriations of eastern religious ideas of reincarnation, yoga, Zen, chanting, etc. Generally departing from the path of organized religion, new age sensibilities seek spiritual wholeness primarily by recognizing and harnessing the forces within—a personalized and inner self-help effort. There is no way to count the number of adherents, for there is no formal movement and individuals appropriate new age mechanisms and methods in various degrees and mixtures. The voluminous output of new age books and associated paraphernalia that fill the shelves of book stores witness to a considerable market for this kind of spiritual quest.

NORTH AMERICAN RELIGIONS

In the 1800s and 1900s, numerous new movements were established in the United States. Most of these were part of the Christian tradition. They often saw themselves as a very distinct part of Christianity—a pure remnant in the midst of a corrupted Christianity. They generally saw their teaching in terms of a newly restored original apostolic message. A few had a sense that America offered a place for the establishment of a utopian state; most saw the world as profoundly decayed and facing an immanent apocalyptic end of human history, which would be followed by a dramatic establishment of the kingdom of God for the remnant who had identified with the "restored truth." The Church of Christ, founded by Joseph Smith Jr. in 1830, attempted to establish a religious state. Its largest branch is The Church of Jesus Christ of Latter-day Saints, popularly known as Mormon. Those such as Seventh-Day Adventists (1863), Jehovah's Witnesses (1872), and Pentecostals (1901) sensed that the end of the world was fast approaching. All the groups had a prominent interest in the propagation of their message, idealizing the life of a missionary, or in some cases of the door-to-door evangelist. Such a strategy provided considerable growth, both in North America and throughout many parts of the world. The most recent of these movements, Pentecostalism, has had the greatest success, outnumbering several times over all the other new North American religious movements mentioned here. Pentecostalism is now the largest Protestant group, significantly larger than several of the groups examined in this text as world religions in their own right. Of these new North American groups, all but the Pentecostals have, in additional to the Christian Bible, a new body of literature that they consider more or less authoritative.

THE CHURCH OF SCIENTOLOGY

Founded in 1954 by science-fiction writer L. Ron Hubbard, the movement's tenets are expressed in the book *Dianetics: The Modern Science of Mental Health* (1950). Scientology maintains that individuals are essentially immortal, spiritual beings (called Thetans), whose dilemma lies in unconscious memories of hurtful experiences (called *engrams*), which the techniques of Scientology are said to confront. Members, who are known as *auditors*, go through a number of levels, listening to instructional material and being aided by more advanced members in confronting such memories. Although numerous criticisms of Scientology's methods and recruiting practices have hounded the movement, it has benefited from a number of high profile Hollywood stars who have joined. It has gained a reputation of being among the most secretive and litigious of religious groups.

UNIFICATION CHURCH

Popularly known as the "Moonies," the official title of this movement, established in 1954 by ex-Presbyterian Korean minister Sun Myung Moon, is the Holy Spirit Association for the Unification of World Christianity. Moon's theology, expressed in *The Divine Principle* (1952), reflects the influence of Christian and eastern beliefs. Moon contended that he and his wife (the Lord and Lady of the Second Advent) would institute a holy kingdom on earth, and Moon appropriated much of the language of the Christian concept of messiah to describe his role. The Unification Church has grown through its recruiting techniques, which have often been criticized for "brainwashing." The group is perhaps best known for its arranged marriages and mass weddings.

ZOROASTRIANISM

Zoroastrianism was for centuries the primary religion of the mighty Persian Empire. With the rise of Islam and the collapse of the Persian (Sasanian) Empire, Zoroastrianism declined; it now has only a little more than 100,000 adherents. Most of these are Parsis or Parsees (lit., Persians), who live in the area of Bombay (Mumbai), having fled to India as refugees. The dates of Zoroaster (Greek: Zarathustra), the founder of the religion, are difficult to determine. The traditional dates place him in the

600s to 500s B.C.E., though some argue for dates much older. Indeed, Zoroaster may be largely legendary. Although without much presence today, Zoroastrianism's monotheistic worldview, with dualistic tendencies and eschatological emphases, seems to have left its mark on Judaism, Christianity, and Islam, though the extent of that influence is debated. Concepts such as angels, a final judgment, and hell are shared by these traditions. Its sacred text is a collection called the *Avesta*.

Spelling Guide to Terminology

The list below provides alternative spellings for much of the basic vocabulary of foreign terms used in Religious Studies. Variations have arisen for a number of reasons. Sometimes the traditional English spelling of foreign terms did not accurately capture the sound. In the interest of accuracy, new spellings were introduced. Another source of variations in spelling is found on the internet, because web browsers often are not capable of easily or consistently displaying characters beyond the Latin alphabet used in English. Various non-English religious sites offer a range of transliterations, with no set standard even within a tradition. Often a letter that would normally have a diacritical mark is simply underlined, which alerts the scholar to the special mark but does not distract the general reader.

Note the three most common variations of Sanskrit transliteration: w/v; m/n; and sh/s/ṣ.

Often long vowels are written by duplicating the vowel, thus ā would be written as aa.

In Text	Transliterated	Other (* = traditional; ** = offensive)
Abbasid	ʿAbbāsid	
Adi Granth	Ādi Granth	
ahimsa	ahiṃsā	ahiṃsā, ahinsa
akhand path	akha	

Ali	ʿAlī	
Allah	Allāh	
Amitabha	Amitābha	
Aranyankas	Āraṇyankas	
Ashkenazi		Askenazi
Ashoka	Aśoka	Asoka
ashram	āśrama	
atman	ātman	
avatar	avatāra	avatara, avtara
Baal	Baʿal	
Bahai	Bahāʾī	
bodhisattva		bodhisatta
Brahmana	Brāhmaṇa	
brahmin	brāhmaṇa	
caliph	khalīfa	khalifah
Divali	Dīvālī, Dīpāvalī	Diwali, Dipavali, Deepavali
duhkha	duhkha	dukkha
Durga	Durgā	
Fatima	Faṭima	
Fatimids	Fāṭimids	
fatwa		fatwaa
Ganesha	Ganeśa	Ganesh, Ganupati, Ganapati
Ganga	Gaṅgā	*Ganges
hadith	hadīth	hadeeth
hajj	hajj	
halal	halāl	
Hasidim	Ḥasidim	Chasidim
ijma	ijmāʿ	
Ismaili	Ismāʿīlī	
jiva	jīva	
jnana	jñana	jyana, gyan
Kaba	Kaʿba	Kaaba, Kabah, Kabaah, Caaba
Kali	Kālī	Kaali, Kalee, Kaalee
Krishna	Kṛṣṇa	
Kshatriya		Khati
Lakshmi	Lakṣmī	Laksmi
langar	laṅgar	
lingam	liṅgam	liṅga
Mahabharata	Mahābhārata	
Mahavira	Mahāvira	
Mahayana	Mahāyāna	
mandala	maṇḍala	mandal
Manjushi	Mañjushi	
maya	māyā	
Mecca	Makkah	

Medina	Madīnah	Medinat-en-Nabi
moksha	mokśa, mokṣa	moksa
Mughal		*Mogul
Muhammad	Muhammad	*Mohammed
Muslim		*Moslem, musulmān, **Mohammedan, **Muhammadan
Navaratri	Navarātrī	Navarātra
nembutsu		nenbutsu
nirvana	nirvāṇa	
om	oṃ	aum
Parsi		*Parsee
Parshva	Pārśva	
Patanjali	Patañjali	
path	pāṭh	
prajna	prajña	
Prayag	Prayāg	*Allahabad
Quran	Qur'an	*Koran
Ramayana	Rāmāyaṇa	
Rig Veda	Ṛg Veda	Ṛigveda
sadhu		saddhu
Sakyamuni	Śākyamuni	
salat	ṣalāt	
samsara	saṃsāra	sansara
Samaveda	Sāmaveda	Sāma Veda
sangha	saṅgha	
samnyasin	saṃnyāsin	samyasin, sannyasin
sati	satī	suttee
Sephardi		Sefardi
shahada	shahāda	shahadah
Shaivism	Śaivism	Saivism
Shakti	Śakti	Sakti
Shankara	Śaṅkara	Sankara
sharia	sharī'a	
Shiva	Śiva	Siva
Shaivas	Śaivas	
Shaktas	Śāktas	
shudra	śūdra	sudra
shruti	śruti	
smriti	smṛti	
Sufi	Ṣūfī	
sutra	sūtra	sutta
swami	svami	
svastika		*swastika
tawhid	tawhīd	
Tirthankara	Tīrthaṅkara	

Tripitaka	Tripiṭaka	
Upanishads	Upaniṣads	
Vaisakhi	Vaiśākha	Baisakhi
Vaishnavism	Vaiṣṇavism	Vaishṇavism
vaishyas	vaiśyas	
vajna	vajña	
Varanasi	Vārānasi	*Banāras, *Benares, Kashi, Kāśī
varna	varṇa	
Vishnu	Viṣṇu	Visnu
Wahhabi	Wahhābi	
Zoroaster		Zarathustra

CHINESE: Pinyin (lit., "spelling") was adopted in 1958 by the Chinese Post Office and, since 1979, all news releases to foreign countries use Pinyin. Many scholarly publications in the western world have adopted Pinyin, replacing the Wades-Giles system, which had been in place since 1892. Although both schemes are phonetic, Pinyin is more systematic. The differences are particularly noticeable in the spelling of personal and place names. Frequently, the Wades-Giles spelling is closer to the way the word is actually pronounced. In particular, note that the Pinyin Q (Wades-Giles CH) is pronounced as CH, the Pinyin X is pronounced as SH, and the Pinyin ZH is pronounced as J.

Pinyin	Wade-Giles	Other
Amituofo	Omitofo	
Budai	Pu'tai	
Chan	Ch'an	
Dao	Tao	
Daodejing	Tao-te ching	
Daoism	Taoism	
Daozang	Tao Tsang	
De	Te	
Di	Ti	
Guanyin	Kuan-yin	
Han Feizi	Han Fei-tzu	
Huayan	Hua Yen	
Jingtu	Ching-t'u	
junzi	chün-tzu	chun-tzi
Kong Qui	K'ung Ch'iu	
Kongfuzi	K'ung fu-tzu	Confucius
Laozi	Lao-tzu	
Mao Zedong	Mao Tse-tung	
Mengzi	Meng-tzu	Mencius

Mozi	Mo-tzu	
po	p'o	
qi	ch'i	
Qiging	Ch'i-kung	
Qin	Ch'in	Chin
Ren	Jen	
Sanhuang	San-huang	
Tang	T'ang	
Tian	T'ien	
Tiantai	T'ien-t'ai	
Taijichuan	T'ai Chi Chuan	
wuwei	wu-wei	
Xia	Hsia	
Xi'an	Ch'ang-an	
Xunzi	Hsün-tzu	Hsun-tzu
Yijing	I-ching	
Yu	Yu	
Zheijiang	Chekiang	
Zhou	Chou	
Zhu Xi	Chu Hsi	
Zhuangzi	Chuang-tzu	
ziran	tzu-jan	

Subject Index

Page numbers in this index are distinguished in the following way:

plain text–term occurs in text on that page

bold text–term occurs as main entry in sidebar

[square brackets]–term occurs in sidebar but not as a main entry

(parentheses)–term occurs in spelling guide

canon (Jewish), 105. *See also* Tanak
canon (Sikh), [235], 236, 238, 244,
246-47, 248-49. *See also Adi Granth*
Canterbury Cathedral, 109
cantor, **57**, 74
Carolingian Empire, 88
caste, 151, 154, 156, [159], [161], [167],
175, 176, 180, 183, 192, 233, 234,
237-38, 240, 243
cathedral, 109
caturmas, **229**, 230
C.E., **15**
Celestial Masters Sect, 260
celibacy, **7**, [7], 72, 100, 101, 168, 172,
180, 192, 208, 227. *See also* asceticism
Centenary Perspective, 76
Ceres. *See* Demeter
Chaitanya, [159], **163**
Chalcedon Definition of Faith, 96
Ch'an. *See* Chan
Chan, [187], [189], 194-96, 210, 212,
261, 270, 276, (314)
Chandragupta, 220
Chang Taoling. *See* Zhang Daoling
channeling, 210, 307
Charismatic Movement, 91
charity, [133], 140, [169], [171], 174,
178, [203], [209], 210, 215, 229,
238-39, 244, 287. *See also* alms
Charlemagne, 88, 102
Chekiang. *See* Zheijiang
ch'i. See qi
Chicago, 161
Ch'i-Kung. *See* Qigong
Children's Festival, **299**
Ch'in. *See* Qin
Ch'in Shi-huang-ti. *See* Qin Shi Huangdi
Chinese dynasties, **271**
Chinese Religions, **253-77**
Ch'ing Dynasty. *See* Qing Dynasty
Ch'ing-tu. *See* Jingtu
Chi-Rho, **101**
chit, 172, 173
Chogye Order, 195
chosen people, 59, 78
Choson Dynasty, 195
Chou. *See* Zhou Dynasty
Christ, 16, 37-38, 79, 83, [89], 93, [93],
94, 96, [101], 106. *See also* Jesus
Christianity, **79-113**
"Christ-killers," 52, 82
Christmas, 69-70, 82, **93**, 102, 110-11
Chu Hsi. *See* Zhu Xi
Chuang-tzu. *See* Zhuangzi

Chun-tzu. *See junzi*
church and state, [81], 84, 101-2
Church History, **81**
Church of England. *See* Anglican
Church of Jesus Christ of Latter-day
Saints. *See* Mormon
Church of Scientology, 308
church structure, 108
Cilappatikaram, [223]
circumambulation, 230
circumcision (Jewish), 49, [57], 58, **63**,
64, 70-71, 74, 77, 83
circumcision (Muslim), **139**, 142
City of God, **81**
civil rights, 102, 222
civil rights movement, 174
class system (Hindu), 154-55, 157, **161**,
164
Classic of Rites. See Five Classics
Clear and Bright Festival, **275**
clergy, 11-12, 74
clergy (Christian), **87**, 101, 105, 106-8,
110, [139], 305
Code of Discipline, 209
coffee, 112
cohen, 73. *See also* priest (Jewish)
colonialism, 95, 124, 241
colored powder and water, 167, 182
Columbus Platform, 76
Common Era. *See* C.E.
communion. *See* Eucharist
communion of Saints, [97]
communism, 195, 215
companions of the prophet, 118-20
Conciliar Movement, 89
confession. *See shahadah*
confessional perspective, 8-9
confirmation, [95], 110
Confucianism, **5**, 256-58, **259**, 265-67
Confucius, 254, **255**, 256, 258, [259],
[261], [263], 265-67, 268, 273-74,
(314)
congregational (church structure), 108
conqueror, 218, [219]. *See also jina*
consensus. *See ijma*
Conservative Judaism, [47], **53**, 77
Constantine, 84-85, **85**, [93], [99], 100,
101, [101], 106, 109
Constantinople, 64, 86, 87, [89], 95, [99],
107, [119], 122, [123]
Coptic Christianity, 96
Cosmological Symbol (Jain), **225**
Council of Constantinople, 95
Council of Nicea, 95, 96

lunar calendar, 66, [135], [167], 182, 214, 275, [275], [299], 301. *See also* calendar
Luther, Martin, [81], **85,** 89, [91]
Lutheranism, 89, **91,** 108
LXX. *See* Septuagint
lying, 15, 172, 202, 203, 208, 227

Maccabees, 49, **49,** [49], [55], 69, 80
Madhva, **163,** 175
Madhyamika, [189], 190, 191
Magadha, 187, 220
magen of David, **69**
magi, 81, 82, [93], 111
magic, 6, 28, 34, 38-39, 130, 154, [189], 245, [259], 303, 307
Mahabharata, **153,** 155, [155], 162, 165, 167, (312)
Mahadevi. *See* Devi
Mahaprajapati, 198, 200
Maharashtra, 182
Maharishi Mahesh Yogi, 161
Maha-sanghika, 189-90
Mahashivaratri, **167,** 182
Mahavairocana, 214
Mahavira, 186, 207, 217-18, 219, **219,** [219], 220, 222-23, 225, [227], 230, 231, (312)
Mahavira Jayanti, 231
Mahavira's Birthday, **227,** 231
Mahayana, **187,** [187], 188, [189], 189-91, [191], 192-94, [193], [197], [201], [203], 205-7, [259], 261, 269, [273], 283, [283], 287, [289], [291], [293], 294, 296, 303, (312)
Mahayuga, 162
Mahdi, **141**
Maimonides, 45, **47,** 63, [67]
Maitreya, **193,** 207, [269], 270
Malli, 223
Manchu Dynasty, 258
mandala, 159, **197,** 210, 213, 214, [283], [289], 294, 303, (312)
Mandate of Heaven, 264
Manimekalai, [223]
Manjushri, 207, 214
mantra, 159, 161-62, [171], [173], 176, **211,** 212, 213-14, [283], 294, 302
Mao Tse-tung. *See* Mao Zedong
Mao Zedong, 258, (314)
mappo, 269, 294-95, 296. *See also mofa*
Marcionites, 92, 94
Mardana, 237
Marduk, [23], **25,** 29, 39

marga, 202, **205**
Marranos, 52
marriage, [11], [23], 308; marriage (Buddhist), [203]; marriage (Chinese), 272, 274; marriage (Christian), [96], 110; marriage (Hindu), 154, [159], **171,** 176, 180-81; marriage (Japanese), 302; marriage (Jewish), 50, 70, 72, 74; marriage (Muslim), 142-43; marriage (Sikh), 246; marriage (temporary), 143
Mars (planet), 182
Mars (god). *See* Ares
martial arts, [189], 270, 276
martyr, **9,** 84, 94, 99, 100, 109, 148, [235], [237]
martyrdom. *See* martyr
Mary, 82, [89], 96, [97], [105], 126
Master Chuang. *See* Zhuangzi
Master Han Fei. *See* Han Feizi
Master Kong. *See* Confucius
Master Meng. *See* Mencius
Master Mo. *See* Mozi
Master Xun. *See* Xunzi
Master Zhuang. *See* Zhuangzi
matrilineal, 72, **73**
matrimony. *See* marriage
Matthew (Gospel of), 82, [83]
matzah bread, [55], 68
Mauryan, 188, [189], 220
Mawlid, **135**
Maya (Queen), 198
meat offered to idols, 144
Mecca, [15], 115-17, 118-19, 120, [123], 125, 127, 128, **129,** [129], 135, [135], 136, [137], [139], 140-41, 143, 147, 237, (312)
Medes, [21]
Medina, **131**
meditation, 157, 161-62, 172, 173, [173], [177], [187], [189], 194, [197], 198, [203], [209], 210-12, [211], 216, 221, 228, 229, 230, [255], 261, 269-70, 274, 276, 279, 283, [283], 285, 294, 296, [297], 303
meditation posture, 153, [177], [193], **209,** 211
Meditation School. *See* Chan
Mediterranean, 20, [21], [31], 35, 79, 80, 85, 87-88, 94, 113, 116, [117], 119, 120
Meiji (Emperor), 196, 288
Meiji Era, 286-88, [287], 302
Memphis (Egypt), 24

Shunyata. *See* emptiness
Shvetambaras, 218, 219, 220, 221, **221,**
    [221], [227]
sick man of Europe, 124
siddha, 225
Siddhartha. *See* Gautama
siddhi, 159
Sikhism, **233-51**
Silk Road, 194, 260
sin, 31, 36, 57, [71], 98, [101], 129, 276.
    See also original sin
Sinai, [59], 66. *See also* Mount Sinai
Sind, 234
Singh, **247,** 250
Siri Chand, [245], 249
Sita, 164
six obligatory actions, 228-29
Sky-clad. *See* Digambaras
SLM, **143,** [143]
slow adopters. *See* Sahajdharis
Small Feast. *See* Id al-Fitr
Smith, Joseph, Jr., 307
smriti (Buddhist), **211,** (313)
smriti (Hindu), 157, 164, 166, **179,** (313)
Sociology of Religion, 7
Solomon, 46, 126
Soma, 164
Son (of God), 86, [89], 95-96, [97], 98,
    [101], 112, 126
Son Dynasty, 195. *See also* Chan
Son of Heaven, 264
son of the commandment. *See* Bar Mitzvah
Songsten Gampo, 196
Soto school, [187], 212, [283], 285,
    [285], 303
South Africa, 174
Southerners. *See* Dravidians
Soviet Union, [119], 215
Spain, [3], 51, [51], 52, 53, 62, 87, [119],
    120-21, 122
speaking in tongues, [91]
spice trade, 124
Spring and Autumn Annals. See Five Classics
Spring and Autumn period, 254
Sri Lanka, 186, [187], 188, 189, [189],
    192, [211]
Sri Ramakrishna, 174
Srimad Rajchandra, 222
St. Nicholas, 111
St. Peter's Basilica, 88, **99,** 109
Star of David. *See magen* of David
state church, 85, 89-90, [91], 102
statue. *See* Buddha images; images
    (Hindu); images (Jain)

stele, **35**
Sthanakvasi, 221, **221,** 226
Sthavira-Vada, 189
stone pillars (Buddhist), 188
Story of Rama. See Ramayana
Student (Stage of Life), 164, **169,** [171],
    178, 180, 182
stupa, 189, **197,** [199], [211], 214, 215
suffering (Buddhism), 198, 200-201,
    202, 204, **205.** *See also* duhkha
Sufi/Sufisim, [117], **121,** [121], 122,
    123, 124, 126, 136, 137-38, [141],
    145, 236, [237], 242, (313)
Sui Dynasty, 194
suicide, 229
Sukhavati-vyuha, 269
Sukkot, **55,** 68
Suleyman I, 123
sultan, **141,** 145, [235]
Sultanate of Delhi, 123, 159, 234-35,
    235, 238, 239
Sumatra, 193
Sumer/Sumerian, 20, **21,** [25], [35]
Summa Theologica I, **81**
Sunday, 12, 70, 77, 93, [93], 98, [135]
sunnah, 133, 142, 147
Sunni, [117], 118, 121, **121,** [121], 125,
    133, 136, [141], 145-46, 147
surah, [125], 128, [131], 136
Surya, 163
Sutra Pitaka, 187, 200
svasti, [173]
svastika, **173,** 225, **225,** [225], 231, (313)
Swami, **159,** 179, (313)
sweat lodge, 306
Switzerland, 89, [91]
syad, 224, 225
syadvada, 225
symbol (Jain), **225**
synagogue, [57], **59,** 61, [63], 66, 67, 70,
    71, 74
Syria, 20, 30, [31], [55], 119, 122, 147
Syrian Christianity. *See* Jacobite (Syrian)
    Christianity

Tabernacles (feast). *See* Sukkot
Tablet of Destiny, [25], 39
taboo, 5, **13,** 15. *See also* dietary taboos
T'ai Chi. *See* Taiji
T'ai Chi Chuan. *See* Taiji
Taiji, [259], [265]. *See also* Yin/Yang
Taijichuan, 256
T'ai-p'ing. *See* Taiping Rebellion
Taiping Rebellion, 195

Taj Mahal, **129,** 239
Takht, **245,** 249. *See also* Akal Takht
taking the hukam, **241,** 245, 246
Taliban, 136, 148, 194
talisman, 154
Tallit, **69, 76**
Talmud, **45,** [45], [47], 50-51, [51], 52, 60, 65
Tamerlane. *See* Timur, the Lame
Tamil, 192, 219
Tammuz, [25]
Tanak, **45,** [45]
Tang Dynasty, 194, 257, 260, **271,** (315)
Tanjur, **191,** 196
Tantras, **153,** 158-59, 160, [179], [189], 190-91, 213
Tao. *See* Dao
Tao Tsang. *See* Daozang
Tao-chia. *See* Daojia
Tao-chiao. *See* Daojiao
Taoism. *See* Daoism
Tao-te Ching. See Daedejing
Tara. *See also* Guanyin
tarot, 307
"*Tat tvam asi,*" 172
te. See De
Tea, 112, [287]
Tefillin, **69,** 76
tel, **35**
temple, 12, [13], 22, 24, 30, [31], [35], 84, 109, 153, 157, [157], 159, [159], 160-61, [173], 175, 177-78, 182, 193, 195, [211], 215, 221, [221], 231, 234, 238, 239-40, 248, 272-73, 277, [281], 282-83, [283], 286, [287], 298, 303, 304, 306
Temple (Jewish), 24, 37, 47, 48-50, [57], **59,** [59], 60-61, 64, 68, 69, [69], [71], 72-74, 75-76, 77, 79-80, [129]
Temple of Apollo, 262
Temple Priest (Japanese Buddhism), **293**
Ten Commandments. *See* Decalogue
Ten Gurus, **245.** *See also* Guru (Sikh)
Ten Lost Tribes, 47
Tendai, **289**
Tenzin Gyatso. *See* Dalai Lama (XIV)
Tephillah. *See* Eighteen Benedictions
Terapanthi, 226
terracotta soldiers, 272
Tetragrammaton, [61], **69**
Thailand, 158, [187], 192, 209, [211]
Thebes (Egypt), 24
theft, 15, [65], [133], 172, 203, 208, 227
theodicy, **13**

theological approaches, 8
Theravada, **187,** 189, [191], 192, 193, [193], [201], [203], 216, 261, [273]
Thetans, 308
Thich Nhat Hanh, 215
Third Buddhist Council, 188
Third Jain Council, 219, 220
Thirteen Attributes of God, 56
thirteen principles of Judaism, [47], 63, **67**
Thirty Years War, 90
thirty-two major signs, **207**
Thoreau, Henry David, 165
Thousand and One Nights. *See Arabian Nights*
Thousand Years of Peace. *See* "Millennium"
Three Baskets. *See* Tripitaka
Three Caverns, **263.** *See also* canon (Daoist)
Three Jewels of Jainism, 225, [225], 228
Three Jewels of Buddhism. *See* Three Refuges
Three Refuges, 195, **197,** 208
Three Sovereigns, 263, **267**
Thunderbolt Vehicle. *See* Vajrayana
Ti. See Di
Tiamat, [23], **25,** [25], 29, 37
Tian, 263-64, **269,** (315)
Tiantai, [191], 194, 196, [259], 261, 269, [273], 283, [283], (315)
Tibet, [187], [189], 191, 192, [193], [195], 196-97, 213, 215-16
Tibetan Book of the Dead, **191,** [203], 210
T'ien. *See* Tian
T'ien-t'ai. *See* Tiantai
Tigris River, 20, [25]
time. *See* calendar; cyclical view of time; linear view of time
Timur, the Lame, 235
Tirthankaras, 217, 219, [219], 222-23, [223], 224, [225], [227], 228, [229], 230-31, (313)
TM. *See* Transcendental Mediation
tobacco, 112, [243], 250
Tokugawa Shogunate, 196, 258, [281], 285-86, 294
tolerance, 9-10, 54, 84, [85], 102, 123-24, 133, 160, [175], 235, [235], 238-40, 306
Torah, 44, 45, **45,** [45], 47, [47], 48, 49, [49], 50, 51, 54, [55], [57], 58, 59, 60, [63], 65, 66, [67], 69, 70, 71, [73], 73-74, 76, 82, 93-94, 126, 128, 130, [131]